THE BIG BOOK OF HOME LEARNING
Volume One: Getting Started

Also by Mary Pride:

The Way Home
All the Way Home
Schoolproof
The Child Abuse Industry

With Paul deParrie:

Unholy Sacrifices of the New Age
Ancient Empires of the New Age

THE
BIG
BOOK
OF
HOME
LEARNING

Volume One: Getting Started

Mary Pride

Crossway Books • Wheaton, Illinois
A Division of Good News Publishers

The Big Book of Home Learning: Volume 1.

Cover Design by Mark Schramm.
Interior Design by Mark Schramm and Mary Pride, based on the
original concept by Karen L. Mulder.
Layout by Bill Pride and Mary Pride.
Cover illustration by Guy Wolek.

First printing, 1990.

Printed in the United States of America

Library of Congress Cataloging-in-Publication Data
Pride, Mary
   Big book of home learning / Mary Pride
     v.   cm.
   Includes bibliographic references.
     Contents: v. 1. Getting started — v. 2. Preschool and elementary —
v. 3. Teen and adult — v. 4. Afterschooling and extras.
     1. Home schooling—United States. 2. Home schooling—United
States—Curricula. 3. Education—United States—Parent
participation. 4. Child rearing—United States I. Title.
LC40.P75 1990   649'.68 ' 0973—dc20   89-81254
ISBN 0-89107-548-8 (v. 1)

99	98	97	96	95	94	93	92
15	14	13	12	11	10	9	8	7	6	5	4

TABLE OF CONTENTS

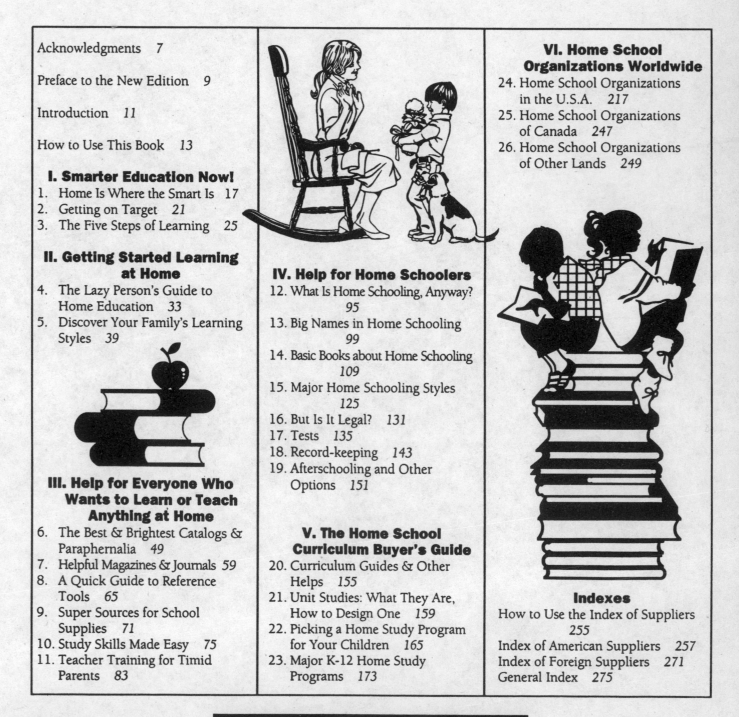

ACKNOWLEDGMENTS

First, I would like to thank my husband, Bill, and our children: Ted, Joe, Sarah, Magdalene Joy, Franklin, Mercy Grace, and Gregory, who arrived just before this book was finished!

Authors typically thank their families for leaving them alone long enough to finish the project. In this case, nobody left me alone. Instead, they all dug in and helped! Bill set up databases, helped mail umpteen thousand letters to suppliers, previewed software, and typeset the book. Ted and Joe tested software, science kits, and engineering and hobby resources. Sarah, Magdalene, and Franklin gave the preschool and early elementary goodies a workout. *Everyone* worked and played with the music and art resources and put up with weeks of watching educational videos at mealtimes. And of course, the five oldest children (representing all three major learning styles!) have shown me a lot about which resources work best in our daily home school.

Authors also typically thank their typists for dedicated work on illegible manuscripts, and their publishers for all those other things that publishers do. I did the typing, so I don't have to admit whether my handwriting is legible or not! I would like, however, to acknowledge the fine work the Crossway Books staff did in helping these volumes to get out. First, Jan Dennis shepherded the project from the proposal stage through final development, a process that required mammoth patience and unflinching belief that the manuscripts finally *would* arrive. Ted Griffin had the difficult job of writing little red marks all over my beautiful manuscript. (If that sounds easy, *you* try memorizing the *Chicago Manual of Style!*) Mark Schramm did some amazing things with cover design and interior layout and spent hours getting everything just right. Lila Bishop was always warm, helpful, and organized, and let me cry on her shoulder when it seemed that I would *never* get through all four volumes in time. Finally, Lane Dennis deserves credit for approving this very ambitious project, and for having the fortitude not to call me and ask how it was coming along in the ten months before he saw any return on his investment.

ACKNOWLEDGMENTS

I would also like to thank my home schooling friends, especially Pam Lancaster, for sharing their opinions of what works and what doesn't in their home schools. Sue Welch of *Teaching Home* magazine also was a big help, not only by her general enthusiasm and support, but by publishing my review column in her magazine, which helped me keep up with new products between editions of this book.

Thanks also are due to all the assorted computer geniuses out there who designed such great hardware and software that we could actually do this whole project, from the first letter to suppliers to the final typeset book, with one-tenth the people and in one-tenth the time it would have taken ten years ago. The people at

Apple ought to get some of the credit, because frankly their product has done most of the work!

But my biggest thanks go to the readers of the first editions of these books. You wrote to me, encouraged me, and shared your honest opinions of resources I had written up and resources I had never seen. You contacted suppliers and suggested that they send me review samples of their products. You remembered to tell suppliers that you had read about them in *The Big Book of Home Learning,* so that this time around most were anxious to be included again. Mostly, you cared enough to give your families the very best education you could find. I thank you and applaud you and admit right now that I couldn't have done it without you!

PREFACE TO THE NEW EDITION

This four-volume series, believe it or not, started out as a single chapter. I was writing a book about the exciting things families can do at home and thought of including a chapter on home schooling. My editors agreed that was a good idea. The chapter grew into a section. The section grew into a smallish book. The smallish book grew into a biggish book, and was published in 1986 as *The Big Book of Home Learning*.

The first edition was surprisingly well received, encouraging me to do another edition two years later, this time including such amenities as a General Index so people would actually be able to locate products they remembered reading about. The home education market was growing rapidly, and my original one book soon turned into two, published in 1988. We called them *The New Big Book of Home Learning* and *The Next Book of Home Learning*.

Several years passed, and it was time for another edition. The home education market had been really booming all this time, and I saw the handwriting on

the wall. In order to have a decent chance of including even just the best products, we would need *four* volumes this time. Introductory material alone, including the Curriculum Buyer's Guide and the ever-expanding list of home schooling organizations, would take up one volume. Readers had been asking us to separate preschool and elementary resources from teen and adult resources—presto, another two volumes. That left one book's worth of afterschool resources: art, music, videos, computer hardware, drill material for all subjects, and general enrichment.

These four volumes are not only bigger; we hope they are better as well. In this edition new reviews are highlighted, so that readers of previous editions can immediately turn to the new items. Products that have undergone significant revision are also highlighted as "updated" or "improved." All prices and reviews have been updated, and the Suppliers' Index now includes fax numbers. We even have an (admittedly scanty) Foreign Suppliers' Index for readers in other countries. Altogether, this edition has several hundred new suppliers and over a thousand new products. All this is laid out in a way that should make it easy for you to instantly find the resources you need in any school or afterschool subject area. And the best news of all—the products themselves are better! I keep telling you, people, that education suppliers are listening to you! This edition includes products that are better, more colorful, more educationally sound, simpler to use, and sometimes even cheaper than ever before.

So if you need to learn more about education, to set up a home education program (whether home school or afterschool), or to find out what's happening in packaged home schooling curriculum—turn to Volume One.

If you are looking for resources for a preschooler or elementary-level child in the basic school subjects—turn to Volume Two. (A quick note: Many of these resources are great for older people, too!)

If you need more advanced resources at the junior high, high school, or adult level—turn to Volume Three. (Most home-taught preteens are ready for this!)

And if you are looking for the resources to round out your family's education, and want to have some fun—turn to Volume Four.

All four volumes have been designed for the everyday, normal family. I'm assuming that you are no more interested in boring textbooks and tedious worksheets than I am. So the Engineering chapter in Volume Three, for example, prominently features hands-on model construction kits and innovative pre-drafting programs. You'll find lots of posters, videos, software, and make-it kits throughout each volume, along with the better traditional resources, including some revived classics from yesteryear. Simply reading about what's available in all these areas is an education in itself. Not to mention how it can spice up your Christmas shopping list!

Education is one of the very best investments you can ever make. And home education is the best educational investment. Here are the tools to help you make the most of it!

INTRODUCTION

This book is not by experts or for experts. It's for *anybody* who wants to learn at home or to help another person learn.

You might be a home schooler, a would-be "after-schooler," a grandparent, neighbor, friend, or just an average person who wants to finally learn what the schools failed to teach you. Maybe you're an independent-minded teacher or administrator looking for ways to help your students. Whoever you are, I wrote it for you!

Today we need to become our own educational experts. We can't afford to stay dependent on education that doesn't educate, but rather produces an unending (and unnecessary) stream of woeful, self-doubting "failures," among whom may be our own children and grandchildren, or even ourselves.

What's more, we *can* become experts.

How? By *discovering* what's out there, *comparing* the different programs, philosophies, and resources, and then *choosing* the best for our own particular needs. That's how anyone becomes an expert in any field. First, he learns what exists in that field. Second, he compares the different options. Finally, he forms his personal opinion based on knowledge and puts it into practice.

In order for you to do this, obviously the first step is *finding out what's out there*. I've done my best to help you with this in the four volumes of this series.

We then go on to the next step, *comparing the options*. Over the years, hundreds of companies have graciously allowed me to see samples of their products. The result has been that I have not only had the opportunity to *review* them, but to *compare* them. Very few people have the means to try thirty different phonics programs, say, or twenty different language courses. Your problem is not so much finding a program, but finding the *best*. If I have been successful in explaining the features that make different products different, so that you can confidently choose the one that's right for you, I will feel amply rewarded.

All you have to do is to find the subjects that interest you, read the reviews, and make your choices.

INTRODUCTION

And since each chapter discusses the educational philosophies *behind* different products and programs, you will be able to intelligently evaluate any products or programs you come across. Addresses for all these are given in the Index of Suppliers at the end of each volume in this series.

The first step to educational success is discovering which teaching and learning methods work and which don't. That's why I devoted several chapters in this book to explaining how people really learn. It's also why you will find so many resources in this book to help you learn how to learn and teach. While Volumes Two through Four of *The Big Book of Home Learning* mainly are made up of educational product reviews, Volume One gives you the foundation to make those products work—including basic resources for everyone who wants to learn or teach at home.

You can use Volume One two ways:

(1) Dive right in and start working your way up to the rank of Educational Expert. I have reviewed enough books, magazines, catalogs, and training products to keep you busy at this fascinating task for quite a while!

(2) Picking and grinning. You may decide that just reading the reviews is enough of an education! Even so, you probably will be interested in some of the fascinating catalogs and super products reviewed in this book. Almost any child can benefit from the resources in the Study Skills chapter, for example. And wouldn't you like to know the learning styles of everyone in your family? With the tools in this book, you will be able to evaluate *and do something about* your children's educational progress, even if they are enrolled in regular schools.

Those of you who intend to home school, or who are thinking about home schooling, will naturally find the information about home schooling particularly useful. Even those who do not intend to home school have to at least be impressed by the depth and range of complete curriculum packages now available to families who teach their children at home. And if you truly are just "getting started" on home schooling, picking one of the packaged curriculum programs in this book is the best way to start.

"But *can* parents really teach their own children at home? *Can* teens and adults really learn anything significant at home on their own?" I don't blame you for asking that question. I'm a bit of a slow learner when it comes to these things myself. Even though my father taught me to read at home before I entered school, and even though he taught me math through the eighth-grade level the summer I was six, it took me the next fifteen years of grade school, junior high, high school, college, and graduate school to figure out that I could learn on my own, outside of institutions.

What clouded the issue was people telling me for years, because of my early educational acceleration, that I was specially bright. *I* wasn't special: my father's teaching was special. Learning at home was special. Access to interesting educational products was special. Reading, instead of watching TV, was special. You can have the same, or better, results by following the simple methods outlined in this book.

Bill and I are now teaching our own children, all of whom perform well above grade level. Ted, for instance, at age ten is well into high-school algebra. He studies woodworking and Greek on his own and makes lovely full-perspective drawings. Joseph, age eight, can read high school books and is teaching himself to play the piano. Sarah, age six, has been reading for years, and is now able to handle any reading task from an encyclopedia article to science fiction. She also enjoys her daily French lessons and her third-grade math text. Magdalene (age four) and Franklin (age two) are now racing to see who will learn to read first. They can both count anything in sight and recite all the books of the Bible (with some highly creative pronunciations!).

I'd like to think that our children are especially brilliant, but the fact is that *most* children show themselves highly creative and intelligent . . . if they are given a chance to learn the way God intended.

And that is what this book is about!

HOW TO USE THIS BOOK

You know how to read a resource book. Just turn to the section that interests you and browse through the reviews until something pops out at you from the text.

Well, guess what?

You can do the same thing with this book!

The editors and I have, however, incorporated a few innovative features that, we hope, will make each volume of *The Big Book of Home Learning* more useful than the average resource book.

If you'll flip to the Index of Suppliers you can see that it is more than just names with addresses attached. We're added all sorts of helpful information: toll-free telephone numbers for ordering, best times of day to call, methods of payment allowed, refund policy, whether or not the supplier has a free brochure or catalog and what it costs if it *isn't* free, plus a brief description of the supplier's product line. In this edition we even have added fax numbers, for those among us who have become addicted to those very helpful machines!

It is easy to find the address of any given company. Instead of searching through a chapter to find the company, as you have to when full addresses are given in the text, just flip to the index.

What all this means is that you can relax and enjoy *The Big Book of Home Learning* without having to write down reams of information about every product that interests you. Just jot down the name of the supplier, the name of the item, and its price on a handy index card or Post-It.™ When you get your whole list together, then you can turn to the index and highlight or underline the companies you intend to contact. Stick the card you were taking notes on in the index and go your merry way. When you are ready to sit down and send away for catalogs, or to call up and order, all the addresses are in one convenient location and you have all the item names and prices handy, too. And you can always find any item whose review you want to reread by turning to the General Index.

The information in *The Big Book of Home Learning* is as current and up to date as we could possibly make it. After the reviews were written, both they and the index information were sent back to the suppliers for verification. Even so, *it is always wise to write or call the supplier to check on prices before ordering*. The prices in this book are included to help you compare different products for value and are not permanently guaranteed. Prices go up and down (usually up!). Both you and the supplier will feel better if the supplier does not have to return your order because the check you enclosed was not for the right amount.

Lastly, this book would not have been possible without the active cooperation of many of the companies listed. Those who supplied me with samples and free catalogs bravely ran the risks of review, and I have not hesitated to point out their products' warts. I would like them to feel they gained more than a critical going-over by their generosity. Both the publisher and I would be grateful if you would mention *The Big Book of Home Learning* when you contact a supplier whose product is mentioned here.

SMARTER EDUCATION NOW!

CHAPTER ONE

HOME IS WHERE THE SMART IS

Are you one of those people who was not in the 99th percentile on every test? Have you learned to think of yourself as an "average" person, or perhaps even "slow"? Are you one of the millions who entered kindergarten with bright-eyed enthusiasm but who lost their love of learning along the way? If you are, then this book is for you.

Or perhaps you *were* in the 99th percentile. You soared gracefully through school while others waddled. This book is for you too.

Has your child been labeled "learning disabled" or "dyslexic" or "retarded" (or even "gifted")? Have you have gone around and around with the school trying to find out what the label means and what the school plans to do about it? Are you looking for a sensible way to help your child, one that doesn't depend on federal funding or special programs? Would you like to see *dramatic* improvement in your child's academic progress? The sources that can help you are right here.

Maybe you have already decided to teach your children at home. You look at the schools near you and are not thrilled at the prospect of incarcerating your children in them for thirteen years. You have precious values that you want to pass on, and you are determined to fight for your children's souls and minds. This book is *especially* for you!

Learning at home is the magic key that millions of people have used to unlock the educational treasure-chest. No longer must you or your children climb the academic beanstalk in competition with a hundred other Jacks, each of whom can only succeed by knocking his fellows off into the depths. No longer must you spend a fortune on college credits for knowledge offered elsewhere for a pittance. No longer must you watch your child shrivel up under the burden of a "label" that some trendy educrat has stuck on him or her. In the comfort and privacy of your own home you can learn whatever you want to, whenever you want to—and so can your children.

The advantages of learning at home are *price*, *options*, and *freedom*. Home educational products come wrapped in Kraft paper and delivered by the mailman. Classroom products come wrapped in classrooms (very expensive) and delivered by the school administration (likewise, very expensive). Home learning can be done at your convenience, and in most cases there are no deadlines at all. You cannot, however, *physically* attend a class and take a bubble bath or groom the dog at the same time. At home, you have thousands of choices at your fingertips through this book alone. Away from home, you either are limited to whatever options are offered in your geographical area—or forced to pay exorbitant sums for transportation in order to get to that great seminar in San Diego or that workshop in Bangor, Maine. At home nobody nags you or grades you unless you want them to. Schools, however, *run* on grades and you must do the work *they* require when *they* want you to do it and in the way *they* want you to do it, or you come away empty-handed.

Let's look at how you can reap the advantages of price, option, and freedom by learning at home.

PRICE

What do you think you'd pay for a private lesson in Country Guitar from Merle Watson? $100 per hour? $200? Homespun Tapes will sell you one solid hour of the master on cassette, teaching you all his tricks for just $12.95. This amounts to actually three hours' worth of lesson, as in person you would be taking a considerable amount of lesson time practicing the techniques. Further, you can rewind the tapes and hear Merle over and over again. No real-life teacher is *that* patient! When you count these latter factors in, the price of a lesson from a musical master comes to less than the price your next-door neighbor would charge.

What would it cost for you to send your child to one of the top private schools in the country? The going rate is now over $5,000 per year for these elite schools, and even those who have money are often turned away because there are fewer places than would-be students. You can, however, get the entire Calvert School program, including teacher grading and counseling, for just a tad over $400. Calvert's home-taught graduates consistently demonstrate the same achievement as its classroom students. You have thus purchased virtually all the benefits of one of the nation's most exclusive schools at a fraction of the in-person price.

Every volume of this series is loaded with bargains like these. What are you looking for? Personal training for your daughter that will improve her study skills? (Right here in Volume One.) The same kind of phonics instruction given at the most exclusive private schools? (Volume Two.) Special tutoring in geometry for your high schooler? (Volume Three.) Art lessons from a fa-

mous teacher? (Volume Four.) Thanks to audio, video, computers, and the written word, you can have private lessons from the best teachers in the world—at home, and at prices that won't make your checkbook scream.

OPTIONS

Lovers of the offbeat and unusual are sure to be delighted with the educational offerings available at home. From make-your-own-globe kits to authentic pioneer stories to science riddles, the home market is popping with surprises! Buy a natural science coloring book for your granddaughter! Find out how to teach math with colorful felts! Dance about the room to grammar songs! Cut out and assemble a covered wagon, complete with horses! Play a computer game where you twirl disks about on the screen to practice your spatial skills!

Some items you need are available *only* at home. You can't just bop down to the local Wal-Mart and pick up the organizers reviewed in this volume, for example. And I am seeing an increasing number of products specifically designed for families learning at home, from the National Writing Institute creative-writing program (Volume Two) to do-it-yourself calligraphy courses (Volume Three).

On reading instruction, are you stuck with whatever method the local school uses, no matter how poorly your children respond? Not at all! There are dozens of excellent programs, and although most public schools and even a goodly number of private schools pass them by (witness our national illiteracy), that doesn't mean *you* can't rescue *your* children by reaching for *Play 'n Talk* or *Sing, Spell, Read and Write*.

FREEDOM

In the spring a young man's fancy lightly turns to thoughts of . . . final exams. If you have ever fallen in love while enrolled in school, you will remember how very inconvenient that was. There you were, struggling with papers and reports and deadlines when your heart was emphatically elsewhere.

School, like time and Amtrak, waits for no man. The oldest grandfather in graduate school has no more freedom than the youngest preschooler when it comes to deciding *when* he wants to learn. The whole class must lurch forward at once, and laggards are left holding a lonely "F."

Under our present inefficient "credentialing" system, which focuses more on classroom attendance than actual knowledge and experience, education becomes a form of involuntary servitude. You give up control of your own life in order to (you hope) gain that coveted credential. You are not allowed to proceed at your own pace, or select the educational content or method you prefer. This applies equally to children and adults, with the major difference being that adults can switch from one institution to another or walk away from the whole thing if they are totally disgusted, whereas children usually have no choices at all.

At home, you are in control. You can pick and choose from a variety of sources instead of being tied down to whatever is physically available in your area.

You can do the work when it is convenient for you. If you are looking for knowledge, not credentials, you can skip the whole stupefying mass of busywork and tests, and concentrate only on what interests you. Learning becomes a pleasant adventure rather than a burden.

Browse through this series. See the vast array of educational products all begging for your attention. The people behind these products are all eager to please you. They are not interested in making you jump through hoops, but in meeting *your* needs, since they know that if they don't you will turn to someone else who does. See how clever, unusual, helpful, and inexpensive many of their products are. Then you will know why the smart learn at home!

CHAPTER TWO

GETTING ON TARGET

The recruits were lined up in the shooting trench, rifles to shoulder. At the signal, "Fire!" each man in turn shot his bullet at the target. All except for Private Smith. As the sergeant bellowed "Fire!" Smith raised his rifle and shot almost straight up in the air.

Seething with anger, the sergeant strode over to Smith's position. "You have to be the worst shot I have ever had in my barracks!" he fumed. "What in the Sam Hill do you mean by gosh-awful shooting like that?" Before he could continue, a large, fat duck tumbled out of the sky, nearly hitting him on the head.

"Well, Sergeant," Smith replied mildly, "seems we were shooting at different targets."

Everyone today is "for" education, but we are not all shooting at the same target. Some of us see education as the Great Rainbow Hope, leading our children on to a future of world peace and prosperity. In their view, education's most important task is indoctrination rather than academics. Presumably Janie will be better off if she learns to aspire to the role of brain surgeon (although she cannot read) than if she actually learns the math and verbal skills needed by a brain surgeon (and chooses a traditional role). Even better, Janie should become an activist fighting for the right of all Third World children to become brain surgeons.

I am not going to argue the pros and cons of this view. Suffice it to say that children do not need manda-tory kindergarten and all-year school, plus afterschool programs, to learn this. Simply make the kids watch Ted Turner specials.

Another view of education is that children need to learn something besides politically-correct attitudes. Stuff like skills and facts. This is what most of the public has in mind when we allow government officials to spend more than $5000 per pupil per year on the public education system.

The good news is that you don't need anywhere near $5000 a year to teach your kids what they really need to know. Just aim at the right target, use the right resources, and enjoy the great results!

So what is the right target?

There are actually *lots* of right targets. Our kids can become speed readers, geographical whizzes, and sports stars. They can learn to write with verve and style and speak with dramatic persuasion. They can have enormous vocabularies (in several languages) and draw, paint, and sing. They can also become decent human beings while doing all the above, since the discipline of learning and the discipline of spiritual growth are not mutually exclusive.

Children have a built-in need to succeed. They need to be able to do something well and see the results. Towards that end, I would like to help my children *master* what they learn *as quickly* as possible, eventually becoming *independent* learners. If you agree with me that these targets are worth shooting at, then read on and see how we can aim so as to hit them!

MASTERY—A FINITE TASK

Here is one simple thought that can greatly reduce stress in learning. *You can master any new skill in a reasonable amount of time.* This idea does not sound earthshaking. But when you compare it to the way schools usually teach, you'll see how revolutionary it is.

Say Johnny wants to learn to read. Does his teacher say, "O.K., Johnny, I'll teach you to read. It should take about twenty hours total, and then with practice you will be able to read anything you want"? No way! Johnny is facing up to *eight years* of reading instruction. No matter how well he can read, every year he will be reviewing his sight words, writing out spelling lists, filling out endless "reading comprehension" tests, and on and on and on. Would this discourage *you*? Of course it would! And it discourages Johnny too. The task seems endless. Nothing he does will make it shorter.

For dramatic results in your home program, just make it clear to the student that this task will *not* go on forever. If he applies himself, he *can* finish it more quickly. Promise *not* to review him constantly on his skills. Instead, immediately put those skills to work.

How do you do this? Well, let's say you are teaching your daughter arithmetic. Once she has learned addition, throw a party. Buy her a present. Treat her to a yogurt popsicle. Do *something* to celebrate. Any ceremony you come up with will help cement the fact that an era is over. Addition study is over. (Celebrating will also make her more anxious to finish the *next* step!) Now you are not going to study addition any more. Rather, you are going to *use* addition. Let her help you tally up the checks when you balance your checkbook.

Have her keep running tabs on the cost of your shopping trip. Addition is used in multiplication and division, which she will be studying next, so if you don't do anything special at all she will still be using it.

If you are trying to teach your child something that he never gets any practice using in daily life, you probably didn't need to teach it in the first place.

ACCELERATION—GETTING UP TO SPEED

Another reason school seems like such a hopeless burden to many children is that it goes on so long. Thirteen years is a longer sentence than most murderers get nowadays. Yet we toss kids into school and lock the door on them for thirteen years and expect them to be enthusiastic about it!

Nobody needs thirteen years to learn what the schools have to teach. At the most, you need three or four.

Let me explain why I said that. It's really pretty obvious when you see how our forebears handled education. In those olden golden days, kids didn't start school until age eight or nine. They attended classes for, at the most, three six-week sessions a year, six hours a day, and by the time they were sixteen they could read, write, and cipher rings around modern children. Nor was their instruction confined to the Three R's. American children of the 1700s through the early 1900s learned history, theology, geography, practical science, and hundreds of practical skills that are now only tackled in college, if at all. When you add up the total time in school, it comes out to eight years of eighteen weeks each. Modern children go to school thirty-six weeks a year; so by simple arithmetic four years of old-time instruction should be all it takes for similar results.

In actual fact, it has been shown again and again that twenty hours of phonics instruction is all that children need in order to read. As for math, you may recall that my father taught me eight years of math in three months, two hours per day. That amounts to 120

hours for *all* basic math, as opposed to the 1,440 the schools now spend. Surely I am not 12 times smarter than everyone else! Similar reasoning applies to the other subjects: history, geography, handwriting, composition, and so forth.

Every child who attends school, public or private, is retarded. "Retarded" means "held back." Schools are in the business of keeping children off the street and out of the job market for twelve years. So they drag out learning needlessly for years, and fill up the time with mindless, boring exercises.

You may wonder what to do with a child who flashes through the standard school subjects. Don't worry. *He'll* know what to do! The whole point of learning the basics is to get to the good stuff—other languages, literature, serious writing, theological studies, designing and inventing, art, music, and on and on. By the time your children finish their basic education, it should be clear what subjects interest them enough to qualify for further study. Let Junior start a business. Send his articles to magazines. Patent his amazing arcade game. Give him a one-man show and invite the artistic community in to admire his work and suggest improvements. With the whole wide world out there, who wants to spend eight years with reading comprehension worksheets!

Some states, in an attempt to save high school dollars, are letting teenagers take the GED at sixteen. But why stop at sixteen? Any wide-awake ten-year-old who is home-taught ought to be able to pass it . . . *without* excessive studying in advance. And wouldn't *that* be a motivator!

INDEPENDENCE— GETTING ON WITH THE JOB

John Holt became famous for suggesting that kids can teach themselves *without* adult interference. Although this idea can be carried to extremes, it is undoubtedly easier to learn without someone hovering over you and babbling in your ear while you are trying to work.

Anyone who has a fine crop of youngsters to teach at home quickly discovers the importance of letting students do as much as they possibly can by themselves. One of my favorite lines is, "Try it. If you have trouble, come and ask for help."

Only children, and adults, who are allowed to work through a problem on their own ever discover the thrill of accomplishment. Throw away those crutches!

The koala may carry her baby until he is as big as she is, but this does not work well for humans.

Robert Doman, head of the National Academy of Child Development, has said that the average child gets only *three minutes* of individualized instruction daily in school. Three minutes! I don't know where Mr. Doman gets his figures, but my own school experience sure validates them. Do you think you can beat this at home? Even fifteen minutes a day is five times more personal instruction than your children get in school!

And your time at home can be much more efficient than school time also. Discover how with the Five Steps of Learning!

CHAPTER THREE

THE FIVE STEPS OF LEARNING

If I had a hammer . . . I'd probably use it to knock nails into wood. If school bureaucrats had a hammer . . . they'd probably hold it by the wrong end, punch feebly at one or two nails, and then call it "nailing disabled" and throw it away. Even more likely, some educrat would announce a "Nailing Crisis" and call for a few billion bucks to buy hammers with heads on *both* ends.

The more the schools fail, the less they learn. Educrats have become experts in blaming their students for the educrats' failures. We now have a bumper crop of "learning disabled" children and "functionally illiterate" adults. Blame the educrats? Never! Yet it is a tiny bit suspicious that a nation which had achieved *99 percent literacy* in 1910 (according to U.S. Bureau of Education figures issued at that time) all of a sudden is supposedly bursting with mental cripples!

Is learning *really* mysterious and difficult? Do we really need hordes of federally-funded educational experts? Let's put a pin to this bubble and see how ridiculously simple learning can be—once we understand a few very simple facts.

HOW YOU USE YOUR BRAIN

Take a look at the brain. It's that roundish mass inside your skull that looks like the Green Giant's left-over chewing gum. Understand how the brain operates and you will know why some educational methods work and others don't.

Oversimplifying grossly, we see that thinking involves two main operations: storage and retrieval. You store everything that comes in through your senses in infinitesimal brain cells. If you could remember all of this, you'd probably go crazy; but you can't remember it, since you lose track of what is stored there quite easily.

Learning is the art of connecting your memories in a way that makes enough sense for you to be able to retrieve them rapidly. *Thinking is the act of making new connections* between your memories. In the brain, thinking causes physical connections to grow between the brain cells. The more connections you have, the better your thinking powers. The brains of geniuses are convoluted and heavy with all the connections they have made. Newborn babies, on the other hand, have smooth brains with almost no connections.

Let us, then, develop a very simple theory of education based on these two observable truths: (1) You can't connect what isn't there. And (2) you can't find what is there without a logical connection. Thus, it is vital to expose the student, whatever his age, to a lot of raw data *before* trying to "teach" him anything concerning that data. After he has soaked up hundreds of facts and experiences, then it is equally vital to supply him with a means of connecting them all. You could call this the "Data-Connection Theory," but since there is actually nothing original about it, call it anything you like. It works like this:

Say you want to teach a child to read. You do not shove a book in front of his face and start teaching. First, you expose him to a lot of print. Big print, little print. Newsprint. Books. Cereal boxes. Meanwhile, you read to him. Snuggled in your lap, he is both cozy and unafraid—ideal conditions for learning. Slowly he will get the idea: those black marks are letters, letters make words, and words are what Mommy is reading to me. Once he understands what reading is all about, he will probably ask you to teach him to read. Your task, then, is to provide the logical patterns (phonics) which translate all those letters into sounds.

True, reading is a complex subject, and we haven't discussed the idea of physical readiness (i.e., brain maturation) or methods of teaching yet. But I want you to understand that there are really only four basic approaches to teaching, three of which are wrong.

Number One is to begin laying a logical framework *without* first supplying any individual data. You can actually feel the strain on your brain of trying to learn this way. You see, you are not only trying to connect your brain cells, but to fill them at the same time! It's easy to see that a lot gets lost in the shuffle this way.

Number Two is to supply the original data, but fail to show how the individual facts hang together. This is what the schools do when they load a kid up with "Readiness" activities and then spring sight-word reading on him. He is stuck trying to memorize zillions of seemingly unconnected facts. Some kids do manage to invent their own phonics patterns and survive, but it's in spite of, not because of, the way they are taught. This rote memorization approach is used all over: in history, in math, in spelling, in my college engineering courses. Learners are handed hundreds of little "rules" or "facts" without any reasonable way of hanging them all in order. The brain does not want to work this way, and so although individual students can stuff the facts down for a test, they promptly forget it all in a week. This is not real learning.

Number Three is to provide *neither* initial experiences *nor* a framework. Fluffhead professors with no communication abilities are the chief perpetrators of this style of "teaching." Others are deluded into thinking the profs are brilliant because nobody understands them. But flunking all your students is *not* a sign of genius. If a teacher gets garbage out, it's probably because he put garbage in.

The only way that works consistently, because it is based on the way the brain operates, is Number Four: providing the learner with raw data and after he's had time to digest it, with a permanent framework for storing the data. New data can then be connected to the old with minimal effort.

In history, the framework would be a time line. In geography, the framework is a globe. The learner must have some way of getting a panoramic view of the field he is studying or he will be, as he puts it, "lost." Once he has that panoramic view, he can fill in the details as long as he lives.

Some educational products provide data (which, as you remember, includes experiences). Others provide a learning framework, such as a good phonics program. Some provide both. As we learn to discern which product does what, we can educate ourselves and our children much more efficiently.

What I am going to say now is even less original. Since the beginning of time, mothers and fathers have mastered these five simple steps of learning. Only in our science-worshiping age have we tried to bypass the wisdom of our grandparents—with the dismal results you now see. *Their* generation was 99% literate, remember?

THE FIRST STEP—PLAYING

Let kids be kids. That's step one. *Play* is the first step of learning. Earthshaking, isn't it? Any kindergarten teacher could tell you that! Ah, but do we *act* on this knowledge? How many times do we or Johnny's teachers try to rush him into "mastering" some new skill without giving him any chance to play around with it first?

Play is not just for babies. Play is the stage where you fool around with something before settling down to get serious about it. When you riffle through a book before starting to read, you are playing. When your husband picks up his new chain saw and makes passes in the air, he is playing. When your wife tries on a new dress that she doesn't intend to actually wear anywhere today, she is playing. Play turns the strange into the comfortable, the unknown into the familiar. Dad hefts his new chain saw because he wants to know how heavy it feels before he risks his fingers using it on a piece of wood. Mom tries on her dress because she needs to feel comfortable about how she looks in it before appearing in public. In the very same way, children need to get comfortable with new words, new objects, and new ideas before they can be reasonably expected to do anything serious with them.

Several writers on education have noticed that children who are allowed to play with learning equipment before being put through any exercises with the equipment do much better than those who are immediately forced to use the equipment for its "proper" use. In his book *How Children Learn* (Dell Publishing Company, 1983, revised edition) John Holt tells about his friend Bill Hull's experience with the attribute blocks he invented:

> They found a very interesting thing about the way children reacted to these materials. If, when a child came in for the first time, they tried to get him "to work" right away, to play some of their games and solve some of their puzzles, they got nowhere. . . . But if at first they let the child alone for a while, let him play with the materials in his own way, they got very different results. . . . When, through such play and fantasy, the children had taken those materials into their minds, mentally swallowed and digested them, so to speak, they were then ready and willing to play very complicated games, that in the more organized and businesslike situation had left other children completely baffled. This proved to be so consistently true that the experimenters made it a rule always to let children have a period of completely free play with the materials before asking them to do directed work with them.

If you're going to open up unfamiliar new territory in your brain, your best move is to send out some scouts. Survey the terrain. Get to know what it looks like. Then you'll feel confident about building a town out there. Play is the brain's scouting expedition.

How does this apply in real life? Here are some examples:

- Children should *see* print and *hear* it read before trying to learn to read. If possible, they should also *manipulate* letters (like alphabet puzzle pieces) and *write* letters before beginning their reading lessons.

- Children should be allowed to scribble freely before you try to help them make specific marks on the paper. Allow them to use any color they want, and to color outside the lines in the coloring book. So far, three of my children have gone through the scribble stage and the color-it-any-color-but-the-right-one stage, and *without any help from me* all three have gone on to neat, accurate coloring.

- Words like *noun* and *verb* should be used well in advance of any grammar lessons. Ditto for all terminology and every subject. Making a student of any age learn both unfamiliar words *and* unfamiliar concepts at the same time is cruel and unusual punishment.

- Grabbiness is part of learning. See how quickly a baby explores the box his Christmas present came in! He is not satisfied until he has gone thoroughly over it with eyes, ears, nose, fingers, and mouth. Babies, more than the rest of us, are determined to make the unfamiliar familiar. They know they don't know, and are trying to catch up. (Incidentally, knowing we don't know and unself-consciously humbling ourselves to learn may be part of what Jesus had in mind when He said we must become like little children.)

THE SECOND STEP—
SETTING UP YOUR FRAMEWORK

A child learning to read and an adult studying aeronautical engineering both need the same thing: a framework to help them organize their data. This framework is like a filing cabinet loaded with files. It provides slots in which to fit the ever-accumulating new data. In history, the time line; in geography, the globe; in reading, the alphabet; in language, the web of grammar; these are frameworks under which myriads of new facts can be filed.

A good framework answers the question, "What in all tarnation is *this?*" History is about people and movements and dates; hence the time line. Geography is about where things are; hence the globe. Engineering is about putting little pieces together to make a building (or airplane, or circuit board). Grammar is about putting words together to make a sentence. Handwriting is about making marks on paper that people can read.

A framework is the big picture, the panoramic view of your subject. Your framework is what's going to glue together all the thousands of facts and ideas you are going to learn.

One big reason kids flounder in school is because the teachers are so wrapped up in skills and subskills and testing and grades that their students forget what they are trying to accomplish. If a student can't see the relationship between filling out fourteen workbook pages on beginning consonants and beginning to read (and believe me, the connection is pretty tenuous), his mind will not be storing the new information under the right headings. Reading will seem a succession of unrelated hoops the teacher is trying to make him jump through, and it won't "come together" for him. This is also why students shy away from those fuzzy graduate courses where the teacher wanders all over the landscape without ever making it clear what the course is *about*.

It's not hard to set up a learning framework. All classical instruction included frameworks. Just giving a subject a *name*, like Oceanography or Weaving or Renaissance Art, is the beginning of a framework. If you know what you're trying to learn—whether TV repairing or gourmet cookery or the story of Ethelred the Unready—you're on your way!

THE THIRD STEP—CATEGORIES

Think of your filing cabinet, if you have one. Can you easily find papers you have filed away, or do you have to grumble your way through umpteen folders every time you need a paper?

Those of us who have expanded into several filing cabinets quickly find that we need a system to keep it all straight. Some use colored folders, some use colored dots, some use each drawer for a special purpose—it doesn't matter. The main thing is that without organization our bulging files are as useless as if they were in Timbuktu.

You see, a framework is only half the story. You can have a filing cabinet (framework) without an organized arrangement of files. Without organization, though you can happily file new facts by the ton, you can't find them except by accident.

Efficient learners make it their practice to break every new subject down into manageable categories. They don't study the American Revolution all at once, for instance. They study Famous Loyalists, Famous

Generals, Spies and Traitors, Naval Battles, the Continental Congress, or whatever categories give them most insight into what they are trying to learn.

It invariably happens that, as you go deeper into a subject, your original categories become too broad and you have to make sub-categories. In our example above, the Continental Congress quickly becomes too wide a field for the serious student. So he might break it down further into Congressional Leaders, Congressional Committees, Southern Congressmen, or other sub-categories, each of which in turn can be further divided.

Let's take another example: reading. Why do phonics courses always spend so much time talking about Vowels and Consonants and Short Vowels and Long Vowels and Blends and Digraphs and Diphthongs? Those are *categories*, that's why! Anyone can remember five Short Vowels and twenty-one Consonants. These little boxes make the data much more findable. Contrast this with the sight-word method used in 85 percent of public schools, where Junior is trying to memorize the individual shapes of all the words in the English language, and you'll have a clue as to why we have a national reading problem.

The difference in learning efficiency between a product or course that organizes the data for you into categories, and one that doesn't, is immense. Although the latter may contain gobs of useful knowledge, you'll have a real struggle walking away with any of it. Keep this in mind as you shop.

THE FOURTH STEP— ORDERING YOUR DATA

Once you've become comfortable with your object of study, the next step is to pick up more information about it. You can do this by memorizing categories of facts, but your task will be much easier if you can sort the information into patterns.

Patterns are your method for filing new facts into a category. Going back to our example of the file cabinet, let's say you have organized your file cabinet by categories. The top drawer is for family records and the bottom one is for your home business. Within each drawer you have file folders (sub-categories), also organized by topic. You have, for example, one file folder exclusively for Personal Correspondence. All is well and good so far. But if you want to quickly find the letter your Aunt Theresa wrote you six months ago, you'd better have a method for filing letters inside that folder.

You could have filed your letters with the most recent to the front of the folder and the oldest correspondence to the back. You could have filed letters by the names of the people writing to you, or by the topics on which they wrote. Although some of these schemes would be more efficient than others, *any* of them would be more efficient than simply shoving each letter helter-skelter into the folder.

In the same way, you will hold onto new facts much better if you can arrange them in order using a systematic pattern.

What do I mean by a "pattern"? As I said, *patterns are your organizing method.* When you have a category of related facts (such as, in phonics, words ending with "at"), the systematic way you file them (in this case, alphabetic order) is your pattern. Let's look at the pattern for our example of "at" words (alphabetically, by digraphs, by diphthongs):

at	pat	plat
bat	rat	slat
cat	sat	spat
fat	vat	sprat
hat	brat	splat
mat	drat	chat
Nat	flat	that

Once a child gets used to writing out families of words in alphabetic order, he has a tool for generating dozens of new words from *every* word ending or category he learns.

Some facts need to be sorted alphabetically, as in our example above. Others have a natural chronological pattern (as when studying the battles in a war). Still others sort out numerically, starting with the smallest and ascending to the largest. Arithmetic is full of these kinds of patterns, e.g.:

$$1 + 1 = 2$$
$$2 + 1 = 3$$
$$3 + 1 = 4$$
$$\cdots\cdots\cdots\cdots\cdots\cdots$$
$$10 + 1 = 11$$

Learning the "one-pluses" by this pattern is much easier than trying to memorize individual "math facts" out of order.

Matter can be organized by its physical layout. You will notice that this series you are now reading follows a definite pattern. Each chapter begins with text that discusses the issues in an educational field. The text is followed by reviews, sorted in alphabetical order. Each review has similar information in its heading. This makes the book easier to use than if all the information were jumbled together.

Why are we spending so much time talking about patterns? Because patterns are what make or break many educational products. If data is not patterned, or is ordered according to the wrong pattern, it becomes much harder to use. Try this simple example. Which of the following foreign language programs would be easier to use? The first categorizes phrases together that deal with, say, table manners, and leaves it at that (this one has categories, but no patterns). The second categorizes the phrases and lists them in alphabetical order (category plus pattern). The third categorizes phrases, and lists them in *grammatical* order (e.g., "I like the meal. You like the meal. He likes the meal. She likes the meal . . ."). The third program sorts the data into *the form in which you need it*, since you talk in terms of I or he or she, not in alphabet lists.

Similarly, it is easy to learn the days of the week in chronological order, which is the way we use them, whereas if you memorized them in random order, or alphabetical order, it would be extremely difficult to use them quickly.

Not every individual fact can be sorted into a pattern. You've just got to memorize the value of pi, for instance. But the vast majority of useful data does follow systematic patterns. It's the scientist's job to find these patterns, and the teacher's job to use them.

If you want to learn effortlessly, and remember what you learn, insist on products that provide both categories and patterns.

THE FIFTH STEP—FUSION

Have you ever had a brainstorm? Suddenly you could almost hear the clicking as light turned on inside your head. Misty ideas suddenly coalesced. Hundreds of previously unrelated facts joined arms and marched along singing.

That marvelous experience is what some writers call "synthesis" and I prefer to call "fusion." Fusion is when frameworks link. All at once electrical impulses can take the express from Point A to Point B, when they used to have to make detours and swim muddy streams of consciousness to make the trip.

Fusion *feels* good. It unclogs your brain, and lets you spend the energy that used to be wasted hacking through jungles of confusion on more edifying pursuits.

Fusion is the opposite of *confusion*, which is what happens when our carefully-built frameworks turn out to be all wrong and we have to start rebuilding them from scratch. This confusion is the eternal lot of those who are heedless about looking for answers to the deep questions of life.

We live in an age when people are being taught that there *are* no answers, so one might as well not bother asking the questions. The only consistent responses if this is true are despair or ruthless hedonism. And these are the lifestyles we are seeing today.

Although the antiphilosophy of relativism—that there is no right and wrong—has had great success, it is not correct. The human brain was not constructed to be open to *everything*. People have a built-in need for right and wrong, for security, for an integrating philosophy of life. Perhaps the best books ever written on this subject, that describe our present confusion and the timeless solution, are *Escape from Reason* by Dr. Francis Schaeffer (published by InterVarsity Press) and *L'Abri* by Edith Schaeffer (published by Tyndale House). Great Christian Books sells both these books, which between them cost less than $10.

We don't need to understand the meaning of our lives in order to eat, sleep, and park the car. But human beings are not worms in the mud; the more we learn about the world and the joys and injustices of life, the more every thinking person asks, "What is this all for?" How tragic if we, and our children, have been taught to strangle these questions before they can even be spoken. Tragic because there is Someone home in the universe; God is not dead; and everyone who seeks, shall find.

PART II

GETTING STARTED LEARNING AT HOME

CHAPTER FOUR

THE LAZY PERSON'S GUIDE TO HOME EDUCATION

One of the fascinating things that happens to people who write books is that *readers write back!* On any given day, our old family mailbox is jammed full of letters. It takes me at least five hours a week just to sort and read my personal mail—never mind *answering* it!

After *The Big Book of Home Learning* came out, many mothers and fathers wrote to share about the fantastic time they were having teaching their children at home. Meanwhile, I received a small but significant number of letters with sad stories to tell. Typically, a mother of one or two would tell me she tried home schooling or afterschooling and gave it up because it was "too hard" and "wasn't working out."

I really wondered about those last letters for a while. We have seven children and a home business, plus both Bill and I write books, teach Sunday school, and try to remain reasonably involved in our community. How come we, and other parents of large families who had written to us, could manage to teach our children at home, while parents with much more time and fewer children were struggling? Why was the question readers most frequently asked, "How do you find time to do it all?"

It could be, of course, that Bill and I are just utterly amazing Superfolks, and I could try and put this explanation over were it not for the large number of people still living who know us personally and know bet-

ter. (That's why it's better to wait until you're 90 to write your memoirs!) It could also be that we have given birth to seven infant prodigies in a row, an explanation their grandparents favor. It's certainly not that we have maids or hired help (don't I wish!).

We do have a secret for our success. It's . . . laziness! Like other survival-oriented parents of a large brood, for many years now we have been searching for easier, simpler ways of doing things. And surprise! There *are* easier, simpler ways to learn at home. Now let's take a look at some shortcuts.

ACCESS

The best way to teach is to not have to teach at all. Ideally, our children should learn how to learn and begin to teach themselves.

How can we help our children reach this stage? In part, by giving them access to educational tools.

Let's define what we're talking about here. Access does not mean simply having educational items available somewhere in the house. It means having them ready to hand, right where the child can get them when he wants them or when you want to direct his attention to them. Children blessed with access to the tools of learning will tend to use them on their own much more frequently than those who have to climb stairs, navigate stacks of clutter, or ask you to get out the items in question.

Here is how the access principle works.

FOR A BABY: Alphabet letters, numerals, and educational pictures clutter our homes. *But* how often do you have the time to sit down with your little one and help him play with all his educational toys? Instead of all those fancy toys, try taping a simple sheet of paper with the ABC's on it on the wall next to your changing table. You have to spend what seems like hours there every day anyway, so why not give your baby something interesting to look at? You will have plenty of opportunities to point to and say each letter, and your youngster will have lots of time to become familiar with the shape of print. The same can be done with color and shape charts, "touch 'n feel" strips with different fabrics glued to them, numeral strips, and so on.

FOR A TODDLER: Is the piano lid often left rolled back so he can plink away at the keys? Are there lots of hard-to-destroy books around that he can "read"? Even better, have you trained him how to handle *your* books properly so he doesn't have to be shooed away from them? Do you have special places for his toys so he can find one easily when he wants it, or are half of them lost and the rest scattered all over? Have you taught him how to put cassettes in the cassette player or just stuck them up high somewhere? Remember, if a child is taught how to use it, he won't abuse it.

FOR AN OLDER CHILD: Do you leave that expensive pint-size violin out between scheduled practice sessions, or is it carefully put away in some hard-to-reach spot? Is art material a mere drawer pull away, or is it locked up in a cupboard somewhere? Is the encyclopedia in your family room (or whatever favorite reading spot your family has chosen) or displayed under glass in the den?

Human nature being what it is, you can be sure that if it is hard to find, hard to get out, or hard to put away, children will avoid it. But when parents make the materials of learning accessible, amazing things start to happen! I once read the story of a Suzuki mother who decided to hint that her daughter should put her violin away by leaving it out in plain view. The daughter never did put the violin away that day. Instead she practiced for half an hour more than usual. Every time she saw the violin she picked it up and

used it. You can imagine how this astonished the mother, who had been used to meeting resistance to music practice. In exactly the same vein, Maire Mullarney, an Irish home school mother, tells in her book *Anything School Can Do You Can Do Better* (available from Holt Associates) how she used to let her children paint all over their ancient kitchen table and walls, serving dinner around the latest masterpieces before wiping them off. Several of her children won national art competitions. This interest in art continued unabated until the family received an inheritance. With the money they bought fancier furniture and redid the house. The unexpected side effect was that the children no longer felt free to paint all over the new, expensive walls and table, and consequently started spending far less time on their art.

In short, if you put it where they can get it and teach them how to use it properly, children will use it. Provided, of course, that you have a good relationship with them and they are not trying to prove something by upsetting you, and also that your home is not loaded with time-wasting distractions that divert them from better pursuits.

The principle of access applies to all subjects, not just art and music. Our children are surrounded by math and science texts, thanks to all the companies that have let me review their wares. It's not at all uncommon to see Ted or Joe browsing through one of these in an odd moment. All our children have free access to crayons, pencils, pens, and paper, and in return we receive a never-ending stream of poems, stories, and art. When Sarah was only three already she was writing great sentences like "HA HAL NAO PHH," and at the age of one Magda would sit for minutes creatively scribbling (if you knew Magda, you'd know getting her to sit for *anything* is a major event!). Everyone bonks on the piano, and with only casual instruction the older ones are becoming quite good at picking out tunes. The knowledge the children pick up entirely on their own by their free foraging through our books helps schoolwork zip along and makes for interesting mealtime discussions. I'll probably never have to teach them art appreciation because of our art books and art cards, and the same goes for laser technology and robotics.

So the secret of making learning accessible is really

- good resources that the children know how to use
- happy children, and
- getting rid of worthless distractions (more on this later).

CLONE YOURSELF

Wouldn't it be wonderful if you could hire a private tutor for some minimal sum like, say, 5¢ an hour, to drill your children on all those memory facts and to tell them fascinating stories? You want it, you have it. Introducing . . . the Tape Recorder. Faster than a speeding mother! More powerful than a tired father! Able to leap tall buildings on either Fast Forward or Rewind! This remarkable visitor from our own planet has powers and abilities far beyond those of mortal men. Perfect recall of every story. Perfect patience. Perfect manners—talks at mealtimes without ever having its mouth full. Yes, friends, the humble audio cassette recorder can teach you and your children how to sing or play a musical instrument, how to speak a foreign language, or how to win in business. It can give you math drill set to song in stereo or read you the entire Bible. Art instruction, phonics courses, great literature, even sports tips are all available on cassette direct from the famous people who invented them. It's like having an army of tutors! And the best part is that you and your children can learn together or separately as the fancy takes you.

We listen to a lot of cassettes at mealtimes. I reviewed virtually all the cassettes for this book at lunchtime. The children also like them at breakfast, suppertime, and in between. Adults can listen to cassettes while washing dishes, nursing the baby, or driving to work, or (in my case) walking on a treadmill.

Video cassettes are also becoming popular, but will never be as versatile as the audio versions simply because you have to give video your full attention. Try to picture a video Walkman. Ugh.

Audio lets you learn while you do other things—a classic example of time-sharing.

INCREMENTAL LEARNING— THE HITS JUST KEEP ON COMING

We are indebted for this next suggestion to John Saxon, the developer of the world's greatest algebra series (read all about it in Volume Three). Saxon's idea is brilliantly simple: Teach one skill at a time. And then *let students keep practicing that skill*. He calls this "incremental learning"—learning one little thing at a time and then building on it.

Obvious, you say? Not in *practice*. In *practice*, once a student learns a new skill, do we ever reward him again for his achievement? Isn't the standard response a sigh of relief and "Now let's get on to the *next* subject"?

Whether in kindergarten or college, students spend their whole lives constantly struggling with the unfamiliar, only to be rewarded for their successes by *more* hoops to jump through. The constant pressure to learn *new* things never relaxes.

Math instruction has been an arid field when it comes to praising the student. Children are taught new skills, and then the skills are abandoned until final exam time, when they spring from the shadows on hapless test-takers. Saxon, seeing the fruitlessness of this "method," decided to *not* jump from skill to skill, but to include questions on previously learned concepts in *every* lesson. This is *not* the same thing as teaching the same old tired idea over and over again, that odious practice of unnecessary review. Saxon's students get to *use* their learning, and be praised for it.

How does this apply to other subjects? Here are some suggestions:

- Every multi-syllable word decoded is cause for rejoicing, not just the first one, until the student gets so good at reading that it would be insulting to praise him. (At this point, accepting his reading as just as good as yours, and asking him to read things for you, is praise enough.)

- Can Johnny color inside the lines? That doesn't mean he has just graduated from coloring books and never gets to color again. It does mean he can experiment with hard and soft coloring, with density, with different kinds of crayons and markers and coloring pencils, meanwhile being praised for his fine coloring.

- Just because Suzy is now in Book 3 of Suzuki piano, she shouldn't think she can never play her old Book 1 pieces again. Rather, encourage her to give them a whirl every now and then. She'll be able to see how much her expression and dynamics have improved, and see her progress.

Seeing how much you have improved is always great encouragement. So is feeling really competent at a task. Incremental learning makes learning *fun!*

LEARN THE LINGO

Shakespeare was wrong. A rose by any other name definitely does not smell as sweet. If you'd like a dash of quick encouragement, learn how to give fancy names to what you are doing with your children. A walk down the street can be a Science Excursion. Reading *Tintin Goes to Tibet* is Social Studies (your child is being exposed to the culture of Tibet, after all). That half-hour with the paint pot is Artistic Self-Expression. Weeding the walk is a Hands-On Nature Investigation. And don't forget all the time you spend answering their questions (stop thinking of those as "interruptions"—the official term is "teachable moments"). Write it all up in a daily journal and you'll be astonished at how much you are getting done.

THE TEACHER'S ROLE—TEACHING AS PUTTING IN

Lastly, here is how to make *teaching* more enjoyable.

You know, teachers are the most overworked and harassed bunch of people around—and that includes parents who try to teach their children. Why is that? In large part, it's because so much of their assigned job is *pulling facts out of people.*

I've never plowed with a mule, but I do believe that it's no harder to get an ornery mule to pull that plow than it is to get an ornery kid to divulge what's in his mind. Especially if *nothing* is in his mind. You can't pull out what isn't there—yet 90 percent of school time is spent on tests, quizzes, seatwork assignments, and verbal cross-examinations ("Who can tell us when Charlemagne was crowned Holy Roman Emperor?"), instead of on giving children information and giving them a chance to ask their *own* questions.

These demands for feedback are not teaching. Teaching is *telling or showing people what they don't know.* And it is so much easier to concentrate on input (telling) than on output (dragging feedback out of students)!

To make the most of your teaching time, and to make it easier on yourself, *tell your children what they need to know.* Don't be afraid to repeat yourself. Increase the proportion of input to output. A few simple oral questions will tell you whether your offspring are on track. Forget those piles of workbook exercises!

Read history to your children. *Read* science books together. *Read* the Bible at meals. Whatever the knowledge you want to impart, put it *in!* Don't wear yourself out checking whether they are learning. *After* they've received ample instruction is the time for a little low-pressured feedback.

Nobody tests your children on TV commercials. But if you still have a TV, you can see they have learned the ads. TV taught them. Unless your children are actively hostile, or so lazy that they won't even bother to listen, or so illiterate that they never read anything, you should be able to do at least as well as a TV set.

I don't mean that we should expect to play all the time. Learning can be hard work. But it should lead to the pleasure of success and be as pleasurable for our students as we can make it. If it's nothing but unalloyed drudgery for them and us, the fault is almost certainly to be found in the teaching materials or method.

When you find yourself working too hard, stop and ask

- Am I overdoing it? Am I making a simple subject too fancy? Am I trying to do *all* the suggested activities in the teacher's edition (this will kill any program)?

- What can I eliminate? What is essential in this course and what is extra?

- Do I need to be doing this at all? Is my child too young for this subject? Am I just trying to show off? Could I or my child live a worthy life in the world without mastering this material?

• Should I give it a rest? Are there other worthwhile things we would like to study or do instead of this until we can come back to it later?

Your goal should be to do the essential (teach Johnny to read, clean the kitchen before the Board of Health condemns it) and to get to the rest when you have time. Don't exhaust yourself trying to imitate all the success stories you read in home schooling magazines. Forget the fancy projects and the field trips that need two weeks to plan. You can always get to them later when your children have more enthusiasm for them and you have more time.

At various times I have had to give up piano lessons for the children (too young, not enough interest), art appreciation (overdoing it, neglecting more essential subjects), and Latin (not enough time, not needed at the moment). In the meantime I have learned a lot more about teaching each of these subjects and located better materials. Art appreciation and piano are now being handled by the children themselves and we have substituted French for Latin. The world did not end because we let some things slip that were giving us no joy for the present.

If it's something basic like reading or math that's giving you headaches you need to check out some of the other resources for these subjects. But even these subjects can be laid aside for a bit while you all recover.

Let's make learning as simple as we can, and learning will be fun!

CHAPTER FIVE

DISCOVER YOUR FAMILY'S LEARNING STYLES

Every trade has its tricks. A blacksmith knows how to make a horse stand still while he hammers on a new horseshoe. Fly fishermen know how to snap the rod and make the line float out over the water. Knowing these tricks makes work a sport, and sport more enjoyable.

Learning can also be a sport. The difference between the duffers and the champions is that the champions know the tricks of the sport, and care enough to put them into practice.

I would now like to share with you some very simple tricks and resources that can make a huge difference in how much you and your children *enjoy* learning.

YOUR SPECIAL LEARNING STYLE

Jack Sprat could learn by chat
His wife could learn by sight
Their son, named Neil, could learn by feel
They were a funny sight!

Everyone is born with a special learning style. Some, like Jack Sprat in the ditty above, learn best by listening. Others, like his wife, learn best by seeing. Still others are sensuous types who need to have real objects to handle. If you are taught through the channel that suits you, fantastic! If you're not, it's frustration time.

Educrats, in their slow grappling with reality, have recently rediscovered learning styles and christened them "modalities." Don't expect any sudden changes in the schools from this discovery, though. Mass-produced education and individualized learning styles do not mesh. The best you can hope for is that *after* your child has been labeled "dyslexic" or "hyperactive" or "learning disabled" some up-to-date remedial teacher will discover that Johnny really just has a learning style that his classroom did not accommodate.

Now let's discover *your* learning style.

SEEING IS BELIEVING—THE VISUAL LEARNER

Are you easily distracted by new sights? Do you remember where you put things? Are you good at catching typos and doing puzzles? Are you very aware of visual details in drawings? Do you remember names better when you see them on a name tag? If you answered "yes" to these questions, you are a *visual* learner.

Visual learners need to *see* what they are supposed to do. You should write out a model, or demonstrate visually the skill to be learned. Some materials that are good for visual learners are:

a. flash cards

b. matching games

c. puzzles

d. instruction books

e. charts

f. pictures, posters, wall strips, desk tapes

g. videos

h. simulation software

The visual sense is, if anything, *over*developed in many children of the TV generation. That is why it's so easy to find instruction geared to the visual learner. The visual learner often gets an artificial "head start" in academic success, thanks to the match between his favorite learning style and the school's favored teaching style. Later on, though, visual learners can get into trouble. Being able to follow printed directions is not the same as being able to follow oral directions, for example—and neither necessarily translates into knowing how to assemble the bikes you bought the kids for Christmas!

Even though such great stress is put on visual learning in our culture, visual learners should be encouraged to develop their auditory and hands-on abilities.

LEARNING BY HEARING—THE AUDITORY LEARNER

Do you like to talk a lot? Do you talk to yourself? As a child, were you a "babbler?" Do you remember names easily? Can you carry a tune? Do you like to "keep the beat" along with the music? Do you read out loud or subvocalize during reading? Can you follow oral directions more easily than written directions? When taking tests, do you frequently know the answer, but have trouble expressing it on paper? Then you are an *auditory* learner.

Auditory learners learn best by hearing. They need to be *told* what to do. Auditory learners will listen to you reading for hours, but you may not think they are paying attention because they don't look at you. They like to memorize by ear and can easily develop a good sense of rhythm. Naturally, auditory learners have a head start when it comes to learning music. Good materials for auditory learners are:

a. cassette tapes

b. educational songs and rhymes (like the ABC song)

c. rhythm instruments

Let's talk for a second about how musically-minded instruction can help auditory learners. Even before Mary Poppins ever informed her rapt young charges, "You know, a Song Will Help the Job Along," parents and teachers were using music to teach

- The Alphabet
- Phonics Rules
- Arithmetic Facts
- Character Lessons ("Dare to Be a Daniel!")
- Bible Verses
- Manners
- Handwriting ("Down and Over/Down some more/That's the way we make a Four!")
- Cultural History (Mother Goose)
- General History ("We fired our guns and the British kept a-coming . . .")
- Science ("The hipbone's connected to the . . . Legbone")
- Oh, yes, Music itself
- and a few thousand other things!

You will find musical resources sprinkled throughout the volumes of this *Big Book* series. Some of the best are in the Phonics, Geography, Bible, Foreign Languages, Storytelling, and of course, Music chapters. Try balancing these with a variety of interesting visual and hands-on resources to both encourage your auditory learner's natural talents and help him develop more visual and tactile learning strengths.

LEARNING BY DOING—
THE KINESTHETIC/TACTILE LEARNER

Now for the physical types! Here are your so-called "hyperactives." As a child, did you have difficulty sitting still? Were you always grabbing for things? Did you always run your finger across the boards when walking past a fence? Do you move around a lot, and use animated gestures and facial expressions when talking? Can you walk along the curb without losing your balance? Do you prefer hugs from your spouse rather than verbal praise? Do you like to take things apart? Are you always fooling with paper or something on your desk when you're on the phone? If so, then you're a *kinesthetic* learner.

Hands-on learning is a must for kinesthetic learners. They need to mold or sculpt or whittle or bend, fold, and mutilate in order to express themselves. Kinesthetic learners learn to read best by learning to write. They like math manipulatives and sandpaper letters. Kinesthetic learners do *not* like sitting at a desk for hours staring at the blackboard—it's like blindfolding a visual learner to do this to a kinesthetic learner.

For kinesthetic learners, try:

a. long nature walks

b. model kits

c. yard work and gardening

d. textured puzzles

e. typing instead of writing (it's faster and less frustrating)

Be sure to have kinesthetic learners write BIG when they are first learning. Large muscle action zips through to the brain more easily than small, fine movements. Manipulative materials and a good phonics program cure reversals in kinesthetic learners, who are the group most frequently labeled "dyslexic." Couple this with small doses of rich visual and auditory materials to increase your kinesthetic learner's attention span for these different types of learning.

You *can* be all three: visual, auditory, and kinesthetic. God designed people to learn through *all* their senses. But since most of us lean more to one learning style, you can increase your learning enjoyment by adapting most input to fit your style.

DANGERS OF "PERSONALITY STYLES"

Learning Style theory can be taken to extremes. The first mistake is to narrow yourself down to fit into a single Learning Style slot. Few people *only* learn visually, or auditorally, or kinesthetically. Categories are useful for defining major areas of interest, strength, and weakness, but they are not good for defining your total personality. Most of us fit into many categories at the same time. Take, for example, People Who like Ice Cream for Dessert and People Who Like Chocolate Candy. Or Sports Fans and Philosophers (there's more crossover between these than you think!). Or Energetic, Outgoing types and Sympathetic, Listening types (you can be each of these at different times).

There is also a danger of accepting everything about a person as that person's "style." Taken to extremes, immature or bad behavior could become enshrined as a valid temperament difference. It was Hitler's style to be fanatical and Goebbel's style to be mean. Some people are fanatical *and* mean. Shall we call this the "National Socialist Temperament Style"?

Yet another problem is the introduction of occult Eastern religious techniques under the umbrella of "helping children with their learning styles." One book, for example, under the heading "Visualizing Success in Learning," says the following:

> Picture a teacher that knows everything. This is your very own "inner teacher." Anytime you have a question about something, you can ask this teacher and get the answer. If you're taking a test and the answer doesn't come to you, ask your inner teacher for the right answer. If you're reading a book and see an unfamiliar word, ask your inner teacher to help you with it. If you're having a hard time understanding a new idea in school, have a conversation with your inner teacher about what is unclear, and your inner teacher will help you understand the idea.

If the author of that book really believes this "inner teacher" is just the child talking to himself, he is making unrealistic promises. If the child doesn't know a word, he doesn't know it, and no amount of chatting inside his head will substitute for looking the word up in the dictionary. However, if the author actually expects the "inner teacher" to provide information the child does *not* know, what we're looking at is boys and girls being encouraged to call upon supernatural beings *other* than God (our forebears called these "demons") and to submit to them as infallible guides.

Long-dead psychologist Carl Jung, a favorite of many involved in learning type theory nowadays, actually had frequent experiences of this nature, although he never recognized that the "beings" he was chatting with could have been more than simple projections of his subconscious mind. I find it ominous that Jungian theory is being repackaged for Christians nowadays, via the Jung-derived Myers-Briggs Type Inventory. The bottom line of all these Jungian "discover your temperament" books and packages is their insistence that character flaws like self-centeredness and the refusal to bow to any absolutes are perfectly valid temperament styles. Some of these books go even further and insist that even our basic beliefs are simply reflections of our temperaments. This amounts to saying, in an exceedingly doctrinaire fashion cleverly disguised by the rhetoric of tolerance, that Jung was right and Jesus Christ was wrong.

The buyer, in other words, must learn to beware. Just because a theory claims to be cutting-edge doesn't mean it is scientifically valid or religiously neutral.

Temperament, in any case, is not an inflexible king to whom we are doomed to submit. As renowned nineteenth-century educator Charlotte Mason said in volume 1 of her *Home Education* series (now republished by Tyndale House and available from Charlotte Mason Research & Supply),

> The problem before the educator is to give the child control over his own nature, to enable him to hold himself in hand as much in regard to the traits we call good, as to those we call evil. Many a man makes shipwreck on the rock of what he grew up to think his characteristic virtue—his open-handedness, for instance.

For terrific insight into how we parents can help our children not only recognize but also rule their natural temperaments, I highly recommend the Charlotte Mason books.

I am listing some popular Jungian resources below, both so you will recognize them when you see them and because once you understand where these are coming from, you can actually find out some useful things about yourself and others. Just don't make the mistake of believing that there's something sacred about being domineering, or wishy-washy, or selfish,

or greedy, just because those tendencies are associated with a particular set of initials on a graph somewhere!

NEW**
Multnomah Press
One of a Kind, $7.95

Jungian psychology packaged for Christians. This book from a Christian publisher starts with sixty pages introducing type theory. You take a quickie word choice quiz based on part of the Myers-Briggs Type Inventory, picking one each of 36 word-pairs to describe yourself, family, and friends. Author LaVonne Neff then gives you some warm, well-intentioned advice on how to apply what you now know about yourself and others to become a more relaxed mom (the book is basically written for women), more mellow wife, more effective child evangelist (of your own kids), etc. Again, the book is very accepting of all approaches to life. The mom who can't bear to let kids come before her career, for example, is validated as much as the self-sacrificing mom—the difference is seen as one of temperament only.

NEW**
Prometheus Nemesis Book Company
Please Understand Me, $11.95. *Portraits of Temperament*, $9.95.

As you can probably tell from the name of the company that distributes these two books, here we have some Jungian psychology applied to the study of temperaments. Professor David Keirsey has refashioned the "psychological types" of Carl Jung and Isabel Myers into "sociological types." Net result: two books about discovering your personality type.

Please Understand Me starts with a personality test. After scoring your answers, you end up as one of four types, each with four variants, for sixteen total possible combinations:

- *The Dionysians*—promoters, artisans, entertainers, artists
- *The Epimetheans*—administrators, trustees, sellers, conservators
- *The Prometheans*—field marshalls, scientists, architects, inventors
- *The Apollonians*—pedagogues, authors, journalists, questers

These are based on four pairs of preferences: extrovert/introvert, sensation/intuition, thinking/feeling, perceiving/judging. The rest of the book first explains Dr. Keirsey's views on how temperament and character determine your behavior in marriage, child-training, learning, and business, illustrated with various literary excerpts featuring different temperament types.

Portraits of Temperament, by the same author, takes a more popular approach to the same subject. Here you get both the Person Classifier and the Temperament Sorter, but instead of personality types being named things like Promethean NJs, the four types presented earlier are now described as:

- *Artisans*—operators and players
- *Guardians*—monitors and conservators
- *Rationals*—organizers and engineers
- *Idealists*—mentors and advocates

Both books strongly stress the belief that even our beliefs are simply the reflection of our basic temperaments, and that we owe it to others to accept them exactly the way they are. This actually is an argument for the Dionysians/Apollonians being right in their basic outlook on life and the Epimethean/Prometheans being wrong. (Is that why the distributing company calls itself Prometheus Nemesis?)

Shekinah Curriculum Cellar
Learning Patterns and Temperament Styles by Dr. Keith Golay, $9.95. Add 10% shipping ($2.50 minimum).

Different ways people learn. Which subjects are easier or more difficult for each type of learner. Strategies for presenting specific subjects in ways that best reach your child. A test to determine your or your children's learning patterns and temperament style. Scholarly tone. Over 100 pages long.

This book presents four basic temperaments: the Dionysian (free spirit), Epimethean (dutiful citizen), Promethean (natural scholar), and Apollonian (crusader for self-actualization). I seriously question the use of these categories, mainly because the Bible says *everyone* should make the search for wisdom his top priority (the Promethean). The Bible also has some severe things to say about self-love and the consuming desire to be a self-actualized big shot (the Apollonian) and the rejection of absolute laws in the quest for personal autonomy (the Dionysian).

In fact, the four "temperaments" turn out not to be four equally valid personality types, but to be unbalanced to one degree or another. The Dionysian, for example, is like a baby that has never grown up. He lives only in the present and has no patience. The Bible would say this person needs to learn endurance and perseverance, and also needs to start putting others ahead of his own impulses. Golay, however, says that "to assign this type a paper-and-pencil task is deadly," ignoring the fact that millions of this type of boy could and did sit in rows in rural schools working with papers and pencils in the days before learning theory. This is not to say that some people are not validly more physical or action-oriented than others—just that we can and should grow to be more than our "natural" selves.

MORE LEARNING STYLES

Having said all that, it is worthwhile to understand one's basic tendencies, whether to cultivate them or fight them. Parents, in particular, can benefit enormously from the knowledge that their "difficult" child is just a different personality who doesn't necessarily respond to the same things in the same ways as the parents. You can then play to the audience—give the kiddies assignments they will really like—while fostering growth in the less-liked areas. One good example would be buying Junior a fishertechnik construction kit (Junior loves working with his hands) and teaching him to type (Junior hates to write, but you want him able to put creative thoughts on paper). A less savvy mother or father would be fighting it out every day with Junior over undone writing assignments, whereas you have successfully navigated to your real goal.

Children do owe their parents obedience and honor, and not every childish rejection of a task calls for negotiation. It's also important to recognize that such things as character flaws, weaknesses, and downright sins do exist. In real life, I'm so-so and you're so-so and we both have things we need to work on. Still, wise moms and dads take care to understand each child's fundamental gifts and preferences.

So here at last are some resources that (a) recognize that we all have weaknesses as well as strengths and (b) will help you discover more about your family member's inborn tendencies, and how to make the most of them.

Alta Vista College
Learning Styles packet by Cheryl Senecal, $10.

Very helpful kit comes with • a description of learning styles (contrasting six different terminologies) • detailed description of how each type behaves in action, and its strength and weaknesses • parent's learning style test (reusable if you fill in the answers in pencil) • children's learning style test for the parent to fill out (also reusable) • and, most valuable of all, hints on how each type of parent can best work with each type of child. Easy to use, very helpful.

NEW✶✶
Keys to Excellence
Personality Keys program, $49 plus $4 shipping.

This has got to be the most complete home personality profile I have ever seen. The Personality Keys program comes with •Adult and Child profiles • two cassette tapes that explain how to use and apply the profiles • a card you send away to receive an in-depth analysis of the Child profile results and • a special pen used in filling out the profiles.

First, let me tell you what it's all for. The idea is to discover how to motivate each individual in your family, to find out what communication style works best with them, and (when necessary) what disciplinary tactics will cause each child to sit up and take notice.

Why do you need this? Because, as Keys to Excellence president Simone Bibeau points out: "You send your children to their rooms. One child may see this as a *reward* and another as a devastating punishment! You keep telling one of your children how wonderful she is, but she just doesn't seem to care about your praises, yet when you praise your other child she responds enthusiastically!"

Nothing drives parents crazy more quickly than this kind of personality mismatch within a family. Yet once every family member is made aware of his or her basic personality type and the personality types of other family members, it becomes *easy* to work together as a team.

The Adult Profile is a largish workbook. Inside the front cover you find 24 blocks of personality charac-

teristics. Using the special pen, you fill in the blocks that most and least describe you. Little shapes appear in the blocks you colored in. You then tally the shapes and transfer the data to "Most," "Least," and "Difference" graphs. At this point you are ready to find out all sorts of fascinating things about yourself!

The first and most obvious result is discovering your basic Stage One personality type: dominant, influencing, steady, or compliant. Under each type you get a list of tendencies, desired environment, and an Action Plan which lists what kind of input you need from other people and what kind of people you work best with. You then go to a Stage Two page, where you use your special pen to uncover adjectives that apply to your specific profile results (such as *decisive, sensitive, fidgety*). Now comes the *really* interesting part. Based on the shape of your graphs, you fit into one of 18 more-precise personality patterns, each coming with a rich amount of insight into how you are motivated and how you motivate others. This includes insight into your basic emotions, goal-achievement styles, judgment style, method of influencing others, how you react under pressure, fears, areas of needed growth, and what your greatest value is to the organization (the profile was developed for businesses). You also get a long paragraph describing your personality pattern.

Bill and I both took the Profile and concluded that its results were right-on, at least in our cases!

The Child Profile uses the same format, but with the difference that instead of initially choosing between different adjectives, the child has to pick the cartoon figure that most or least describes him. These are outlines of full-body poses that are supposed to express different emotions. To save my life, I couldn't figure out what some of those cartoons represented, so I am wondering just how useful this profile is. Theoretically, its cartoon format helps children aged 4-14 take the test by themselves; in our case we found that everyone from the six-year-old on up had a sufficiently good vocabulary to pick adjectives from the Adult Profile.

The Child Profile is not completely self-scoring, like the Adult Profile. You have to count the little symbols, fill in the graphs, and then copy them onto an enclosed card that you return to get the analyzed results. In the meantime, you can get a concise summary of the first-stage results from a chart in the back of the workbook.

The accompanying cassette tapes, available exclusively from Keys to Excellence, explain how to use the profiles and give further valuable advice on putting what you learned to use.

Obviously, one Adult and one Child profile don't go very far, and they *are* somewhat pricey. (This is because Keys to Excellence has to purchase the profile workbooks from the research organization that developed them—and it costs a bunch to develop this kind of analytical tool!) We found we could, with a little effort, reuse the Adult Profile for several people in our family. Just have the second person circle his choices before coloring them in, have the next put a square around his choices, and so on. It gets a bit messy, but it works!

NEW★★
Timberdoodle
Growing Up Learning, $8.50. Shipping extra.

Growing Up Learning is an upbeat book designed to help you uncover your family's learning modes. Author Dr. Walter B. Barbe explains the importance of the basic visual, auditory, and kinesthetic learning styles. He then helps you identify your own learning style (he calls this your "Learning Strength") with his own special checklist. Next you apply the checklists he has developed for different age groups to your children. Finally, he devotes the rest of the book to showing how you can apply your understanding of your natural teaching style and your child's natural learning style to get the best results in your home life and home education efforts. Barbe deals specifically with the mixed-mode child as well—the child who has strong preferences in more than one learning area at once. A helpful, easy-to-read, inexpensive book that could save you a lot of grief. From the publishers of *Highlights* magazine for children.

PART III

HELP FOR EVERYONE WHO WANTS TO LEARN OR TEACH ANYTHING AT HOME

CHAPTER SIX

THE BEST AND BRIGHTEST CATALOGS AND PARAPHERNALIA

It's time to admit my terrible secret. I am a catalog junkie! Other people go to the mall; I go to my file cabinet full of mail-order catalogs. Not only does this mail-order shopping and browsing save time, but you can get all sorts of offbeat and extremely helpful items by mail order that never appear in a regular store.

I highly recommend a trip to your local teacher's supply store, but even these educational Disneylands can't possibly carry all the idea-sparking materials out there. When it comes to home education, a good catalog collection is a gold mine of fantastic resources.

Lots of these resources are handy in any family, or for single people, or for classroom teachers. Here are such goodies as a catalog of catalogs (for dedicated mail-order shoppers), discount book clubs, and a family catalog featuring wool-stuffed dolls and imported art material. Spark up a blah day with some of these ideas!

ALL-PURPOSE HOME EDUCATION CATALOGS

NEW★★
Alpha Omega Publications
Free 140-page color catalog.

Alpha Omega Publications, a well-known publisher of worktexts for Christian and home schools, launched their very impressive *Horizons* home school catalog in 1988. This catalog not only features some items unavailable elsewhere, but boasts a much more visual format than most home school catalogs. This means you get big color pictures of the resources offered, plus more text describing what each is and what it is good for. Lots and lots of hands-on kits and manipulatives, basic tools like microscopes, learning games, how-to books, an extremely large age-graded literature section, computer software, music-makers, calligraphy and crafts supplies, books on home schooling, and a whole lot more. Plus, of course, in-depth looks at all the Alpha Omega curriculum options, from the *Readiness, Set, Go!* preschool program through *Little Patriots* kindergarten to the regular Alpha Omega LIFEPAC program for grades 1-12.

Brook Farm Books

The First Home-School Catalogue, second edition, revised. $8 U.S. plus $1 postpaid.

Absolutely scads of unusual items, freebies, and fascinating information about home schooling. You can order more than 1,000 of the 2,000-plus listed items directly from Brook Farm Books.

Categories: • Activities • Adolescence (the selection proves it's better to skip the pimpled stage and go straight from diapers to college.) • Art (includes sources for art reproductions) • Baby & Birth (supports natural family life) • Badges (buy 'em from Brook Farm Books) • Beginning to Read (Richard Scarry, Dr. Seuss, and other easy readers) • Biographies • Book Clubs • Books, Discount • Books, Technical • Brown Paper school books • Cards (game rules) • Classics (nice large selection from different publishers, including illustrated classics and classics in beautiful bindings) • Coloring Books • Crafts • Dictionaries • Education Books and Cassettes • Games • Geography • Gifted • Global Education (Donn Reed's for it) • High School Subjects Self-Taught • History (posters, activity units, American and Canadian) • Ladybird Books • Languages • Literature (includes Marguerite Henry, Tintin, and the Tarzan series) • Logic (two books) • Made Simple books • Math (includes Saxon math) • Music • Parenting • Radio and Recorded books (hundreds of hours of cassettes) • Religion (liberal) • Resources and Teaching Aids (includes pages of freebies) • Science (cosmic, fun stuff) • Vocational Education (Exploring Careers series) • Writing (the three best books on the subject). I left out a few of the minor categories—hope you don't mind! All is indexed for easy use.

The First Home-School Catalogue stresses challenging, constructive, informative, fun, and worthwhile items. You won't find much regular curriculum stuff here, due to the Reeds' unschooling philosophy. Think of it as a Whole Enrichment Catalog.

IMPROVED**
Builder Books

Creative materials for all subjects, including the Hewitt Research Foundation programs (Math-It, Winston Grammar, Moore-McGuffey readers, etc.), quality Christian kid's literature—discounted (!), and resources for all subjects and ages. Parent's helps, felts and flannelgraphs, Bible, devotional, character-builders, literature, biographies, critical thinking skills,

science, creation science, history and geography, government and cultures, music and art, and integrated curriculum helps. Lots of hands-on items, e.g., American History paper dolls, toy money, fractions manipulatives, Usborne books, Aristoplay games, tons more. The 1989-1990 catalog was 32 pages. Catalog seems to double in size each year.

NEW**
Didasko

"Home Educators Resource Catalog." The word *didasko* is Greek for *I teach.* This energetic catalog features Aristoplay games, Audubon Society nature guides, Dover educational coloring books, Steve Wilkins' fantastic history cassette series, Crossway Books, the Harper and Row "I Can Read" books, Master Books creation science, classics from Random House, and (unique to this catalog) the Ravensburger wooden games and puzzles from West Germany. Some very unique items, like *George Bourne and the Book of Slavery Irreconcilable,* writings of the first American abolitionist (a Presbyterian minister), and the Art for Children series sold as individual books (I have only been able to find them as sets elsewhere).

HearthSong

"A Catalog for Families." Everything is natural and beautiful, from the wool-stuffed dolls to the holiday specialties (colorful egg-wrapping tinfoil for Easter, and a handcrafted natural wood Nativity set for Christmas, for example). Books for children and adults, music instruments, arts and crafts, and more. The catalog should appeal to those who read *Mothering* magazine, as it has that same slightly New Age profamily flavor.

NEW**
Hewitt Research Foundation

Hewitt's *Educational Resources Catalog* is a nice general-purpose home schooling catalog heavy on (naturally) Hewitt Research Foundation programs. The entire Math-It series; an innovative safe drawing compass with no sharp point to prick young fingers; the Lauri Build-a-Skill series; a "Godly Heroes" biography series; math manipulatives; lots more.

Holt Associates

John Holt's Book and Music Store catalog is a source of creative inspiration. John Holt was a lover of good literature and fine music, and Holt Associates is carrying on the tradition. As brevity is the soul of wit, Holt Associates reviews are both pungent *and* brief. The book list, of course, includes many books about children and/or learning, plus lots of books for children to read or adults to read to children. Many are unusual or hard-to-find; all have a sense of fun and wonder. I really appreciate the work Holt Associates did in providing this selection. You can also order some art supplies and musical instruments through this catalog. We've obtained many of these items and have never been disappointed.

NEW**
The Home School Books and Supplies

Enormous spiral-bound catalog with thousands of home school items. Unless I'm getting this confused with another company, these are the people who ran the "Home School Book Bus" and who now have opened a for-real store in a for-real shopping center offering all these nifty items for home schoolers where people can actually come and *see* them! Catalog covers a lot of ground, from preschool through high school: Weaver curriculum. Spelling, phonics, and vocabulary. Reading and comprehension. Grammar and composition. Math. Science. Bible. History. Coloring books and projects. Art. Music. Foreign languages. Latin. Thinking skills. Economics. Children's literature. A Beka books, Alpha Omega. Lauri. Duplos. Legos. Lots of unusual and hands-on items. Format is name, price, and short description of each product.

NEW**
Home School Supply House

Pretty, smaller-sized (8-1/2 x 5-1/2) black and white 32-page catalog with product descriptions and photos. This catalog has items you won't find in other home schooling catalogs, such as literature program packages designed especially for home schoolers and a wider selection of public-school textbooks. The usual Aristoplay games, poetry books, math manipulatives. Science kits, textbooks, and experiments. Handwriting. Creative writing. Spelling. Social studies. Research and reference. Introductory French, Spanish, and Latin. "Unschooling" flavor.

IMPROVED**
Learning at Home

You'll find reviews of Learning at Home's home school teaching guides and test prep series elsewhere. This Hawaiian-based company is now a major distributor of K-12 books and workbooks, science supplies, reference tools, math manipulatives, and lots more. You can now consider this a full-service home schooling catalog, without the devotional aids of the strictly Christian catalogs. Great oaks from little acorns grow; it's amazing to see how fast they have expanded.

NEW**
Lifetime Books and Gifts
The Always Incomplete Catalog

I just love the title of Tina Farewell's new *Always Incomplete Catalog*. Tina, a home-schooling mom from Lake Wales, Florida and the daughter of the owners of fabulous Chalet Suzanne Country Inn, has put together a marvelous little catalog majoring on the Principle Approach and the Child-Light philosophy.

The best of just about everything I recommend in *The Big Book of Home Learning* is offered in these pages! Those of us looking for children's classic literature are especially going to be pleased, as Tina has made available the entire "Children's Classics" and "Illustrated Junior Library" sets, as well as inexpensive paper editions and individual books from other sets, all laid out very neatly and simply side-by-side so you can compare prices. Lots more books here: the entire Anne of Green Gables series, all of Beatrix Potter, Laura Ingalls Wilder, Jean Fritz (wonderful historical books), C. S. Lewis, Marguerite Henry, J. R. R. Tolkien, and a whole page of the best early reader books. Books for adults: every home-schooling book your little heart desires. Little Patriots series. McGuffey's. *Learning At Home* (both volumes). Ray's Arithmetics. Saxon Math. Usborne books (the whole line!). A great little poetry section. David Macaulay books. Principle Approach books. Puzzles, games, activities, research, resource books. Creation science for children and adults. History. Biographies. Bible. Art. And on and on . . .

Tina keeps right on top of things. Some items she offers have just recently come out: *Keyboard Capers* and its manipulatives, for example, or Dr. Gary Parker's great *Life Before Birth* book and cassette.

I don't see one item in this catalog that I don't like, and I own an awful lot of them. Tina says, "If you don't see it, we can get it for you." She keeps adding to her stock as she discovers new items, hence the name, *Always Incomplete Catalog.* This indeed could be one-stop shopping for everything but crayons. No discounts, but a truly excellent selection.

NEW**
Riverside Schoolhouse
Free; nominal postage charge if you want additional supplier catalogs.

"The Complete Resource Center for Home Educators." Riverside tries to carry it all, rather than just stock a limited number of fast-selling titles. Complete *Weaver Resource Guide* lists products you can use with each unit of this unit-studies curriculum. Large literature sections features many titles listed in *Books Children Love* and *Honey for a Child's Heart.* New in 1990: foreign language section with children's books in foreign languages, beginning with Spanish. Large devotional section includes the hard-to-find Suzie and Johnny books from the Radio Kids Bible Club of thirty years ago. Plus the complete line of Usborne books, Ladybird books, Betty Lukens Felts, Little Folks Felts, Saxon Math, and lots more. Some of these lines are described in their own catalogs, others are illustrated in separate brochures from the manufacturers.

Shekinah Curriculum Cellar
Catalog, $1.

Shekinah Curriculum Cellar advertises itself as "More than a *catalog*—A commentary on quality books and teaching aids for home educators." Lots of good stuff, some hard to find elsewhere, extremely wide selection with thousands of products, many discount prices. Terrific children's literature section. A must-have catalog.

Sycamore Tree
Catalog costs $3, refunded with first order.

One-stop shopping with this super catalog of home education products, all of which you can obtain through Sycamore Tree. Great choices in every subject area—over 3,000 items in 1990! The reviews are terse but informative. Very few products are pictured. Another must-have catalog.

Timberdoodle

Best source for top-notch hands-on and creative thinking materials for home schoolers, such as fishertechnik construction and robotics kits, Midwest Publishing thinking skills workbooks, *Creating Line Designs* books, Lauri crepe rubber puzzles, Pacific Puzzle Company puzzles, Cuisenaire math rods, and lots more! A home business run by home schoolers for home schoolers. Large black-and-white catalog gives truly useful descriptions of each resource. Timberdoodle doesn't try to cover every single subject category; rather their materials fit in the niches everyone else leaves out! Good prices, great service.

DISCOUNT AND USED HOME EDUCATION RESOURCES

NEW**
Christian Teaching Materials Company
Latest list of available items, $2.

Used and new home education materials at discount prices. Tens of thousands of books, all major publishers. Accepts trade-ins. Listings organized by subject, author or publisher, and grade level. Retail cost and your cost are both shown. New books are marked with an asterisk. Used books are marked down according to the amount of wear and tear. Teeny type in the listings. Some advertisements from other companies included in each catalog.

So how good are the discounts? Used textbooks 53-80 percent off retail. New textbooks 15-35 percent off. Used workbooks 50-80 percent off. Curriculum, answer keys, and teacher guides 25-50 percent off.

NEW**
Rainbow Re-Source Center
One issue, $1. One year (8 issues), $6.

Rainbow Re-Source Center has a unique business designed to help both buyers and sellers of used education materials. They sell your used education materials on a consignment basis and return 70 percent of the selling price to you in cash when each item sells.

Here's how it works. You send them anything you think a home schooler might want to buy—textbooks, workbooks, science tools, educational games, whatever. You also fill out their book/material review form (one line per item), telling them the item's original cost (if known) and whether or not you want it returned to you (at your expense for postage) if it doesn't sell. They send you a postcard acknowledging receipt of the item, its assessed condition, and the planned selling price based on that condition and the likely demand for the item. Your item is then listed in the next issue of the *Rainbow Re-Porter.* Your name is not listed, only your item. If it fails to sell after several months, they will keep discounting it until either it sells or you request its return. When it sells, you get a check!

Rainbow Re-Source Center also maintains waiting lists for buyers who want to get in line for particular items, and publishes listings of items in special demand, so you can see what items you have might be especially hot.

The inventory list is now printed—a big step forward from the dot-matrix type in the first issues! Items are listed by subject and publisher. Prices are listed in columns labeled Unused, Excellent, Good, Fair, and Poor, so you can see the item's condition at a glance. Retail prices are listed, where known. The *Rainbow Re-Porter* also includes a small section of teaching tips and reviews.

You don't send in money with your order. As soon as they receive your form listing the items desired, quantity, preferred/acceptable conditions, and whether you are willing to wait for the item (and how long!), they will reserve available items in your name and send you a postcard listing the reserved items and the amount due. Send in your money within two weeks and the items are yours!

BOOK CATALOGS YOU CAN USE

I definitely read too much. Some of it people just drop on my doorstep, but most of it is my own fault. The problem is that I get so many wonderful book catalogs—the best of which are these below.

NEW**
American Citizen Catalog

A division of Regnery Gateway, Inc., a middle-sized conservative publishing house. Wonderful reading for thinking people. The catalog itself is a good read, consisting of longish, insightful reviews of the books offered. Every home-schooled teen and college student should browse through it.

Barnes & Noble

Barnes & Nobles is similar to Publishers Central Bureau in offering frequent catalogs with hefty discounts on a wide range of books and some other special-interest bestsellers at retail price. They are to be commended for avoiding PCB's wretched tendency to promote porn and anti-Christian nonsense. I no longer will order from or even look at the PCB catalog, since they freely intermix porn and sexual materials with family books.

If you like literature, history, and art, you will doubtless be entranced with Barnes & Noble. Some recent offerings: *The Oxford Illustrated Dickens,* a complete set of 21 volumes for $185. *Columbia History of the World,* published at $25, offered for $9.95. Everything David Macaulay ever wrote, and the new Macaulay videos at $10 off apiece, plus a Barnes & Noble exclusive: David Macaulay prints, hand-signed by the artist. Hundreds of other offbeat, distinguished, humorous, artistic, silly, or educational books, cassettes, and videos, most discounted. Some stuff you discover to be yukky after you get it. Not to worry, just send it back for a refund. Get a catalog and see the selection for yourself!

NEW**
Bluestocking Press

Books-only catalog featuring alternative education and home schooling, free market economics and philosophy for parents and kids, and work options for entrepreneurially-minded folks of all ages.

Examples: *Teach Your Child the Value of Money. Capitalism for Kids. Learning Vacations, The Young Thinker's Bookshelf.*

Book-of-the-Month Club

Appealing to a more predominantly male audience than Literary Guild (see below), Book-of-the-Month Club selections lean less on the romantic and more on the practical.

You get the bulletin featuring Main Selections (sent automatically unless you send back the card and request not to get them), Alternate Features, and others. The deals for new members are great. A recent offer in *Insight* magazine, for example, gave the prospective member a choice of six great tragedies of Shakespeare on cassette for $19.95 (17 cassettes in all, list price $179.60), the Compact Edition of the *Oxford En-*

glish Dictionary for $27.95 (list $195), six Julia Child cooking videos for $39.95 (list $179.70), *The Story of Civilization* by Will and Ariel Durant for $29.95 (eleven hardback volumes, list $335.45), and *The Encyclopedia of Philosophy* for $24.95 (four hardbound volumes, list $225).

NEW**
Cahill & Company

Here we have yet another division of Regnery Gateway, Inc. The Cahill & Company catalog is addressed more to things spiritual and artistic and less to the political and historical topics covered in the American Citizen catalog. Like that other catalog, this one will open your eyes to a tremendous array of sparkling thought. Lengthy reviews bring you up-to-date on what's new. Some offerings partake of a non-evangelical mystical spirit.

Christian Book Distributors

Very large mail-order source for Christian books. Huge discounts on commentaries and other pricey sets, decent discounts on other books. All shades of doctrine, from liberal to fundamentalist. Popular with pastors and seminary students. Three-dollar membership entitles you to the large newsprint catalogs where you may then dig for bargains. You don't have to be a member to order. Bestsellers, counseling, youth ministry, missions, church history, Christian living, religious reference books, Greek and Hebrew language study helps, Bibles, music, and tons of bargain books, all in mint condition. Excellent shipping, packaging, and service. Free sample catalog.

Conservative Book Club

You've seen the full-page ads offering you Sam Blumenfeld's *Alphaphonics* for free or the entire hardback McGuffey readers for just $10 if you'll join CBC. "Gotta be a catch," you think. No. There isn't. All you have to do is buy four books at discounted prices over the next two years (or some such similar offer: check the latest deal). Every six weeks or so you get a newsletter with the latest offerings, one of which is sent automatically unless you request otherwise. The newsletter is not too long—you can read it over lunch—and if you are not the totally disorganized type you can easily handle sending back the enclosed postcard when you don't want the featured selection.

CBC is very friendly to home schoolers, and many of their more recent offerings are good home-schooling and education books. Besides that, they carry the hottest (and most readable) titles about economics, politics, literature, and other civilized issues, all at discount. Nothing the least bit risqué or iffy. I've been a satisfied customer for years.

Great Christian Books
$5 for one-year membership ($8 Canada, $12 overseas). Membership automatically extended one year each time you order.

Generous discounts on just about every Christian book (classic or just-released), tape, children's book, or reference work you might want to own. GCB's large Home Schooling section offers discounts on a wide line of curriculum and books, including A Beka and Alpha Omega. Many Buying Power Specials at up to 60 percent off list price. Fine service, huge selection.

Laissez-Faire Books

"The World's Largest Selection of Books on Liberty." What that means is that they carry a huge array of libertarian books. Politics, economics, philosophy, history, even fiction, all from a notably different slant than the public schools present.

Libertarians believe in limited government and personal responsibility for our own behavior. Some are more mellow, others more demanding. Laissez-Faire appears to follow the hard-core Ayn Rand philosophy—if you can't hack it at the game of life, that's tough, bub.

LibertyTree Network

You may have seen ads for this company in various home-schooling and conservative publications. What we have here is a sharp, good-looking, creative selection of books and other products with a libertarian flair, but without all the heavy dogma. LibertyTree concentrates on highly readable books and fun items such as history books and puzzles for children. Wide range of topics. Many items especially selected for home schoolers.

Literary Guild

Most of Literary Guild's stock is current best-sellers. This means sexy romance novels and gory mysteries, along with a smattering of how-to books. Literary Guild does offer free books to new enrollees, and they do also stock some nonfiction and children's books. Unlike Barnes & Noble and Publishers Central Bureau, the iffy stuff is sequestered by itself and labeled as to content (e.g., "Violence. Explicit sex"). You have to stay on top of their catalogs and send in your little cards faithfully or you get stuck with the wretched Featured Selection.

Master Book/Creation Knowledge Catalog

Books, audio cassettes, videos, and Bible studies—hundreds of items all from a Biblical and creationist viewpoint. Most items are for teens and adults. Small but growing selection of creationist books for young children. Plus new Good Science program for K-3 and 4-6. Find out what California Superintendent of Education Bill Honig doesn't want school kids to know—get this catalog!

Publishers Central Bureau

Similar to Barnes & Noble. Publishers' closeouts, bestsellers, and arcane stuff for history buffs, military fans, art lovers, and the like. Something for literally everyone, from nerdy college sophomores (e.g. a "humor" book on the male organ) to thinking folks. Unhappily, there seem to be a lot of nerdy sophomores out there, judging from the PCB catalog! PCB has separate video and tape catalogs from time to time.

Quality Paperback Book Club

We agree with QPB: "Just because books come from trees doesn't mean their leaves should turn yellow and drop to the ground." QPB, whose books don't shed pages because they are printed on good quality paper, is one of these we-send-you-our-brochure-every-six-weeks, selection-sent-automatically-unless-you-tell-us-differently jobbies. If you stay right on top of your mail, this should pose no problem. If not, watch out! You may end up buying Madame Mao Tsetung's biography.

QPB carries books beloved by the Northeast literary elite. We, therefore, pass by their fiction (Norman Mailer and his ilk have always bored me silly), but

sometimes can pick up instructive books. Examples: a book on recognizing architectural styles, another on the history of mathematics, a collection of Greek mythology. These are never the Featured Selections, so make sure the little card gets sent back *promptly*.

You can easily rack up Bonus Points and earn free books and all that fun stuff. And yes, they sell *only* quality paperbacks.

WHERE TO FIND EVEN MORE CATALOGS

NEW**
Baby Love Products
The Catalogue of Canadian Catalogues, $7.95 plus $2.95 shipping (Canadian).

One of my big embarrassments in writing this book was the puny number of Canadian distributors of educational products that I have been able to unearth. Although I wrote to every single supplier in this book asking for the name and address of Canadian distributors, the results were disappointingly slim.

So, just for you North-of-the-border types, here is a source with "names and addresses of hundreds of mail-order catalogs for everything from art and craft supplies to log homes." It's sold by Baby Love Products, a company that itself has a very worthwhile Canadian catalog featuring cloth diapers (many kinds), baby aids of all sorts, children's toys, books for parents and children, and lots of other good stuff. The Baby Love folks pepper their fascinating catalog with folksy wisdom and answers to common child-rearing questions, like, "Why do my baby's diapers fill up with water-repellent white curds?" (Answer: You're using soap instead of detergent. Switch!). One hundred sixty pages of useful info and products in the early 1990 Baby Love issue—including, as mentioned above, *The Catalogue of Canadian Catalogues*.

NEW**
Catalogue Revue

You may have received one of these in the mail once upon a time—a small four-color brochure listing hundreds of catalogs you can send away for. Circle the number of the catalog(s) you want, enclose the catalog price plus $1 shipping, and have a full mailbox. Eclectic selection ranges from vitamins and crafts to discount aquarium supplies and "sexy swimsuits" (as if you could find an *unsexy* swimsuit anywhere these days!). Or for $3 you can get the *Catalog Revue* itself, consisting of 52 color pages displaying over 150 catalogs for "fashions, gifts, gourmet, collectibles, crafts, and special interests."

Pinkerton Marketing.
The Great Book of Catalogs. 192 pages. $12.95 postpaid.

Oh, boy! What a joy! Pinkerton's *The Great Book of Catalogs* really is "All You Need to Know to Shop by Mail." I've wasted hours, and more money than I care to admit, tracking down a good catalog for mail-order shoppers. All the others I've seen are too yuppy ("Honestly, darling, you can't find a *better* source for Dior seconds") or too strange ("We have great buys on Latvian air-whistles!"). *The Great Book of Catalogs* shares none of these defects. Perhaps that's because a real, live American couple, Steve and Betsy Pinkerton, put it out instead of a committee of jaded journalists.

TGBOC is updated frequently. The revised fourth edition for 1989 lists more than 2,600 U.S. consumer mail-order catalogs, all tidily sorted into 80 logical sections and traceable through the excellent index.

TGBOC does *not* contain educational items (or why would I be writing this book?). It *does* have a good cross-section of everything else, from Animals and Art to Toys and Travel. Crafts! Gifts! Hardware! Sports! Music! Business Supplies! You can overdose your VISA just by browsing here.

The book is available only by mail. Order directly from Pinkerton.

PARAPHERNALIA

NEW★★
Honeymoon Point
Child's T-shirt, $8. Adult's, $10. Add $1.50 for first shirt, 50¢ per additional for shipping.

T-shirts for home schoolers, made by a home-schooled teen. Cara Green named her home business after her grandparents' summer cottage on Hobb's Pond in Hope, Maine. Since Cara is particularly fond of the loons that swim on the pond, she designed a T-shirt with a family of loons on the front, and underneath is the saying, "When it comes to school there's

no place like home!" (The loons and printing, by the way, are very professionally done—this is *not* cutesy kid art.) All sizes are available. Child sizes: 6-8, 10-12, 14-16. Adult sizes: S, M, L, XL. Colors: Ice green, red, teal, light blue, and fuchsia.

NEW★★
Lord's Fine Jewelry
Class ring prices range from $95 for a Ladies Sterling Silver to $350 for the most expensive men's 14K gold model. Many different styles. Shipping $5.

Are you ready for Lord's of the rings . . . ?

I always get a chuckle when I hear some public-school type complaining that home-schooled students miss out on all the social experiences of public school. Come on, people! Not only do home schoolers have graduation ceremonies, art fairs, and even (in some places) marching bands, home schoolers have their own high school class rings. No kidding!

In 1987 the Oklahoma Central Home Educators Consociation (yep, that's really their name!) accepted bids from four national ring companies. From these bids, Lord's Fine Jewelry was chosen to be the official Home School class ring manufacturer, due to their lower cost and ability to fill single retail orders. Sheri Collins won the home schoolers' ring design contest for that year. Her original design has now been joined by several additional ring designs, with new styles added almost every year.

Your home-school ring will read "HOME SCHOOL HIGH SCHOOL" or "CHRISTIAN EDUCATION" around the stone. To have it personalized with your school name is an extra $65 charge.

The synthetic stone for each ring is placed over the outline of a cross with rays flaring out from it. You have your choice of stone color. You may also have your initials engraved on the inside of your ring for free, or your whole name for an extra $6.

And, in case you're not a "ring" person, Lord's Fine Jewelry is coming out with a line of Christian Home School Jewelry in mid-1990—necklaces, earrings, tie tacks, charms, etc. Watch for their "Apple" series!

CHAPTER SEVEN

HELPFUL MAGAZINES AND JOURNALS

Magazines are the lifeblood of the home education movement. You can teach your children at home all alone. You can join a local support group or a state organization. But national magazines and newsletters keep you in touch with the movement—its excitement, its political unity and educational diversity.

You might also want to stay in touch with the struggle for true academic freedom and public school reform, or the world of professional schoolteachers. Resources for these areas are also provided below.

HOME SCHOOL MAGAZINES

UPDATED★★
Growing Without Schooling
$20/year (6 issues), $36/12 issues, $48/18 issues. Group subscriptions and back issues available. Single issue, $3.50. Published by Holt Associates.

GWS has been around longer than any other home school magazine. It started out as a forum, and has kept this format. Most of the tabloid is given over to readers' comments, which makes a nice change from columns written by "experts." The GWS philosophy is that normal home schoolers *are* the experts!

Although the GWS staff are staunch believers in "invited" learning and globalism, the philosophies of GWS's late founder, John Holt, they allow readers to express other points of view. Within limits; anyone who tries to make a case for traditional child-training methods in GWS is likely either to not see the letter published or see it rebutted. I have found it easier to get a letter published in a national newsmagazine than to get GWS to print anything I write to them! However, there is no nasty mudslinging; GWS is about as close to a genuinely pluralistic magazine as you will find anywhere in the world today.

Many articles are chronicles of home schoolers' actual experience; reading GWS is inspirational as well as informative. More: up-to-date legislative news and court decisions from every state. Plus excellent reviews of books and products of use to home schoolers, and a very handy mail-order bookstore from which you can order resources the GWS staff particularly like. All back issues are available—a great teacher training resource!

UPDATED★★
Home Education Magazine
$24/year (6 issues), $12/6 months (3 issues), $4.50 current issue.

Very professionally-done home-school magazine with an unschooling flavor. Features include Kids' Pages with simple, fun activities; articles from all perspectives on the joys and tribulations of home schooling (some wildly funny); philosophical ruminations and hard-hitting poetry (imagine that!); and great ideas galore. Somehow the publishers, Mark and Helen Hegener, manage to scoop the world again and again with the best new resources—which they review and sometimes even advertise before anyone else has heard of them. Issues are now 56 pages, with six regular columnists and 8-12 feature articles in each issue.

The Home School Researcher
$12/year (4 issues). Back issues, $1 for subscribers, $3 for others. *Annotated Bibliography of Home Centered Learning*, $8.

This is a bit different. Brian Ray, a researcher at Seattle Pacific University, collects and comments on research having to do with home education. Scholarly, not at all glossy or glitzy publication. Home school leaders should consider subscribing to this valuable ammunition.

NEW★★
Konos Helps
$18/9 monthly issues. Back issues, $2.50 each.

A newsletter for people who like the unit-study approach to education. Although each issue is tied to one theme from the popular KONOS curriculum, editor Kathy von Duyke and her partner Nina Watts stress that their newsletter is meant for *any* family interested in integrated learning. Published nine months of the school year, each issue is packed with hands-on activities and ideas for teaching a houseful of kids. 1989-90 issues cover Indians; Rocks, Plant, and Animal Classification; Kings and Queens; Christmas; Great Feats; The Eyes and Senses; Frontier and Pioneers; Plant and Animal Reproduction; and Olympics.

UPDATED★★
The Teaching Home
$15/year (6 issues). Back issues available.

The Teaching Home is *the* national and even international Christian home school magazine. The editors have a great idea: your state newsletter is copublished with *The Teaching Home*! Then, instead of having to publish (or pay for) two magazines, local and national news are covered at once! Presently 23 editions of *The Teaching Home* are published: Alaska, Arizona, California, Colorado, Florida, Idaho, Illinois, Indiana, Iowa, Louisiana, Mississippi, Montana, New Mexico, New Hampshire, New Jersey, New York, North Dakota, Oklahoma, Oregon, Tennessee, Texas, Utah, Washington, and (can you believe it?) Australia and New Zealand. This list changes, but you get the idea. Check with your state newsletter editor about doing this in your state.

The magazine has everything: philosophical articles, news, theme sections, success stories, reviews (yours truly is the Senior Resource Editor), and ads. Bonus: *Teaching Home* not only has a hefty section of letters from readers, but a department of articles selected each issue from more than 100 home-school newsletters all across the nation and around the world. Their news section is not only legal news, but news of workshops, conventions, and other services as well. The ads are directed to Christian readers, so you are aware of the products' theological content in advance.

Editor Sue Welch has put a considerable effort into continually upgrading *Teaching Home*, and it shows, not only in the new color covers and fancier interior layout, but in the fact that this is presently the only home-schooling magazine you can find on a magazine stand. Spring Arbor Distributors has added *Teaching Home* to their Christian bookstore distribution program.

As a service to home schoolers, *Teaching Home* keeps its entire list of back issues in print. These are "themed" issues, meaning most of the info is still relevant and useful. For a full list of back issues available, see the Teacher Training chapter.

NEW★★
Wisdom Publications
Home School Digest, one year (four issues), $10.

Founded a few years ago, *Home School Digest* is a thick magazine loaded with ads. Articles are a potpourri, including straight reprints from advertisers' books and articles by advertisers promoting their philosophies or products. You will also find quite a few articles of the "Why you ought to home school" and "How horrible public schools are" varieties. Most issues have one or two decent articles, but issues lack unifying themes and clear editorial focus.

EDUCATIONAL ISSUE JOURNALS

Blumenfeld Education Letter
$36/year (12 issues), $18/6 months, $9/3 months.

Talk about hard-hitting! Sam Blumenfeld, author of *How to Tutor, Is Public Education Necessary?, Alphaphonics,* and *NEA: Trojan Horse in American Education,* reports on all the educational news the standard media seem to miss. Like, for instance, the alarming upswing in teen suicide with death cult overtones. Blumenfeld digs behind the philosophy to actually get at the story. Example:

> Are "death educators" normal human beings or are they the purveyors of a satanic death cult that has taken hold in the schools?

> The only "death educator" I've met is the one I interviewed at a high school in Massachusetts where they've had an unusually high incidence of suicides. He was a tall, slim man in his late thirties or early forties who taught "health education." I asked him if he knew why the children were killing themselves. He said he didn't know. . . . I then asked him if he expected the situation to improve or get worse at his

school. He asked me what I meant by improvement. I said I meant a decrease or an end to the suicides. His reply was quite unexpected. "It's a matter of opinion whether that would be an improvement or not," he said.

That issue then went on with articles like "NEA Promotes Death Education and Values Clarification," "Boy Murdered in Satanic Sacrifice" (that happened in Monroe County, Michigan), "Fifth Grader Kills School Principal," "Student Kills Self in Class," "Third Suicide in Pennsylvania School" (Palisades School District in Springtown, PA), "Sixth Suicide at Leominster High" (Leominster, MA), "Cluster Suicides Hit Schools," "Suicide Epidemic Stuns Omaha," "Teen Kills Self on TV," "Death Video Becoming Popular." After reading all that, Mr. Blumenfeld's question about where all these kids are getting this elaborate communal death ritual starts to sound a lot more serious.

The Blumenfeld Education Letter covers all the terrain, not just death ed. You won't fall asleep reading it.

The Christian Educator
Published by Christian Liberty Academy. Quarterly. $4/four issues.

If you like sassy cartoons, success stories, and newspaper articles with interested headlines like "Teachers Oppose Drug Test" (Long Island public school teachers would have been tested for drug use like major league baseball players, but they were "violently opposed"), you'll love *The Christian Educator.* With a newspaper format and mainstream newspaper articles, *TCE* manages to cull article after article showing the shortcomings of government education and prints them alongside its own articles on home education. Who's being persecuted today, and what does the judge think about it? What teachers' union is opposing testing for its members? What percent of teachers just flunked their skills test? Why aren't public school students good at thinking? How many signers of the Declaration of Independence were educated at home? Stay on top of the struggle and get a few laughs.

NEW**
Education Reporter
One year, $25 (twelve issues). Back issue, $2. Published by Eagle Forum Education and Legal Defense Fund.

Heavy-hitting reporting in newspaper format on what's good, bad, and ugly in public education today. Recent issues have focused on the "censorship" controversy (e.g., are public schools allowed or even required to stock books promoting "alternative" philosophies and lifestyles such as witchcraft and lesbianism for the sake of "freedom of choice," while the traditional religious viewpoint is banned from the classroom), battles over sex education curriculum, the attempt by educrats to mandate a new standardized "reading" test that quizzes pupils on their beliefs rather than their reading ability, and other fun stuff like that. Occasional bright spots surface as a school district here and there decides to exercise some common sense when parents complain. Conservative viewpoint, which is no surprise, since it is published by Phyllis Schlafly's group, Eagle Forum. Includes suggestions about what parents can do to protect their children from the worst of the political and New Age power plays in public education. Not too many pages—you can read it in one sitting, though due to the subject matter I would not recommend picking mealtime for this!

Educational Freedom
One year, $5 (two issues).

The name says what this journal is all about: freedom of choice in education. Articles by well-known thinkers. The issue in my hands has articles by Richard John Neuhaus ("Moral Leadership in Post-Secular America"), Frank J. Russo, Jr. ("The Economic Argument in Favor of State Tuition Tax Credits"), Russell Kirk ("An Establishment of Secular Humanism?"), Daniel D. McGarry ("The Creationism Decision of the Supreme Court"), and others, some with a strong what-we-should-do-now flavor. It also includes extracts from other books and publications.

On Teaching
Published by the American Reformation Movement. Available for donation. $5 a year is good; more is gladly accepted.

Provocative, quality newsletter that explores education from a Christian viewpoint. Philosophical. Reconstructionist. Witty. Catch this choice morsel from a past issue:

Poor little San Diego. The home of mediocre sports teams, a sub-mediocre state university, the most expensive utility rates in the nation, sunny beaches and empty heads. The eighth-largest city in America, but still thought of as Los Angeles' little brother. San Diego has had little reason to rejoice . . . until now.

For reasons known only to the intellectualoids, San Diego was chosen as the locale for the unveiling of the Carnegie Forum on Education. . . . Our humble little Hotel Del Coronado housed such educational superstars as NEA chief Mary Futrell, (yes, *the* Mary Futrell), Albert Shanker of the American Federation of Teachers, and California's own educational top-dog, Bill Honig. (I am leading a campaign to have the Hotel declared a national monument). . . .

First, the report called for the creation of a National Board for Professional Teaching Standards. This Board will establish national certification standards. . . .

This proposal is fascinating. Already, 99.9% of the public school teachers in America, plus many private school teachers, have State teaching credentials. (I used to have a California State Secondary Teaching Credential. I have repented, and God has forgiven me.) Does the need for this new National Board mean (horrors!) that what I have been saying for years is true—that the State teaching credential is worthless? If the State credential is worthless, then why have we been told for so long that *every* teacher needs one? If the State credential is the greatest thing since sliced bread, then why do we need a new National Board? . . .

Before I go on to the next point, I want to say one more thing. There is probably a small group of rabid ultra-right-wing fundamentalist kooks out there who believe that this is just another attempt to unify and socialize and control the education of every child in America under one all-powerful Board of evil intent. Well, I don't believe that for one moment. I believe the intent of this proposal is entirely benevolent, and that this proposal only reflects the concern these people have for the well-being of the children of America. I also believe that, 32 years from now, when I turn 65, I will be able to live comfortably on my Social Security income. . . .

The Carnegie Forum found quite a number of scapegoats . . . the absence of a National Board, or the absence of a "lead teacher," or the fact that we don't treat teachers as "true professionals," or the preponderance of white teachers, etc., etc., ad nauseam. The only people *not* responsible for our problems are the NEA, the Federal Department of Education, the graduate schools of education, the administrators and the teachers. . . .

The Carnegie Forum conveniently missed two "minor" changes which have taken place in the educational history of this nation. These two "minor" points account for the mess we are in. Unless and until the Carnegie Forum (or anybody else) addresses these two issues, it is missing the point completely. These [are the] changes: the shift from Christian education to "secular" education; and the shift from "secular" education to social programming. . . .

Someone needs to gather these past issues into a book. It would be at least as good as Richard Mitchell's *The Graves of Academe*. In the meantime, you can get your dose by writing away for it.

CHAPTER EIGHT

A QUICK GUIDE TO REFERENCE TOOLS

The world is divided into two classes of people: those who read the encyclopedia and those who don't.

I must confess, not without some trepidation, that we are a family of encyclopedia-browsers. Many is the time that we have gone to the encyclopedia to look up some specific entry, such as "Attila the Hun" and found ourselves engulfed in a journey through Attic Greek architecture, atlas production, and so on through the A's.

This is not how it is supposed to work. You are supposed to look up your entry and then browse through the cross-references, not the next-page articles. Open-ended learning then results, so they say, from all the fascinating linkages between subjects you discover by your dutiful pursuit of cross-references.

In defense of our unorthodox study methods, let me say that we unearth many fascinating things we would never have known enough to look up. Research skills are all very well. But it's also nice to feed your curiosity.

All of which is to say, *reference tools should fuel your passion for learning.* Think of reference tools as the pathway to new and interesting facts and ideas, rather than just sources for answers to specific questions. Curiosity is great, and I'm sure you have lots of it. After all, the world is divided into two classes of people: those who read resource books (like this one) and those who don't . . .

DIGGING INTO DICTIONARIES

Dictionaries are not what they used to be. As all of life has become politicized, so has the humble dictionary. Many dictionaries now are saturated with obscene words, Marxist political definitions, and the like. A bigger problem *academically* is the stuffing of dictionaries with slang, to the detriment of the old words your child is more likely to need to look up. College student dictionaries, especially, often are ludicrously overloaded with bureaucratic jargon and technological terms, while literary vocabulary gets short shrift.

TEEN AND ADULT DICTIONARIES

I'm not really happy with any of the modern dictionaries on the market. The *Oxford Dictionary of the English Language* ought to have definitions for the words I actually want to look up—if I feel like mortgaging the house and adding a few yards of shelf space to hold it! American productions leave me flat, since they refuse to define words that have gone out of use (i.e, the ones I want to look up when I read an old book). They aren't all that hot on new words either. Try to find the word *jacuzzi* in my fairly-new *American Heritage Dictionary,* for example!

For these reasons, and many more, quite a few home schoolers are investing in the unique dictionary reviewed below.

Foundation for American Christian Education (F.A.C.E.)
Webster's, $50 retail, $35 to Christian schools, churches, study groups, and home schoolers.

This is no ordinary dictionary. FACE sells a facsimile edition of Noah Webster's 1828 *American Dictionary of the English Language*. A stunning addition to your library shelf (hardcover, gold-embossed, and over two and a half inches thick), it also is a fascinating landscape of the American language as spoken when people believed in God and grammar. FACE calls this edition of *Webster's* "the only American Christian dictionary," and although Bob Jones University may dispute that, this classic *Webster's* certainly breathes a refreshing air.

One very evident use of this volume would be to look up those obscure words with which old literature is dotted. Thus, if in perusing Chaucer one is puzzled by the word "swinker," flip to the spot in FACE's *Webster's* and discover that the term once meant "laborer" or "plowman." Webster gives a literary reference for many words, á là Dr. Johnson in his famous lexicography, as well as an etymology. The definitions clearly emanate from a sober and serene mind, and for that reason reading *Webster's* is very calming. The print is decently large and the definitions absorbing.

DICTIONARIES FOR ELEMENTARY SCHOOL KIDS

Children's dictionaries are a different story. The idea is to present kids with a dumbed-down, colorfully illustrated "dictionary" of their very own. Trouble is, they already know the definitions of all the included words. My elementary school taught us to use the *real* dictionary in second grade, and I see no reason why this should be impossible today.

However, a special kids' dictionary does have some virtues. Larger print, bigger pictures, and (sometimes) more sensible pronunciation guidelines for words can make life easier for young students.

You can find a child's dictionary in any well-stocked bookstore. But for a dictionary that's really different, check out the review below.

Bob Jones University Press
Christian Student Dictionary, $16.90. Shipping extra.

Highly attractive, quality hardbound dictionary designed for elementary students. Oversized, one and a half inches thick. Definitions and usage illustrations reflect a Christian perspective. This does not mean that you will find Biblical references or usages for every word. As the editors say, "Our intent was to create a good balance and not make an exclusively religious dictionary." Often the illustrative sentence refers to everyday life. As an example, these usage illustrations are all found on the same page: • For the verb *perk*—"The dog perked up his ears at the sound of footsteps coming up the sidewalk" • For the verb *permit*—"Will you permit me to leave?" and "The heavy snow permitted sledding." • For the verb *persecute* —"The Romans persecuted the Christians" • For the verb *perish*—"Ten people perished in the accident," "Whoever believes in Christ will not perish," and "Elephants are perishing from the African continent."

Each entry word is followed by its pronunciation (pronunciation key on each left-hand page throughout), part of speech, and a simple definition using only words found elsewhere in the dictionary. Nice open margins contain many colorful illustrations. Plus the *Christian Student Dictionary* includes an introductory "Guide to the Dictionary" with simple practice exercises to familiarize students with the dictionary; a Spelling Table that shows all the different ways every sound can be spelled, to aid in looking up unfamiliar words; a visual history of each letter of the alphabet; and word histories of selected words (printed in colored blocks in the margins, not hidden under the word entries). The vocabulary contained in this dictionary is quite decent, too. My only wish is that Bob Jones University Press had included *more* Biblical usages.

DICTIONARIES FOR LITTLEST KIDS

We have all seen the picture dictionaries produced by famous children's illustrator Richard Scarry. These sorts of books are fun and colorful, designed more to teach vocabulary than for looking-up exercises. Fun value is max, educational value not necessarily so.

For dictionaries designed to fit with your children's academic studies, look below.

NEW**
Scott, Foresman Picture Reference Books
My Pictionary: hardbound $10.95, softbound $8.50. *My First Picture Dictionary*: hardbound $13.95, softbound $10.95. *My Second Picture Dictionary*: hardbound $15.95, softbound $12.95.

Not too long ago I received a really special review set of dictionaries for children in grades K-2. Unlike most children's dictionaries, these were designed to accompany children's school studies.

My Pictionary is 144 pages with over 850 colorfully-illustrated grade-appropriate entries for grades K-1. Words are grouped in categories, such as People, Animals, Storybook Characters, Numbers, Months of the Year, and so on. It comes with a complete alphabetical index, making it useful for beginning look-up exercises as well as browsing and study, and a two-page alphabet chart.

My First Picture Dictionary, for grade 1, has 312 pages with 1,500 grade-appropriate entries and simple definitions in sentence format, sometimes including "thinking" questions. E.g., "The alphabet is all the letters from A to Z. Can you say the alphabet?" Lots of colorful illustrations. Special 12-page reference section includes maps, shapes, measurement and numbers, time, parts of the body, healthy snacks, the calendar, holidays, opposites, and colors.

My Second Picture Dictionary, for grade 2, is up to 448 pages with 4,000 entries. This book also has a special 12-page reference section covering the entire school curriculum for this grade.

I checked these books out and was delighted to find no political or social bias in them at all. You can actually find a mother with her baby as well as a father playing with his child; family is defined in the traditional sense; and there is no nonsense about indoctrinating kindergartners about the evils of nuclear warfare and the terrors of AIDS. Plaudits to Scott, Foresman Inc. for sticking with the charming and interesting and not loading these heavy burdens on little backs.

EXPLORING THE ENCYCLOPEDIA

Two hot spots for encyclopedia buying are your living room and your neighbor's yard sale.

Advantages of the yard sale: El Cheapo prices, and the set probably has never been used anyway. Disadvantages: Out of date sociological information, e.g., the names and political setup of African countries. On the other hand: Really old encyclopedias often contain less philosophical propaganda than the newer.

Advantages of talking to an encyclopedia salesman in your living room: You get the most current version of the encyclopedia, and are allowed to purchase subsequent Yearbooks to keep your set up to date. You may be offered other sets from the publisher, such as a science encyclopedia or children's literature, at substantial savings when you buy their encyclopedia. You get to feel like a big shot and a wonderful mother or father every time you look at your *very own set* of *brand new encyclopedias*. Disadvantages: You may not like eating lentils and pea soup for the next six months. And what if you find an encyclopedia you like *better*, after blowing your retirement fund on another set?

I will admit it. We bought a new encyclopedia. Like the vast majority of home schoolers, ours is one of the two listed below. (Bet you can guess which one!) And boy, does that baby get a beating! If we see a funny-looking spider or a strange tree on a nature walk, back home the first thing after taking off coats and jackets is a dash to the encyclopedia shelf to look up the critter or plant in question. After we saw a video about Sergeant York, the great World War I hero, we found and read the encyclopedia entry about him. When historical questions arise, like "When exactly did Galileo live?," instead of arguing fruitlessly about it, someone triumphantly proves his point from the encyclopedia. Not to mention the times we sit down and just *read* it . . .

If you have an encyclopedia and your children read it, they are getting a well-rounded basic education. No ifs, ands, or buts. Come to think of it, pea soup and lentils taste pretty good . . .

Encyclopaedia Britannica, Inc.
Available in several bindings, priced from merely expensive to outrageous.

Over the last few years *Britannica* has been updated so the entries will support elitist social change theories. See, for example, the Mel Gablers' report on *Britannica*. All that noted, *Britannica* is by far the most thorough encyclopedia available. You get the 12-volume Ready Reference (this used to be called the Micropedia), 17 volumes of Knowledge in Depth (formerly known as the Macropedia), a two-volume index, and the "Unique One-Volume Outline of Knowledge!" The latter surveys every major field of study in a dry, scholarly fashion, and then directs you to places you can study further in the encyclopedia.

Let's take a deeper look at *Britannica*, section by section. The Ready Reference section contains over 86,000 articles and cross-reference entries, plus almost 16,000 graphics of various kinds: photos, drawings, and maps. These are supposed to be the "easy" articles for younger people to use and for adults who want a quick overview of the subject. Next, the Knowledge in Depth section is loaded with long, heavy articles that give up to full book length to the treatment of selected subjects—only 680 articles in these 17 volumes. Biosphere and Excretion are among the favored subjects chosen for the Big Treatment. This is what *Britannica* calls "changing with the times" and being "contemporary in outlook and coverage."

Britannica has the user interface of medicine. It's supposed to come from people who know much more than you do and be good for you. This makes it less than uproarious fun to use. Face it—the typeface they use is *ugly*, and *Britannica* seems to have a fixation about not pampering the reader with colorful or interesting graphics. The text is right in line with this philosophy. They don't pamper the reader with colorful or interesting writing, either.

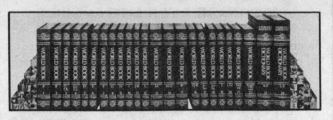

UPDATED**
World Book, Inc.
Available in several bindings, priced from affordable ($579) to moderately expensive ($899). Combination pricing available when you buy with *Childcraft* and or *Early World of Learning*. Buy last year's edition when available and get a special deal from your salesman.

The World Book Encyclopedia is Number One among home schoolers. It's also Number One in sales to the general public, outselling its next three direct-selling competitors combined. Four out of every 10 families in the U.S.A. and Canada that own an encyclopedia own this one. Why? Because it's more fun to read than *Britannica* and has lots more info than cheaper competitors. Easy-to-read, appealing articles start in newspaper fashion with the main points in simple vocabulary, and then progress to a fuller treatment of the subject. Over 29,000 terrific graphics (24,000 in color), annual revision policy, less philosophical bias than most encyclopedias. Designed for use in public schools, *The World Book Encyclopedia* covers every subject in the K-12 curriculum, plus a lot of other useful material. You won't find book-length scholarly articles here, but then, you can always go to the library and take out a book on a particular subject if you need that much more info than you find in the encyclopedia. And only *World Book* is continually tested in more than 400 classrooms throughout the U.S. and Canada. Twenty-two volumes include separate Research Guide and Index volume. Choice of bindings.

Your World Book salesman will also try to sell you a set of Childcraft books. These are meant as a learning and reference set for younger children, and include everything from three volumes of stories and poems to read aloud (or silently) to engrossing volumes on plants, animals, different cultures, and so on—plus a not-altogether-encouraging Parents' Guide. The latter subscribes to the theory that it's normal for children to reject their families in favor of the peer group and current cultural fads. This doesn't happen in cultures that don't encourage it. The child-training advice in the Parents' Guide is more of the same—how to graciously surrender your children to the Youth Culture, the Media Culture, the Sex Culture, and so on. Otherwise, most of Childcraft is fun reading, and it certainly is kid-appealing.

He or she also will try to sell you a set of *Early World of Learning,* a "research-based school readiness program." World Book asked a lot of kindergarten teachers what children needed to know in order to perform successfully in their classrooms. Based on the answers to this question, World Book developed a big boxful of 19 program books, 10 cassette taps, three activity books, 60 activity cards, "Amy" and "Zak" hand puppets, a Playboard, and Parents' Guide, all to teach the 105 skills targeted by the early childhood educators as most-necessary to success. Will you buy it? If you do, you get a combination-offer discount on the encyclopedia. (Find out more about Childcraft and Early World of Learning in Volume 2 of *The Big Book of Home Learning.*)

World Book underwent a major revision in 1988. This is the first "sweeping revision" since 1960. The new version has 70 new articles, almost 1,000 completely revised articles, and over 6,000 partially revised articles. Among the revised articles were those on countries and cities, all of which are now up-to-date. *World Book* now has four-color maps of all the world's independent countries, except for Vatican City, the postage-stamp papal republic that fits conveniently in a photograph. More than 10,000 color illustrations were added, and an entirely new typeface was used.

Frankly, I am not that excited about the new "World Book Modern" typeface, even if it was designed by Hermann Zapf, one of the most famous type designers of the century. It is blockish and sterile. Even so, *World Book* still looks better than *Britannica.*

I also should mention the other World Book reference products: *The World Book Encyclopedia* (text only—no pictures) on compact disc read-only memory (CD-ROM); *The World Book Dictionary; The World Book Atlas; The World Book Encyclopedia of Science* (see Volume 3 for review); *The World Book Medical Encyclopedia; The World Book of America's Presidents* (fascinating—see review in Volume 3); *The World Book Year Book* (encyclopedia owners get a shot at updating their set annually by adding the Year Book volume); *The World Book Health & Medical Annual: Science Year: The World Book Annual Science Supplement;* and *Childcraft Annual.* It's a fairly impressive lineup if you are looking for mainstream "expert" thinking on any of the covered subjects.

Bottom line: If you just have to have the most recent information acceptable to your local public school

system and want to enjoy the expanded color and graphics, get the latest edition of *World Book Encyclopedia.* If you prefer a friendlier, though less glitzy, format and don't mind missing out on the latest changes of government in political hot spots, look in the classifieds and see if anyone in your town is trying to sell one of the later pre-1988 editions.

GENERAL REFERENCE TOOLS

NEW★★
Kay Milow
Home Schooler's Complete Reference Guide, $25.

This spiral-bound 208-page oversized book is an encyclopedia of learning for K-6. Home schooling mother Kay Milow draws on her experience teaching at both school and home to provide all the lists, rules, definitions, project ideas, and teaching tips you are likely to need for reading, English (including an extensive section on sentence diagramming), spelling, math, social studies, science, health, Spanish, and art. Everything is organized by subject in a sequential manner, so it is ultra-easy to use. Need to find a glossary of geometric terms? Information on noun suffixes? How to outline? Conservation projects? State abbreviations? Roman numerals? Basic math exercises using money? Irregular English verbs? Literature reading lists for each grade level? All this and tons more, plus sample exercises and projects and suggested library books to read for each topic, are in this one handy volume. You won't have any holes in your home curriculum if you diligently use this book. In fact, you may not *need* any home curriculum if you diligently use this book! As Jill Johnson of Waverly, Nebraska, a satisfied user of this book, says, "Kay's book, a set of encyclopedias and the occasional use of the public library are all you need."

NEW★★
World Book, Inc.
The Student Information Finder, $34.95. Also available in combined offer with *How to Study* video (see Study Skills chapter).

The two volumes of *The Student Information Finder* contain important facts most often taught in school. The Language Arts and Social Studies volume has facts about writing, language, and spelling; places around the world and important dates and people in history. The Math and Science volume has basic info about math and all the sciences, e.g., a periodic table of the elements with concise explanations of how to use it and info about each element. The brochure says these books are designed to help students review material they have learned and to supplement information in their textbooks, as well as providing quick answers as needed for reports and other assignments. Colorful, lots of pix.

SAVING MONEY ON REFERENCE TOOLS

Barnes and Noble
Publishers Central Bureau

These two discount houses often offer great bargains on reference sets. Drawbacks: You may have to spend an hour with the catalog to be sure you don't want anything this time. Another drawback: Remaindered reference sets sometimes (not always) deserve it. Also, each catalog carries a mixture of sophomoric "erotic" material, which many of us would just as soon avoid.

NEW★★
Bluestocking Press
How to Stock a Quality Home Library Inexpensively, revised edition, $5.45 postpaid.

Do you know how to make your home library pay for itself? How to get a complete set of *The World Book Encyclopedia* for $60? How to find free or almost-free books that you really want? How to avoid duplications in your book shopping? The new edition of this how-to-find-it-for-less book has even more leads on sources for cheapo or freebie books. The appendix alone lists 22 sources of discount books stores, mail-order books suppliers, and remainder dealers who sell to the general public. More: advice on *what* books to put on your shopping list, covering all ages and subject areas. Encouraging style, fun to read. A must-have for bookish families. Following its advice, I myself can hardly *move* without tripping over a book we bought at discount!

SUPER SOURCES FOR SCHOOL SUPPLIES

School supply stores (sometimes called teacher's supply stores) are my very favorite places to shop. These companies have a selection of toys that makes Child World look sick. They sell fairy tales and Dr. Seuss. They carry chemistry sets and ant castles. They have music and filmstrips and art supplies and playground equipment. They sell games, and flannelboard figures, and puzzles. And just to prove they are really education-minded, most of them even sell workbooks!

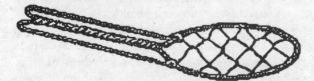

Parents and grandparents, you have been missing out if you have been doing your birthday shopping without a school supply catalog handy. Unlike the textbook market, which is dry and boring and loaded with ideology, the school supply market is bursting with creativity. You can teach your children the shapes of letters over 35 different ways with just the products Constructive Playthings carries (I counted). For just this one skill area, you can get: crepe rubber puzzles with alphabet pieces; textured, grooved alphabet blocks; alphabet letter molds: an alphabet stamp set; alphabet blocks; an alphabet flip book; alphabet sten-

cils; and an alphabet worm puzzle. And these are just some of the less innovative products! Whether you are studying handwriting, or math, or science, or history, or you name it, the school supply people carry a constellation of exciting materials in your subject area. You can hardly keep from getting ideas for fun ways to learn just by reading one of these catalogs.

Why are textbooks so dull and school supplies, which sound at least as dull, so exciting? Because textbooks are "approved," a doctrinal ritual which demands adherence to whatever religious dogmas are currently in vogue among the elite, and school supplies are not. Teachers have *much* better sense than the bureaucrats who actually run the schools, and when they get a chance to pick which materials they use, they demand good products. School suppliers are also heavily used by private schools, and this helps keep the school supply market more geared to materials parents would approve.

Since textbooks are supposed to carry the teaching load, school supplies can afford to be fun. Virtually everything in a good school supply catalog has kid-appeal. Kids *want* to use this stuff! Which leads us to a semi-serious suggestion for the schools. How about throwing out the textbooks and using only school supplies? I know that it's un-American to teach kids without testing them every two minutes, but still it would be an interesting experiment.

SUGGESTED SUPPLIES FOR YOUR HOME CLASSROOM

Almost every book on home learning that I have seen includes a list of supplies for the home classroom. Almost every list that I have seen is a mile long. In time, you probably will accumulate all of those items, but at first glance it looks like home learning would break the bank and clutter up your home! I would like to offer the following thoughts in an attempt to simplify and economize.

First, desks. The kind with a storage space under the lid are great. Now, where to get them? *Big Book* reader Maria Warren of Florida points out, "Desks and school chairs can be purchased for a nominal fee from your local county's school surplus store. They have everything a school can possibly use, from sewing machines and audio-visual equipment and accessories to flagpoles and clocks." So if you want desks, now you know where to get 'em cheap! If you don't have room for desks, don't worry. Children can study at the kitchen table, or on the living room floor. Some of our family's best lessons have been given sitting on the living room couch! Just be consistent about whatever spot you pick, and in time it will develop that special "study area" feel during lesson hours.

Second, blackboards. The best kind is the white mark 'n clean style that you write on with special colored markers. These are much easier to read and work with, and don't get chalk dust all over your rugs. The old-fashioned kind you write on with chalk aren't bad, either, although these are no longer *black*boards but green. For kinesthetic kids, blackboards are great, since the kids can practice BIG letters and numbers without a lot of paper clutter. You can make your own with special chalkboard paint (available at your teacher supply store) painted on a wall or a sheet of heavy cardboard or Masonite, or get one ready-made. You can permanently rule lines on your board with permanent marker, for writing practice, or leave it as pristinely green as Kermit the Frog. You can have *several* boards, one ruled with lines, one with empty grids for math problems, one just for drawing and free play. It's up to you!

Third, paper and pencils. These you must have. Almost every office has reams of used computer paper whose backsides you can use for scribble paper. Tracing paper is helpful for drawing exercises and tracing letters. Colored construction paper can be used for almost everything. But watch out! Art paper also now comes in foil, tissue, fadeless, and corrugated. It's possible to go overboard when you see the selection!

Actually, you don't even *need* paper and pencils for most activities. Our great-grandparents used slates and chalk, thus eliminating paper litter and saving money. Although slates are hard to find today, every school supplier has kid-sized chalkboards, some especially designed to be held on the lap, and kid-sized mark 'n clean boards. When first learning to write, these boards are a boon. Kids can erase their mistakes and try again, and make letters as large as they like without wasting paper. If you only have one or two children, you might prefer these lap-sized chalkboards or markerboards. For a larger family, a nice big blackboard saves a lot of trouble, as you can all do your work in the same place at once.

Fourth, art media. After trying markers, watercolors, yarn, Cray-Pas, charcoal, colored pencils, clay, toothpick art, and too many other materials to mention, we have settled down to scissors, glue, crayons, and modeling beeswax as the "bare essentials." (Modeling beeswax, available from HearthSong in many colors, doesn't get stuck to the table and the bottoms of tennis shoes, and is easy to remove if it does—unlike clay and play dough.) Older children who are responsible enough to work with expensive and messy materials on their own can accumulate whatever they can afford to buy; but when you don't have much time to hover over kids' art projects, ye olde cut 'n paste is great. Get rid of those scuzzy old bottles of wheat paste and get some glue sticks, and pasting becomes a neat activity. Anything a youngster wants to do with line and color, he can do with crayons. Anything he wants to do in 3-D he can do with beeswax. Until he learns the basics of drawing and modeling, you don't need all the glitzy stuff in the art catalog.

Once you have your basic art media, your basic writing stuff, and a place to sit, you have enough to get started. The beauty of learning at home is that home is not a classroom. All the other classroom paraphernalia—globes, an American flag, bulletin boards, chalkholders that draw musical staffs, and so on—can be added when and if you feel the need. It's better to get too little and have to make a second shopping trip than to buy too much and have it cluttering up your house.

SCHOOL SUPPLY CATALOGS

Besides being sources for all sorts of creative teaching tools, these catalogs are also the place to get your teaching supplies, such as chalk, crayons, blackboards, protractors, paper, and the like. If you're into stickers and happy faces, these people will be glad to oblige you. If your pressing need is for a BIG bottle of glue, or a small American flag, you can find it here. The only school supply I wouldn't get from a school supply firm is a student desk. Modern desks have just a flat writing surface and no place to store the books. This is realistic, considering the rate of theft in schools, but not functional at home. We got our desks (which we have sold) second-hand through an ad in the local paper. As Maria Warren pointed out above, your county might have a school surplus store that would love to trade you an old but durable desk for a little of the green stuff. My best friend got hers *free* when a school district threw out their old ones. See what kind of deal you can work out, or save your money and stick with the kitchen table. But for every other item, let your fingers do the walking!

A&D Bookstore & Educational Supply (formerly Sentinel Teacher Supply)

Decent medium-sized catalog with a good selection of teacher's supplies, plus the usual kiddie goodies. Less toys than Lakeshore, more curriculum-style materials than most.

ABC School Supply

Gorgeous color catalog of materials of early childhood education, elementary, and special education. Most materials are for preschool through third grade. ABC carries a few Christian products and seems geared to the private school market. Shipping sluggish at "rush" seasons of the year.

Chaselle

More of an emphasis on office supplies and art supplies than most others. Chaselle has separate catalogs for arts and crafts, basic "lifeskills" materials, preschool and elementary school materials, general school materials, and microcomputer materials. A smattering of the best of everything is in the general catalog, which is the one you'll probably want.

Christian Light Publications

Besides their own Mennonite version of the Alpha Omega Publications curriculum, Christian Light also vends science lab equipment, a smattering of literature and textbooks, and record-keeping forms for private schools. All prices are very reasonable, as CLP obeys the Christian injunction not to gouge one's brethren.

Constructive Playthings

Curriculum materials, supplies and equipment for everyone from newborns to preteens; also special education materials. Full-color catalog features some exclusive items, such as their pretend play food. Constructive Playthings manufactures many pieces themselves in their line of hard maple children's furniture. Large selection of children's books and records.

Hoover's

Hoover's motto is "Everything Educational" and they're not kidding. Their catalog is *huge*. We've shopped at their Teacher's Store here in St. Louis and admire the vast selection. Hoover's has other outlets throughout the Midwest—mostly under the name "The Teacher's Store." Check your Yellow Pages for one near you.

If you ever think of starting a private school, Hoover's can even get you all the furniture you need for the library, gym, auditorium, etc. Much of this heavy-duty furniture is not listed in the catalog—contact them directly.

Since Hoover's carries so many products, you may find the catalog overwhelming. The selling point here is "completeness," not glamor or layout.

Ideal School Supply

Elementary products, all subjects. Ideal is a manufacturer/supplier of materials sold in other catalogs and in teachers' stores. Full-color catalog features items by subject area. Lots and lots of manipulatives and games for early childhood, special ed, math, language, science, and social studies. Good quality items.

Lakeshore Curriculum Materials Center

Colorful catalog, slimmer than most, zippier items, upscale selection, faster shipping (Lakeshore guarantees three-day shipment). Categories: infants, preschool, elementary, and special education. It is impossible to thumb through this catalog without being tempted.

Your Local Yellow Pages

Look under "School Supplies" or "Teacher's Supplies." These stores are increasingly anxious to sell to parents; you don't have to worry that you will be spotted as a non-teacher and hustled out! The typical teacher's supply store has a lavish selection of art supplies, workbooks, educational games, bulletin boards and stuff to put on them, and lots more, generally more geared to elementary school than to high school. If you're looking for posters of the U.S. presidents, or geography flashcards, they are very likely to have what you want. You will get all sorts of ideas for your home education program by visiting one of these friendly stores.

FREEBIES AND CHEAPIES

World Book, Inc.

Reprints of selected articles from *World Book*, many of which include color pictures, are available *free* in quantities of one to teachers and librarians. If you are home schooling and have a school name and stationery, you are a school and need not feel embarrassed about sending for some of these. But don't abuse the privilege—give them a shot at selling you their product!

More inexpensive offers: World Book has a booklet, *Through the Year with World Book*, designed to put their encyclopedia to use ($2.50), and a set of classroom posters for $1 each, or any four for $2. Some of these, like the *Physical Map of the World*, are quite useful.

CHAPTER TEN

STUDY SKILLS MADE EASY

Teaching is to learning as preparing the feast is to eating it. As each teacher needs the tools of teaching in order to prepare an inviting and digestible educational feast, so each student needs to master the tools of learning. He needs to learn how to chop up the lesson into smaller, more digestible parts. He needs to learn how to thoroughly "chew" new material until he has digested it. He needs to learn how to refresh his mind ("take a drink") in the midst of arduous study. Then, after all that, he needs to know how to turn around and prepare the same feast for someone else—since you don't really know a subject until you can teach it yourself.

Study skills don't come naturally to all of us. Although a child might spend hours poring over a book, unless he has been trained, or has trained himself, to study for meaning, he will most likely just remember the parts that especially interest him. Thanks to television, which has trained almost all modern children in the habits of inattentiveness, he may not even remember anything at all! Learning, for such a child, is the process of being entertained, and hardly any residue is left in his mind after the "educational experience" is over.

So, although this is a chapter of study skills resources, let me suggest that the first step to improved understanding and better grades for any child or adult, whether in school or out of it, is to minimize or elimi-

nate passive entertainment such as television. The habit of attentiveness is the first study skill to cultivate. Try reading books aloud to your students to develop auditory attentiveness. Nature walks, in which you try to observe and identify the flowers, trees, birds, and so on along your way, are great for developing visual, tactile, and auditory powers of observation. Is the tree's skin *rough* or *smooth?* Does it have *pointed* leaves or *round?* Does that bird *warble,* or *chirrup,* or *screech?* By pointed attention to the real world and to real words, you can lay the framework for disciplined habits of mind that will benefit your family for the rest of their lives.

Now here are some products especially designed to focus your listening skills, memory skills, note-taking skills, research skills, and general study skills.

STUDY TECHNIQUES

Perhaps the most familiar study method is SQ3R. As I recall from my elementary school days (the recollection is a bit fuzzy), SQ3R stands for Survey, Question, Read, Recite, and Review. First you *survey* the material, getting a feel for it, but not actually studying it. You scan the table of contents, read the blurbs on the back cover, browse through the book noting headings, if any, and so on. Next, you *question.* You decide what information you will look for in this material. For example, when reading a book on King Henry the Eighth, you might ask, "Why did Henry decide to break with the Catholic church . . . who were his wives . . . what were their names . . . was Henry a good king or a bad king?" As you study, you will be looking for answers to these questions. Now you *read* the material through carefully. You then *recite* your questions aloud. Finally, to tamp down what you learned, you *review*, skimming through the material and reminding yourself of the important facts you wish to remember.

The reason SQ3R is so popular is that . . . it works. Surprise! Look at SQ3R from the data-framework standpoint. First you play with the data, then you try to structure it (by means of preformed questions), then you assimilate data into your structure, then you modify your structure to include even more data, and finally you cement the connections by reviewing the newly-gained data. All very natural.

As you get better at asking questions, and come to your studies already loaded with relevant data from previous study, you will find the process easier and easier. I still find myself using SQ3R unconsciously when reading a particularly important book, taking my yellow highlighter to significant passages on the Revise and Review steps. There just seems to be no way to skip any step profitably, unless you are one of those rare people gifted with a photographic memory. (Or perhaps "cursed with a photographic memory," depending on how much network television you watch!)

Audio Forum
Secrets of Successful Study, $29.95. Add $3.50 shipping.

Three cassettes—*Time Management, How to Study a Chapter,* and *Taking Tests*—all in one binder. This series is geared towards those suffering through traditional high school and college courses. Thus, much emphasis is put on overcoming panic attacks before tests, and the *How to Study a Chapter* tape gives you strategies which work best in textbooks (e.g., read the chapter summary first, then the subheadings, then the chapter). Good advice for those with little control over their academic lives.

NEW**
Chesterbrook Educational Publishers, Inc.
College, High School, Grade School video seminars each $69.95, audio seminars each $39.95. Add $3 shipping.

You may have seen the colorful full-page ads in your Sunday paper for this "Where There's a Will,

There's An 'A'" program taught by Professor Claude Olney. The ad features a plug from John Ritter, testimonies from parents, teachers, and students, and promises that the course will teach your student to study "smarter," not "harder." Beyond this, the program content sounds similar to others reviewed here—specific techniques for studying, writing term papers, taking tests, increasing retention, and so on. The video seminars are two videos plus a manual; the audio seminars are four cassettes plus manual. I could not get a review copy in time to tell you anything more.

NEW**
Dale Seymour Publications
How to Study student text $10.95, parent's guide $8.50. Teacher's guide also available, $5.95.

This set is one of Dale Seymour Publications' bestsellers. Each book is organized around five basic study skills: managing time/setting priorities, active listening and note-taking, how to study textbooks, how to prepare for tests, and test-taking skills.

Some contributions of this series: An emphasis on breaking studies into reachable 15-minute goals. Speed writing based on abbreviations, not shorthand. How to team-study. Using memory keys to improve retention. How to set up an effective study area. The TI-3R method (similar to SQ3R)—Think, Index, Read, Record, Recite—and how to personalize it. How to use a solitaire-like card game to effectively review class material for tests. The Splashdown method for reducing test panic.

The parent's guide explains the basic principles of success in studying and gives specific suggestions for what you can do to help your son or daughter form the proper study habits. This is not fluffy general advice, but very practical training in how to train your children. Inspirational quotes scattered throughout. The student book, in larger print, covers the same information in a more personal way, with discussion questions at the end of each chapter.

UPDATED★★
Learn, Inc.
Speed Learning, $125 for each of these modules: Medical, Science/Engineering, and Finance/Accounting. *Speed Learning* video (VHS or Beta), $150 for each module listed above. Standard Edition of *Speed Learning*, $120 audio, $150 video. *Super Reading Jr.*, $39.95. Add $3 shipping.

The bestselling self-study reading program in the world. *Speed Learning*, billed as "much more than speed reading," is supposed to help you understand, remember, and use more of what you read. Not a rehash of the eye-training exercises and speed drills offered by other programs, *Speed Learning* concentrates (according to the ad) on improving your thinking skills. Special modules are available containing an additional workbook with reading material and exercises from particular professional fields. One million people have taken this course.

The junior version, *Super Reading Jr.*, is billed as "a system that actually teaches children how to think." It is supposed to double your child's ability to read and remember. The course, designed for eleven- to sixteen-year olds, should take 30 to 60 minutes per day, five days a week, for eight to twelve weeks.

So, what does *Super Reading Jr.* cover? Setting purposes for your reading. Deciding what you need to learn, and what parts of the material you are reading are relevant to that purpose. Predicting what the author will say. Adjusting the rate of reading to the difficulty of the material. Adjusting the *style* of reading to the purpose of reading: skim-reading for the answers to straight questions, scan-reading to interpret content, study-reading to decipher an assignment and apply your reading to it, and pace-reading, for quicker coverage of ordinary reading. Also covered are how to survey reading material and the use of reference resources in the book such as indexes, tables of content, charts, and graphs. You get a biggish (256 oversized pages)

study/instruction book, two cassettes, and a parent's guide, all in a very nice binder. The parent's guide includes basic information about how to use the course and a pre- and post-test with answer keys, so you can evaluate how much your child has learned. The study/instruction guide contains many fascinating reading exercises along with the basic instruction, plus work pages and self-tests.

NEW★★
World Book, Inc.
The Student Information Finder, $34.95. *How to Study* video, $29.95 (VHS only). Both plus free copy of *101 Easy Ways to Get Better Grades*, $49.95.

From the people who brought you the *World Book Encyclopedia*, here are several study skills aids designed for upper elementary and high school students.

For simple reference needs, the two volumes of *The Student Information Finder* have all those basic lists of facts, dates, people, places, scientific terms, etc.

World Book's *How to Study* video explains the SQ3R method of studying. It has won all kinds of awards, including "Best Educational Video of the Year" from the American Video Conference. The brochure tells us it's not "old fashioned" or "preachy," but "upbeat, positive" and "entertaining." Funny characters like Scoop Newsworld and real kids sharing their concerns about studies and school. Free book when you buy both the *Info Finder* and video.

LISTENING SKILLS

NEW★★
Achievement Basics
What Is Listening? and all three volumes of *Stories for Quiet Listening*, each $7.95 plus $1 shipping.

Cassette with self-checking activities in listening skills for elementary-grades children. *What is Listening?* also gives short dramatized examples that show young children why it is important or helpful to listen for safety, information, understanding, success, and pleasure. The Listening Song summarizes this information. A dramatic story on side two shows the use of listening as a social skill. Also available: three volumes of *Stories for Quiet Listening*. Each of these cassettes is told and sung by the late Harold Peary—the original "Great Gildersleeve" of the old radio show. Volume One is designed to help children tell sounds apart better, with stories like "Sammy the Garter Snake" (focusing on letter S). Volume Two features sound effects to recognize, rhyming words, and so on, all wrapped into stories. Volume Three takes this a step farther, culminating in "Songs by the Mystery Guest," where animals gather and sing their words and sounds in a contest.

NEW★★
Keys to Excellence
Creative IQ program, including *Active Listening* and *Helping Your Child Achieve in School,* $69 plus $4 shipping.

For kids aged 3-13 and their parents. Seasoned schoolteacher Simone Bibeau has now added to her original creativity program a two-tape set, *Active Listening* and *Helping Your Child Achieve in School.* Side one of *Active Listening* is for the parents, providing games we can play with the children to make them better listeners, and Side two is for the kids themselves. *Help Your Child Achieve in School* covers the politics of dealing with the teacher, problems schoolchildren experience, and what you can do to assist your child short of teaching him yourself. Upbeat common sense, blended with pertinent stories from Simone's years as a classroom teacher. The two cassettes come in a nice binder, along with the original four cassettes, workbooks, and binder of the Creative IQ program. For details of the latter, see its writeup in the Creative Writing chapter in Volume Two.

NEW★★
Learn, Inc.
Listen Your Way to Success by Robert Montgomery, $59.95.

This nicely-packaged listening skills course is directed to adults already out in the workforce. Serious-minded teens can also use it. They will find much good advice pertinent to their future careers here.

You get three cassettes, a guidebook, listening test, and workbook, all designed to help you *hear, question,* and *understand.* The course includes • six shortcuts to better learning • three principles of active listening (e.g., identifying the speaker's motive) • eight pitfalls to

avoid in the business and social worlds • nine personality/attitude types and how to identify them through their body language • ten ways to improve your relations with workplace peers and bosses • five ways to improve your telephone listening, including the questions to ask and how to ask them. All of this is much more motivating than the usual "learn this method to do well in school approach," and many of the principles are transferable to the school environment.

NEW★★
R & E Publishers
Power Study series by Sondra Geoffrion, each guide $3.95 or $17.50 for complete set of five.

A very practical, inexpensive series of study skills guides for people in junior high through college. The Power Study series includes guides for English, Math, Social Studies, Science, and a guide on improving your general grade-point average. Each short (32-page) guide packs a lot of useful information about how to take class notes, how to best write down assignments, how to maximize your study time for the particular subject, how to "power cram" for and skillfully take tests, and how to use the returned tests as study tools. Each guide also includes a "40 Ways to Earn Higher Grades" chart that summarizes the most important Power Study tips. A good choice for teens and young adults.

MEMORY TRAINING

I have a mind like a steel sieve. From earliest childhood on, I have been absentmindedly putting the paper towels in the refrigerator and the milk in the cupboard. Many times I have found myself standing in the middle of the kitchen (or bedroom, or living room) wondering just what I came into it to get.

My grandmother loves to hear about my latest fits of absentmindedness. It cheers her up to remember that young people can forget things, too! She is not actually any more absentminded than I am, but, as she points out, when someone her age forgets things, everyone assumes it is because she is getting older.

Most of us don't remember anywhere near as much as we'd like to. To some degree or other, we go through life absentmindedly not noticing our environment. Some of us can't remember people's names. Others forget street directions, or need a shopping list to remember more than three items, or forget the subjects we were studying the minute we have passed the test.

Meeting this need for improved memory, a number of companies now market memory training programs. The most prominent of these lean heavily on word-picture associations and a variety of techniques designed to increase your attention to the item you are trying to remember.

Now, increased attentiveness is the key to improved memory. One hundred and fifty years ago British educator Charlotte Mason was pointing this out, and thousands of years before her Aristotle had noticed the same thing. But word-picture association has its limits. For one thing, it is a highly *visual* approach—and not all of us are visual learners. For another thing, it takes far more energy to recall an elaborate picture and translate it back into words than to simply recall the words themselves to mind.

I mention this because one memory-training company now claims in its ads that learning from pictures is natural for people, whereas learning from print causes frustration and inability to retain information. Now if this is true, the only logical response is to turn *all* learning into "sight" learning—bring back hieroglyphics and abolish the English alphabet.

What do I mean by "word-picture association"? Say you want to memorize the Bible verse, "Thy word is a lamp unto my feet and a light unto my path." What you get in this company's case is a picture of a word-finder book facing a numeral two who is dressed in underwear. A myna bird is pecking at the numeral's feet. Behind this, an ampersand is holding up a light and another numeral two also dressed in undies is walking toward a myna bird on a path. Lamps, the key word for this verse, are displayed in green in several places on the card. You memorize this picture and from that memory reconstruct the exact words of the verse.

Will this method work? Of course it will work, given enough attention, especially since certain pictures are always used for certain words—e.g., a HOOt owl for the word WHO. However, it's a long hike from

here to proving that the tried-'n-true method of memorization through repetition (simply rereading or repeating Scripture aloud sufficient times) is utterly worthless. In fact, many people have memorized chapters and even entire Bible books by the old method.

As you can see, as a Bible memorization method the picture association method is limited. Nobody has time to make a picture of every verse, and if you did, the commonness of certain images would tend to cause confusion and forgetfulness. For other times of learning, though, particularly when you are trying to associate a number of words that have no natural connections (e.g., states and their capitals), the visual memory method is excellent.

How about memorizing math facts? Some people will point out that multiplication has its own set of built-in regularities, such as "To multiply by 9, subtract 1 from the number multiplied and add as a second digit the number required to make a sum of 9—e.g., to find 2x9, subtract 1 from 2 for the tens place, then note that 1+8=9, and you have the answer, 18." The question is, "How well will children note and remember the regularities?" Even if a subject to be memorized is semi-regular, if the child is a visual rather than an intuitive learner, he might well grasp the facts in question more quickly with a visual method.

The long and short of it is this—word-picture memory methods may be fun and clever, but they are not the answer to our national educational woes. Hieroglyphs are useful in associating unrelated objects, like names and faces or states and their capitals, but are not an effective substitute for written words as a vehicle of learning. Picture-learning is no more "natural" than imagination-learning, which is what happens when we visualize in our minds while reading. I learned (and still remember) the multiplication table without visuals, and so did you. So recognize visual memory tools for what they are—fun and exciting ways for special-purpose learning, and don't buy the pitch that we need picture-words to cure us of the Learning Blues!

CASSETTE AND VIDEO COURSES

Arthur Bornstein School of Memory Training

Memory Training Course Book, $22.50. Complete Home Study Memory Training Kit (includes book, review book, 100 visual key practice cards, numerical dictionary, study guide, and 8 cassette tapes), $125. Individual tapes: *How to . . . Retain Facts and Ideas for School and Business, Develop Concentration and Visualization Techniques, Remember Names and Faces, Develop and Retain Your Vocabulary, Retain and Master a Foreign Language, Remember Numerical Data*, $9.95 each. Video Memory Training Course, 10 sessions, VHS or Beta (includes book and practice materials, training guide, and test question book), $395. Video *Memory Training Methods for Students, Memory—How to Improve It* one-hour courses, $39.95 each. Add 10% shipping.

Arthur Bornstein has trained over a million people to remember things better. You may have seen him on major network TV programs rattling off 40-digit number strings, or teaching hundreds of Bible verses to audience volunteers in less than an hour. The core of his method is association, and the more exaggerated the association, the better. This means fun times for the learner! Bornstein has association systems for remembering names and faces, vocabulary, numbers, foreign languages, spelling, and more. More than mere memory, his course is designed to improve your study habits: listening, concentrating, observing, classifying, and of course remembering.

Bornstein's complete ten-session video memory course was designed for business, and the price places it out of the average person's reach. To fill this gap, he has developed two new one-hour video courses: one for students that concentrates on memory techniques for retaining academic material and good study and listening habits, and one "for all ages" giving basic techniques for remembering facts, ideas, names, faces, and numbers, plus concentration techniques.

Bornstein also has programs for memorizing the multiplication tables and basic arithmetic facts, spelling facts, states and capitals, and improving your vocabulary. See reviews elsewhere in this book.

Learn, Inc.
Memory Made Easy by Robert Montgomery, $39.95

Engaging, not terribly expensive memory course that uses all the tricks: stacks, links, visual association, picture rhymes, number alphabet, and so on. Robert Montgomery (no relation to the famous actor) with the help of his studio audience shows you how it's done. Three cassettes, booklet, binder.

NOTE-TAKING TECHNIQUES

Conversa-phone Institute, Inc.

Variety of home steno and shorthand courses, plus lots of foreign language, dance, and self-improvement courses. This company has been around a good long time.

RESEARCH TECHNIQUES

Center for Applied Research in Education
Guided Research Discovery Units, $7.95 each. Shipping extra.

Here's a new idea! Guided research projects that students ages eight to 14 can complete at their own pace and learning level. Each unit has three to six projects and uses a wide variety of research skills. Kids actually get to use the library card catalog and the encyclopedia . . . to take notes . . . to find the right book and pull out the appropriate information . . . to categorize . . . summarize . . . rewrite . . . and so on. In the Animals unit, for example, the student picks a mammal, then describes it, finds out about its family life and reproduction, where in the world it lives, its habitat, food and eating habits, and so on. When finished, he can make a mobile of his research information.

Units available are: Animals! Animals! Animals! (nature science) • It's a Small World (geography) • Fascinating People (history) • Fun Pac (language arts) • Bookshelf Adventures (covers mystery, poetry, historical fiction, and science fiction) • Blast Off! (space science). Teacher's guide included in each unit.

NEW★★
World Book, Inc.
Through the Year with World Book, $2.50.

If you own or have steady access to the *World Book Encyclopedia*, you can do real research projects with *Through the Year with World Book*, a 48-page booklet with a whole year's worth of activities, games, and puzzles based on that encyclopedia. A question a day brings the encyclopedia into play!

CHAPTER ELEVEN

TEACHER TRAINING FOR TIMID PARENTS

Fear. Gut-gripping fear. Why should parents and others who contemplate teaching children outside of a school setting feel fear?

A silly question like that deserves a silly answer, and here it is. It's because we've been taught to think of T • E • A • C • H • I • N • G as a mysterious ritual requiring years to master. From the cradle, we are drilled to believe that only experts (meaning people with paper credentials) are equipped to understand basic life skills. To reinforce this, the experts have developed a language of their own, especially designed to mystify the outsider who thinks he or she is actually capable of T • E • A • C • H • I • N • G. "Behavioral objectives," mumbles one expert to another. "Um, ah, yes, and cognitive assessment interface modules back to you," responds the second. "I'll see that cognitive assessment and raise you one postpubescent learning gradient," confidently interjects a third. Baffled, the onlookers whisper among themselves, "Gee, those experts must really know their stuff. Don't understand a word they're saying, but it sure sounds important!"

Now, you don't want to be an expert. You just want to know what you're doing so you can get on with doing it. Therefore, this chapter contains resources with the no-frills philosophy and teaching how-tos you need to get started. Really, T • E • A • C • H • I • N • G is a lot simpler than you think!

PSYCHOLOGY OF LEARNING

Education Services
Biblical Psychology of Learning, $8.45 postpaid. Hardback.

A sizzling title it's not. All the same, this is a *great* book!

Dr. Beechick, a long-time teacher who has also worked as an editor on educational projects at major publishing houses, wittily exposes the shortcomings of what she calls "rat and couch psychologies." Method matters less than heart, she contends, basing this on Scripture. She then builds a case for family discipline as the initial building-block of education. The book goes on to say much more, all well worth reading. Start with this book.

Holt Associates

How Children Learn, 1983 revised edition, $9.95. *How Children Fail,* 1982 revised edition, $9.95. Shipping extra.

Readable, fascinating, mind-stretching. John Holt was perhaps the keenest, most honest observer of children in this century, and these books are full of his observations. I find his writings remarkably *real,* unusual in a day when researchers commonly twist the facts to fit their theories. Holt's outlook could be called libertarian, and he sometimes goes to extremes for the sake of consistency. All the same, he raises good questions that deserve answers.

DISCIPLINE IN LEARNING

Aletheia Publishers (a division of Alpha Omega Publications).

What the Bible Says About . . . Child Training, $6.95.

If, as Ruth Beechick asserts, the first step in education is establishing the teacher-disciple relationship (see above), immediately the question arises: "Do parents have any right to take an authority role, and if so, how should they handle it?" Here are answers for these questions.

Subjects include: the need for controlling young children; how and when to use chastisement; devices children use to avoid obeying, and how to respond; and developing self-controlled teenagers. Remember to balance this book's emphasis on the hows and whys of discipline with plenty of encouragement; kids need both!

The author, Richard Fugate, has a prominent position at Alpha Omega Publishers, a major curriculum supplier for Christian and home schools, and is the father of several good kids.

What the Bible Says . . . is endorsed by many Christian leaders, from Dr. Paul Kienel of Association of Christian Schools International to Jerry Falwell.

Aletheia Publishers also has a seminar based on this book, available on both cassette and videotapes. Write for a free brochure.

Pecci Educational Publishers

How to Discipline Your Class for Joyful Teaching. 42 pages. $4.95. Add 10% shipping.

This many not sound like a home schooling book, and in all honesty it isn't. It is the shortest, best book on motivation that I've ever seen. Written for class-

room teachers, the book is just as helpful for parents. *How To Discipline . . .* is a guide to help children *want* to please you. Mary Pecci realistically faces the question of what you should do when you've *already* blown your stack, and other vital questions that most books blithely ignore. A book with "soul."

HOW TO DO IT

Baker Book House

Excellence in Teaching with the Seven Laws, $4.95.

Excellence in Teaching with the Seven Laws summarizes and updates John Milton Gregory's *The Seven Laws of Teaching.* Gregory, a Baptist minister, served as Michigan state superintendent of public education, head of the Classical School in Detroit, president of Kalamazoo College, and president of the University of Illinois. More importantly, he did all this in the 1800s, when it really meant something!

Gregory's seven laws are simple statements of essential teaching principles. The Law of the Teacher, for example, states that teachers have to know the material they want to teach, and then tells them how to improve in this area. Also included are the Law of: the Learner, Language, the Lesson, the Teaching Process, the Learning Process, and Review and Application. Taken separately, each Law seems self-evident; together, and combined with the supporting text that illustrates and explains how to put them into practice, they'll put you on the road to becoming a great teacher.

NEW**
Carden Educational Foundation

Quality Teaching, Successful Learning, $14.20 hardcover. *Let's Bring Them Up Sensibly,* hardcover, $13.50. Shipping extra.

The more I look into the history of education, the more I find that we have no good excuse for being "A Nation At Risk." All the "reforms" and "innovations" which have led to our national educational malaise were vigorously opposed and exposed decades ago by talented teachers.

Miss Mae Carden was one of these. The scion of a wealthy family, she quit her postgraduate program at Columbia Teachers College when it became evident that the faculty were hellbent on pushing their theories of "look-say" reading instruction on the American public. She opened a successful private school in New York, where she developed materials for teaching her own classical approach to languages, arts, and all the other school subjects. Once these materials were developed, Miss Carden would go to an area upon invitation and instruct the public school teachers in her methods.

Now we come up against the crunch of reality. The educrats fought back. One elementary school principal of a school using Carden methods was hooted down by his peers when he tried to explain in a meeting that his school had *100%* reading successes. The people at the meeting had been taught that such success was impossible—so never mind the *facts!* In district after district, Carden materials were banned, *even after they had been shown to work far better* than the materials with which they were replaced. Teachers could only continue to use them in many cases by "bootlegging" them into the classroom.

Not all parents would sit still for this, so over the years a small but flourishing network of private schools for nursery school through high school has been founded using the Carden method and materials. Until recently, only persons having taken the Carden teacher-training courses were allowed to purchase these materials. The Carden Educational Foundation, however, is willing to make exceptions for homeschooling families and others with special circumstances that prevent gathering together a group of 10 for a three-day training course. Also, anyone can buy the books listed above containing Miss Carden's educational philosophies. You also can send for two free brochures: *The Carden Curriculum in the Carden School* and *A Carden Nursery School.*

NEW★★
Charlotte Mason Research & Supply
Complete slipcased six-volume set of Charlotte Mason books, $49.95 plus $5 shipping.

This is the only series of how-to-teach books I know about that comes endorsed by Her Majesty Queen Elizabeth of England!

Charlotte Mason, as some of you might know, was a nineteenth-century British educator with some marvelous insights and ideas into how to teach children. Inspired by her philosophy, the Parents National Education Union of Great Britain and a number of schools were founded.

Charlotte Mason understood the need to respect the child while not worshiping him. She stressed the importance of the "fallow" first six years of life, when according to her children ought to spend much time out-of-doors playing and observing nature. Among her other contributions: geography taught the way adults like to learn it, through the medium of interesting travel stories; history centered around interesting people and their environments rather than as a list of dates to memorize; the importance of beauty in the child's life and the value of living with great art (in the form of inexpensive art prints); and how to train children in the habit of perfect obedience. This is only the tip of the iceberg, as Miss Mason had many fascinating things to say, all based on her personal experience of decades of teaching.

Having heard of Charlotte Mason, I went years ago in search of her books, only to find that they were not available anywhere, even in the entire St. Louis library system! Dean and Karen Andreola have solved this problem for us. While visiting England a year or two ago, they tracked down the books in the library of Charlotte Mason College and got an American publisher (Tyndale House) to put out this very nice facsimile edition of six Charlotte Mason books. The series includes *Home Education, Parents and Children, School Education, Ourselves, Formation of Character,* and *A Philosophy of Education.* All are easy reading—remember, British *parents* were inspired by these books!

Those inspired by these books will be happy to know that Dean and Karen's future plans include importing or developing materials to help us all put Charlotte Mason's ideas into practice. Write to Charlotte Mason Research & Supply for details of their latest projects.

NEW★★
Crossway Books
Schoolproof, $7.95.

Schoolproof is my own contribution to the how-and-what-to-teach genre. My main concern was to show parents how to *simplify,* and how to avoid getting entangled in unproductive philosophies. Towards that end, *Schoolproof* provides twenty ways to present a lesson, twenty ways to get feedback, how to tell enriching educational resources from time-wasting clutter, how to organize your environment to make home education natural, plus information on the stages of learning and how to respect your children/students without falling into the error of reversing your roles. Chatty style, an easy read.

NEW**
Dove Christian Books
Never Too Early: Rearing Godly Children Who Love to Learn, by Doreen Claggett, $7.95.

Doreen Claggett, the author of the Christ-Centered Curriculum for early childhood (reviewed in Volume Two), has prepared this book as an antidote to the better-late-than-early school of educational thought. Mrs. Claggett believes that very young children *do* benefit from semi-formal instruction and that it lays the foundation for a disciplined life. After sharing her reasoning on this subject from Scripture and her experiences, she includes many how-to teaching and training tips for this age group.

EDC Publishing
Parents' Guides to Entertaining and Educating Young Children, . . .Babies & Toddlers, $5.95 each.

Two books, each 48 pages of colorful illustrations, encouraging advice, and creative suggestions on how to entertain and educate your little ones from birth to the preteen years. Like all the other Usborne books from England, the Parents' Guides feature colorful cartoon graphics that teach along with the text. Warm, truly helpful, and free of patronizing put-downs.

NEW**
Education Services
You CAN Teach Your Child Successfully. $13.70/softcover, $18.95 hardcover. Each *Teaching* book, $6.45.

Ruth Beechick's new book, titled *You CAN Teach Your Child Successfully*, is (a) designed to help you teach children from 4th to 8th grade and is (b) absolutely wonderful! Like all Beechick books, this has gems on every page. Her comments about time lines and how best to use them are alone worth the price of the book. Considering how little advice on instruction is available for anyone whose children are past the learning-to-read stage, this book is a must-buy for home-schooling parents.

Fans of Ruth Beechick will be delighted to discover that she has also written a series of four books for Sunday school teachers, directed to teaching the different age groups. Although these books focus on teaching Sunday school, you will find their insight and practical tips useful in general home schooling as well. Dr. Beechick, with her knowledge of secular research and famous ability to criticize it biblically, brings up topics you may never have thought of, such as "How do children think? Do they learn differently at different ages? What is the best way to teach memorization? Are behavioral objectives in Christian curriculums good or bad?"

Beyond a refreshingly Christian view of child development, you also get explicit instruction in how to teach each age group about Christ, sin, salvation, and essential doctrines. She also deals with the mundane how-tos such as how to present flannelboard and puppet lessons, the uses of singing games, and so on.

The series includes: *Teaching Preschoolers: It's Not Exactly Easy But Here Is How to Do It* • *Teaching Kindergartners: How to Understand and Instruct Fours and Fives* • *Teaching Primaries: Understanding How They Think and How They Learn* • and *Teaching Juniors: Both Heart and Head.*

Sarah Yoder of Indiana just recently wrote to me pointing out that Ruth Beechick's books provide wonderful how-tos for those interested in the Charlotte Mason approach. Even though Ruth developed her own approach quite independently of any Charlotte Mason influences, since great minds think alike she has come up with some excellent practical ideas that mesh beautifully with the Charlotte Mason philosophy. As Sarah says, "She discusses how to narrate (essentially), how to *use* the living books, and how to teach *making the most* of the home environment, instead of mimicking the classroom." Take heed, Charlotte Mason fans!

Elijah Company
How to Tutor by Samuel Blumenfeld. $11.95 plus $2.25 shipping.

Sam Blumenfeld's excellent *How to Tutor* presents far more than advice on the basics of tutoring. *How to Tutor* covers the how-tos of presenting Readin', Ritin', and 'Rithmetic. Stripped-down, no-frills, easy to read and easy to do. Step-by-step instructions, with explanations of *why* Mr. Blumenfeld has such success with his approach. This last feature, the reasoned explanations of why you should follow classic methods of instruction, sets *How to Tutor* apart. It would be quite possible to take your child from zero to Grade 6 in the three R's armed with this book alone.

Gazelle Publications
The Home School Manual, second edition. Revised edition, 1988, $16.50 postpaid. 432 pages. Hardcover. 31 chapters, 9 appendices, index.

Thoroughly Christian in content, *The Home School Manual* tries to establish a Christian approach to home schooling in general and each school subject in particular. This is a lofty objective, and the book makes a good beginning. The wealth of suggestions had me gasping for breath (count on at least two readings to master this book).

Non-Christians can also gain a lot from the *Manual*. The teaching tips and ideas are useful in any home.

Written by many contributors, the *Manual* nonetheless is readable and even entertaining in spots.

If you like to have a reason for what you are doing, and if you're looking for *lots* of teaching ideas, *The Home School Manual* is worth the money.

UPDATED**
Growing Without Schooling
$20/year (6 issues), $36/12 issues, $48/18 issues. Group subscriptions and back issues available. Single issue, $3.50. *For subscribers only:* Back issues are $2/issue, plus $2 handling charge per order. Example: 10 back issues are $20 plus $2.00 handling. Complete set of back issues (as of early 1990), $100. Published by Holt Associates.

New home schoolers have a potential gold mine in the *Growing Without Schooling* back issues. Together they contain as much material as several books, and cover every home schooling viewpoint. The teaching suggestions alone, all of which have been "field-tested" by the contributors, normal parents like you and me, are worth the price. Indexes of back issues are available, for those who are not speed readers and who need to find help on specific points.

NEW**
Pennsylvania Homeschoolers
The Three R's at Home, $7.95 postpaid. Paperback.

Veteran home schoolers Susan and Howard Richman share their earthy educational philosophy along with tons of stories about how they and their friends "did it." You get everything from teaching reading (begin by reading *to* your children), how to raise a creative writer (PA Homeschoolers has a strong emphasis on this, both publishing kids' writing and including it in their regular newsletter), math from the fiddle-with-Cuisenaire-rods stage and up, tests and record-keeping, ways to write a curriculum and get organized, and more! Lots of warmth and common sense. A really fun book to read, especially for those who tend to be intimidated by the "professional" approach.

Multnomah Press
Teaching to Change Lives, $7.95. Paperback.

This book is subtitled "Develop a Passion for Communicating God's Word to Adults or Children—in the Church, in the Home, in Bible Study Groups, or in School." Howard Hendricks, a Dallas Seminary professor and a writer whose vigor will leave you breathless, has his own set of seven laws of teaching: the Laws of the Teacher, Education, Activity, Communication, Heart, Encouragement, Readiness. Taken together they spell t-e-a-c-h-e-r (cute). I promise you, you will read this book all the way through. Every page has some nugget (usually more than one) slipcased in an anecdote from Dr. Hendricks's years of teaching.

NACD
Teaching at Home, $18.

The National Academy of Child Development philosophy on two cassettes. Unlike other organizations, NACD believes strongly in parents' desire and ability to work with their children. NACD was producing customized home programs of physical and academic therapy for handicapped and well children long before home schooling became a noticeable movement. The NACD approach, as applied to every child, first focuses on helping parents create a warm and encouraging family environment. (Sure, I know everyone *talks* about this, but NACD shows you exactly how to recognize what is good or lacking about the way you treat your children, and what to do about it.) Next come exercises to help children "organize" their brains to be either all right-handed, right-footed, right-eyed, etc., or to be left-handed, footed, and so on. NACD believes this increases both coordination and mental function. Robert Doman, NACD's founder, also presents strategies for organizing home study time. Very interesting listening.

R & E Publishers
Effective Teaching, $6.95. Add $1.50 shipping.

Author Allene Mandry has served in the educational trenches, and her book *Effective Teaching* is both amusing and instructive. Here's a taste:

> If the purpose of the English class is to teach students to speak and write effectively, then why do most assignments consist of underlining or filling in the blank with the correct word? Seldom are students asked to write original sentences or compositions using what they have learned. In fact, as I look back on my daughter's short school career of six years, I can only recall one composition that she was required to write, and that was last year in the fifth grade. This is indeed sad. Why do we require students to learn rules and terms if they are never required to use them? Certainly, real life does not involve daily underlining exercises.

The theme of this book is that it's our job as teachers to relate the subject to the child's world so he really understands it, rather than resting satisfied with mindless parroting of uncomprehended facts. The author covers all school subjects, including testing and use of the library, in a brisk, common-sense style.

Rod and Staff Publishers, Inc.
Handbook for Creative Teaching by David Martin, $18.50. Very durably hardbound, 900 text pages plus index.

This tome is intended to serve as your comprehensive guide to everything about teaching and learning. Written primarily for the beginning, inexperienced teacher, the *Handbook* is designed so you can readily find the sections you need, rather than having to wade through the whole book at one go. I don't have space to list all the 84 chapters and five appendices, but believe me, it covers just about everything a classroom teacher could ever want to know. Lots of case histories, anecdotes, strategies. Most of the content applies easily to home teaching. The Rod and Staff philosophy of orderliness and seriousness comes clearly through. So do warmth and understanding. Those who are teachers at heart can count on many invigorating hours curled up with this book.

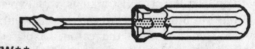

NEW**
Teaching Home Magazine
Back issues: 1983-84 complete set $10, 1985 complete set $12.50, 1986 complete set $15. 1987, 1988, 1989 complete sets $17.50 each. Single copy of issue in last three years, $3.75.

As a service to home schoolers, *Teaching Home* keeps its entire list of back issues in print. These are "themed" issues, meaning most of the info is still relevant and useful. Older reprints are trimmed down and mostly ad-free. These are nicely-presented, well-written magazines with a variety of articles on the theme subject. For specific advice on how to handle specific subjects and common home-teaching problems, you can't beat *Teaching Home* back issues.

Topics in the 1983-84 back issue set are Principle Approach, Christian materials, summer activities, support groups, socialization, discipline, and the father's involvement in home schooling.

Topics in 1985: February/March—Principle Approach. April/May—teaching history, lobbying for legislation. June/July—the Classic Approach ("Lost Tools of Learning"), time and household organizational helps. August/September—teaching several grades at once. October/November—educational uses of the computer. December/January—motivating children to learn, unit studies, and how to write your philosophy of education.

Topics in 1986: February/March—evaluating and choosing curriculum. April/May—teaching children to read/phonics, art, general legal information, "What Works" from the Department of Education. June/July—work education, achievement tests, art. August/September—teaching math and art. October/November—teaching children to think, godly priorities (a very good issue!). December/January—teaching teens.

Topics in 1987: February/March—teaching preschool and kindergarten. April/May—learning styles and the 87-88 Basic Resource Guide. June/July—teaching science. August/September—music in the home school. October/November—teaching creative writing. December/January—teaching Bible.

Topics in 1988: February/March—ten common approaches to home education, how to combine approaches. April/May—home school support groups, lesson plan for unit studies. June/July—teaching literature. August/September—teaching geography and missions. October/November—teaching health and physical education. December/January—report on 1988 National Home-School Convention, family relationships.

Topics in 1989: February/March—teaching political science and economics. April/May—preparing your children for adulthood. June/July—new thinking about art and phonics instruction, solutions to problems in teaching math. August/September—home school questions and answers, family prayer album, review of home education research, teaching your child to know God. October/November—organizing for success. December/January—hot new ideas in home education.

Warren Publishing House/Totline Books
Teaching Tips, $3.95 plus $2 shipping.

Attractive little booklet with over 300 helpful hints from *Totline* subscribers, geared to preschool and early elementary classes. Classroom tips: equipment, decorations. Curriculum tips: art, music, and general learning. Special times tips: transition times, quiet times, outdoor times, snack times, group times, cleanup times. Sample hint: old plastic shower and window curtains make great table or floor coverings for messy play! Or how about using a pizza pan as a magnet board for learning games? And did you know that glossy magazines, such as *Time* and *Newsweek*, make better paper chains than ordinary construction paper? If you love this kind of lore (and what mother doesn't?), send for a copy.

PHILOSOPHY OF EDUCATION

NEW**
Crossway Books
Schoolproof by Mary Pride, $7.95.

My father is a professor of philosophy, so I have an excuse for mixing educational philosophy into my how-to book on teaching children. Besides the how-to features mentioned above, *Schoolproof* also deals with the questions "What is a child? What should the teacher/student relationship be? May we try to motivate children, and if so, how? What is the purpose of education, and how can it best be served?" The last part of *Schoolproof* presents my view of a model school, including both a new outlook on curriculum and suggestions on how and why we should restructure children's schools more along the lines of community colleges. [Hint: it's because education should fit the child, rather than the other way around!]

NEW**
Trinity Foundation
Education, Christianity, and the State, by J. Gresham Machen, $7.95. *A Christian Philosophy of Education*, by Gordon Clark, $8.95. Foreign orders, add 20% postage.

Here are two amazing books about *why* and *what* we should teach: *Education, Christianity, and the State* by J. Gresham Machen, and *A Christian Philosophy of Education* by Gordon Clark, and both published by Trinity Foundation. These two men (both now deceased), working from a Scriptural understanding of education and government, exactly predicted the situation we now find ourselves in.

Presbyterians know who Dr. Machen was. Founder of Westminster Seminary and vigorous opponent of theological liberalism in the 1920s, he had a rare keenness of mind and clarity of style. *Education, Christianity, and the State*, a collection of essays and speeches on these subjects, covers all the subjects

Allan Bloom dealt with in *Closing of the American Mind*—only Machen did so years *before* the problems really took root. Here is Machen at his ripest: "If liberty is not maintained with regard to education, there is no use trying to maintain it in any other sphere. If you give the bureaucrats the children, you might just as well give them everything else." And "The undergraduate student of the present day is being told that . . . what he is really in college to do is to think for himself and to unify his world. He usually makes a poor business of unifying his world. And the reason is clear. . . . He is being told to practice the business of mental digestion; but the trouble is that he has no food to digest. The modern student, contrary to what is often said, is really being starved for want of facts." The latter could have come straight out of *Profscam* (reviewed above)!

Machen went to bat *for* Christian schools and home teaching, and *against* a Federal Department of Education, non-Christian "values education," and the attempt in his day to take over the home through a Child Labor amendment to the U.S. Constitution, which would have given federal bureaucrats total control of family life under the guise of protecting children from exploitation. (Sound familiar?) Those battles of the Roaring Twenties are being fought again, and it should hearten all of us to see how parents won them the first time around.

Machen also ably makes the case for Christian scholarship and Christian culture, while defending civil liberties. Both those who favor and those who are concerned about Reconstructionism will find much food for thought here.

In *A Christian Philosophy of Education*, Gordon Clark, chairman of the Department of Philosophy at Butler University before his death in 1985, takes Machen's reasoning a step farther. Clark carefully explains the different philosophies of education, shows where they fall short, and puts forth his own philosophy of education.

Like Machen, Clark had the whole thing all figured out years before Allan Bloom was born. He asks all the important questions—Can education be neutral? what kind of curriculum should we have? what makes education Christian?—and answers them, too.

References to folks like Kant and Heidegger and most especially Dewey are sprinkled throughout, but Clark always explains who the philosopher was and what he taught before ripping up his philosophy.

Clark is more professorial and subtle than Machen, and he likes to sting. Example: "The liberal

arts requirements were altered to cater to a group of students who, having found German and mathematics too difficult for them, thought they were competent to reform economics and sociology." Ouch!

Special bonus: John Robbins' excellent introduction clears up the question of the basic purpose of education in just seven pages!

TEACHER MAGAZINES

This section includes all-purpose magazines for teachers. Specialized magazines, like those for teachers of gifted children or magazines with lots of activities but no teacher improvement articles, will be found in the appropriate sections of the other volumes in this series.

Educational Oasis: The Magazine for Middle School Teachers
One year (five issues), $20. Sample copy, $4.50.

This Good Apple publication, like the others, is upbeat and full of activities for the teacher to try in the classroom, as well as articles about teaching. Individualized units for all curriculum areas. Reproducible pages with answers to the quizzes and riddles in the back. Not too glitzy or colorful. No ads except those for Good Apple products.

Good Apple

One year (five issues), $13.50. Sample copy, $2.

This is Good Apple's magazine for grades 3-8. Like the others, it's loaded with reproducible activities, games, posters, task cards, bulletin board ideas, you name it. You also get how-to and philosophy articles. Big issues; no ads to speak of.

Instructor and Teacher

$20/year (9 issues). $27 Canada and other countries.

The biggest and best magazine for (mostly public school) elementary school teachers. Some articles you will find extremely helpful; others might jar you. In the latter category, I am thinking of a recent article on AIDS education that urged teachers to tell their students AIDS is *not* a judgment from God (interesting what kind of theology one can teach in the public schools). Most articles, however, are practical and helpful.

Regular features include • a look at what the editors think are "A+" public schools • educational philosophy from several experts (mostly good, invigorating stuff free of edubabble) • monthly calendar • pull-out art reproduction-of-the-month • "Speak Out" op ed section (the January '88 issue had a great op ed on home schooling) • Newsfront (what's new in public ed legislation and trends). Other articles run the gamut of everything from special ed to student motivation. I find the ads particularly interesting: not the full-page puff jobs asserting how great some textbook line is, but the little ads for new or unusual products. That's how I found many products reviewed in this book!

Kappan

$20/year (10 issues) USA, $22.50 foreign. Single copy, $2.50.

Publication of Phi Delta Kappa, the professional fraternity in education. Erudite, thoughtful, not as effervescent or polemical as other teachers' magazines. Example: a *Kappan* article by Charles L. Glenn, director of equal educational opportunity for the Massachusetts Department of Education. Titled "Textbook Controversies: A 'Disaster for Public Schools'?," it pointed out that parents who complain that their children's textbooks systematically exclude religion and traditional values have a point. As a sidebar, the article included quotes from Paul Vitz's *Censorship: Evidence of Bias in Our Children's Textbooks* (reviewed in the Basic Books chapter). This is more fairness and open-mindedness than I have seen in other teachers' publications. Departments include an Editor's Page, Washington Report, Stateline, Peer (interviews of influential researchers and research implementors), De Jure, Prototypes (cutting-edge programs), Books, Newsnotes, and Backtalk.

Lollipops: The Magazine for Preschool and Early Childhood Educators

One year (five issues), $15. Entire issue reproducible for home or school use. Sample copy, $2.

Teaching tips and philosophy mixed with *lots* of activities! Activity calendar, games, motivational charts, poems, science, songs, language arts, crafts, stories, book reviews, riddles—anything you can think of for the preschool curriculum. A Good Apple publication.

Shining Star

One year (four issues), $16.95. Sample copy, $2.

Christian education magazine loaded with 80 pages of reproducible puzzles, games, and work sheets, plus teacher tips, family worship suggestions, stories, and a three-month Activity Calendar. *Shining Star* work sheets are divided into units including New Testament Heroes, Christian Values, and Memory Verses. Mainstream evangelical flavor (self-esteem, etc.) The merciful editors include an Answer Key in the back in case you or your little ones can't figure out the puzzles. Another Good Apple publication.

STORYTELLING

Christian Life Workshops

The Family Storytelling Workshop. Six-tape set by Gregg Harris with notes and three-ring binder. $32.50 postpaid. Money-back guarantee.

Can teaching your kids be as easy as telling them stories? You betcha!

The Family Storytelling Workshop shows how you can use casual storytelling in character education, child discipline, holiday celebrations, and Sunday school lessons. You can be as tongue-tied as the Rock of Gibraltar—it doesn't matter. All you need is to be willing to talk to your children while you're working together around the house.

I warn you, your children are going to like this! Ours now clamor for their favorite stories. "Tell me my birth story!" "Tell us the story of the Red Ink!" Storytelling is also great for developing your dramatic talents. Fathers would find it more fun to be around their families if they were the center of excited attention more often as the family storyteller. And storytelling mothers get more respect!

This six-tape set may do more good for your family life than any other one thing (besides maybe getting rid of your TV set).

HELP FOR HOME SCHOOLERS

CHAPTER TWELVE

WHAT IS HOME SCHOOLING, ANYWAY?

Nothing is new under the sun. Two thousand years ago the Sanhedrin was flabbergasted to see men preaching confidently who hadn't been to their approved schools, and today Americans are astonished at the idea of children learning at home. After the first shock passes, though, most people are sensible enough to judge the movement by its results. After all, what can you say about:

- An 11-year-old girl who entered Oxford University, and two years later received her mathematics degree. Ruth Lawrence was one of only two math students to receive special commendation for her work. Ruth had never been to school. Her father taught her at home.

- Ishmael Wallace, a boy who the public school considered "not musically gifted," and who they were in the process of labeling "slow" when his parents withdrew him. Ishmael is now nationally recognized as a talented musician, and is the author of an award-winning musical. (For the full story of this home schooling miracle, see his mother Nancy Wallace's book, *Better Than School,* reviewed in Chapter 14.)

- Grant Colfax, a totally home-schooled lad, made national news by getting accepted at college. Of course, Grant didn't apply to just *any* old college—he sent in his forms to Yale and Harvard, and was accepted at *both.* Two of Grant's brothers (one is adopted) are also now at Harvard. (For the Colfax family's story, see their book, *Home-schooling for Excellence,* also reviewed in Chapter 14.)

All throughout human history, children have been educated at home. Virtually none of the signers of the Declaration of Independence had formal schooling. Thomas Edison was taught at home (the school said he was "addled" and his mother disagreed). Until compulsory attendance laws were passed, which is a fairly recent development in our history, children were normally taught to read at home *before* attending school, and many well-educated people never went to school at all.

As I said, home school is nothing new. What *is* new is the mass movement out of public school and back to private education, including home-based private education—e.g., home school. These are your three choices: public school, private school, and home school.

WHAT ABOUT PUBLIC SCHOOL?

This section is not about what is wrong with public education. Heck, *you* know what's wrong with public education! Any contestant on "Family Feud" could quickly list Ten Things That Appall Me About Public School: crime, drugs, illiteracy, lack of discipline, plummeting standards, lack of respect for authority . . . You see how easy it is? The question is not so much, "What is wrong with the public schools?" as, "What should we do about it?"

Most people, while agreeing in principle that the public schools are not what they should be, are quite pleased with *their* particular public school. After all, with $4,000 per year per child ($7,000 in the city of Boston), you get football fields and trampolines and art rooms and video players and a lot of other impressive stuff. You also get hundreds of nice people employed by the school, some of whom you know personally, such as your children's teachers. It's hard to admit that all that money and all that effort are not necessarily producing the best results—especially when you get free baby-sitting for your five-and-ups thrown in!

Public education has so captured the Western mind that most of us can't even conceive of a world without it. We'd rather live with millions of illiterate graduates, a shocking dropout rate, kids who can't communicate with anyone but their agemates, textbooks that deride traditional values, and so on, than admit that all that money and all those buildings can't and won't solve the problems, and in fact may be *creating* the problems. Schools, for example, are now the prime marketplace of drugs in the nation. Schools are training children to get pregnant (because sex is just for fun and not for marriage) and then sending them off for abortions when they put their sex ed lessons into practice. Schools are fostering racism by misguidedly teaching kids to focus on whether they are black or white or Asian or Hispanic, rather than stressing our common heritage and opportunities.

This is what is bound to happen when education is centralized. Smart people will notice that they have a golden opportunity to build up their faction if they can only be the ones who control what the children are taught. Inevitably, education becomes a political battleground, with each side striving to control the curriculum, the training of teachers, and the textbooks. Learning has to take a back seat to all this. So now we have Nuclear War Studies, Women's Studies, Black Studies, Hispanic Studies, instruction in how to hotline your parents, condom education, New Age "thinking skills," World Peace studies, and a whole host of other stuff eating up the curriculum. This is exactly what we should have expected.

Many people see the problems public school bureaucrats have brought upon themselves and, with virtuous zeal, are crusading to "reform the schools." I have never considered this as an option, for the following reasons:

(1) As a Bible-believing Christian I do not believe that education is a function God has granted to the government. We have never needed public schools, and we don't need them now. (See Sam Blumenfeld's *Is Public Education Necessary?* for the facts on how America got along fine without public schools for hundreds of years.)

(2) As an American citizen I do not believe that bureaucrats have the right to force their values on other people's children. The Bible says we can try to persuade others "with gentleness and respect." Civil government may punish evildoers for their crimes, but under God it has no right to prevent parents from passing on their morals and beliefs, whether Christian or non-Christian, to their children. This does not mean that public schools, as long as they exist, should outlaw *voluntary* Bible reading and prayer. It does mean that school should not be a vehicle of compulsory religious indoctrination. Which it is.

(3) As a very concerned mother, I am not about to make my children into guinea pigs for my, or anyone else's, social experiments. Nor am I going to send my six-year-old out into the public school as a "witness" when adult Christian public-school teachers refuse to talk about Jesus during or even after school hours. If the grown-up Christians in the public schools can be intimidated into not reading their Bibles silently on school property or having a Bible study with other teachers, why should I expect my children to pick up the load that the adults are refusing?

(4) As an educator of some nine years' home experience, I do not think the public schools can even come close to the education Bill and I can offer our children at home. How many government schools teach Latin to elementary-age children, or give them oil-painting lessons, or have six-year-olds reading *Macbeth*? We and our friends have done all of these at home!

I just can't see the point of making our children study the same subjects over and over again for years at a time when they could be learning important and interesting things *right now*. Why should they have to wait for high school to take drafting, or college to learn electrical engineering?

School is, after all, supposed to be where you go to get educated. The fact that so many of us think first about "socialization" and only later about education just proves how successful the educrats have been at redirecting us away from the basic purpose of school. Not that the results of public school socialization are all that great. The jails are filled with people who had ten or more years of public school socialization!

Public school does have one big advantage. It is "free." I put that in quotes, because there are hidden costs. I'm not talking just about the increasing number of fees, though those can add up to hundreds of dollars nowadays. The truly big advantage of public school is how it is supposed to free up the parents' *time*. Take your kid to school and you can have the house to yourself for the next six hours; or you can enroll him in the latchkey kids program and take a full-time job without worrying. Where else can you get free all-day baby-sitting, and even feel *good* about what a fine parent you are being to put your children there?

But the mother who drops her child off at kindergarten with a sigh of relief, secure in the thought she can trust the teacher to do all the teaching, will find that the game is not played that way these days.

Parents are supposed to be "partners" with teachers, meaning that if the kids don't learn it's the parents' fault for not teaching them at home.

Parents are supposed to make sure kids do their homework, drill them on their studies, provide all the extra educational opportunities the teacher recommends, and bake cookies for the PTA. Parents are supposed to prepare children for reading by reading to them extensively; help them succeed in school by driving them back and forth to the library; surround them with educational tools like globes and atlases; and even (if you take those little home hand-out papers seriously) give them "experiences" in weighing and measuring in your kitchen.

Then there's carpooling, volunteering as a classroom aide, helping in fund-raising drives, attending Parents Night, boosting the sports teams, etc.

If you don't do all this you are considered a lousy parent with no interest in your child's education.

If you do do all this, you might as well be home schooling!

WHAT ABOUT PRIVATE SCHOOLS?

You probably agree with me that public school is not exactly what it should be. You might be considering home schooling. If you are not home schooling already, you are wondering about whether perhaps private school would be a better choice.

Private education differs from public education in the following ways:

(1) It costs money. Sometimes lots of money. This is reason enough for many lower- and middle-class families, or large families, to seriously consider home education.

(2) It is more parent-controlled. This is more significant in a small school than in a large one. Some of the large parochial schools are every bit as hard for parents to deal with as the public schools.

(3) It may offer an alternative approach to education. I say "may" because many private schools are merely public schools in disguise. Their teachers have been taught in the same schools as public school teachers, they have the same mania for "educating the whole child" (a euphemism for forcing their values on children instead of teaching them skills), they use the same offensive methods and the same curricula. Do not assume that because the school is "private" it is different.

Private school is certainly a valid choice, once children are mature enough to know what they believe and defend it from their peers. But because parents cannot always find a private school that supports their educational philosophy and values without totally draining their pocketbook, for many the choice comes down to simply public school or home school.

WHAT ABOUT HOME SCHOOL?

Every mother and father is a teacher. The question really is, "How much of what my children need to know should I help them learn?"—not "Should I try to teach them?"

This section is designed to help you make that decision. The more you know about your options, the clearer the choices become. This next chapter gives you a simple introduction to the major people and methods in the home school movement. I've also included a list of books that you might want to read, and resources especially for home schoolers, with reviews to help you pick the ones that can help you most. Since there are many home schooling styles, from California Mellow to Little Red Home School, you'll find a chapter on these as well. Finally, the Curriculum Buyers' Guide gives you a complete overview of the correspondence programs that your fellow parents are using. Or, if you have educational expertise and a hefty hunk of confidence, the reviews in the other volumes of this series will give you plenty of options from which you can fashion your own program.

Let's take a look now at some of the leading thinkers in the area of home education. By becoming familiar with their ideas you will not only sound much more erudite ("they laughed when I stood up to talk about education—but when I mentioned John Holt . . ."), but you will be able to make informed decisions about whether and how you'd like to do it.

CHAPTER THIRTEEN

BIG NAMES IN HOME SCHOOLING

Little kids are people. That is the message of three of the most respected names in home education: Charlotte Mason, John Holt, and Maria Montessori. Miss Mason, a British educator of the nineteenth century who founded a very prestigious College of Education; Mr. Holt, whose career as a teacher spanned several decades and who was the founder of *Growing Without Schooling*; and Montessori, whose work began early in this century in Rome and who has since passed away, all agree that children *want* to learn. Further, the things children want to learn are *adult* things: how to take care of themselves, how to cook, how to drive a car, how to read the newspaper.

CHARLOTTE MASON AND "LIVING EDUCATION"

Charlotte Mason saw the business of education as not only preparing the child for life, but helping him to live to the fullest *right now*. Based on her evangelical Christian view, she embraced both the child's need for discipline and parental guidance and the child's inbuilt ability to learn and grow.

Miss Mason firmly believed that Nature is the best teacher of many lessons, and that children need a rich background of real-world experiences for their education to make any sense. Her educational method began with the mother teaching the child to be more observant—to recognize and classify trees, shrubs, flowers, birds, clouds, landscape features, and so on. This was to be coupled with nurturing the child's sense of wonder and awe.

Young children were not to have formal lessons at all, but to spend a great deal of time out-of-doors playing and enjoying nature. Charlotte Mason had a number of misgivings about the Kindergarten movement, which at that time was not an immovable national institution but a rather recent German innovation, and her thoughts on the subject of why a teacher-centered structured environment may not be the best educational foundation make fascinating reading.

Parental discipline was to be based on the importance of forming good habits, since "a habit is ten natures." In other words, whatever your natural tendencies or temperament, a learned habit will be ten times more powerful. This is extremely refreshing to those of us who have been told umpteen times that we have to just live with the worst of our children's personalities (and our own)!

For almost every subject, Charlotte Mason had a way of making it more fun and more meaningful, without ever lapsing into silliness. She absolutely derided what she called "twaddle," the dumbed-down sentimental nonsense that adults then, as today, feel compelled to spoon-feed children. Instead, she advocated the use of "living books." Thus for literature the children would read real classics. For history, the best historical biographies. For geography, well-written travel books. In art the child would begin by learning to appreciate the great paintings of the past. Children who did not yet read would be read to—and they would learn to narrate back everything they had heard or read. None of this was to be *forced* upon children. It was the parent's or teacher's job to kindle enthusiasm—or, rather, to find a channel for the child's natural enthusiasm.

In the Mason method, children got lots of free time to themselves. She stressed that, for younger students, school should ideally take only the mornings, with the afternoons for free play, preferably out-of-doors. Homework was anathema; the school or parent should be able to teach the material in the lesson time, without burdening the child's free time.

Charlotte Mason's main interest was in the children's classical education, rather than in teaching vocational skills. She trusted parents to take care of that department themselves without a lot of help from her. Her ultimate goal was to help parents train their children as worthy members of the Kingdom of God, knowing the truth not because someone had indoctrinated them in it, but because they had seen it for themselves. This is many times removed from the poor, watered-down Sunday-school philosophy of nowadays, that neither expects our children to be great nor trains them to be good. Hence the great and growing interest in her work by Christian parents and educators today.

Charlotte Mason's books are available from Charlotte Mason Research & Supply, as will be, in time, a number of resources to help implement her methods.

MARIA MONTESSORI AND THE "NORMALIZED" CHILD

Montessori had a great devotion to the inner goodness of children. So intense was this devotion that interviewers spoke of her as establishing a "new religion," and she in fact spoke this way herself. In those days, a lot of people talked like that. Socialism was relatively new, and heady in its insistence that people were naturally good and only society was bad. Unhappily, some Christian preachers had laid it on a bit thick about our carnal nature, to the point where the church seemed to be saying that children were nothing but bad. Montessori's experience did not bear this out, and neither does the Bible, for it teaches that all people, saved or unsaved, are made in the image of God. Therefore, though all people, including children, have a tendency towards selfishness and its attendant evils, and nobody is as good as he ought to be, nobody is as bad as he could be. This is the ancient doctrine of Common Grace, and it means that children, though they like the rest of us fall short of God's standard of perfection, do have the ability to love others and enjoy obedience.

Theology aside, we find Montessori, a medical doctor, carefully observing children and making notes about what they liked and disliked. Asked to take over the education of some Italian slum children, she put her theories into practice and stunned the world by turning these children into adept scholars.

What did she do? She gave the children pieces of equipment carefully designed to help them learn adult skills: wooden frames with canvas attached and string for practicing lacing, frames for buttoning, frames for using the button-hook devices of that day. She gave them materials they could feel with their hands: textured blocks, letter stencils, number stencils. She gave them grown-up tools scaled down to child's size: pots and pans, brooms and mops. She gave them responsibility for doing as adult a job as possible. Children in Montessori's own school served themselves lunch and cleaned up afterwards, although they were only three to five years old.

Having prepared the environment as carefully as she could to be free of distractions, Montessori and her teachers sat back and watched. They might show a child how to use a piece of apparatus; then they would withdraw and let the children learn as much as they could totally unaided. The data was there—hands-on experiences by the roomful. The framework was there—carefully graduated exercises led the children almost imperceptibly to reading, writing, and figuring.

The children learned.

Awed by Montessori's success, teachers all over the world descended on her. She was less than delighted by their attention, since she was very busy and most of her callers did not speak Italian, a prerequisite for intelligent conversation with this Italian-speaking doctor. In time she ended up writing several books and teaching others to carry on her work. The "Montessori method" is now taught by several different societies and in hundreds of schools and preschools, as well as home schools.

Many Montessori schools use her special equipment, but do not follow her spiritual ideals. The two *are* separable; using Montessori's materials need not compromise your religious beliefs.

The three fundamental Montessori principles are:

(1) "Observation." According to Montessori "the teacher must refrain from interfering directly."

> The child educates himself, and when the control and correction of error is yielded of the didactic material [she means when the stuff you hand the kid doesn't confuse him], there remains for the teacher nothing but to observe . . . the teacher teaches little and observes much.

In "true" Montessori education, adults do not teach at all. Instead, they closely watch the children in order to see how the environment should be changed to meet their needs. The closest an adult comes to "teaching" a child is in showing him how to use Montessori's materials.

(2) "Individual Liberty." Children are turned loose and allowed to do whatever suits their fancy. This does not result in random play, however, because of the next principle.

(3) "Preparation of the Environment." In Montessori's thought it is very important to "control for error" by only presenting materials that logically relate to one another. Shapes must fit neatly into their allotted slots, graduated cylinders must go up by uniform sizes, color-coded items must logically follow the code, and so on. Thus children are not confused.

The point of this all, as is obvious, is to build a framework for the child. Montessori provides many experiences, and by concentrating deeply on the work provided, the child is able to build his own framework. Montessori called this process "normalization" and attributed mystical significance to it. A "normal-

ized" child learns, in time, to build frameworks for himself even when he is not provided with a perfect environment. He learns to look for patterns on his own and to try to fit reality into categories.

Much of what Montessori recommends makes a lot of sense, once you realize that "normalization" is just framework-building and the concentration required is merely the brain making lots of little connections. God did make children and adults able to learn without being "taught," and it is marvelous.

For more information on the Montessori approach, you can purchase the *Parents' Guide to the Montessori Classroom* from Parent-Child Press for less than a dollar. Montessori apparatus is available from a number of suppliers listed in Volume Two. Finally, for Montessori training materials, you can join the International Montessori Society. Membership fee of $20 includes subscription to all Society publications and discounts on books. They offer an expensive home-study course ($2,100, includes materials, tuition, and registration), Montessori conferences, a Montessori newspaper, a journal, and run a mail-order bookstore that sells (naturally) books by and about Montessori and her methods.

JOHN HOLT AND "INVITED LEARNING"

If Maria Montessori is the high priestess of "prepared environment," John Holt is the prophet of real-world learning. For years Mr. Holt quietly but insistently taught that children can learn *all by themselves,* without any well-intentioned adult interference. He sees the idea of programmed learning as positively evil. As he so tellingly put it in *How Children Learn,*

> The difference between fond and delighted parents playing "This Little Piggy Went to Market" with their laughing baby's toes and two anxious home-based would-be clinicians giving "tactile stimulation" to those same toes, so that the child will one day be smarter than other children and thus get into the best colleges, may not on the face of it seem to be very much. But in fact it is the difference between night

and day. Of two ways of looking at children now growing in fashion—seeing them as monsters of evil who must be beaten into submission, or as little two-legged walking computers whom we can program into geniuses, it is hard to know which is worse.

John Holt did not reject all of Montessori's thought, but he fiercely defended the right of children to tackle the *real* environment. Where Montessori would carefully create a lacing frame for children to practice on, Holt would let them mess with Daddy's shoes. Where Montessori would carefully exclude from her prepared environment all randomness and chance, Holt would be happier in the mess of normal living.

In this area of disagreement, I would follow Holt, as God certainly didn't create children to need a special, isolated world of their own. In fact, Montessori's apparatus is, if you examine it, just a child-centered copy of what every normal home contains: pots and pans, buttons and laces, round things and square things, soft things and prickly things. Her genius is in letting children actually handle these things, rather than forbidding them to touch or try to use adult possessions.

John Holt's motto was "Trust Children." Based on his own observations of children learning and not learning, garnered in real-life situations, Holt believed children really want to learn and that they will learn what they need to know if left entirely to themselves. In actual practice Holt advocated involving children in our adult activities rather than begging them constantly, "What do *you* want to do today?" Still, his theory almost eliminates "teaching" as a profession, other than a master/apprentice type of relationship where the apprentice is eager to learn a particular difficult skill. What a person can learn on his own, Holt says, he should learn on his own—our teachers are not there to tyrannize us, but to offer the help we need.

John Holt's books and much literature supporting his views is available from Holt Associates, as is the newsletter he founded, *Growing Without Schooling*.

If I could pause here a moment and contrast the three home education celebrities we have looked at, I would summarize as follows:

- Charlotte Mason was interested in introducing children to God's world.

- Maria Montessori was interested in changing the world to fit the children.

- John Holt was interested in introducing children to the adult world.

Now we come to a matter of some debate in home schooling circles. Should children get "lessons" while they are young, or should they wait? Is it Better Late Than Early, or Never Too Early?

RAYMOND MOORE: BETTER LATE THAN EARLY

Based on his own experience as an educator and on analysis of more than 8,000 early childhood studies, Dr. Raymond Moore and his associates came to the following conclusions, as summarized in a January 1, 1984 bulletin from Hewitt Research Foundation:

Readiness for Learning. Despite early excitement for school, most early entrants (ages 4, 5, 6 etc.) are tired of school before they are out of the third or fourth grades. . . . They are far better off *wherever possible* waiting until ages 8 to 10 to start formal studies (at home or school). . . . They then quickly pass early entrants in learning, behavior and sociability. . . .

The eyes of most children are permanently damaged before age 12. Neither the maturity of their delicate central nervous systems nor the "balancing" of the hemisphere of their brains, nor yet the insulation of their nerve pathways provide a basis for thoughtful learning before 8 or 9. The *integration* of these *maturity levels* (IML) comes for most before 8 and 10.

This coincides with the well-established findings of Jean Piaget and others that children cannot handle cause-and-effect reasoning in any consistent way before late 7's to middle 11's. *And the bright child is no exception.*

Socialization. We later became convinced that little children are . . . better socialized by parental example and sharing than by other little children. . . . Contrary to common beliefs, little children are not best socialized by other kids; the more persons around them, the fewer meaningful contacts.[5]

For these reasons, the Moores have been writing, lecturing, appearing on radio and TV, organizing seminars, and otherwise getting out the word that *little children don't belong in school*. Parents who are convinced by their arguments must de facto elect home schooling for their younger children, since even a private school means formal education.

The Moores don't believe that young children should even be taught formally at home—unless the child himself or herself requests it. Instead, they advocate an unschooling approach to the early years: "more loving firmness, less indulgence; more work *with you*, fewer toys; more service for others—the old, poor, infirm—and less sports and amusements; more self-control, patriotism, productiveness and responsibility—which lead to, and follow, self-worth as children of God." Through a rich relationship with their parents and a rich exposure to real life, children will then approach their formal school studies unwearied, with minds ready to learn and sufficient abilities to master learning quickly.

The Moores' books are available from Hewitt Research Foundation.

DOREEN CLAGGETT: NEVER TOO EARLY

A feisty opponent of the better-late-than-early approach to education, Christian educator Doreen Claggett laughs the idea of "readiness" to scorn. In her view, children need to learn discipline and good study habits, and the earlier the better. She has authored an early childhood education curriculum based on her beliefs (Christ-Centered Curriculum: see Volume Two), and a book, *Never Too Early*, published by Dove Christian Books.

Let me note here that the differences between the Late and Early approaches may not be as large as first appear. The Moores do think young children should learn something, and that if the children themselves request instruction they should not be denied. Mrs. Claggett also recognizes the benefits of home teaching, and is not unalterably wedded to the vision of rows of

four-year-olds sitting at desks. She is trying to build character, not Superbabies.

My personal view on this controversy, for what it is worth, is that early *informal, at-home* instruction in *small doses* does not hurt young children at all, provided the parents are sensitive to whether the child is indeed able to handle and enjoy the lessons. Children can and should be learning self-discipline through other means than lessons, such as household chores and table manners.

There is room for both the Lates and the Earlies in this world. I like my children to learn to read as early as possible; reading is one of my own greatest sources of learning and pleasure, and I could not possibly read to them as much as they can read to themselves. On the other hand, some of my friends are taking the Late approach, and their children learn to read just as well.

THE PRINCIPLE APPROACH

The Principle Approach is a relative latecomer to the home education community. Briefly stated, it is the belief that God has given us principles that govern every area of life: politics, education, business, and even such mundane things as dress and fashion. Followers of the Principle Approach also believe that America, being founded by users of this approach, has a unique opportunity in history to bring the gospel to the world. Their concentration so far (in writing) is on "the relation between Christianity and America and its form of government."

Now bear with me, because I'm trying to explain something that has confused many people. Although the Principle Approach as it now stands involves much study of American history, it is *not* a history course. Rather, the history is shared in order to give us an example of how to apply the "seven minimal Biblical principles" to all areas of our lives, since many of America's founders strove to do so. These principles are supposed to be the basis of the American republic (as it then was), including such things as the Principle of Self-Government and the Principle of Individuality.

Central to the Principle Approach is the heavy use of notebooks for recording information. Children are expected to study in the old-fashioned way and develop strong powers of abstract thinking. The whole emphasis is on reasoning through to basic principles rather than simply regurgitating facts.

Now, where can you find out about the Principle Approach? The ladies at Foundation for American Christian Education (FACE) have already assembled a weighty library of material based on the Principle Approach as it is applied to American history, and the Plymouth Rock Foundation is working to apply the Principle Approach to today's issues. See the History and Government chapters in Volume Three for more details.

James B. Rose's book, *A Guide to American Christian Education for the Home and School: The Principle Approach*, is *the* book on the Principle Approach. Contents include a philosophy of education, how to apply the Seven Principles to your home, school, and home school, and specific grade-by-grade and subject-by-subject suggestions, contributed by a phalanx of educators who actually use this approach. Cost: $25, for over 500 large pages. You can order it through American Christian History Institute.

DOROTHY SAYERS: BRING BACK THE TOOLS OF LEARNING

Another woman whose ideas about education are becoming increasingly popular is Dorothy Sayers. One of the Oxford Christians associated with C.S. Lewis, and herself the writer of witty and erudite murder mysteries featuring the unflappable Lord Peter Wimsey, Miss Sayers was an Anglican Christian of no mean intellectual powers. Like Lewis she was very concerned about the lack of thought that seemed to characterize the rising pre-World War II generation. Also like him, she wrote about it. Her best thinking is found in the classic essay, "The Lost Tools of Learnng?," found in her book *A Matter of Eternity*, published in America by William B. Eerdmans Publishing Company, from which the following quotes are taken.

Do you ever find that young people, when they have left school, not only forget most of what they have learnt (that is only to be expected) but forget also, or betray that they have never really known, how to tackle a new subject for themselves? . . .

Is not the great defect of our education to-day . . . that although we often succeed in teaching our pupils "subjects," we fail lamentably, on the whole, in teaching them how to think? They learn everything, except the art of learning.

What answer does Dorothy Sayers propose? Hang on to your hats, folks—she wants to bring back the Middle Ages! This is not as flaky as it sounds. Miss Sayers is primarily interested in the first half of the medieval syllabus, called (believe it or not) the Trivium. As Miss Sayers point out,

The whole of the Trivium was, in fact, intended to teach the pupil the proper use of the tools of learning, before he began to apply them to "subjects" at all. First, he learned a language; not just how to order a meal in a foreign language, but the structure of language—what it was, how it was put together and how it worked. Secondly, he learned how to use language: how to define his terms and make accurate statements: how to construct an argument and how to detect fallacies in argument (his own arguments and other people's). Thirdly, he learned to express himself in language: how to say what he had to say elegantly and persuasively. . . . At the end of his course, he was required to compose a thesis upon some theme set by his masters or chosen by himself, and afterwards to defend his thesis against the criticism of the faculty. By this time he would have learned—or woe betide him—not merely to write an essay on paper, but to speak audibly and intelligently from a platform, and to use his wits quickly when heckled. . . .

The great difference of emphasis between the two conceptions holds good: modern education concentrates on *teaching subjects*, leaving the method of thinking, arguing and expressing one's conclusions to be picked up by the scholar as he goes along; mediaeval education concentrated on first *forging and learning to handle the tools of learning*.

Miss Sayers then proceeds to lay out her ideal course of study. She recommends beginning with Latin grammar,

. . . not because Latin is traditional and mediaeval, but simply because even a rudimentary knowledge of Latin cuts down the labour and pains of learning almost any other subject by at least fifty per cent. It is the key to the vocabulary and structure of all the Romance languages and to the structure of all the Teutonic languages, as well as to the technical vocabulary of all the sciences and to the literature of the entire Mediterranean civilization, together with all the historical documents.

She prefers the livelier postclassical, medieval Latin to the Augustan style.

Recognizing that the healthy child is capable of absorbing an astounding number of facts before he or she can yet connect them with adult logic (here is our Data again!), Dorothy Sayers suggests beginning foreign languages in the early years, as well as memorizing stories and poems, historical dates and facts, geographical facts, the identifying and naming of specimens (science), and the multiplication table, geometric shapes, and the grouping of numbers (math). This she calls the Grammar stage. Any amount of memory work may be done: memorizing Scripture in outline form, the Catechism, the Psalms, the Ten Commandments. "At this stage, it does not matter nearly so much that these things should be fully understood as that they should be known and remembered. Remember, it is material that we are collecting."

Now the child moves on to Formal Logic. When? "When she shows herself disposed to Pertness and interminable argument" (i.e., "when the capacity for abstract thought begins to manifest itself"). In Language, we examine the logical construction of speech. In Reading, we move to "essay, argument and criticism, and the pupil will learn to try his own hand at writing this kind of thing." Mathematics—Algebra, Geometry, and so on—comes into its own as "a sub-department of Logic." History will now be examined in the light of Theology. Theology itself now blossoms into Systematic Theology. Miss Sayers, as a devout Christian, is concerned that the pupil learn to analyze all that is presented to him according to the teaching of the Bible. "Criticism must not be merely destructive; though at the same time both teacher and pupils must be ready to detect fallacy, slipshod reasoning, ambiguity, irrelevance and redundancy, and to pounce on them like rats."

What of the "subjects"? "The 'subjects' supply material; but they are all to be regarded as mere grist for the mental mill to work upon."

At last the child advances to the Rhetoric stage of full mental maturity. At this point, he chooses and develops his own style of writing and speech. Aptitude for a particular branch of knowledge now leads naturally into training for real work in that branch.

Is the Trivium, then, a sufficient education for life? Properly taught, I believe that it should be. . . . For the tools of learning are the same, in any and every subject; and the person who knows how to use them will, at any age, get the mastery of a new subject in half the time and with a quarter of the effort expended by the person who has not the tools at his command. . . .

For the sole true end of education is simply this: to teach men how to learn for themselves: and whatever instruction fails to do this is effort spent in vain.

I have no criticisms of Miss Sayers' educational theory at all, except to note that although geniuses may be more readily produced by teaching Latin, still our children can do quite well even without it. We all need the tools of learning—man, woman, and child—and let no fear of Roman grammar deter us!

SOCRATES: MAKE THE STUDENT THINK

Going back even beyond the Middle Ages, we find an enduring educational theory taught by an ancient Greek philosopher.

Was Socrates the first Rogerian counselor? He liked to ask questions rather than give his students any answers. Unlike Carl Rogers, though, Socrates had a definite end in mind. The teacher was not just an echo to bounce the student's ball back into the student's court a la Rogers. ("Why does E=MC², Professor?" "Hm. I see you have some questions about relativity.") Socrates would nudge his students along in the right direction. ("Well, what does E stand for, Jim? And M, and C? Have you read the text pages on quantum theory?")

You need to know what you're doing to mess around with the Socratic method. You also need patient students, since a teacher's constant refusal to give his students a direct answer can quickly become infuriating. For this reason, I suggest that you mix Socratic nudging with occasional merciful answers, following Jesus' example with His disciples.

JOHN DEWEY: PROGRESSIVE EDUCATION

No discussion of educational theory would be complete without a nod to John Dewey, generally regarded as the father of Progressive Education. Progressive Education is distinguished by its emphasis on socialization (the "affective domain") rather than on academics (the "intellectual domain"). Thus the goal of Progressive Education is to produce "well-adjusted citizens," that is, compliant followers, rather than to impart any particular skills.

It is fair to say that the majority of home learners are seeking rather to escape Progressive Education than to implement it.

ALLAN BLOOM: BRING BACK THE GREAT BOOKS

Let us now close with the educational movement that can build on the best of all others and works equally well whether at home or school.

This unusual movement is led by, on the one hand, a long-dead English Christian educator (Char-lotte Mason, mentioned above) and a very alive American Jewish professor (Allan Bloom, author of *The Closing of the American Mind*). Its theme? Dump the textbooks and trendy pop wisdom, and let kids dig into the classics of all ages. Let them come to grips with the best thinkers of the past—and let those thinkers speak for themselves.

I say this is unusual, because for the longest time all education has been filtered to the student through committees. Committees write the textbooks. Committees write the teacher manuals that tell the teacher how to teach (and increasingly teachers are following the manuals). Committees censor our cultural heritage by straining all history through a feminist/socialist/globalist net and throwing away any odd fish that don't fit the grid. In consequence, today's students are pathetically ignorant of everything except current fads, which their textbooks project back upon history. Furthermore, the student never gets a chance to argue with the individual thinkers—to grapple with Rousseau or Adam Smith or Nietzsche, or see what Jesus said instead of what everything says He said.

I am 100 percent for the Great Books approach. It is human. It is real. It knocks the pins out from under the From-Mount-Sinai tone of secular Western teaching (just who *are* these committeepeople anyway who dare to present their current prejudices as The Truth?). It is exciting and enlightening. Furthermore, it works. Children and adults who delve into the Great Books find their minds stretched and filled with fair flowers of thought. They gain perspective on our culture, such as the insight that McDonald's Restaurants and video games have not always been, that intelligent people have been known to believe in right and wrong, and that there was life before TV.

It helps, of course, to choose the *right* Great Books. Encyclopaedia Britannica Corporation sells a set, "Great Books of the Western World," that distinguishes itself by the number of major Christian works it neglects. There might be some value in a few rounds with Freud and Marx—although even Marxists find Marx tough sledding—but Christians will find more grist for the mill in *The Complete Works of Francis Schaeffer* or anything and everything by C. S. Lewis. Not to mention the Bible, which precious few people have ever read straight through, especially those who claim they "know" it is full of myths and absurdities. (I used to be one of them!)

The Great Books approach works for other fields as well. Art, for instance. We all have heard of Picasso. Ah, but what about Dürer and Fra Angelico? Or music:

is the sound of Middle Ages *chansons* as familiar to our children as punk rock? Architecture and design: compare the grandeur of a medieval cathedral to today's box-of-blocks buildings or the warmth of an Early American cannonball bed to El Plastic progressive furniture. I may sound nostalgic, and with these comparisons, I have a right to be! But awareness of the past cuts both ways. It helps us appreciate true advances without a slavish belief that modernity always means progress. It gives us the raw data from which to make *informed* choices, and a place to stand. And that is real education.

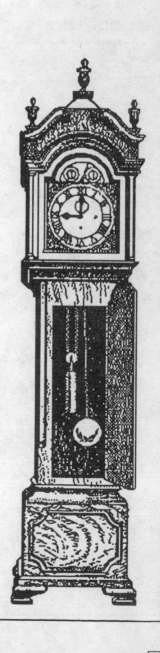

CHAPTER FOURTEEN

BASIC BOOKS ABOUT HOME SCHOOLING

When Bill and I realized we were expecting our first child, neither of us had ever heard of the home schooling movement. We thought (I blush to say it) that we were going to be pioneers. Surprise! Before our first son was even three, I was invited to my first home school seminar. And as we delved more deeply into home schooling, we were delighted to find that all the really hard work had already been done. Court cases had been fought and won. Books had been written. Curriculum had been developed.

Because those who blazed the way have worked so hard, we have a flood of increasingly professional books about home schooling. These range from charming how-we-did-it books to tomes that resemble a Ph.D. dissertation. I have personally read at least 95 percent of what's out there on this subject. So, out of this rich array of home schooling books, here are the best for you.

BOOKS FOR BEGINNERS

Alpha Omega Publications
Parent Starter Kit, $19.95. Full refund if returned within 30 days.

Excellent introduction to home schooling with Alpha Omega materials. Kit includes: Alpha Omega's *Home School Manual* (not to be confused with Ted Wade's manual of the same name), a sample language arts LIFEPAC, Alpha Omega's large Scope & Sequence that outlines the entire Alpha Omega program from K-12, a catalog, a brochure describing Alpha Omega's "Little Patriots" kindergarten series, and an informative home schooling cassette tape.

The Scope & Sequence and *Manual* make this more than a promotional packet. From the Scope & Sequence you get an idea of what ought to be learned when. The *Manual* then covers just about every question of interest to home school parents, from daily schedules and discipline to field trips and penmanship. It also includes a very helpful section on how to use Alpha Omega curriculum using the sample LIFEPAC enclosed with the packet. If you work through this, you will gain a good understanding of basic teaching, whether or not you decide to use Alpha Omega curriculum.

NEW**
Alpha Omega Publications
Starting a Home School, $2.95. 1989. Booklet, 64 pages.

Subtitled "Solutions to the Most Commonly Asked Home School Questions," this inexpensive booklet by veteran home schooler and well-known leader Richard Fugate covers all the basic issues. Section I explains why you should consider home education and answers the most common objections. Section II discusses the main reasons for home-school burnout and shows how to avoid failure. Section III has practical steps for starting a home school and selecting a curriculum. Although Alpha Omega, a work-text publisher, publishes this book, the treatment of different curriculum options is fair-minded.

Starting a Home School is an especially good booklet for busy dads, who often balk at reading a full-sized treatment of these questions. Several state groups are already using it as their main handout to novice home schoolers. This is really nitty-gritty advice that can save prospective home schoolers a lot of trouble. Heavy Christian emphasis.

NEW**
Christian Life Workshops
The Christian Home School, $13.95 plus $2 shipping. Wolgemuth & Hyatt Publishers, 1988. Hardcover, 168 pages.

Gregg Harris's *The Christian Home School* is a delightfully refreshing, easy to follow, basic book on home schooling. *The Christian Home School* does simplify while it explains, and that perhaps is why it is Number Six on the Spring Arbor Distributors hotlist of Christian books as I write this. This is now the best first book for home schoolers, although veterans can learn from it, too. Gregg Harris, who has spent years presenting his justly renowned Home Schooling Workshop, leads you from the reasons for home schooling through how to answer arguments against it. He tells you how to get started, pitfalls to avoid, and why and how to link up with support groups. Even veteran home schoolers will enjoy the confident feeling you get from reading this book!

Crossway Books
A Survivor's Guide to Home Schooling, $7.95. 1988. Paperback, 177 pages.

A Survivor's Guide to Home Schooling is an absolutely delightful book, written by two experienced home-school moms who have also run a *very* large extension program/support group, answers the nitty-gritty questions other books ignore like, "How am I ever going to get my laundry done?" The book has great stuff on subjects like Making Them Do It, reasons why *not* to hastily volunteer to teach other people's kids, ways to *realistically* schedule your days, and bushels more!

As the name implies, *A Survivor's Guide to Home Schooling* is not so much designed to enchant people with the idea of home schooling as to help them make it work. The authors deal with questions like • What about the father who works outside the home and is unavailable for extended help in home schooling? • What if your child is a slow learner or has difficulties? • How to avoid being suckered into loading up on expensive curriculum we will never, ever use • What experienced home schoolers' schedules *really* look like • How to realistically cope with teaching many children of different ages at once.

On top of this are valuable sections with information you won't find elsewhere: • Plain Talk About Teaching Other People's Kids (the authors' advice is, "Don't, except in very unusual, limited circumstances") • Serving Other Home Schoolers (how to start a support group and make it run) • Mom, Will You Read Us a Story? (some fantastic insights into why and how reading aloud to your children is *the* essential preparation for their successful reading) • Making Them Do It (why you should).

Luanne Shackelford has been called the Erma Bombeck of home schooling, giving you an idea of the book's sense of humor. She and Susan White have lots of experience and lots of children. A very warm book, salted with humor and peppered with vivid real-life examples. When you see the cover, you'll want to buy it!

Crossway Books
For the Children's Sake: Foundations of Education for Home and School, $7.95. 1984. Paperback, 161 pages.

I have never read a book that was more full of joy. Addressing the relationship of Christianity and education, Susan Macaulay shares with us the insights of Charlotte Mason, a teacher extraordinaire from the last century. The sweeping freedom that a child raised God's way can know, and the depth of beauty he or she can enjoy, shines through on every page. The author includes many of her personal experiences as a home-schooled child, and the experiences of her own family as they searched for appropriate education for their children.

For the Children's Sake is not a "how to" book as much as a beautiful "why to" and "in what manner."

NEW**
Fleming H. Revell Company
The Peanut Butter Family Home School, $7.95.

I just love Bill Butterworth's column in *Moody Monthly*. In a world full of depressing deep thinkers, Mr. B. always points out the peanut-butter lining. He and his wife, Rhonda, are perfectly normal parents who happen to love their kids and each other a lot, and who are still capable of being amused by the small, funny incidents of everyday family life.

So what happens when the wife in this perfectly normal family suggests they consider home schooling? First, the perfectly normal husband scratches around for ways to discourage her. Then he gets convinced that it's an OK idea to try for at least a little while. Next, the wife gets all fired up over hands-on learning . . . and gets pregnant. Good-by to the educational home bread-baking business and hello to Daddy learn-ing to cook "pasketti" while Mommy lies on the couch. During that year the new fixer-upper house didn't get fixed up much, but kids learned to read and picked up gobs of history. Mom and Dad threw themselves into it all with enthusiasm, taking some wrong turns along the way. A heart-warming chronicle of home schooling for just plain folks.

UPDATED**
Hewitt Research Foundation
School Can Wait, qpb, $8. *Home-Style Teaching*, hardback, $10. *Home-Spun Schools*, qpb, $6. *Better Late Than Early*, qpb, $6. *Home Grown Kids*, qpb, $7. Add 10% shipping plus $2 handling fee.

Dr. Raymond Moore has assembled a formidable corpus of work bearing out his hypothesis that little children belong at home. With the help of the Hewitt Research Foundation staff, and with wife Dorothy coauthoring in some cases, Dr. Moore has branched out into home schooling "how-tos."

School Can Wait makes the argument that delayed formal education makes the best academic sense. Impressive footnotes, written in the educational jargon that school folk love.

Home Grown Kids contains a short case for home education, followed by the Moores' views on child-rearing and teaching, from birth to age ten.

Home Spun Schools has inspiring examples of families who have successfully home schooled, interspersed with the Moores' suggestions and philosophy.

Home Style Teaching is the Moores' how-to book. Engagingly written, with lots of common-sense arguments and wisdom distilled from experience, *Home Style Teaching* is a book well worth owning.

Home School Burnout, the Moores' latest book, repeats a lot of information found in their earlier works. Unlike their other books, it has an unfortunate negative tone, with long passages directed against proponents of other learning methods.

Of these books, I would first get *Home Style Teaching.* A book to read and re-read!

NEW**
Home Education Press
The Home School Handbook, 40 pages, updated annually, $6.50 postpaid. *The Home School Reader*, 164 pages, $12.75 postpaid.

An upbeat handshake to home schooling, *The Home School Handbook* has brief, pungent articles on

Why Home School?, Does Home Schooling Really Work?, Community Resources and Services, and Choosing a Curriculum. Your questions about socialization, legalities, support groups, college (for those inclined to waste their money on it), and preschool education are also covered. Plus a list of over 100 resources. Yes, you'll find most of them in *The Big Book*, but these reviews are still worth reading. Hey, for $6.50, who can complain?

The Home School Reader is a "best of" anthology drawn from articles published over the years in *Home Education Magazine*. Wide range of perspectives, wide range of subjects. Some of the more famous contributors: John Holt, Nancy Wallace, Mario Pagnoni, Susannah Sheffer, Chris Klicka, and Clint Bolick. Everything here but the kitchen sink. Over forty lively articles in all.

ICER Press

School at Home: Teach Your Own Child, $6.95. 1982. Softcover, 173 pages. Appendix. Index.

School at Home is a decent beginner's book. Author Ingeborg Kendall, a home-schooling mother, has done her research, as the copious footnotes show. The book deals with nitty-gritty areas such as motivation and scheduling, as well as educational philosophy and legalities. Mrs. Kendall is enthusiastic about correspondence programs, in contrast to others who prefer to completely develop their own curriculum. Her book discusses the advantages and disadvantages of both the programmed curriculum approach and the self-designed program.

NEW**
Teaching Home

Home School Information, by *Teaching Home* staff. 48 pages. Magazine format. $5. Quantity discounts: 5-20 $4 each; 21-99 $3 each; 100+ $2.50 each. A great resource for support groups and state organizations. Free *Questions and Answers* brochure.

An excellent place to start is by asking advice of the people who have been helping home schoolers for years, namely the good folks at *Teaching Home* magazine. Their *Home School Information* booklet is an oversized 8-1/2 x 11" guide that includes: • answers to the most-asked questions • a Basic Resource Guide to the most popular and useful curriculum and resources • several articles on socialization • general legal infor-

mation • a list of state home school organizations • and more! The 1988-89 version also includes an article on "Ten Common Approaches to Home Education" (written by the leaders promoting each viewpoint) and a review of home school research as well. Lots of info in a compact, nice-looking, user-friendly package. As a community service, *Teaching Home* also offers a *free* "Questions and Answers" brochure. Nice folks!

MORE ADVANCED READING ABOUT HOME SCHOOLING

IMPROVED**
Gazelle Publications

The Home School Manual, 3d edition, $16.50 postpaid. Hardcover, 31 chapters, 9 appendices, index.

Ted Wade's *Home School Manual* has been revised again. As in previous editions, Ted has included chapters and excerpts by many other writers, most of whom will be familiar to veteran home schoolers.

The book is, like previous editions, thick and packed with information on why and how to home school—and why some people, in Ted's estimation, should not.

The first section, "Principles of Home Education," covers thirteen subjects from why and why not to home school through how to structure your home school and how to run a support group. The "Areas of Learning" section is eleven chapters, some influenced by a Seventh-day Adventist perspective, on how to teach different subjects, from early education and values through the normal Three R's and on to art, work education, and social development. This section contains some debatable points, such as the idea that reading can be taught with almost no phonics. The last section, "Theory Into Practice," shows how several veteran home-school families handle the toughies, like teaching several children at once.

Ted has added six new chapters and two new appendix sections. The Regional Information appendix, which lists legal information highlights, sources for state government information, and state home-schooling groups, is excellent. The list of educational service organizations also has a lot of fine information in a very small space, thanks to Ted's system of using letter codes to define various program options. With this list and the info in my own Curriculum Buyer's Guide, you would have an extremely complete overview of the possibilities from two complementary perspectives.

Ted has done a really good job of integrating a lot of material from a lot of different people into a fairly uniform, information-packed book.

Obviously, one book can't do it all (although *The Home School Manual* gives it a good shot!). For this reason, I would encourage readers to supplement this book with a few others that delve deeper into the philosophy of teaching, such as Susan Schaeffer Macaulay's *For the Children's Sake*, Ruth Beechick's *A Biblical Psychology of Learning*, and my own *Schoolproof*.

IMPROVED**
Home Run Enterprises
Christian Home Educators' Curriculum Manual, now in two volumes: *Elementary Grades* and *Junion/Senior High*. Tentative pre-publication prices are $14.95 each or both books for $24.95. Add shipping: book rate, $1.50/one book or $2/two; UPS, $2.50/one book, $3.25/two.

Cathy Duffy has been producing helpful resources for home schoolers for many years now. Her *Christian Home Educators' Curriculum Manual*, while lacking the glitz of some newer home-schooling resources, gives you a lot of solid help. Now in two volumes, it will be especially helpful to those who already are familiar with a number of resources but need help making up their minds.

In the *Elementary Grades* book, Cathy gives general advice on how to choose curriculum. She then gets extremely specific about recommendations for each subject area and age level for kindergarten through sixth grade. For each area, you get one or more of the following: a list of children's natural preferences of how to learn the subject, by learning style; basic suggestions and educational philosophy for how to present the subject; and a mini scope and sequence list of what the student should be learning in this area. Occasional charts also appear here and there.

The meat of each chapter, however, is the very specific resource recommendations. These generally include the resource's title, a supplier for the resource, and descriptions that vary in length from brief and punchy description to lengthy and detailed. Cathy is quite down-to-earth when explaining what she thinks is good and bad about each resource. Resources are listed alphabetically under each topic. Price information is not included.

The *Junior/Senior High* book provides detailed information on planning and goal-setting, including discussions of career and college preparation. Cathy suggests many options for providing those hard-to-do-at-home courses. She also covers motivation, learning styles, record-keeping, transcripts, and graduation. Then, as with *Elementary Grades,* she devotes a lot of space to recommending specific materials. Cathy also has included several unique planning and record-keeping appendixes that you can photocopy and use to help plan assignments and schedules, create transcripts, and so on.

In both books, Cathy includes reviews of individual textbooks from major publishers (e.g., A Beka) whereas other writers tend to review an entire publisher's line as a whole rather than separating each textbook out by grade and writing it up separately.

These books are good investments for serious home schoolers.

NEW**
Mountain Meadow Press
Home School: Taking the First Step, by Borg Hendrickson, 323 pages, 1989, $14.95 postpaid. Three appendices, glossary, index.

Home School: Taking the First Step is a big, thick book designed for serious reading. You won't find the fun anecdotes and how-we-did-it flavor of other home-schooling books. Unlike other introductions to home schooling, it is extremely detailed, with lots of lists of things to do and pieces of paper to fill out. For that reason I don't recommend this as the *first* book you read on the subject. Start with a home-school magazine or one of the lighter beginner's books.

Section I is extensive answers to thirteen common questions, from "How do I know if I have what it takes to home teach?" to "What if my child is 'exceptional'?" Section II, the heart of the book, shows how to develop your own curriculum, lesson plans, and record-keeping while still presenting a structured, orderly appearance to outsiders such as school officials. Lots of checklists, sample records. Detailed information on how to write a "statement of intent to home school" and other forms beloved of government officials is covered in Section III. Section IV overviews state regulations and procedures. Section V lists support groups and services. Section VI, "Reading and Resources," has a *long* bibliography of recommended books on the topics of education and home schooling, plus 17 pages of names, addresses, and one-line descriptions of 232 suppliers. This section is definitely not the most helpful part of her book, and could have been easily left out, as it does not provide anywhere near enough information to purchase products, or even to know which companies you should ask for catalogs. The appendices, however, do have a whole pile of information about teaching methods and approaches (31 different ones, all described in detail), effective teaching practices (here's where Borg shares her professional educator's lingo and outlook), and more info than you ever thought you'd need on how to prepare and cement a lesson. You also get a glossary of common educational terms, an Index of Checklists, Worksheets, and Samples, etc.

This book should be most valuable to those who need to keep professional-looking home-school plans and records.

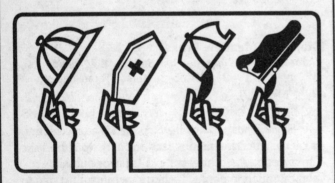

REASONS FOR HOME SCHOOLING AND PROOF IT WORKS

NEW**
Black Fox Productions
Homeschooling for Excellence by David and Micki Colfax. $8.95 plus $1.45 shipping. Warner Books, 1988.

The true story of a family that headed off into the California wilds with their four sons. Life on the homestead did not include daily bus rides to public school, but it did allow the Colfaxes to put their educational

theories to work. So far three of their sons have gone to Harvard on full scholarships, straight from their home school. (One son is still too young for college.) "But they were probably naturally extra-intelligent." Quite possibly so—but you see, two of the Colfax's sons are adopted. The Colfaxes are white; one son is black and one is Eskimo. Obviously whatever the Colfaxes have going for them can't be confined to heredity!

So, what *did* the Colfaxes have going for them? First and foremost, no TV reception in their area. (They count this as a blessing!) Second, a busy homestead and parents who actually needed their sons to become good at real work, such as building sheds, gardening, and caring for dairy goats. Third, willingness to invest in serious educational supplies (the section on recommended reference books is one of the best parts of this book). Fourth, having the boys each keep a daily journal with important information about their homesteading projects and other areas of real-world interest. Fifth, an open-minded attitude that allowed the boys to learn material when they were ready for it, not when it was "time to learn it" according to some public-school scope and sequence.

The Colfaxes have a lot of previous experience as teachers, researchers, and writers about education. That, plus the fact that their oldest children had a taste of classroom experience (enough to convince them of the merits of home schooling!), makes it hard to ignore their critique of the public schools. And they *do* criticize the public schools, mainly for having become "industrialized" to the point of almost dropping education itself from the curriculum! The chapter "The Trouble with School" is worth reading several times. Once you get over the shock, you'll understand the *root* cause of public educational decline in a way you never did before. The part of the book I personally liked best was the down-to-earth advice on how to keep home schooling simple. Most of us keep forgetting how easy it really is to teach the basics.

All in all, *Homeschooling for Excellence* is a friendly, insightful, short-enough-to-read-in-one-sitting book that I think you'll enjoy.

Blue Bird Publishing
Home Schools: An Alternative. Third edition, 1989. $11.95. Add $2 shipping.

This is one good little book. Author Cheryl Gorder coolly and logically presents what home schooling is, why people do it, and why we should be allowed to do it. Those ignorant of and/or actively hostile to home schooling will not be put off by the book's tone, and the numerous graphs, quotes, and lists all give the book a professional, authoritative air. Included: • profile of home schoolers • reasons for choosing home schooling • controversies • psychological and emotional problems school causes some children • social aspects • religious and moral issues (including a definition of "secular humanism" and an explanation of why home schoolers are so wrought up about it) • academic failures of public education • academic advantages of home schools • historical, political, and ideological issues • legal aspects • harassment v. cooperation • state laws and home schoolers • a survey of 200 public-school teachers that checks out their ideas about home schooling • helps and resources • home-school organizations • bibliography • index. Wonderful for convincing yourself or others that home schooling is OK.

NEW⋆⋆
Christian Life Workshops
Dr. Brian Ray's Home School Research Clinic, $19.95 plus $2 shipping for 2 cassettes and workpacket.

The man who knows most about research related to home schooling is Dr. Brian Ray, an Assistant Professor of Education at Seattle Pacific University. For years Dr. Ray has been editing *Home School Researcher,* which critically reviews the research in the area of home education. He himself does home-school research.

OK. So what does all this mean to you?

It probably would mean a lot less had not Christian Life Workshops put together a nifty little clinic on the subject of home-schooling research, featuring (of course) Dr. Ray. You get the entire clinic on two 90-minute cassettes, plus a nicely-designed workpacket that both summarizes major points and provides space

for you to follow along with your own notes. Or you can chop it up and use it for transparency masters, enabling you to present the clinic to a large audience (such as your friendly local court or your state legislature).

Dr. Ray has the gift of making the technical both simple and entertaining. By the time you have finished going through this clinic, you will understand a lot more about research in general, home education in particular, the characteristics of home educators and their families, what kinds of results home educators have been getting, the reasons why families choose home education, and the major historical and legal research on the subject.

Dr. Ray is also a regular contributor to *Teaching Home* magazine; so if you want to stay on top of the very latest home-school research, consider subscribing to *Teaching Home.*

Crossway Books
The How and Why of Home Schooling. 1987. $6.95.

Passionate introduction to home schooling from Ray Ballman's strong anti-government-school perspective. The first part of the book exposes the nakedness of public education and pleads strongly for a rediscovery of Christian educational principles, while the second half offers practical suggestions for getting started in home schooling. Chapters include: • Home Schooling: The Return of a Biblical Model of Education • Is Home Schooling for You? (a chapter that makes it hard to answer, "No") • Public Education: The Assault on Excellence • Why Home Schooling Is the Best Alternative • The "How" of Home Schooling (goals and objectives subject-by-subject, organization, things to watch out for while choosing curriculum, the roles of mother and father, team teaching, multilevel teaching, evaluation, character education, teaching by example . . .) • How to Begin • Why Grandparents Should Support Home Schooling.

Hewitt Research Foundation

School Can Wait, qpb, $8. Add 10% shipping plus $2 handling fee.

As mentioned above, *School Can Wait* makes the case for delayed formal education, based on the Hewitt staff's research into hundreds of studies of early childhood education.

Hearth & Home Ministries, Inc.

Home Education: Is It Working? $1/copy (5-copy minimum).

Pretty little pamphlet, nicely prepared with attractive graphics on good paper. Includes graphs that show the superior performance of students in Alaska's home-study program and cites numerous studies that show home education's effectiveness. Also presents historical, legal, and moral arguments, all footnoted. On the back are quotes from the Bible, President Reagan, the U.S. Department of Education, the Secretary of Education, and a former Chief Justice of the United States, all supporting the principle of parents teaching their children. Very convincing; an excellent handout to your mother-in-law, neighbors, friends, and legislators.

Larson Publications

Better Than School, $14.95 postpaid. 1983. Hardbound, 256 pages.

Another beautiful book about home schooling, this one is entirely personal. Nancy Wallace's son, Ishmael, was having a terrible time in school until she and her husband decided to pull him out. Their struggles in doing so were amply rewarded, as Ishmael first blossomed emotionally, then academically, and finally musically. The family's love of learning and life comes through, and we are delighted but not surprised when Ishmael becomes an accomplished musician and when a play he writes gets performed by serious (well, in the case of this play, humorous) actors. All this from a child the school considered very ordinary musically, and below average academically.

The Wallace's daughter, Vita, is likewise home-schooled and likewise musical. Holt Associates sells a tape of the Wallace family playing music together.

What is amazing about this book is how a whole family can thrive when they stop accepting artificial limits. Nancy wants to learn to play the piano, and so

she starts taking lessons. Ishmael wants to write a musical, and so he does. Vita wants to do everything, and so *she* does!

Better Than School reads like a novel and is better than a fairy tale. Bring home the boy the school considers an "ugly duckling," and he turns out to be a swan. What hath God wrought?

BOOKS ON "FREE" OR "INVITED" LEARNING

NEW**
Afore-the-Wind

Skipping School in Earnest, $13.60 postpaid, or $16.20 Canadian postpaid. 1988. Paperback, 158 pages. Two appendices, bibliography, index.

Much "alternative" educational philosophy from a humanist perspective, plus much information about home schooling in Canada.

Author Freda Lynn Davies has subtitled this book "Just Cause for Leaving a Mired System." She goes into such topics as materialism, prejudice against children, inappropriate use of scientific methodology to capsulize children, and the evils of unthinking acquiescence to institutional authority. A strong socialist-progressive perspective informs the philosophy in this quite intellectual book produced with a grant from the Explorations Program of the Canada Council.

Of primary concern to many Canadian parents are the actual laws in their provinces, and the current judicial interpretations of these laws. Here *Skipping School* excels. You get not only the actual laws themselves (in Appendix A), but a history of the major legal cases and how they were argued. Ways to argue for the right to home school are spelled out in the text. All this to provide elbow room for the family to live its own educational life, mind you!

Brook Farm Books
The Homeschool Challenge, $8.95 plus $1.50 shipping.

Veteran home schooler Donn Reed tells all! Legal stuff, an irreverent history of home schooling, what subjects the Reeds teach and why, structure, TV, discipline (he's against punishment), religion from a liberal viewpoint, computers, high school at home, and so on.

"We would better wait and see" are words from the Provincial Minister of Education that start off a chapter on the illiteracy of educrats. Revealing quote: "'The only reason Charlie got to be Minister of Education,' a neighboring farmer told me recently, 'is that he sat behind me in grade school and copied all my answers.'"

Reed, who has spent time in jail as a conscientious objector, is unintimidated by authority and suspicious of dogma. This includes feminist dogma (he has a funny chapter, "Pesky Pronouns," on unisex language) as well as traditional Christianity (Reed shares his distress over one of his daughters' conversion to fundamentalism). Breezy writing, typewritten rather than typeset—pioneer home schooling.

Holt Associates
How Children Learn, How Children Fail, and *Teach Your Own* are available through Holt Associates. Try your library for the others. *How Children Learn.* 1983 revised edition, $9.95, qpb. 303 pages. *How Children Fail.* 1982 revised edition, $9.95, qpb. 298 pages. *Teach Your Own.* 1981. $10.95 qpb. *Escape from Childhood.* 1974. $7.95.

How Children Fail and *How Children Learn* are John Holt's firsthand observations of children doing both, along with some very penetrating analysis of the causes.

Teach Your Own is his book about home schooling: why and how to do it. It is an excellent introduction to the subject. Holt's chapter answering objections against home schooling is particularly valuable.

The Underachieving School and *What Do I Do Monday?* come from a period when Mr. Holt was still trying to reform the public school system. Both contain brilliant insights, and *What Do I Do Monday?* also has long sections of suggestions on how to teach some difficult subjects, with the thoughts on math being especially helpful.

In *Instead of Education* Holt starts to look beyond the "school" system, whether public or private. He raises some serious questions in this book.

Holt's book on children's rights, *Escape from Childhood,* while provocative, is utopian in tone and therefore not as valuable. Holt's basic thesis is that children are people just like adults, only smaller, and should be allowed the privileges and responsibilities of adults, including sex, drugs, employment, and property ownership. About the latter two I agree. But what about the sex and drugs, you may ask? Holt is not a maniacal pervert: he is reasoning coldly and logically from our society's current beliefs in these areas. If, as so many seem to believe, sex is primarily for "fun" and procreation merely a sorry afterthought, then we have no good reason to protect children from it. Disgusting, but true. Similarly, if society permits adults to drug themselves (not that Holt approved of this), then it is hypocritical to forbid tobacco, booze, and marijuana to children. Similar arguments apply to child-parent "divorce" and all the other shocking suggestions in the book. If you are unhappy with Holt's conclusions in these areas, you might want to look over my book *The Way Home* (Crossway Books, 1985, $8.95), which sets forth a different set of initial premises, based on the Bible. *Escape from Childhood* at least raises all the right questions, and if we are not willing to look for God's answers we'd better be prepared to live with the alternative.

Home Education Press
Alternatives in Education: Family Choices in Learning. $10.75 postpaid.

Here you have a *thorough,* well-organized introduction to alternative education at home or elsewhere.

By Mark and Helen Hegener, veteran publishers of *Home Education Magazine.* Chapters are • Alternative Education • Alternative Educators (Steiner, Montessori, Piaget, Dewey, A. S. Neill, Illich, Holt, Kohl, Kozol, Herndon, George Dennison) • Home Schooling • Alternative Schools and Learning Programs • Correspondence Schools and Programs • Public School Alternative Programs • High School and Higher Education • Resources • Advertisers • Index. Well-written.

Larson Publications
The Complete Home Educator, $10.95 postpaid. Larson Publications. 248 pages.

No, Mario Pagnoni's book is not complete. It is, however, very funny, and does contain more info per square inch about the use of a personal computer in home school than any other book. Also helpful are the suggestions on how to teach the Three R's in a *relaxed* way. (Mr. Pagnoni, a schoolteacher by trade, has had plenty of experience with the alternatives!)

The book is brash and irreverent, covering such topics as Christmas gift sexism and why the Lawrence-Haverhill, Massachusetts area, where Mr. Pagnoni teaches, was rated the worst in the USA. As one of Mr. Pagnoni's students so aptly remarked, "What do we need that cultcha stuff for anyhow?"

John Holt wrote the Introduction. Unschoolers everywhere like this book.

ONE-STOP SHOPPING FOR HOME SCHOOL BOOKS

NEW**
Home Education Press
Free catalog.

Now you can get many of your home-schooling books in the same place! Mark and Helen Hegener of

Home Education Press have put together a catalog that at the time of writing already had over forty standard home-schooling titles. Old favorites such as *The Home School Manual, Home-Spun Schools,* and *Teach Your Own.* New releases such as *Homeschooling for Excellence* and *The Three R's at Home.* Write for their free catalog and experience convenience shopping!

BOOKS ON THE HISTORY OF SCHOOLING

Delphi Schools, Inc.
The Leipzig Connection by Paolo Lionni, $4.95.

You wanna know who to blame for the current state of public education? It's true, as Sam Blumenfeld and others have shown, that pointy-headed intellectuals were eagerly pushing for weirdo approaches to education 150 years ago. Chief of the pointy-heads was Wilhelm Maximilian Wundt, a fellow who invented the theory that human beings were just animals to be trained to respond to various stimuli and that education consisted of providing the right stimuli. In other words, forget about mental skills and hello to social conditioning.

But where did those guys actually get the oomph to put their ideas across? Nobody in America except for a few other pointy-heads was salivating with eagerness to turn classrooms into psychological laboratories. The answer, documented in this book, was John D. Rockefeller, Sr., the oil monopolist. Rockefeller's assets in 1910 were equivalent in 1980s dollars to over $10 billion. Such success, however, did not come without a price. The man in the street, Congress, and and the newspapers cursed him as the epitome of the soulless capitalist, piling up monopolistic millions at the expense of everyone else. To counter this bad P.R. and all the Congressional investigations it was fueling, Rockefeller determined to become a philanthropist. The main cause he chose to fund was education. The way he chose to fund it was to bankroll the Wundtians operating in the U.S.A. and to offer matching funds to universities that would set up Wundtian departments of education. And lo, the rest was history.

The Leipzig Connection chronicles the whole sorry mess in less than 100 well-documented pages. Amazing to think how many of our sacred modern educational dogmas were birthed in John D.'s pocketbook. Reads like a detective story, answers a host of questions about "modern" education that most of us didn't even know enough to ask.

Research Publications
Is Public Education Necessary? and *The NEA: Trojan Horse in American Education.* Each book $9.95 plus $1.50 U.P.S. delivery. 1985. Appendices, index, fantastic documentation.

Sam Blumenfeld strikes twice!

Is Public Education Necessary? is a great book, not so much for its readability as for its thorough documentation of why we even have public education and who put it there.

The NEA: Trojan Horse in American Education shows how the schools have been turned into a political football and why our declining national intellectualism is no accident. Written in a lively, intelligent style, this is undoubtedly Blumenfeld's most important book, and essential reading for anyone concerned about curing America's educational inferiority. (The solutions are surprisingly simple.)

Oxford University Press
David Nasaw. *Schooled to Order: A Social History of Public Schooling in the United States.* 1979. Look for it at your library.

Find out how, from the very beginning, public school has been first and foremost a vehicle for social propaganda and secondarily a device for producing submissive employees. Find out how the elite control the poor by means of schooling. Though not an entertaining book, *Schooled to Order* is eye-opening.

BOOKS WITH THE FACTS ABOUT PUBLIC SCHOOL TODAY

Yes, yes, I know. *Your* local public school is the best, the teachers are all wonderful people who would not dream of supplanting parents' values, the facility is grade-A. Let's assume all this is true. If you'd like to keep it that way, you'd better find out about the movements committed to undermining education in *all* public schools—including yours!

Barbara Morris Report
Change Agents in the Schools, $12.95.

A shocker. Relentless documentation of how humanists (in the religious sense of the word) are forcing their peculiar doctrines on our children under the guise of "educating them for the real world." Drug education that teaches kids to use drugs. Sex ed that promotes incest. "Values clarification" designed to unfreeze kids from their parents' values. The use of questionnaires as the first step in invading a child's mind. How "Back to Basics" is a phony cover-up for presenting mere survival skills (label-reading, simple addition) to secondary students while taking the heat off the schools. All of this in the educrats' own words. *They* said it!

Barbara Morris Report
The Great American Con Game, $8.95 postpaid.

Impeccable research, scary reading. I read this three years ago and am forced to say that Barbara Morris knows what she is talking about. The media are just now starting to gear up to push these "progressive" proposals, such as: The plan to require *all* U.S. children to participate in "mandatory voluntary" community service (translation: involuntary servitude, or slavery). The bureaucrats' plans to control our leisure activities. Compulsory exchange of U.S. children with hostile countries—pushed by Jacques Cousteau and seriously endorsed by some of our top leaders. How "parent-school partnerships," so strongly urged by education leaders, are actually a device for retraining and neutralizing opposition to the bureaucratic agenda. The push for master files on every schoolchild, to include personal data about his family, his beliefs, and (when he is older) his political participation. None of this is fiction or scaremongering. The book is mostly quotes from our "educational leaders"!

Books for All Times, Inc.
Glad You Asked! $5.95 plus $1.75 shipping.

Subtitled "Provocative answers to today's urgent questions about public 'education.'" Unusual book, set in a question-and-answer format based on the questions most frequently asked the author in his radio and TV interviews. Joe David gives some trenchant answers to the common questions. Like socialization:

How about making our students into good citizens?

When this becomes the primary focus, as it has, and you neglect the intellectual needs of the children, which we have, you will create what we seem to have in abundance, automatons. . . .

Some philosophy, some debunking, all served up in easy-to-digest portions. The author is pro-Montessori, pro-home and private school, non-Christian, and wittily opposed to the posturing of educationists.

Crossway Books
Child Abuse in the Classroom, $5.95. 1984. Mass market publication, 434 pages. Appendices, index.

A bombshell, this time lobbed by the victims. So many parents were complaining about what was going on in their children's classrooms that the Protection of Pupil Rights Amendment (commonly known as the Hatch Amendment) actually passed Congress. The Department of Education, loath to implement it, finally got around to holding hearings six years later. These all-day hearings were held in seven locations around the country.

Seeing that the Department of Education was equally slow to disseminate the transcript of the hearings, noted conservative activist Phyllis Schlafly dove in and published her own book, consisting entirely of testimony given at the hearings. (There are two appendices, "How Parents Can Evaluate Curricula" and

"What's Happened to Spelling?") Every charge Barbara Morris makes in her books is here documented by the experiences of those victimized by antihuman religion masquerading as "education." Teachers, parents, and students testified. Common complaints were that the public school was teaching: witchcraft, fornication, homosexuality, unisexism, antifamilialism, suicide, drug use, barbarianism (kill the old, the young, the infirm, anyone weaker than you), socialism, one-world government, psychological prying and manipulation, peer group dependence, and values teaching *in place of education*. (The classic example was a sermon on abortion rights in math class.) Parents also objected to the way school staff tried to brand them as troublemakers when they started asking questions or making their wishes known. Teachers objected to the way humanistic content and methodology were forcefully jammed down their throats. (One of the saddest testimonies is that of a teacher who tried to hold out against "Mastery Learning" in her school until the administration drove her to the brink of a breakdown. It seems that teacher manipulation is part of the Mastery Learning program.) Some former students gave testimonies about the way they'd been encouraged to destroy themselves in school. One young lady, living with her boyfriend without benefit of clergy and undergoing multiple abortions, was held up as an example to her Marriage and Family Living class. She now has changed and doesn't want *her* children exposed to this.

If you, or any of your friends, think public school isn't *really* that bad, please get this book.

NEW**
Footstool Publications
Blackboard Blackmail by Suzanne Clark, $8.95. Paperback, 230 pages. Foreword by Beverly LaHaye.

"It never occurred to me the Sunday afternoon I sat at my typewriter to compose a letter to the editor of our local paper that by doing so I was going to be sued for $100,000." So begins the amazing story of housewife Suzanne Clark. She was sued for that sum by the NEA after she wrote a letter to the editor, supported by extensive documentation, rebutting an op-ed written by two NEA (National Education Association) officials.

This book not only is an education in what the NEA and the educrats are *really* up to (Mrs. Clark ought to know, having had to defend her statements under threat of court action!), but into the mindset of this national organization that would sue a housewife for using her First Amendment right to express her opinions, based on evidence, in a letter to the editor of her local paper. As *Human Events* reporter Allan Brownfeld remarked, "The NEA . . . believes that free speech is for itself—not its critics . . . If anyone doubted the NEA's commitment to freedom before this action—and many did, for good reason—few doubts remain."

The NEA continued to play the heavy even after Mrs. Clark started to gain media support, going so far as to threaten boycott of advertisers to a Kansas City, MO radio station that had the temerity to invite Mrs. Clark as a guest. (During the show, by the way, she answered all questions about the NEA's positions by reading directly from NEA resolutions and publications. Dangerous stuff!)

Want to know what the NEA *really* is after? You'll find out through the course of this book. Mrs. Clark shares with us the best research on NEA methods and goals that I have yet seen. What's happening in "our" public schools is no accident. According to testimony from the then-president of the NEA, taken in 1983, as long ago as then the NEA had effectively "declared war against the New Right" (see page 71 of *Blackboard Blackmail*). Why should the NEA be declaring war on anyone? Because the most powerful teachers' union in the world is no longer focusing on *teaching* but on *indoctrinating*, even though many of its own members are unaware of the shift.

You can read the original NEA article, and Mrs. Clark's response, for yourself, since the publisher thoughtfully included both. I would suggest that, after reading these, you skip over Chapter One, a philosophical indictment of NEA methods and goals, and go straight to Chapter Two, where the story properly begins. Then read the unbelievable story for yourself!

Little, Brown and Company
The Graves of Academe, $14.95. Hardbound, 229 pages.

Richard Mitchell, a professor of English at Glassboro State College and publisher of *The Underground Grammarian*, carves up the educrats and serves them for supper. Mitchell exposes the problems in public education, not by telling horror stories, but by quoting the illiterate rascals who perpetrate them. As, for example, in this delightful vignette, titled "The Missouri Compromise":

You will not be astonished to learn that there are some people in Missouri who cannot manage commas, cannot avoid sentence fragments, cannot regularly make verbs agree with subjects and pronouns with antecedents, and cannot help sounding like literal translations from Bulgarian. If you are a regular reader of this column, you'll also be unastonished to hear that those pitiable illiterates are members of the Missouri Association of Colleges of Teacher Education.

These poor saps have finally noticed that lots of irate citizens "have indicated concern of [yes, *of*] the decreasing standardized test scores of students." They even know that a "sensitivity has become quite manifest in the development in state wide [yes, two words] assessment systems." But they don't seem too worried. They've cleared up the whole mess in a "position statement" called *Assessment of Basic Skills Competencies of Potential Teachers.* . . .

"The teacher," they say, "must have a high degree of proficiency in the basic skills. They are expect to transmit to their students through precept and example."

Yeah. And here are some of the precepts and examples through which these Missouri Teacher-training Turkeys transmit: . . .

"There is a question of the relationship of secondary and co-secondary schools in terms of relationships. The authors [!] of this position paper agreed that such an assessment process can have a significant impact [they never discuss *insignificant* or *mere* impacts] on secondary school curriculum in turning to an assessment instrument to which the public schools might be inclined to reach toward."

Why do the good people of Missouri suffer such humbug without turning to some blunt instrument to which they might be inclined to reach toward? We can tell you why. It's because these ugly crimes against nature are committed in private among consenting Turkeys. How many "authors," do you suppose, conspired to write, rewrite, edit, and finally to *approve* all that gibberish? . . .

We have some advice for the good people of Missouri. Turn those rascals out. Pension them off for life at full pay, requiring only that they never again set foot on a campus. Don't worry about the cost. In fifty years or so, there won't *be* any cost. As it is, you're planning to pay more and more of them for ever and ever. . . .

We have forgotten that the storekeepers used to pay miscreants to stay *away*. It worked. We've gotten it backwards. We pay them to hang around and smash the windows. Let's be realistic and pay the miscreants to do that one thing that we most need them to do—nothing, nothing at all.

Mitchell has focused on the real root of our public education problems—the teacher training colleges through which all potential public-school teachers must pass. *The Graves of Academe* pins the rap for the rise of an incompetent elite, jealous of real scholars and real learning, on two prominent, although unintentional, villains: the Wundterkinder (a nineteenth-century school of psychologists named after Wilhelm Max Wundt), and the 1913 NEA Commission on the Reorganization of Secondary Education. The Wundterkinder "viewed education as a science: teaching was a stimulus, learning a response thereto. Wundterkind educators have turned out generations of teachers who don't teach, but instead try to modify behavior." The NEA Commission followed up this disaster by insisting that the true purpose of education was to produce "good citizens" rather than to teach anyone anything. This Commission was the first to introduce Worthy Home-membership, Worthy Use of Leisure (see Barbara Morris's *Great American Con Game*) and other nonacademic goals *in place of* the traditional curriculum.

Recently many citizens in my state went to a great deal of effort to oppose an omnibus Education Act that threw millions more dollars at the public school establishment. The opponents, however, had no positive program of their own. If they had read this book, they would have known what to ask for: removal of the certification requirement for public-school teachers and disbanding of the publicly-funded teacher training colleges.

Mel and Norma Gabler
Educational Research Analysts

What Are They Teaching Our Children? $7.95. Qpb, 192 pages. Published by Victor Books/Scripture Press. Sold at Christian bookstores, or order in bulk from Gablers.

The next time you hear some far-left group screaming about how right-wingers are trying to censor America's textbooks, you ought to pick up a copy of this book and read it through. Laced throughout with lurid little quotes from actual classroom texts, *What Are They Teaching Our Children?* is the story of one couple's fight against the arrogant elite who are determined to instill their peculiar anti-values into America's children. *Your* children may be learning the details of gang rape, cannibalism, and suicide from "approved" school texts. *Your* tax money is paying to indoctrinate children in antireligious values, bureaucratic dependence, antipatriotism, and psychopathic hedonism. Meanwhile, occupations such as motherhood

and fatherhood are systematically weeded out of texts by the very groups which scream the loudest against "censorship"! I'm not making this up—all this stuff is in current textbooks, and the Gablers have provided quotes so you can read them for yourself.

Servant Publications

Censorship: Evidence of Bias in Our Children's Textbooks, $6.95 plus shipping. 1986. Might have gone out of print by the time you read this; I hope not!

American textbooks are designed to undermine religion and traditional values. Here is irrefutable proof, not from a critical outsider or outraged parent, but from within the Establishment itself.

Dr. Paul Vitz, operating under a grant from the federal government, analyzed a representative sample of public school social studies textbooks and language arts readers. He found, among other things,

> Referring to social studies texts:
> Not one text reference to characteristic American Protestant religious life in these books. . . .

> The dominant theme is the denial of religion as an important part of present-day American life. . . .

> Not one reference in any of these books (grade 5 social studies texts) to such major religious events as the Salem Witch Trials; the Great Awakening of the 1740s; the great revivals of the 1830s and 1840s; the great urban Christian revivals of the 1870-90 period; the very important Holiness and Pentecostal movements around 1880-1910; the liberal and conservative Protestant split in the early twentieth century; or the Born-Again movement of the 1960s and 1970s. . . . In spite of these books' emphasis on religious freedom and tolerance, there is not one reference to the large Catholic school system or to the recent Christian school movement as an expression of religious freedom. . . .

When an explicit definition of the family is given, it is seriously deficient or disturbing. . . .

A Strong Partisan Political Emphasis. . . . A reader would think there are no male Republicans in the country, much less any active conservatives, male or female, of any political stripe during the last twenty years. . . .

A Money and Career Emphasis. All of these text sequences present work as having two—and only two—primary meanings. One is to be paid money and then to use the money to buy goods. . . . The other meaning given to work is that it gives status. . . .

Neglect of Charity and Good Works. There is not one mention in the texts of the fact that many people don't work for money, e.g., homemakers; or that many people volunteer their services . . . or exchange goods and services (barter); or . . . work for rewards other than money. *The absence of any concern for non-material values is so extreme that not one book's discussion of a family budget includes any money for charity or for others in need.* . . .

Referring to basal readers approved for use in public schools:

By far the most noticeable ideological position in the readers is a feminist one. . . . Certain themes just do not occur in these stories and articles. . . . The few with a modest promotherhood emphasis are set in the past or involve ethnic mothers. No story clearly supports motherhood for today's woman. No story shows any woman or girl with a positive relationship to a baby or young child; no story deals with a girl's positive relationship with a doll; no picture shows a girl with a baby or doll. . . . There are, however, role reversal "romances." . . . The stories about woman pilots use such words as *courage* or *daring* while stories about men almost never use this vocabulary. . . .There are other types of feminist bias in these books, such as stories that rewrite or misrepresent history by referring to women judges, merchants, and soldiers at times and places where, in fact, there weren't any. . . .

Serious Judeo-Christian religious motivation is featured nowhere. References to Christianity and Judaism are rare and generally superficial. Protestantism is almost entirely excluded, at least for whites. In contrast, primitive and pagan religions, as well as magic, get considerable emphasis. . . .

Even the bureaucrats are finding it hard to dismiss this book, based as it is on observable facts about the content of approved public school texts that children are *required* to study. Groups as diverse as People for the American Way and Concerned Women for America are agreeing that history without religion is bunk.

I would not, however, get too excited about the prospects for real reform, because in our current climate any move towards including teaching about religion in the public schools is bound to be a plug for one-size-fits-all tolerance and understanding, e.g. good old-fashioned pagan syncretism. (In fact, I have already seen one proposed outline, promoted by a Christian group, whose centerpiece is just this plea for "understanding.")

The best we can hope for is a patronizing pat on the head in history class for our forebears and their quaint beliefs. Instead of pretending that Thanksgiving is just Turkey Day, the schools might go so far as to point out that those strange old Puritans wanted to thank God for their survival—while simultaneously teaching kids about "thank" rituals in other cultures and religions.

Meanwhile, any religious group that believes it has The Truth (Mormons, traditional Catholics and Jews, evangelical Christians, Muslims, etc.) is going to find very quickly that such claims are no more tolerated than they ever were. It will also become impossible to exclude witches, Satanist, Pan-worshipers, and so on from "equal time." Under such circumstances, New Age religion is bound to be the big winner.

WORKSHOPS

UPDATED
Christian Life Workshops
The Home Schooling Workshop. Twelve cassette tape set by Gregg Harris, with notes and three-ring binder, $69.95. Now available in four sets of three cassettes, $19.95 each. NEW: Instructor's Choice Tape Series, $5.95 per tape. NEW: Intro to Home Schooling video, 2 90-minute tapes, $25 rental plus $50 deposit or $75 purchase. Add 10% shipping, $3 minimum, $5 maximum.

Great stuff on tape, even better in person. Attending Gregg's workshop in St. Louis was the high point of the year for us. Gregg Harris tells how to help our children develop an enduring taste for righteousness by giving them a taste of it, "touching their young palates" with the best of our own experience and study. He shares practical principles of child discipline and instruction that help our children in the long run rather than just providing temporary relief. He explains how to use casual family storytelling to pass on our values and national heritage to our children without even having to take time out from our household work. Find out how to achieve financial independence and give children needed work experience through a home business and how to develop a ministry of hospitality (Gregg calls this "the original Bed and Breakfast plan"!). An extra: the tapes include insights on home evangelism, one of the modern church's most neglected areas.

The Home Schooling Workshop includes all this, plus the info you'd expect on the advantages of home schooling, the dangers of age-segregated peer dependency, how to begin a home-study program, how to choose a curriculum, legal considerations, and instructional methods.

Though Christian Life Workshops is in fact a household ministry of the Harris family with very little additional staff, it is a thoroughly professional and ethical organization, charging no hidden fees and covering completely the normal costs of hosting the workshop. CLW has helped to establish Christian home education associations from coast to coast and has glowing recommendations from former hosts.

Gregg is cutting down on his live workshop schedule in order to concentrate more on his writing. He has now produced a video version of his Friday evening introductory sessions, which presents strong arguments for keeping children out of conventional schools and teaching them at home. Also covered in this video is the educational strategy of secular humanism, clinic research in schooling readiness, and the Biblical answer to "What about socialization?" Gregg is not given to clichés; I promise you will get some startling new insights from this presentation!

At the workshop you not only get Gregg's message, but you can also roam around the large exhibit hall of curriculum in which nearly every major Christian publisher has a display. Not to mention meeting so many wonderful home-schooling families! Workshop alumni may attend free of charge each year, so the $45 per couple or $30 per individual is a one-time investment. (Note: support groups can register together and save $10 or more each.) Or if you buy the tapes, you'll get Gregg recorded live before an audience of 400.

The complete set includes twelve cassettes. For the convenience of those with tight budgets, these are now packaged as four volumes of three tapes each.

Volume 1, Christian Home Schooling, includes Advantages of Home Schooling, How to Win the Battle for Your Child, Ten Steps for Beginning Right. Volume 2, Motivating Children to Study, covers Training Children to Be Faithful, Delight-Directed Unit Studies, and Teaching History in the Home. Volume 3, The Life-Style of Home Schooling, covers Home School Hazards (passive dads, active toddlers, and teacher burnout), Hospitality and Family-Style Evangelism, and Family Businesses for Teens. Volume 4, Social and Legal Issues, covers Home School Support Groups, Family • Church • State (how they relate), and Laws & Legal Options.

You also have a choice of some fascinating (and inexpensive) special-purpose workshops, thanks to Gregg's habit of leaving a session in each live workshop open to address a special topic of current interest to home schoolers. The series now includes Age-Integrated Sunday Schools & Bible Studies, Learning Disabilities or Learning Differences?, Christian Home School Support Groups, Home Schooling Teenagers, and Learning Styles.

These are *the* home-schooling tapes to buy. And if your Christian home-school support group or co-op is considering hosting a home-schooling seminar, this is the one.

CHAPTER FIFTEEN

MAJOR HOME SCHOOLING STYLES

As the ocean swarms with fish, so the home education market is swarming with ideas. The richness and diversity of home educators' imaginations make it impossible to list *every* possible home-education setup. However, the field breaks down into several general categories, and by looking them over quickly you can see which format fits your family's particular personality. Thus you can avoid "reinventing the wheel," as well as feeling comfortably certain that your choice is based on knowledge.

SCHOOL AT HOME

The first commonly used method of home education is to make home into a school. Mom becomes Teacher, the kids pupils. A room is set up complete with desks, wall maps, ticking clock (to record when one "period" ends and another begins), storage cabinets and bookcases. Each subject is handled in one-hour chunks.

Following the typical classroom method, Teacher lectures all subjects. Pupils must raise their hands for permission to speak. Teacher decides what is to be learned and when and enforces her will on the students.

People who strictly follow this method rarely last long as home schoolers. They burn out from trying to imitate, for the sake of maybe four students, a ritual designed to cope with hundreds.

Many families find it convenient to adopt the physical layout of a schoolroom and to keep records in a professional way while abandoning the "school" mentality. They reason that there is nothing sacred about one-hour-per-subject and schedule their time in a multitude of creative ways. Teacher also gets tired of trying to do it all for the children, and finds it is usually simpler to let them take more initiative for their own scheduling.

In some cases, where children have been brought home to cure their severe discipline problems, parents find that the strict "school at home" method is necessary in order to give some structure. As problems subside, generally so does the strictness.

TRADITIONAL SCHOOLING, OR "BACK TO BASICS"

The cry of "Back to Basics!" has been ringing throughout our land for fifteen years, without any glorious results. Except at home. The public school establishment is unable to implement the much-desired basics because, as one principal put it, "We're too busy teaching the kids other things." Home schoolers aren't all wrapped up in sex ed, death ed, drugs ed, values clarification, nuclear ed, and all the other pet programs of the NEA, and thus they do have time to teach the basics.

At home, getting back to basics means a lot of teacher-led drill. The very discipline required to do a lot of drill is praised by many as character-building. Also, by stressing the academic "survival skills" of reading, writing, and arithmetic, parents insure that their children's academic foundation is solid before trying to build anything gaudy atop it.

Basics, then, means first things first and drill, drill, drill. This need not be boring. You can play games with flash cards (see Margwen Product's Match-A-Fact math series, for example). You can learn the facts in song. Problems arise, however, when believers in basics try to jam the facts down without first allowing children to handle them and become comfortable with them.

When teaching arithmetic, for example, it is easy to get most children to parrot the "addition facts." This is the way the public schools teach them. First kids are taught the "facts" for combinations up to 5—e.g., $1+1=2$, $1+2=3$, $1+3=4$, $1+4=5$, $2+3=5$, $3+2=5$, etc. After they have struggled with these for a year, they get to learn combinations to ten. Sooner or later they learn combinations to twenty. Somewhere along the line the "subtraction facts" are also introduced. But if kids *never actually add and subtract*, handling actual apples and oranges and pieces of gum and pencils, the "facts" mean nothing to them at all. Moreover, this is an awful lot of headwork to do when so many "facts" are really repetitions of each other. $1+4=5$ is the same as $4+1=5$ is the same as $5-4=1$ is the same as $5-1=4$. A rose is a rose is a rose is a rose.

Kids should get to mess around with math. After they are comfortable with numbers, they should be told the various principles that describe the same operation. The commutative principle means that $1+4$ is the same as $4+1$. This eliminates 50 percent of addition memorization. The inverse principle means that $5-1=4$ is the same fact as $4+1=5$. This eliminates another 50 percent. Once they know how to derive the answer, then it makes sense to drill them so the answer comes swiftly. This is reinforcing the framework, not replacing it.

As this thinking applies to math, so it applies to all areas. Rigorous repetition and drill are useful when used correctly. Our country's past experience of this form of traditional schooling bears this out. But drill without understanding produces parrots, not thinkers.

Most Christian home school correspondence programs emphasize basics. Among these are A Beka Video School and its sister Pensacola Christian Correspondence School; Living Heritage Academy, carrying

Basic Education's Accelerated Christian Education series; Associated Christian Schools, with a Baptist flavor; and with an eclectic selection of Christian materials, Christian Liberty Academy. For Catholics, Our Lady of Victory and Our Lady of the Rosary feature a strong basics approach.

Both A Beka Books and Bob Jones University Press offer complete "basics" materials for home schoolers. Both also allow you to order as little or as much of their program as you wish. Bob Jones is especially friendly to home schoolers, offering a toll-free number for information as well as for orders.

THE CLASSICAL SCHOOL

Following the teachings of Dorothy Sayers (discussed in the last chapter), a number of families are resurrecting the "classical" or "medieval" style of education. In the early years they fill their children up with reams of facts: poetry, foreign languages, history, geography, classification of all kinds of animals-vegetables-minerals, and arithmetic facts. Christian families do a lot of Bible memory work in this stage, and some learn the Catechism. Some, following Miss Sayers exactly, pursue the study of Latin, as well as the fine arts (music, painting, and literature).

This first stage is a lot of fun for both parents and students. Most of us adults have never had an extended pleasurable learning experience, and it is a treat to finally learn French or to take up the classical guitar after years of longing to do so. Parents and children thus often end up learning together.

The second stage becomes much more rigorous. Miss Sayers calls it the "Formal Logic" or "Dialectic" stage, because formal analysis (frameworks) are introduced at this point. In language, the student learns grammar. In math, logic. In reading, criticism. In writing, essays and arguments. Theology now becomes Systematic Theology, and history is examined (for Christians) in the light of God's providence. This is the time for asking "Why?" about everything and discovering and testing truth. For the learner this is a very heady stage, as the world begins to blossom before him, and care must be taken to prevent the beginnings of arrogance.

The last stage, "Rhetoric," is where the learner develops his own particular style of writing and speech, and launches into learning his actual calling. For some, this will mean apprenticeship (discussed later in this chapter).

It is possible to go at this medieval thing with a lot of flair: to not only use the classical method, but read the classical writers; to learn calligraphy and other gentle arts of the Middle Ages. One family we know is doing just that. By tenderly admiring what was great in the past, you get a real standard by which to judge the arts in the present.

Classical schooling is not for all, of course. A kid who is a genius with tools, whose fondest wish is to be an auto mechanic, might be hard to settle down in front of a ripe passage from Virgil. But families with an intellectual bent should definitely consider it. As Miss Sayers so pungently points out (again, in her essay "The Lost Tools of Learning"),

> The truth is that for the last 300 years or so we have been living on our educational capital. . . . But one cannot live on capital forever. A tradition, however firmly rooted, if it is never watered, though it dies hard, yet in the end it dies. And to-day a great number—perhaps the majority—of the men and women who handle our affairs, write our books and our newspapers, carry out research, present our plays and our films, speak from our platforms and pulpits—yes, and who educate our young people, have never, even in a lingering traditional memory, undergone the scholastic discipline.

If you are upset by soup cans masquerading as art and pornography posturing as great fiction, perhaps you and your youngsters would like to produce something better. The Literature, Music, and Art chapters in various volumes of *The Big Book of Home Learning* can help put you in touch with the masters.

Calvert School (secular, Christian flavor), Covenant Home Curriculum (Calvinist), and Seton Home Study Program (Catholic) are about as close to a classical program as is offered today in training method. Our Lady of Victory (Catholic) gets deeply into Catholic classics with a "basics" emphasis. Nobody anywhere has a full program that covers Greek, Latin, and the gamut of classical writings. Even Christian programs don't deeply study the Christian classics, leaving that to seminary. Mistake! Will someone out there meet this need?

UNSCHOOLING

Along with traditional and classic schooling, "unschooling" is one of the most popular home-school formats. To avoid confusion, I should mention that the word "unschooling" is used for two separate things. Some people refer to the act of removing one's children from the schools, or refusing to enroll them, as "unschooling." But "unschooling" also describes a very popular home-schooling philosophy: that children learn better from doing real things than made-up exercises.

One might, for example, teach writing by assigning essays, poems, etc. which are then graded and filed away in a little folder. Alternatively, a child might learn to write by writing actual letters to Grandma, writing shopping lists, writing stories to be submitted to a children's magazine, and so on. On the one hand, a child can learn to read by following a strictly tracked "primer" series; on the other hand, he might prefer to begin by reading books he picks out himself from the library.

Unschooling is a far more radical approach to education than enrolling in a traditional home correspondence course or following a planned curriculum. It requires more creativity and flexibility (some say this is also one of its rewards!). Some people find unschooling more stressful, as they are constantly worrying whether Johnny really is learning *all* the math he needs to know, or whether someday they will discover that he is eighteen years old and still has never heard of George Washington! Others, more confident, think unschooling is the most relaxing, friendly way for children to learn.

All unschoolers are not created equal. Since unschooling is actually an apprenticeship to the parents, the parents must be *doing* something in order for the children to learn. Parents also must enjoy answering questions and taking the time to patiently show children how to do things they could do much more quickly themselves. Since unschooling follows the interests of the family, a family that is very deficient in some major area (all extremely poor readers or totally ignorant of math, say) must resort to outside help in order to overcome their own lacks.

No law says that children can learn *only* from their parents, and many unschoolers rely heavily on relatives, friends, and community resources to supply opportunities for their children to learn.

Unschoolers are generally shy of tests—not that their children don't know anything, but because testing is one of the "school" things they dislike. To show the children are making progress, unschoolers often rely on journals of learning experiences and/or folders of projects or other work completed.

Experienced home schoolers, even those who use curricula, often incorporate unschooling into part of their program. "Total" unschoolers, those who use no set structure at all, seem to be a minority (this is my guess based on what I see home schoolers writing about themselves). Parents generally feel less nervous about unschooling "skills" (e.g., carpentry, cooking, sewing) than academic subjects.

In some cases, children who did not respond to any kind of formal learning have demonstrated amazing abilities when unschooled. I don't, offhand, know of any cases where the reverse is true.

WALDORF EDUCATION

A small number of parents are home educating according to the principles of Rudolph Steiner, an Austrian educator, now deceased. Steiner's Waldorf School stressed imagination in the learning process. Children learned their letters and numbers by hearing fanciful stories about each symbol. (The number "1", for example, looks like the letter "I" because there is only one of me.) Math follows the adventures of little gnomes who add, subtract, multiply, and divide the king's treasures. Much attention is given to storytelling and delighting the children, rather than to rote learning. This translates into a heavy emphasis on artistic creativity; children learn to play the recorder and do a wide variety of crafts.

Steiner's philosophy was rather mystical, and New Age people seem especially fond of it. Now that there is so much attention being brought to "right-brain" (i.e., creative thinking) as opposed to "left-brain" (i.e. logical thinking), Steiner's work is undergoing a mild revival.

Oak Meadow School in Blacksburg, Virginia offers a Waldorf home-schooling curriculum.

THE "PROJECT" OR "INTEGRATED" APPROACH

Followers of Dr. Raymond Moore (see the previous chapter) adopt an "unschooling" method for their youngest children, followed by a "project" or "integrated" approach (now frequently called "unit studies") for those they consider old enough for more formal learning. By learning to cook, for example, children deal with fractions (one-half cup, one-quarter teaspoon), measurements, multiplication and division (doubling or halving recipes), some properties of chemistry, neatness, and so on. This is an excellent way to collect data, but it does not create a framework. Thus the more enlightened believers in projects also teach reading and arithmetic as separate disciplines and use history time lines.

For Christians, the Hewitt Child Development Center curriculum provides planned projects. The Konos Character Curriculum, also for Christians, is a year's K-6 activities correlated with a history time line (you have to buy your own math and phonics programs). Alta Vista College's home-school program, Becky Avery's "Weaver" curriculum, and Bill Gothard's Advanced Training Institute all also feature a project approach (again, for Christians). You will find more information on unit study programs and how to make your own in the Curriculum Buyer's Guide.

APPRENTICESHIP

A strange new thing is happening in our day. Families are looking at the universities and colleges and saying, "We should spend ten thousand a year on *this*?" Think it over. Is it smarter to spend thousands of dollars on a credential that will get you a job, or to get the same education on the job for free? Is it better to spend thousands of dollars training to be another man's servant (that is what corporate-industrial careers actually are), or to save that money as capital for your own business?

Not so long ago, it was normal for a man to train his sons to carry on his business. They would start with both experience and capital. If a particular son had no aptitude for the family work, he would be apprenticed to the craft he desired. Mothers taught their daughters the "home" crafts (which, by the way, were *not* demeaning, but at the time were absolutely essential for family survival—try living without food and clothes!). This is the way the world ran for thousands of years, and it worked.

All forms of education described above flow neatly into apprenticeship: classical education, basics, un-

schooling, project/integrated, and even Waldorf education. Children who learn by doing are ideal apprentices, and all forms of home education in some degree prepare children for this responsibility.

Hewitt Research Foundation has a list of several hundred home businesses that the young learner can tackle while at home, thus apprenticing himself to a craft under the guidance of his parents or another community member. Bill Gothard has taken this a step farther, and is even now working with Christian businessmen to set up apprenticeship opportunities for the graduates from his Advanced Training Institute home-study program. Further, the Business Skills chapter in Volume 3 will give you some guidelines for thinking through the question of apprenticeship and independent home business.

CHAPTER SIXTEEN

BUT IS IT LEGAL?

What do you do if, God forbid, Mrs. Busybody should report you on the child abuse hotline for "educational neglect"? What do you say to an irate truant officer or an officious schoolperson? Most home-school families never face these problems. Still, it's good to know what to do if the bureaucracy catches you by the shirt in its grinding gears.

First step, of course, is to join a home school group. There's safety in numbers, and more than one court case has been dropped when sympathetic friends packed the courtroom or picketed the courthouse. These groups are also well-informed about the current laws and in touch with legislators and other leaders.

Remember, you don't need any defense against school laws if your children are under the minimum compulsory attendance age, which varies from five to seven.

Following is a brief list of other legal resources that will help you be confident in your program.

ORGANIZATIONS

Home School Legal Defense Association
$100/year per family. Send SASE for application. Do not send money with your application request.

The purpose of the Home School Legal Defense Association is to establish the fact that responsible home schooling is legally permissible in every state. They will provide experienced legal counsel and representation by qualified attorneys to every member family who is challenged in the area of home schooling. The attorney's fees will be paid in full by the Association.

Run by Concerned Women for America's former legal counsel, Michael Farris, this is a reputable organization with thousands of member families. Knowing you can obtain quality legal counsel is enough to dissuade potential persecutors in some cases. So is knowing what the law says, if your state law is favorable to home schooling. Ask your local home-school group for a copy of the law (someone should have it on file). Then, if you feel you need more protection, or if you just want to contribute to the defense of those families that are on the hot seat, you might want to join the Association.

National Association for Legal Support of Alternative Schools
Membership, $20/year.

See the NALSAS writeup under "U.S.A. National Home School Organizations" in the Home School Organizations section. NALSAS offers help to all types of home-school programs.

BOOKS AND LEGAL INFORMATION

Christian Liberty Academy

National Guide, $5. *Legal Manual*, $5; optional accompanying cassette tape presentation, $5.

The *National Guide to Home School Attorneys and Organizations* is a 115-page directory of names, addresses, and phone numbers, with over 300 listings. CLASS also has a Legal Manual which introduces you to the law and includes such things as a sample affidavit with step-by-step directions for dealing with school officials.

UPDATED**
Dr. Steve Deckard

Home Schooling Laws in All Fifty States, $18 postpaid. Updated annually.

A manual listing the requirements that home schoolers must meet in order to meet each state's compulsory education law. Dr. Deckard starts off with a useful chart summarizing the basic elements of homeschooling law. Each state has check marks in the areas relevant to its particular law. This chart includes Application Process, types (if any) of required Teacher Certification, Record-Keeping, Testing and Evaluation (what kind is required), Curriculum (objectives, scope, sequence, time by day or year, etc.), provision for movement from state to state or reentry into public schools, health and safety requirements, diploma provision, control provision, and "miscellaneous." You also get a listing by state that provides the address and phone number of the person in charge of home-schooling affairs at the State Department of Education and a digested version of the state home-schooling law. An extensive appendix section includes "forms collected from each state regarding the procedures for home schooling." Since not every state has such forms, not every state is represented in this section. Plus, in the most recent version, a few pages of resources, ideas, etc.

The only thing to criticize in this spiral-bound, handy-sized manual is the tiny, hard-to-read type and the poor repro of the state forms. This matters less than it might, since you are most likely to use *Home*

Schooling Laws as a quick reference, not as something you take to wile away the hours on your vacation! For its purpose it really is a bargain at the price.

Home School Legal Defense Association

Florida Legal Seminar Tapes, 12-tape set, $25 postpaid. State Laws Report, $20 postpaid.

Most lawyers know precious little about defending home-schooling cases. So, get your lawyer an education! The Home School Legal Defense Association taped a twelve-hour legal seminar devoted to court strategies for home-schooling cases. Covered were:

- How to Present a First Amendment Case (William Ball)
- How to Use Expert Witnesses in a First Amendment Case (William Ball)
- Constitutional Issues and Home Education, Parts I & II (Michael Farris)
- Survey of Home School Statutes (Chris Klicka)
- Criminal Defense of Home Schooling Families (Michael Smith)
- Federal Civil Rights Litigation (Michael Farris)
- Constitutional Issues and Home Education, Part III (John Eidsmoe)
- Negotiation Techniques (Chris Klicka)
- How to Prepare a Home School Client for Trial (Michael Smith)
- How to Prove That Public Education Violates Your Client's Religious Beliefs (Michael Farris)
- Questions and Answers (all lecturers)

Don't get panicked by some of these titles—"Criminal Defense of Home Schooling Families" and the like. The HSLDA by its very nature gets embroiled in the (mostly rare) "tough" cases, and its lawyers need to know how to handle worst-case situations. Most home schoolers never get hassled at all. If a homeschooling family is threatened, usually a letter or phone call from a HSLDA lawyer, or simply presenting the school authorities with the state law, will settle the matter. Problems mostly arise in the hostile states: Michigan, for example. So if you live in an unfriendly state and don't want to move, you might want to seriously consider both HSLDA membership and obtaining this set of tapes.

Also available: a fifty-page summary of all the state laws in chart form, one page per state. Covered are the legal requirements in each state and what you must do to comply, if you intend to comply. Updated annually.

NEW**
Pennsylvania Homeschoolers
Story of a Bill, $6.95. 1989. Paperback, 152 pages.

"On the one side, two thousand homeschooling families who had never before engaged in political action. On the other side, the teacher's unions, the school board association and the Pennsylvania Department of Education. At stake, the very survival of home education as an alternative to school education in Pennsylvania."

If this beginning grips you, you're sure to enjoy this story of how the 2,000 Davids took on the far more numerous Goliaths . . . and won! You will gain an education in how bills become law in a state capitol as well as be entertained by what is really a very gripping story, full of human interest. Follow the Pennsylvania home schoolers through their legislative breakfasts, children's slide presentations to legislators, committee hearings, and behind-the-scenes lobbying. The fast pace of a novel, the tension of a whodunit, *and* a happy ending!

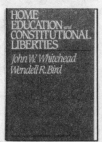

Rutherford Institute
Home Education and Constitutional Liberties, $5.95 plus 10% shipping. Other books by John Whitehead and the Rutherford Institute, see below. Also available from Rutherford Institute: *Home Education Reporter.* $10/state plus $1.50 shipping; $250 complete package.

Every home-school recommended reading list contains *Home Education and Constitutional Liberties,* and with good reason. John Whitehead, a constitutional lawyer, summarizes all the major court decisions affecting home schooling and shares his reasons for believing that home schooling is inherently constitutional. Whitehead's arguments are legally sound and have been the basis of of many home-school legal victories. Whitehead and Bird have done us a great service by showing we are *not* antiestablishment rebels, but are

actually within the American legal tradition. The book is worth reading for your own peace of mind, and "must" reading for your lawyer (or, better, the school board) if you are challenged.

John Whitehead and others at the Rutherford Institute also have produced a series of books and publications on your civil and religious rights—*The Right to Picket and the Freedom of Public Discourse* ($6.95), *Freedom of Religious Expression in the Public High Schools* ($5.95), *Real Threat and Mere Shadow: Religious Freedom and the First Amendment* ($15), *Arresting Abortion* (legal strategies for dissent—$6.95), *Parents' Rights* ($7.95)—as well as Whitehead's contributions to political philosophy—*The Stealing of America* (how bureaucrats took over—$6.95), *The Second American Revolution* (solutions—$8.95), and *An American Dream* (appealing look at America's Constitutional roots—$8.95). All are available from Rutherford Institute.

Also available from Rutherford Institute: the *Home Education Reporter,* a state-by-state analysis of compulsory education laws and relevant court rulings. Each segment includes a synopsis of the state's law; a straightforward explanation of the requirements; and the consequences of violating the law. Updated annually. Order info on just your state, or any combination of states ($10 per state; please specify which state or states you want when ordering). This info is free at your local law library (if you have time to pursue it and know how to look things up) or from your state Department of Education (if you're brave), or available from your state home-school group for a minimal charge to cover photocopy costs (if you're not). However, a couch potato such as myself will find Rutherford's service handy.

The *Rutherford Institute* magazine tells you about the court cases Rutherford is currently fighting, many of which involve home-school rights. Free, but donations are welcome (and needed).

THE BEST DEFENSE

. . . is a good offense. The best defense against legal harassment is a good state law. The best state law, to date, has the following provisions:

- Requirement of a specific number of instructional hours every year, a percentage of which must be in the "core" areas of Reading and Language Arts, Math, Science, and Social Studies, along with related subjects. This requirement also applies to the public schools.

• Parents keep records of how many instructional hours each school-age child receives. These records are considered sufficient proof that home schooling is occurring. Parents may also keep a journal, and are expected to test or evaluate their children periodically. Such evaluation need not take the form of a standardized test.

• Parents may include or exclude any subjects necessary to follow their religious convictions. The state may not require any particular item to be taught.

• No requirement for certified teachers, state inspection of the home school, or any particular percentile performance on standardized tests.

• The child abuse bureaucracy is expressly forbidden to continue an investigation if the only accusation is "educational neglect" and the parents demonstrate they are home schooling. Such cases are turned over to school officials, as being in their proper province. In other words, home schoolers cannot be charged with child abuse and threatened with loss of custody simply because they are home schooling.

Sounds pretty good, doesn't it? The state is Missouri, and the organization to contact if you'd like a copy of the law and advice for how to lobby for it in your state is Families for Home Education (address given under "Missouri" in the "Home School Organizations in the U.S.A." chapter).

CHAPTER SEVENTEEN

TESTS

Nobody is average any more. This we know, for standardized tests have told us so. I reported in the 1988 edition of the book about how a West Virginia watchdog group, Friends for Education, did a mail and telephone survey of the state departments of education. These good folks were surprised to find, in their own words, "no state is below average at elementary level on any of the six major nationally normed, commercially available tests." (The quote is from an AP story of November 27, 1987 entitled "Tests called misleading. Survey finds 'above average' pupil scores in every state.") Two years later, according to an article in the February 1990 issue of *Chronicles,* it's the same thing all over again. Once again *all* the states are "above average" on these tests.

Curious, eh what? We can't *all* be above average, by definition. "Average" means "the middle of the pack," and every pack has to have a middle. When the pack's bottom drops off, someone has been doing some fast shuffling with a sleazy finger.

And it gets curiouser. Not only are today's teachers wasting hours and hours of classroom time teaching to the test (often against their will); not only are today's kids not compared against each other, but against "a norm based on a select group of students who took the test as long as eight years ago"—and that's why nobody is below average; but we, the public, are somehow buying all the propaganda about "improving test scores" and "better quality public education."

Are the wrong people getting the credit? It seems a definite possibility. Consider:

- Millions of families are paying a bundle for private tutoring at places like Sylvan Learning Centers. A recent full-page ad in *Instructor,* a magazine largely for public-school teachers, encouraged teachers to consider recommending these centers for any children falling behind in their classes.

- Millions more families are shelling out big money for preschool phonics games, early readers, math games, and other extras that they hope will prepare their children to be readers and cipherers *before* they ever enter the public school first grade classroom.

- Millions and millions beyond these are paying stiff tuition at preschools and early learning centers, whose programs are often designed to teach kids reading and writing before they even get into kindergarten.

• Like never before, parents are spending time and money *at home* to help their children educationally. Educational games sales have gone up tenfold in the past few years. Home computers loaded with educational software abound.

The point is this: now that teachers are getting into the habit of telling parents that it's *their* job to get their children additional help, work with them on their spelling words, buy them special readers and summer skills practice kits—and the parents are doing this—just exactly how does the credit for "improving test scores," even if they were really improving, belong to the public schools?

If there were no private tutors or private tutoring centers . . . if we didn't hear so much about "parent-school partnerships" (meaning that the parent gets drafted as a home teaching aide) . . . if teachers did not teach to the test, and the tests weren't dumbed down . . . if parents weren't buying educational helps at a phenomenal rate . . . then the public schools might have some reason to boast. As it is, to paraphrase Queen Victoria, we are not impressed.

ABOUT THOSE SACRED TESTS . . .

The world of testing is an unearthly landscape where the inhabitants all have initials rather than names and queer sounds burble out of the gloom. "Raw Scores on Skills Battery," whispers one creature (perhaps the elusive NMSQT). "Diagnostic Subtest Equivalency Norms," giggles another. "Let's SIT down with some fried TOEFL sandwiches and SORT things out . . . if you DARE," suggests the WBSS. "You're a real laugh WRIOT," applaud the Peabodies. "With us, to screen for developmental delay is better than to ACT."

To normal earthbound creatures, the language of testing is mystifying. And so it will stay, because without the jargon that consecrates modern testing, it wouldn't sound scientific. And if testing didn't sound scientific, nobody would make children stake their entire future on it. And if kids' futures didn't depend on how they did on the tests, the testing companies would be out of business.

In some ways, parents who educate at home are in better shape because of the sanctity of modern testing. It's not that hard to teach a child to do well on a standardized test, and since the tests are sacred, good results command respect. Tests that check out objective skills, such as the ability to add and subtract or the ability to tell nouns from verbs, can be helpful in assessing a child's area of strength and weakness. But unhappily the testing story doesn't end there. The prestige that objective standardized tests have achieved is being used to huckster a whole range of *subjective, manipulative tests.* These are mislabeled "scientific instruments," when they are actually being used to promote a political agenda.

As Peter Schrag and Diane Divoky report in their excellent book *The Myth of the Hyperactive Child* (Pantheon Books/Random House, 1975):

> By early 1975, more than 30 states, under pressure from the federal government (which has threatened to make funds for the handicapped contingent on screening), had passed laws requiring local school districts to conduct such tests. In most they cover not only the familiar categories ("learning disabled," MBD, "emotionally handicapped," "visually handicapped") but also include scales rating children for "impulse control," "intellectuality," "withdrawal," and "social behavior." The specific applications and consequences of these tests vary from state to state, but the objectives are similar. *There is money for special education*, for the handicapped and for other categories of disability (real or imagined): *the more clients a system can create for such programs, the more special funds it can claim* from state and federal agencies. . . . What is certain is that since the end of the sixties, the number of special education programs, including L.D. classes, has mushroomed, that available funds have tripled, and that, given the vagueness of the proliferating categories and the lack of effective techniques for remediation, there is no conceivable way that most of the screens can lead to proper placements. In Washington, court-ordered testing of "special" track children revealed that *two-thirds had been mislabeled and misplaced and should have been in regular classes.* Similar results have been reported in Philadelphia, San Francisco and other cities. (Emphasis mine)

Early Childhood screening, for example, is being peddled as the cure for all our national academic ills (as if the same people who can't teach five-year-olds would do better if they got their hands on them two years earlier!). Legislators are being pressured to make Early Childhood screening *compulsory.* The kicker is that some of these screening tests are *designed* to find normal children deficient, so large numbers of little children can get forced into state schooling to "remediate" their supposed problems. It's just another device for dragging children out of the home at an earlier age, and saves the bureaucrats the trouble of passing compulsory attendance laws for babies.

Tests of "Social Development" and the like are also excellent for suppressing nonconformists. Once you get out of the realm of 2+2=4 and start testing *subjective* responses, the test-maker can impose his prejudices on the rest of us. Any response that he doesn't like can be labeled "immature" or "deviant" or "anti-social," and the unfortunate test-taker dragged off to receive compulsory behavior modification.

Since testing is so pervasive, so uncontrolled, and can be so damaging, and since legislators are already under fire to make testing even *more* widespread, I would also like to propose a law. Instead of making testing ever more compulsory, how about making it less so? Nobody should be forced to take a test against his will, or the will of his parents in the case of a minor child. This is the only way we can effectively preserve our civil right to privacy, and it won't hurt legitimate tests one whit, because *people gladly take tests whose benefits they can see.* Even if colleges didn't require the SAT, most prospective college students would take it. Another example: few parents or children object to the Iowa Test of Basic Skills, and those few should be allowed to act on their valid objections. But to make testing a political football imposed on the people from above is plain and simple tyranny.

Even in states where home-schooling families are not required to subject their children to standardized tests, one of the first questions prospective home schoolers raise is, "Where can we get our children tested?" Most parents are more than willing to personally pay to have their children's progress evaluated, without any coercion at all. Those who shun tests, in my experience, have serious reasons for so doing. Even though my own children are grade levels above the norm on standardized tests, I fully support the right of *any* family to choose or reject testing. The power to test is the power to destroy.

WHY WE NEED BETTER TESTS

Now, let's talk for a minute about just how useful American standardized tests really are . . . or aren't. We're not talking about the dubious "screens" used to separate kids into regular, "gifted," and "special" groups, but bona fide, nationally-normed, fill-in-the-little-box-with-your-number-two-pencil tests. As men-

tioned above, every state in the country is currently "above average" on such tests. That being so, how meaningful are the tests themselves?

Albert Shanker, president of the American Federation of Teachers, the nation's second-largest teachers' union, thinks Americans are kidding ourselves about how well our children are doing educationally . . . and that the tests we give our kids are a big reason for the illusion that they are doing well. In a speech given before a conference of teachers and school administrators in Denver in late September, 1989, he said,

> The question is, how many of our 17- to 18-year-old youngsters—the kids who are still there after about 29-30 percent have dropped out—our "successful" kids (not the at-risk kids, not the dropouts)—what percentage of those kids are able to *really* read something that's fairly difficult? What percentage of them can write a letter or an essay of one, two, three, four, [or] five pages and do a good job? What percentage of them can solve a two-step mathematical problem?
>
> Well, the answer is, depending upon whether you take reading, writing, math, or science, the percentage of those still in school at age 17 and about to graduate who are able to function at that top level is: three, four, five, or six percent.
>
> *Three, four, five, or six percent.*
>
> The percentage of those able to write [a] one or two-paragraph letter with lots of errors in it is only 20 percent. In other words, 80 percent of those who have *not* dropped out cannot even write two paragraphs loaded with mistakes [that express] a single idea. . . .
>
> What it means, translated into very rough and nasty terms, is that the overwhelming majority of kids who go to college in the United States would *not* be accepted in any institution of higher education anywhere in the world.
>
> Probably about 90-95 percent of our kids going to college could not get into college elsewhere. They can only get into college here—because we have relatively low standards for college entry compared to all those other countries. . . .
>
> Every American teacher knows that at the end of this year, at the end of next year, and finally with the SATs, my kids are never going to have to write an essay. They're never going to have to organize their thoughts. They're never going to have to worry about how to express themselves. They're merely going to need a passive knowledge of which things to knock out and which one or two to guess from. . . .

THE BIG BOOK OF HOME LEARNING — VOLUME I

137

We need different examinations. We don't write essays here because we've spent all of our lives taking these idiotic multiple-choice examinations. In every other country in the world, the teacher knows, "I'm preparing my kids to succeed, and to succeed means that the kids I'm teaching are going to have to sit for two, three, four, or five days and write essay examinations."

Preach it, brother Shanker! The moral is that we'd better make *sure* Junior can really read and write, and the only way to be sure of this is to have him (1) read aloud to us and narrate back what he read, (2) write out answers to science and history questions, (3) write letters, essays, poems, and stories as part of his regular school work—and have them corrected, and (4) regularly solve intricate math word problems. This kind of informal "testing" will tell you more about what your child really knows than ten tons of computer-graded standardized tests. Then, if your child can, by age 17, consistently solve two-step math problems and write an error-filled two paragraphs that make sense, you will know that he's in the top 20 percent of American schoolchildren. If he can write a decent two-page essay, you'll know he's in the top 2 percent. And if he can write a letter of application to Oxford University that doesn't cause gales of laughter in their Admissions Department, you'll know he's off the scale for our stateside tests.

TESTS PARENTS CAN USE

The bad news is that at present I know of no source that provides and grades essay-question tests. (Anyone out there want to start a business providing them?) The good news is that you won't have any trouble at all getting your children tested with nationally-normed tests (the kind that we all do so well on but that won't get us into Oxford University). Here's how to do it.

The easiest way to run your children through a standardized test is to have them tested at a nearby private school. Your children just come to school on the day everyone is tested, do their thing, and then you take them home. The fee for this service is usually nominal. Be sure the private school is friendly to home schoolers before you ask to do this.

Virtually every home-school program includes testing. Some, like Alpha Omega, include both diagnostic and standardized achievement tests. So if you sign up for one of these programs, your testing problem is solved. Look in the Curriculum Buyer's Guide for more info.

Below are some other test options specifically designed for or commonly used by home schoolers. These can be valuable for parents of schooled children also, especially if you have reason to question the results from the school's own testing.

Alpha Omega Publications
Student Testing Kit, $10. Parent Starter Kit, $19.95.

Designed for use with AOP's Parent Starter Kit, their Student Testing Kit includes: • Parents' Testing Manual with complete answer key, grading information, and word list for reading tests • Language Arts diagnostic testing manual that covers several grades, keyed to AOP's LIFEPAC levels • Math diagnostic testing manual, ditto • four Student Record books for grade-keeping • Parents' Cumulative File, with health and medical history records, yearly progress record, permanent transcript, achievement test profile, and high school academic projection form. Three kits are available: • First and Second Grade Kit (students have learned to read) • Third to Eighth Grade Kit (students have completed second grade) • Ninth to Twelfth Grade Kit (students have completed eighth grade).

Bob Jones University Press
Mental abilities tests, $10 each. Achievement tests, $20 each. Test set combining the two, $25 each. Order by grade as per instructions on order form. Achievement tests for grades 1 and 2, specify first or second semester. Phone or write for info and/or order form.

BJUP's Academic Skills Evaluation Program uses the Iowa Test of Basic Skills to test academic achievement for grades 1-8 and the Tests of Achievement and Proficiency for high schoolers. Also available for grades 3-12 only is the Cognitive Abilities test, "a test to appraise reasoning ability that yields verbal, non-verbal, and quantitative evaluation scores."

In order to administer the test you must either be (1) currently certified as a teacher by a national or state organization, (2) a graduate of a four-year college program, or (3) a current teacher in an operating conventional school. These requirements were established in conjunction with the test provider.

For test security reasons, the tests can only be mailed to the qualified tester, and all testing materials including answer sheets must be returned within 60 days of receipt to BJUP for scoring and interpretation. You get back an analysis of the results in four to six weeks.

The tests themselves take quite a long time. You will need to spend several hours reading the instructions carefully before giving the tests. Then you and your students need to set aside an hour or two a day for a week during which you will be giving the tests. This extra time investment, however, results in much more accurate results.

We have personally used Bob Jones testing for several years now and are quite pleased with the results. Since these are the same tests used in many public and private schools, with the same fill-in-the-boxes-with-number-two-pencil interface, our children are learning test-taking skills they might need later on. They are also being evaluated against a huge group of public-school children, so we have a good idea where they stand relative to this group. The returned scores break down the children's results into specific enough areas that we can see exactly what areas are weak or strong—e.g. capitalization, punctuation, map-reading.

Hints: Be *sure* to follow ordering instructions carefully to insure you get the proper grade-level test for your child. Call Bob Jones University Press (800-845-5731) if you have questions about which test to order. You might also do better to plan on testing in the late spring and summer. During the months of April and August test scores returned will not only include grade placement and percentile rankings, but an "item analysis of test results" as well. This item analysis pinpoints your student's strong and weak areas and provides other useful information.

Bureau of Educational Measurements
Most tests in $1 to $20 price range. Typical specimen set $6 to $16. Scoring services available.

This is it! Piles and piles of tests now available to home schoolers and other parents! The BEM has been in business since 1914 and was one of the first testing companies in the world. For the past few years it provided testing materials for home schoolers in the Northwest. Due to positive response, they have decided to expand their services to other parts of the USA and to Canada.

Unlike most major testing corporations, which only sell tests in bulk, the BEM will let you buy any number or combination of tests from their catalog. All you have to do is fill out the Purchaser Qualification Statement certifying that you are qualified to administer tests (keep in mind that thousands of public-school teachers have never received an official course on the tests *they* administer) and return with your test order. On approval of your request, your materials will be shipped. If for some reason the BEM does not believe you qualify, they will recommend ways for you to obtain approval in the future.

BEM carries all the most popular achievement tests (California Achievement Test, Iowa Test of Basic Skills, Metropolitan Achievement Test, and Stanford Achievement Test), Mental Ability tests (including the Peabody Picture Vocabulary Test), vocational aptitude and preference surveys, personality tests, math and reading tests, plus a number of tests developed by Emporia State University (with which it is affiliated).

Covenant Home Curriculum
K-3, $14.50 each grade. Grades 4-12, $18.50 each grade. Indicate grade level just completed.

Covenant Home Curriculum sells many review and self-test materials. They also carry their own C.H.A.T. Little Windows on Progress series (Covenant Home Achievement Tests). These are meant to give you an accurate reading of your child's grade level equivalence in the two main academic areas of math and language. The tests are easy to administer, taking only thirty minutes for each of the two sections. Scoring by Covenant Home Curriculum staff is included.

The C.H.A.T. series is partially patterned after the sample SAT national standards and grade levels. Standards are also based on curriculum levels established in *Warriner's English Grammar and Composition*, a standard work.

NEW★★
Hewitt Research Foundation
PASS test for grades 3-8, $24. MAT (readiness-grade 12), $30. MAP complete battery (grades 5-9), $35. Kuder General Interest Survey (grades 7-12), $15. 3R's Achievement test (grades 3-8), $30. 3R's Achievement and Abilities Test, $35. Cognitive Abilities Test (grades 5-8), $25. TAP, Complete Battery (grades 9-12), $25. Lower prices on MAT for enrolled students.

This is something new! Hewitt Research Foundation has, as you can see above, put together an impressive array of testing options for home schoolers. First among these is the Personalized Assessment Summary System (PASS). Like other achievement tests, PASS evaluates student achievement in reading, math, and language. Unlike the others, PASS was designed for you to give at home, and takes into account the type of individualized curriculum your child may have been studying.

PASS was "normed" (that is, calibrated for accuracy) using a standardized item bank. The difficulty of each question on the test was figured using a method developed by Danish mathematician Yorg Rasch. All items on any given test fall within a limited difficulty range, which presumably makes it easier to find gaps in learning.

The student taking the PASS first takes a placement test designed to find his or her approximate achievement level. The computer-scored results from the PASS test itself include suggestions for reaching goals in each subject area. You can also compare results with home school and national norms for that grade level.

The Hewitt testing brochure I saw did not give detailed descriptions of their other tests. These include the Metropolitan Achievement Test (MAT) and Tests of Achievement and Proficiency (TAP), as well as an IQ test and a vocational preference test. All of these except the PASS "must be administered by a certified teacher or professionally qualified person." I'm not sure what is meant by "professionally qualified person." If this means that you know enough not to cheat when giving the test and that you are able to interpret test results (about all that is hoped for from classroom teachers), almost everyone is qualified!

NEW★★
Lulli Akin
$30 for first student in family, $25 each additional student. Send in your name, phone number, address, and each child's name or grade, along with your check.

Now, for the first time, the elite Educational Records Bureau tests developed by an independent group of 1100 top private schools are available to families at home! Convinced of the need for tests that were not "dumbed down" and that would provide meaningful practice for the SAT and ACT tests, my friend Lulli Akin had embarked on a search that led her to the ERB. As Lulli says, "Through providential contact with several Christians in these schools, and their subsequent intercession for us to ERB, we were able to become a member school, although the ERB Headquarters had never heard of home schooling!"

Special advantages of the ERB tests:

• They are designed to be administered at home.
• They contain both aptitude (IQ) and achievement tests, so the student's ability can be compared with his actual achievement.
• They are modeled after college-entrance SAT and ACT tests, a feature of especial interest to college-bound high schoolers.
• The tests are totally confidential. Lulli gives your child a special code. The National Testing Service only gets that code, never your name or address.
• Your child is compared against four norm groups, rather than just the usual group of kids who took the test eight years ago. These groups are (1) National Norms—a sample of students from all types of schools nationwide, (2) Independent School Norms—students at independent schools that give ERB tests, (3), Suburban Norms—test results of public school districts that are ERB members, and (4) School Norms—tests results of those who obtained the ERB tests from Lulli, e.g., home schoolers.
• Detailed item analysis gives you a breakdown of your child's performance by subcategories within a topic. In plain English, this means that you will be told exactly what kind of errors (misuse of commas, for instance) your child is making and how many other children tested made the same kind of error.
• More academically challenging than other tests. Lulli says that in her experience the tests are about one year more advanced at each grade lev-

el than other standardized tests. This is important because academically-advanced children (such as home schoolers and those taught at tutor-oriented private schools, such as the ERB schools) tend to test "off the chart" on regular standardized tests. As Albert Shanker pointed out, knowing you did better than 95 percent of public-school kids may not mean all that much when those same public-school kids can't string together two decent paragraphs!

The one real disadvantage of the ERB tests is that you can only take them at one time of the year and you have to wait quite a while to get back the results. You may order the tests any time from January 1 on. You then take the tests and return them by May 1. Lulli batches the tests together and sends them in for scoring; you get the results at the end of June or beginning of July.

The ERB tests do not measure such things as research skills and map use, concentrating solely on classic SAT-tested skills and knowledge. The Iowa Test of Basic Skills from the Bob Jones University Press Academic Evaluation Program does measure such things, and its questions on those topics require higher-level thinking skills. So don't get the impression that all non-ERB tests are utterly worthless! We will be giving both the Iowa tests and ERB tests to our children this year.

READING TESTS

Educators Publishing Service
Introductory Set of Dyslexia Schedule (includes Schedule, School Entrance Check List, and Manual), $4.25. McCarthy IDRI: Info booklet $2.40, Teacher Administration booklet $6.50, pupil booklet $1.60, individual record forms (package of 12) $7.50.

EPS has all kinds of tests of reading ability and disability. Those they consider most relevant for home schoolers are the *Dyslexic Schedule School Entrance List* and *McCarthy Individualized Diagnostic Reading Inventory*.

The *Dyslexia Schedule* is a questionnaire designed to capture "relevant social and developmental information about any child who has been referred for special-

ist attention because of a reading disability." The most important questions from the *Dyslexia Schedule* are now printed separately as the *School Entrance List*, meant for routine survey and screening purposes. The idea here is to find out whether your child's reading difficulties stem from dyslexia (in which case he should demonstrate the common symptoms this test was designed to discover) or if the problem is something else. If the problem should be dyslexia, EPS has lots of materials to help. See the Reading chapters.

The *McCarthy IDRI* (named after its designer, William G. McCarthy, a professor of elementary education and department head at Indiana State University) can be used from grade 2 through adult and covers reading levels from primer through grade 12. "More than just another placement test," it deals with all areas of reading: accuracy, fluency, and comprehension, with the comprehension skills broken down and classified to aid in teaching. Teacher's and pupil's booklets are reusable. This test looks pretty good. The student reads a passage and you note any miscues. That gives you his reading level. Next, you interview him about the passage with comprehension questions that show how well he thinks about what he reads. Optional tests of phonics, word analysis, and study skills are also included.

TEST SCORE BOOSTERS

More and more public school providers are coming out with test preparation series. Students using these workbooks learn how to increase their test scores. It's really a pity that teachers are forced to spend the little classroom time they have that should be devoted to actual learning just prepping kids for tests. My friend Mildred, a public-school teacher, wishes she could spend classroom time on instruction, not test-taking skills, and there are many more like her.

However, since the public school kids are being groomed for test-taking, it behooves those of us in home-based private education to pull up our socks and make sure our students aren't lacking in this area. If your home-schooled child must take a test for some reason, he might need special training if tests are not a big part of your home curriculum.

College entrance tests and the G.E.D. are special cases worthy of special preparation. For that reason they have a chapter to themselves in Volume Three of this series. But for general-purpose test-taking skills, take a look at what the following companies have to offer.

NEW**
Frank Schaffer
Test Taking reproducible workbooks, $3.98 each for grades 1, 2, and 3.

Cute, nonthreatening workbooks with practice tests in reading, language, and math. Tests use the same format as the regular public school standardized tests. The workbooks are designed to help children learn how to record the information they already know, not to teach them new academic skills. Even the most test-phobic child will warm up to these workbooks from this popular publisher of elementary-school enrichment material.

Learning at Home
Set of teacher and student books, $10.25. Separate student books, $3.50 each. Shipping $2.50, orders under $20; $3 orders over $20.

Although, as I said, many public school providers offer test-taking series, I'm only going to mention one elementary grades test prep series here. *Scoring High* is a "full program of instruction in test taking skills and strategies. *Scoring High* is a proven practical series that has already helped millions of first through eighth grade students improve their test taking ability."

You can get *Scoring High* for the California Achievement Test, the Comprehensive Test of Basic Skills, or the Metropolitan Achievement Test. These are the three biggies. You can also get preparation help for 10 other standardized tests, including six at the high school level, and the all-important GED and SAT. (For more info on the latter, see Volume Three.)

Learning at Home is a company for home schoolers, and is glad to take your small order, which is why I suggest you buy your test prep materials there.

CHAPTER EIGHTEEN

RECORD-KEEPING

Remember the lady who wrote the *I Hate to Cook Book?* I'm thinking of writing a sequel: the *I Hate to Plan Book.* By far the most tedious part of home schooling is the record-keeping. It's not so bad if you have only one child and a lot of free time. But when you have three . . . or four . . . or five . . . or ten, all using different materials at different grade levels, keeping records can be a bit, shall we say, time-consuming?

What makes it worse are all those cheery columns in home-school newsletters written by moms who apparently stay awake 24 hours a day. They can reel off every activity each child has done in the past five years. They have neat binders full of completed art-work (at *my* house, it usually gets stepped on or wrinkled by the baby before it gets into a folder!). *Their* children's workbooks never get dog-eared or scribbled over by the toddler. *They* never find themselves at 2 A.M. staring at a planning journal and trying to remember what everyone was doing for the past week. *Their* library book lists are always up to date; they can tell you every book Johnny ever read, starting with *The Cat in the Hat.* Of course, they also have plenty of time for enriching field trips, during which the children happily write in their own well-organized journals.

I have come to the conclusion that some of us were born ABC types—Artistic, Bohemian, and Creative (translation: disorganized) and others were born with a silver To-Do list clutched in their baby fingers. Then all the organized people, once they grow up, develop wonderful organizing systems that only work for *other* organized people. You know the kind of system I mean: 25 cleverly designed planning pages for organizing everything from your shoes to your daughter's wedding, plus hundreds of To Do lists by year, month, week, and day (the latter divided into neat 15-minute chunks).

These organizers meet a real need, since organized people go bonkers if they don't know exactly where everything is and exactly what they are supposed to be doing every single minute. But for disorganized people, they are a disaster. The guilt! The mess!

Ever see one of those organizers after an ABC type gets hold of it? Scratched-out lists, arrows pointing from the day she *intended* to do the project to another day she *hopes* she will get to it . . . then to *another* day, and another . . . The problem is that we ABC's are always coming up with *new* projects we didn't plan into our cute little schedules. These throw the whole system off, which makes us feel miserable.

It only gets worse when we try to keep home-school records. Now we have a fruitful opportunity to mess up other people's schedules as well—namely, our beloved children. If Johnny misses his history lesson on Monday because he got too involved in an art project, and Suzy takes two days to do her English assignment instead of one, already our lesson plans for the week are a mess. If, on top of this, we are trying to use the unit study approach, in which a single activity integrates many different school subjects, and our state likes to see records organized by school subject, the resulting record-keeping decisions can produce mental paralysis. I know; I've been there!

So you can believe me when I tell you that I have *intensely* searched for record-keeping and lesson-planning methods and materials that work for disorganized people. Along the way, of course I found some wonderful organizers for the organized; but I also have finally found some wonderful organizers for The Rest of Us. Now my life is still a disorganized mess, but at least the records look good!

LESSON PLANNING FOR ORGANIZED PEOPLE

NEW**
Mountain Meadow Press
Home School: Taking the First Step, by Borg Hendrickson, 323 pages, 1989, $14.95 postpaid. Three appendices, glossary, index.

Home School: Taking the First Step is a very organized tome designed to get you mentally and otherwise organized. The heart of the book is the very detailed step-by-step instruction in how to prepare and keep your home-schooling records, complete with checklists and sample forms. Author Borg Hendrickson's detailed approach will work best for already neat and organized people. These folks will end up with impeccable records impressive to school officials.

I'd advise reading this book *before* you have to decide what record-keeping system you will use, as deciding what parts (if any) of Borg's very complete system you want to use will take a while.

LESSON PLANNING FOR DISORGANIZED PEOPLE

NEW**
Light of Faith Christian Academy
Lesson Planning with the Card File System, $3 postpaid. Foreign orders, $4.50.

If you like to plan lessons in advance, or if your state requires lesson plans, this is a really easy-to-use method that will get you organized. Each lesson plan fits on a single index card, and you will be able to see

instantly where each child is in each book or program. By using cards you also are freed from the tyranny of having to do any particular thing on any particular day just because it is written down in a planning block somewhere. Cards can be added or subtracted as inspiration strikes or wanes. The author has designed the system so children can even use the lesson plans by themselves, and your lesson plans for one child can be reused by the next when he gets to that level. The system shows what book you were using, what pages, what teacher input is needed, and what grade or evaluation you gave to the work. If you have to write out the dreaded "Lesson Objective" you can also do it on the card, especially if you are using 4 x 6's. It can't be any simpler than this, and at the price, why not learn how it works?

RECORD-KEEPING AIDS

Of course, the *real* record-keeping aid we all need is a faithful servant who will follow the children around and write down every thing they do. Failing that, here is one very helpful set of clever tools designed to save those who give grades from going crazy.

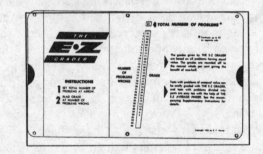

NEW**
E-Z Grader
E-Z Grader, $3.50. Long-Ranger E-Z Grader, $2.50. E-Z Average Finder, $3.50. E-Z Weighted Grade Finder, $3.50. Add 10% shipping, $1 minimum.

The E-Z Grader line is a set of nifty little devices for computing grades, averages, and the like. The original E-Z grader operates like this. Pull out the cardboard tab on the side until the total number of problems on the test shows in the little box. Then find the total number of problems wrong, and read off the grade percent (based on 100 percentile). Works with any number of questions up to 95. Example: 67 total problems with 15 wrong yields a grade of 78 percent. It just took me one second to figure that out using E-Z Grader!

If you like to give tests or assignments with *more* than 95 problems (you nasty you!), or if your student tends to get more than 34 wrong at a time (not likely!) you need the Long-Ranger E-Z Grader. This clever device is a circle within a circle. You turn the inside circle until the arrow points to the total number of problems in a cutout window, then read off the answer on the outer circle that corresponds to the number of problems wrong. It uses logarithmic scales, so can go up to 200 problems. Example: 160 problems with 45 wrong rounds off to 72 percent. *That* only took a second, too!

Since figuring grades on a single test or assignment is only a fraction of the work involved in grade-keeping, E-Z Grader also offers an Average Finder. First you add up the grades. Next, move the inner card until the number of grades to be averaged appears in the little box opposite the arrow. Find the answer opposite the sum of grades that appears in one of the windows on the card. This also takes only a second.

OK. You have average grades in a variety of course segments (homework, quizzes, tests, essays, class participation). Now if you really want to get fancy you need the Weighted Grade Finder. This is also simple to operate. You find the average grade for a segment of the course (e.g., an average of 93 percent on homework). Decide what weight you want to give the homework grades (say, 40 percent). Move the indicator bar until it registers at 40 percent, find the average grade on the outer card, then read off the weighted average (in this case, 37.2) in the inner window. Do this for all the parts of your course, add up the weighted grades, and there's your total grade! Example: For the student who got a 93 percent average on homework (weighted at 40 percent of the grade), an 88 percent average on daily quizzes (weighted at 40 percent) and a 94 on the final test (weighted at the remaining 20 percent of the grade), you would end up with a weighted average of 91.2. That took me a big thirty seconds to figure out, using a calculator to add the weighted averages. Compare that to the head-scratching you'd have to go through using pencil and paper, and then multiply it by several kids in several subjects, and you'll see why the Weighted Grade Finder is so popular!

Each E-Z Grader is made of durable white cardboard die-cut, printed in two colors, and securely fastened together with small metal studs. These inexpensive aids are meant to stand up to rough classroom handling.

The bottom line is this: from now on all your grade calculations can be done using nothing but the adding function of your calculator and a durable cardboard E-Z Grader. Millions sold, and now you know why.

ORGANIZERS FOR ORGANIZED PEOPLE

UPDATED**
Alpha Omega Publications
Bob Jones University Press
Time Minder,™ includes binder, $29.95. Refill package, $17.95, only available to organizer buyers. 20% discount on refills with coupon in book.

An easy-to-use traditionally-styled organizer for home-schooling families who like to keep it relatively simple is Marilyn Rockett's Time Minder™ Alpha Omega Publications and Bob Jones University Press both carry this attractive organizer.

The Time Minder™ includes four sections, all tabbed on the side for easy reference. A brief section at the beginning gives simple, clear instructions in how to use the organizer.

Section 1, Long-Range Planning, includes the year-at-a-glance calendar, on which you can mark your school year and holidays using the little codes at the bottom of the page. On the back of the calendar is a place to mark special occasions. The second form, the Year Beginning Evaluation, includes four pages for four individual family members. On the flipside of this form is the Year Ending Evaluation. Next come the goal-setting pages, four sheets with room for four goals on each. Last in this section is the Curriculum Plan and Info sheet. Just as in CLW's organizer, this is a place to make notes and write addresses of suppliers you are thinking of using.

Section 2, Schedule, is your home organizer. On the first form you write down everything you need to schedule, broken down into daily, weekly, semimonthly, monthly, quarterly, and annual. On the flipside is your basic schedule form. Next comes the Monthly Planner: 12 sides of paper marked with days but not dates, so you can pick up the organizer and start with it at any time of the year. To Do Today, perhaps the most useful form of all, has one column for calls to make and one for meal planning. Two sheets cover one week, in the standard week-at-a-glance format, and you get enough pages for a year. You get a priority column and a check-off column as well. A handy snap-out ruler/tab can be used to mark your place. (You can buy extra rulers!) Last comes four pages of Holiday Planning sheets.

Section 3, School, has a flexible weekly lesson planner (you define the squares however best suits you), Grade/Goal Summary pages (with instructions for use by people who do not give letter grades), Testing forms, Books Read pages, Field Trip Plans, and Special Projects pages.

The last section, printed on heavier paper for durability, is a combination address and phone directory and four-year Christmas card record, plus a People and Resources section.

The new edition has seven new reproducible Master Copy forms: a Journal Page (usable by both kids and adults), Household Responsibilities (very handy—lists work assignments down the side and family members across the top), Mom's Memos (info for baby-sitter), Attendance Record (for states that require it), Student Assignments (a more flexible format that I would personally use to replace the lesson plan pages), Health Record, and Proposed Project/Idea Planner.

Each family has permission to copy extra forms as needed for your own use, so larger families can make enough forms for all family members.

This planner is easy to use, easy to customize, and covers the areas most home schoolers need most.

UPDATED**
Christian Life Workshops

The Home School Family's Complete Household Organizer by Gregg and Sono Harris. 250 pages, with divider tabs in 3-ring binder. $34.95 plus $3.50 shipping. Upgrade packet available for purchasers of original edition.

Here is an extremely complete organizer designed to help Christian families set up a methodical schedule of family ministry and home schooling. It is designed as a tool to help people get into that mindset.

CLW's organizer has a system of major and minor planning keys that allows you to jot only key references on the month-at-a-glance or weekly planner sections. Details are recorded only once, on the Planning/Record sheets.

Now, what do you get? An inspiring introduction on the adventure of family ministry and 13 tabbed sec-

tions. Each section includes blue Master Copies (store and save these), and enough white copies for your first year's use.

Let's look at these one by one.

1) Household Management. Master sheets only. You get a Weekly Menu Planner with a clip-off shopping list, a Recreation Planner (this sheet is my idea of being overorganized!), Lending Library Book Marks sheet, and Borrowing/Lending Record.

2) Personal Records. This includes master sheets only for personal study recording, an Idea Keeper, reading list, and Reading Review sheet. The latter would be quite helpful to any budding author or speaker, since it gives you room to record strong passages to remember, quotable quotes, and bibliographic references, plus your thoughts about the book. You photocopy as many of each of these as you find helpful.

3) The Weekly Planner. Fifty-two sheets. One side covers Phone Calls to Make and Letters to Write, Things To Do (broken down by personal, home school, business, hospitality, and civil influence), Appointments (by day: includes a space for a Bible text), a very complete Household Maintenance chart that gives you an open-ended list of possible maintenance activities for each location plus codes that tell you at a glance whether the job is assigned or done, Projects to Complete, Items to Obtain, and Projects to Plan.

4) The Monthly Planner. Each month covers two sides of the sheet: Sunday through Tuesday plus a column listing the Planning Keys, on one side, and the rest of each week on the other. There's also a section for Notes and Events to Plan. At the end of this section are five Notes to Remember pages, cross-keyed back to the Monthly Planner pages.

5) The Daily Checklist holds a very complete Baby-sitting Instruction Sheet, as well as holding kids accountable for their hygiene, devotions, and personal and family chores. You're going to want to make a lot of copies of this sheet!

6) Family Business. Six Master Pages. One page records names, addresses, and phone numbers of advisors and professionals. There is also an Estate Net Worth Worksheet (find out the sorry truth!), a Household Budget Planner, Auto Maintenance Record, and a Record of Generosity. The Home Business Venture Planning/Report Sheet works better as a take-off point than a sheet to fill out.

7) Church. For personal/family Bible study and sermon recording.

8) Hospitality. Master Pages only. The Guest Room Planning Record is the most useful of these six planning sheets.

9) Civil Influence. Five Master Pages. The most useful ones here are the Prayer List for Those in Authority and the sheet for you to fill out with political and media contacts.

10) The Household Profile Sheet. A place to write down important facts like your passport numbers; vehicle make, ID, and license numbers; children's birthdates, blood types, Social Security and driver's license numbers; where to find your insurance policies, what each policy number is and who your agent is; bank information; and emergency contacts.

11) Home Schooling Plans and Records. Forty pages of Weekly Lesson Plan sheets. Each has room for basic comments, six subjects (you could squeeze in seven kids under each subject), and lesson planning codes down the side so you can condense your info into the smallest possible space. This section also includes eight Quarterly Attendance and Grades by Subject sheets.

12) Home School Helps. Another section with Master Pages only. Some of these sheets are helpful, some are more work than they are worth. Quite helpful is the Weekly Assignments sheet—copy up bunches of these and use them to help your children form independent study habits.

13) The Directory. Two Master Pages. Your basic name/address/phone number sheets.

The organizer comes in a three-ring binder, complete with a full year's worth of materials. You can use it practically forever, because every buyer has permission to reproduce the entire organizer for personal use only for the rest of his life. At year's end, just pop the entire year's organizer in an envelope and

there are your school records for the year in easy-to-find order. Use your Copy Masters to reproduce the new year's sheets, click them into your binder, and you're ready to roll again.

Notice that the CLW organizer does provide schedule and chore sheets for the children, making it a true household (not just parent) organizer. Also, because it is reproducible, large families will have enough sheets for everyone.

This organizing system takes some time to master—learning the codes for the planning keys and what goes where. You probably won't use *all* the sections: select the ones you need now and leave the rest for later.

Once you cut the organizer down to size this way you wind up with a useful planning tool that covers many areas others don't. CLW promises you will like it or you get your money back.

NEW**
Home School Supply House
Instructor Daily Planner, $3.55. Shipping extra.

Here is your basic teacher's planning book. 88 pages, spiral-bound, room for 180 school days.

Reliable Corporation

Reliable is the office supply company with whom we do most of our business. Besides a terrific assortment of inexpensive time-minding equipment (average price of a monthly planner ranges from $2-$5) and project planning charts (we have one on our study wall), Reliable also carries all the paper, pencils, lamps, desks, chairs, file cabinets, index cards, flip-top files, and so on that you are ever likely to need—all at deep discounts. If you'd like to *really* get organized and the old-fashioned methods work for you, Reliable has the stuff.

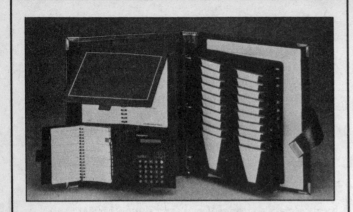

ORGANIZERS FOR CHILDREN AND DISORGANIZED PARENTS

NEW★★
The Executive Gallery
"Traditional Organizer" in vinyl, $39.95. "Budget Organizer," $19.95. "Chairman" in vinyl, $99.95. "ScheduleMate II" in vinyl, $69.95. Extra ScanCard Project Cards, $9.95/500. Lots more models available. Shipping extra.

This is the system I personally use to keep track of our various home businesses, writing projects, household planning, and so forth.

Unlike other planning systems, the ScanCard system uses *cards*. You write the project name of top of a card, jot down whatever you want to remember to do, and stick it in one of the pockets of your organizer. Every day you quickly scan all your cards to see what ought to be done next.

Like most really useful inventions, the ScanCard system happened almost by accident. Founder Marvin Williams was fed up with project lists and overstructured time management systems. So he developed a system of filing project cards into staggered pockets, with the project name peeking out on top. Everywhere he went, his fellow businessmen wanted one. Getting the hint, Mr. Williams formed a product line featuring these organizers, and so far he has sold almost a million.

For myself, the ScanCard system's best feature is that it is not tied to particular dates and times. Instead of writing in the date and time you intend to do a project, you just write the project down on a card. Then, when interruptions inevitably mess up your schedule, you don't have to cross out boxes on your calendar, draw little lines back and forth between pages, and so on. No guilt, no pain, no projects forgotten because they weren't done on the right day and you forgot to write them in again on a later page. If you need to do something by a certain date, just say so on the card. The card format also makes it super-easy to add or subtract projects.

It would take too much space to list all the different styles, colors, and bindings in which ScanCard comes. So here are the most popular:

• The Traditional Organizer "is made to fit the needs and budgets of most people—executives and professionals, homemakers, teachers, students, and the clergy." It is 9x12" and only about 3/4 inch thick. Inside its two covers you find on the left 24 ScanCard pockets and a small year-at-a-glance calendar that sits in a plastic pocket of its own just beneath those pockets. On the right is a yellow legal pad, a one-sheet phone/address index on thick stock with room for 100 names that becomes visible when you flip forward the legal pad, and a "TrapFile" vinyl pocket behind it all where you can hold important papers. In between is a narrow little pocket where you can keep your pen or pencil. It comes with 500 ScanCard project cards.

• The Budget Organizer has heat-sealed edges (instead of hand-sewn and reinforced like the Traditional Organizer) and 250 ScanCard project cards instead of 500.

• The Chairman of the Board is the deluxe model. It comes with three ScanCard panels which handle up to 120 projects, and is expandable (with purchase of additional panels) to a total of 200 projects. It also has an appointment calendar, phone index, built-in multi-function calculator, business and credit card compartments, and concealed pocket files for important papers, plus everything included in the Traditional model. It comes with 500 ScanCard project cards.

• ScheduleMate II is a 3-ring binder. Each panel has a row of pockets for ScanCard project cards on the left and a linear calendar pad on the right. The basic system comes with a supply of four 12-month calendar pads, but you can also get seven-day week, 24-hour diary, and 52-week year pads. The whole system is expandable from 40 projects to 100, so you can set it up with a weekly "To Do" panel, a daily "To Do" panel, a yearly long-range planning page, and a monthly project planning page, all in the same binder. It comes with 500 ScanCard project cards.

If you need something bigger and better, Executive Gallery has expandable executive models. If you're into designer chic, you can get a thin European model in glove leather or a variety of models in cowhide leather. If, like me, you're into survival, there's always the basic (and surprisingly durable) vinyl models. If you need specialized planning cards, they have those too. Something for everyone!

We like these systems so much that we carry the basic models in our own Home Life catalog.

NEW★★
Home Life
"Traditional Organizer," $39.95. "Budget Organizer," $19.95. "Chairman," $99.95. Shipping, add $5 per organizer. Various colors available. Personalization available on all organizers except Budget model. Accessories also available.

Home Life is my own home business. We carry the basic ScanCard systems mentioned above, with a little extra—our own special instructions on how to set up the systems to organize your home management, home business, and home schooling.

The beauty of this system is that you can keep your personal, business, home, and ministry projects *all in the same place.* My own organizer at the moment has a "To Call" card, several project cards for writing projects, a Sunday school card, a Yard card, a Christmas and Birthday card, a Shopping card, cards for some long-range dreams, and project cards for each of our home business projects. Bill's organizer is full of business and ministry projects. The children's organizers have cards for their home-school assignments, chore cards, shopping cards, business project cards, and so on.

Can the ScanCard system be used for home-school lesson planning? You bet! One organizer per child would do it, as well as leaving space for Junior to do his own kid's business and chore planning. Then just save the completed project cards (we show you how to set them up) and you have a complete "paper trail" of your home-schooling activities for legal purposes. Our "How to Use the ScanCard System at Home" booklet (available exclusively through Home Life and included free with each organizer purchase) explains exactly how to set up your organizer for home schooling, home business, household management, home ministry, and so on.

We recommend the Chairman model for business owners, the Traditional model for children (it's more durable than the Budget model) and most other uses, and the Budget model for those who really need to save money, don't care if their organizers are personalized, and are prepared to treat them gently.

NEW★★
Home School Supply House
"My Learning Logbook," $7.95. Blank Books, $4.98 each. Shipping extra.

"My Learning Logbook," a Home School Supply House exclusive, includes "Read," "Create," and "Explore" sections where you can write down what you've done, plus places to summarize what you've accomplished each month. It comes in a sturdy three-ring binder with five dividers, plastic sheet-protectors for artwork or writing samples, and an info sheet that tells you how to use it. Looks good for a child's own record-keeping system. Blank Books, hardbound 5-1/2 x 8-1/4" books with ruled pages, are another source of free-form record-keeping. Choice of three cover designs for the latter.

NEW★★
Kaye McLeod
Daily/School Planner, $5.95 each plus $2 shipping.

Here's a one-year planner for children aged five to twelve years old. It's an 18 x 24" color poster with an set of 12 undated monthly planners in the middle. Around the edges are lines for Phone Numbers of Special People, Special Days to Remember, My Jobs Around the House, What I Can Do to Help Others, Things I Need Help With, Things I Need to Practice, and My Achievements and Rewards. Cute, motivating, and inexpensive!

NEW★★
Pennsylvania Homeschoolers
Plan-It, $9.95 postpaid.

Susan Richman raves about the *Plan-It* teacher's planning/record book in her *The Three R's at Home.* After suffering for a while with a standard teacher's plan book she picked up at the local office supply store, she decided she just *had* to have something she could use for all her varied organizing needs: lists, addresses, ideas, brainstorms . . . Neither spiral notebooks nor homemade booklets did it for her, until she found (ta-dah!) *Plan-It for Teachers: A Comprehensive Planning Tool,* designed by teacher Richard Glaubman. This is a hand-lettered book with all sorts of extras and room for a full school year's records. Susan improved her personal version by punching holes in all the pages and inserting the book in a three-ring binder. Now she can add in oaktag pockets for memorabilia and extra information, slip her piano practice charts in the back, and so on.

I asked Susan to send me a copy of this jewel of a book so I could check it out for myself. She very graciously did so. Looking it over, I noted that you get ten months' worth of records, not twelve. This works fine for those of us who like to take it easy in the summer, but year 'rounders need to know they'll come up two months short.

The book is indeed easy to use. You start each month by filling out the undated monthly calendar and filling in the activities and special events for that month. On the backside of the blue monthly sheet is an overview of each month with weekly priority lists. Then each week you fill out four pages:

1) A page that lists your daily goals, special projects/events, and materials needed for each day of the school week, plus an appointments and "phone calls to make" block for each day.

2) Morning lesson plans (three blocks per day plus a space for "problems and evaluations"). The blocks are big enough to hold two or three children's lesson plans at once, if you write small.

3) Afternoon lesson plans (same format as morning).

4) In Susan's words, "A nice friendly page after each week's little [planning] boxes where you're invited to put down notes about students, problems, concerns, opportunities, and successes, goals needing more attention, and spin-off ideas."

If you need to prepare individual lesson plans for four or more children you'll need more than one *Plan-It.* (You might want to buy one per child anyway, just to have the extra planning space.)

Plan-It is designed to work best with regular *weekly* planning. Like other fill-in-the-block planners, if you get too far ahead and then get off schedule, you'll have a mess. Also, if you tend to do more than three subjects or activities per morning or afternoon, this is probably not the planning tool for you. Otherwise, *Plan-It* is definitely a breeze to fill in and use.

CHAPTER NINETEEN

AFTERSCHOOLING AND OTHER OPTIONS

Not all home-school families necessarily think of themselves as home schooling. My father, for example, didn't think he was home schooling me when he taught me reading and math. It was just a fun thing we did together.

Some of the options in home schooling, beyond choices of educational method, are:

- Total home schooling. Parents take full responsibility for the children's instruction until they are grown.
- Transitional home schooling. The children's early school years are spent at home, with the understanding that later on they will make the transition to formal school (whether college, high school, or third grade).
- Supplemental home schooling. The children are enrolled in school, but Mom and Dad realize they need more, or different, instruction than they receive there. So on evenings, weekends, vacations, or special days off from school, parents and children study together.

The first two options are generally well understood. Most families fall into category two, the transitional home schoolers. The third option, supplemental home schooling, is still valid for many situations, although it does not receive as much attention because it does not conflict with public officials' perception of the compulsory attendance statutes.

Some parents have found it possible to make creative use of their school districts' truancy laws to partially home school their children. If a child is not considered "absent" if he leaves at 1:30, then a parent could conceivably remove him at that time every day without infringing on the school's attendance policy. If departure after 10:30 is considered only 1/2 of an absence, and parents are allowed up to 25 parent-caused absences a year, that can add up to an awful lot of days mostly spent at home. And then there are long family trips (which are not illegal). Some families (not many) live a nomad life precisely to be able to home school without hassles.

When the parents have no fundamental quarrel with the school's policies, but merely feel that their children need additional help in a particular subject area, supplemental home schooling makes a lot of sense.

The subject reviews in this book were designed to help home schoolers *and* those attempting supplemental home schooling.

Beyond total, transitional, or supplemental home schooling, here are other options for parents and children:

• Directed home schooling is making an appearance. The children are enrolled in a "satellite" program of an existing school, or are otherwise taught under the supervision of a tutor. The tutor, or satellite program administrator, is not there to teach the children but the parents. He or she handles the satellite program records, orders curriculum, organizes support groups and field trips, helps the parents when educational problems arise, and in general provides both legal shelter and direction.

• Finally, you have the self-study option. Young people and adults can obtain accredited or unaccredited degrees from a wide variety of sources, studying at home on their own. (See the chapter on Adult Education.) Resourceful people can also learn quite a bit at the library, from "picking the brains" of other people, or by attending some of the numerous workshops, seminars, etc. that are constantly being given on any imaginable subject. This is a good way to learn how to cook or build a house. Self-study can work equally well in academic areas, for those who have mastered the "tools of learning."

So, you see, learning academics is the same as learning anything else. You can learn in the library, at home, in a classroom, or lying on the green grass under a chestnut tree. You can learn with friends, family, neighbors, total strangers, or all alone. You can be structured or unstructured, mellow or disciplined. Our own family has done most of the above at one time or other. The important thing is to *get started*. As they say, "A moving car is easier to steer." Start learning together or on your own, and you will soon discover what works best for you.

THE HOME SCHOOL CURRICULUM BUYER'S GUIDE

CHAPTER TWENTY

CURRICULUM GUIDES & OTHER HELPS

P arents totally committed to standard schooling (but not to standard results!). Parents considering "a little" home schooling or afterschooling. Parents who want to find out in exactly what topics Junior needs tutoring. Budget-minded home schoolers. For all of you, here are the simplest curriculum helps of all. Not strictly curriculum (no textbooks, workbooks, or complicated manuals), the following Teaching Guides and curriculum objective manuals provide you with a a starting point to do (or hire) your own teaching of the basic secular academic subjects. If you want to find out what Junior has been missing, or you know how to teach, this is the simplest and cheapest way to go.

For those of you who need a whole curriculum, we will be looking at unit studies and A-Z packaged curriculum in the next two chapters. Even if you will be using one of these two approaches, you might be interested in purchasing a curriculum guide. A curriculum guide will help you avoid "holes" in your unit study program, and give you an overview of what you are trying to teach in your purchased curriculum.

Community Learning Center/Explore Curriculum
$15 K-3 or 4-6. Both, $25 postpaid.

Very simple, easy-to-use list of curriculum objectives in logical order. Next to each numbered objective are two boxes for date assigned and date completed.

These are labeled by level, so you can see where you should expect to be.

Skill area objectives (reading, language arts, math) help you see where your student stands and what should come next. Content area objectives (science and social studies) suggest units of studies. For example, "Can locate some of the early settlements on the North American continent by Europeans"—list of these settlements follows. This would lead naturally into map work and historical study of the settlements. Another example: "Explain pollination." This could be accomplished through modeling, drawing, or the child telling you how pollination works. The third category, educational experiences, includes art, music, and physical education experiences the student should have in order to function as a well-rounded person. Example: "Can use clay or plasticine to produce human forms in various poses." "Familiar with the four periods of classical music and can name a composer for each." "Can catch a ball while running."

Some suggested objectives are quite open-ended, such as "Has own repertoire of familiar and well-loved music." Others are quite definite: the ability to define musical terms or famous historical personages.

This is probably the simplest "curriculum" to use for those who already know how to teach and know the subject areas. If all you need is an easy-to-follow guideline. the Explore curriculum is a bargain.

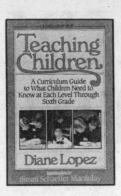

NEW**
Crossway Books
Teaching Children, $11.95

Teaching Children: A Curriculum Guide to What Children Need to Know at Each Level Through Sixth Grade by Diane Lopez is the third in the Child Light series published by Crossway Books. The first two books in the series, *For the Children's Sake* by Susan Schaeffer Macaulay and *Books Children Love* by Elizabeth Wilson were both enthusiastically received. This naturally created a lot of anticipation for *Teaching Children*.

The basic premise of *Teaching Children* is sound—to present a "Scope and Sequence" for each subject area based on the Charlotte Mason style of education. The Scope and Sequence you do get, with a tremendous amount of suggested topics of study, most following the standard public-school curriculum. However, *Teaching Children's* specifically Christian emphasis is not all I had hoped for. Apart from a brief re-hash of the Charlotte Mason methodology and some Christian literature selections, the topics often sound quite secular—e.g., the study of Occupations, which the public schools use to thrust careerism on little girls. The way these topics are studied also is often secular. So under Substance Abuse Prevention (a topic most home schoolers don't feel much need to meddle with), we find "Learn how to express feelings." Charlotte Mason never would have said that! Like the Bible, which says you conquer "drunkenness" (not "Substance Abuse"!) by being filled with the Holy Spirit, Charlotte Mason always stressed developing self-control, a love of the Lord, and habits of Christian character.

Those who expected the gentle approach of *For the Children's Sake* will be surprised at the tone of this book. Skills are rigidly divided into grade levels, par-

ents and teachers are told to do this and do that, and we find the passive tense widely employed (e.g., "It is recommended that . . ."). Again, this is far from Charlotte Mason's own approach to education. Another weakness: The "Developing a Christian Mind and Worldview" chapter is limited to resources put out by L'Abri workers. Yes, I know the Child Light people are all products in some way of L'Abri, the Christian fellowship founded in the Swiss Alps by Dr. and Mrs. Francis Schaeffer, but *Teaching Children* would have been a much stronger book if the author had been aware of the excellent work others not connected with L'Abri are doing in the area of Christian thinking and education.

The series of curriculum and teaching guides put out by Learning at Home is superior to *Teaching Children*, as they contain not only topics for study but how to teach them and why to teach them. For those who mainly want the Charlotte Mason approach, Ruth Beechick's how-to-teach books provide both input into what topics ought to be studied when and practical ideas that work beautifully with the Charlotte Mason philosophy.

NEW**
Kay Milow
Home Schooler's Complete Reference Guide, $25.

This spiral-bound 208-page oversized book is an encyclopedia of learning for K-6. Home-schooling mother Kay Milow draws on her experience teaching at both school and home to provide all the lists, rules, definitions, project ideas, and teaching tips you are likely to need for reading, English (including an extensive section on sentence diagramming), spelling, math, social studies, science, health, Spanish, and art. Everything is organized by subject in a sequential manner, so it is ultra-easy to use. Need to find a glossary of geometric terms? Information on noun suffixes? How to outline? Conservation projects? State abbreviations? Roman numerals? Basic math exercises using money? Irregular English verbs? Literature reading lists for each grade level? All this and tons more, plus sample exercises and projects and suggested library books to read for each topic, are in this one handy volume. You won't have any holes in your home curriculum if you diligently use this book. In fact, you may not *need* any home curriculum if you diligently use this book! As Jill Johnson of Waverly, Nebraska, a satisfied user of this book, says, "Kay's book, a set of encyclopedias and the occasional use of the public library are all you need."

Learning at Home

Teaching Guides are sold both as grade level sets of language arts, math, social studies, and science, or individually by subject area. Prices for the 4-subject Teaching Guide sets: grade 1, $40; grade 2, $44; grade 3, $48. Mixed grade level set (for a child who performs at different levels in different subjects), $44. Single subject Teaching Guide, between $11 and $13.75 each. Resource Units for upper elementary: grade 4, $35; grade 5, $36; Grade 6, $37.

So you say you don't need a lot of expensive services and fancy books? You say you just want a little help in figuring out what Johnny ought to be doing next and how to present it to him? Voila! Learning at Home has exactly what you need.

This medium-sized company offers professionally prepared Teaching Guides with Curriculum Outlines for grades 1-3 in language arts, math, social studies, and science—the four (often state-required) core areas. Hawaiian home schoolers have been successfully submitting Learning at Home guides for eight years to the Hawaii Department of Education.

Curriculum Outlines are written in "teacher talk," and their main purpose is to reassure the authorities that you seriously intend to teach your kids. They also serve as a Scope and Sequence to give you an overview of the skills the schools supposedly teach in that grade and the order in which you should teach them. The Teaching Guides, on the other hand, help you actually teach the stuff. Each new skill is covered step-by-step, so you know how it works and can explain it to your learners. This is all done in such a clean, taut style that you can't get lost along the way.

Let me tell you, these guides are *good*! I would recommend the Teaching Guides to any parents who are concerned about their children's education. By flipping through the "back issues"— i.e., the grades your little one has already finished—you can see very quickly if there are any weak spots, and what's more, you will have the information you need to correct the school's deficiencies right at your fingertips. By going through the Guide for your son or daughter's current grade, you can begin to take an active part in improving his or her education. All this for an absolutely rock-bottom price.

If you are using a unit-studies curriculum such as KONOS or Weaver, you might want to consider getting the math Teaching Guides from Learning at Home, and perhaps the language arts Guide for the grade as well. If you are clever at teaching and don't need a special phonics program, in this way you can provide a complete grade-school education for any number of children at a minimal cost.

Learning at Home now offers Resource Units for upper-elementary students (similar to the lower-grades Teaching Guides except that all four subjects are spiral-bound together). They also have branched out into offering a test preparation series (see the Testing chapter), a line of workbooks, and lots more supplementary material, from poetry anthologies to basic art courses. Write and ask to be put on their mailing list if you're interested.

Learning at Home's staff also provides counseling and standardized testing services for local (Hawaiian) home-schooling families, and tutoring for afterschoolers. If you live in their area, give them a call!

NEW**
The Weaver Curriculum

Skills Evaluation for the Home School, $15 plus 8% shipping.

Skills Evaluation for the Home School is a "framework of educational expectations" covering kindergarten through grade 6 by grade level and subject. You get 175 pages of detailed "what Johnny and Suzie should be able to do," with check-off boxes so you can see if they really are able to do it all. Few projects or activities are suggested (except at the kindergarten level), as you might expect in a publication put out by someone who has designed an entire unit study curriculum full of activities and projects! In other words, *Skills Evaluation* is best *not* used as a starting point for curriculum design, but as a way to check the success of whatever curriculum you are already using. Becky Avery, author of the Weaver curriculum and of this spiral-bound oversized book as well, suggests that you use *Skills Evaluation* three times a year (to oversee your progress) and also use it to prepare for year-end testing.

CHAPTER TWENTY-ONE

UNIT STUDIES: WHAT THEY ARE, HOW TO DESIGN ONE

Unit studies are hot among home schoolers today. I mean *hot*. Speakers criss-cross the country telling appreciative audiences that the unit study method of education is the best/only/God-given way to learn. Home-schooling publications print sample unit studies. Support groups meet to discuss and implement unit study co-ops.

So, what is a unit study?

Unit studies are what used to be called "integrated studies" or "multidisciplinary studies." It is also sometimes called the "project approach." The idea is to develop skills in many school subject areas at once by completing a series of questions or projects on a given topic. Instead of simply studying fractions, for example, Junior could make a double batch of oatmeal cookies, thus having the chance to measure and multiply fractional amounts of flour, shortening, sugar, and oatmeal. Of course, dedicated unit study fans would not stop there! Junior would also perhaps have to write out the doubled recipe (writing skills), do the baking and cleanup (home economics), and analyze the nutritional content of the recipe (health). From this activity he might springboard into, say, a study of the human digestive system (science) or the art of food presentation (art and culinary skills).

Unit study fans tend to look for real-life experiences which can be translated into academic experiences. Thus, a child traveling from Birmingham to St. Louis in the family car might be asked to keep a journal detailing types of transportation he saw along the way . . . or the geography of the terrain on the trip . . . or historical sites the family passed . . . or simply a chronicle of the family's adventures on the trip. Unit study fans also like to translate academic experiences into real-life experiences, by (for example) making Pilgrim and Indian costumes and having an authentic Thanksgiving feast.

Insofar as unit studies are actually based on how children and other people learn, they tend to involve searching out the answers to questions. Mr. Smith might become interested in adding a passive solar greenhouse to his home and thus start subscribing to magazines and reading books about solar energy and home design. One thing leads to another, and five years from now Mr. Smith might find himself the proud owner of twenty books on modern architecture, a home-remodeling program for his IBM PC, and even a new greenhouse! Along the way he would have become (or at least consider himself!) somewhat of an authority on solar energy, home remodeling, basic carpentry, how to deal with contractors, zoning laws, and so on. He didn't gain any of this knowledge through taking a course, but simply through pursuing his own interests.

One big advantage of unit studies, then, is that they force the student to discover new skills in order to answer his questions. You can't make a Pilgrim costume out of fabric without learning something about patterns and sewing. You can't order parts from model train catalogs without learning to read and fill out order forms. You can't bake oatmeal cookies without learning about fractional measurements. Kids who have stubbornly resisted formal school instruction universally break down and learn the needed skills on their own when they see that the skills are needed in order to complete a cherished project.

All this smacks of manipulation . . . but teasing stubborn learners along is not the real point of unit studies. Unit study fans firmly believe that the unit study approach connects kids with the real world, in which we do have to solve real problems with real skills and knowledge. Being able to solve real problems is what motivates adults to learn (so goes the theory), so why not kids? Also, unit studies prevent children from perceiving knowledge as some commodity divided up into subjects, since from the first they are gaily romping across subject boundaries.

Perhaps the biggest charm of unit studies is that, once you understand how they work, you can concoct an entire wide-ranging academic curriculum using almost no money. Anyone can do a unit study anywhere. Whether your child is in private school, public school, home school, or not even old enough for official school at all, there is always time and money for a unit study. The library alone is a virtually inexhaustible source of unit study material. So is the rag bag, the workshop, and the family kitchen! You can do as little or as much as you like. And by their very nature, unit studies can be tailored to fit your family's interests like a glove.

Here let me give a warning. *Some things need to be taught systematically and not by unit studies.* I would not want to try to teach math and grammar using nothing but unit studies. Unit studies are of most value when *reinforcing* the basic subjects. They can also be used to advantage as the sole source of social studies, history, science, and practical skills instruction, as these are all (to one extent or another) hands-on and topical subjects. Happily, the vast majority of home schoolers already understand this, and every packaged unit study curriculum stresses that math, phonics, and grammar must be studied separately and systematically.

The other thing to remember about unit studies is that they can easily degenerate into extended arts-and-crafts sessions that have precious little to do with any academic subject at all. Not every topic deserves the full-blown unit study treatment. We don't need to

spend a week crafting clever valentine containers out of shoeboxes in order to learn about Valentine Day. We don't need to collect all the large shoes we can find in order to spark creative writing projects centering around large shoes. (These were both actual projects suggested in a public-school-teachers magazine!) Reading and lectures are always quicker means of picking up basic knowledge, even if they lack the reinforcement and experiential value of a hands-on project.

Keeping all this in mind, how do you go about designing a unit study? Why not ask someone who has successfully used one? So I asked Christian home-schooling mom Julie Flanagan of San Diego, California, and she graciously gave me permission to reprint her wonderful description of how to design a unit study! Here is how the Flanagans did it.

"UNIT STUDIES" BY JULIE FLANAGAN

A unit study may develop from a question raised by a child.

"What causes earthquakes?"
"Why doesn't he like me?"
"Why can't I have some candy?"
"How much more money do I need before I can buy that toy?"
"How can you get to a place you've never been without getting lost?"
"How do we know what God wants us to do?"
"What does this word mean?"
"How far is it to Indiana?"

The unit study may last only a few minutes, or it may last a whole year. The study should begin in the Bible [Julie's Christian emphasis], proceed to word studies and language applications, and continue into a project, major or minor. Make as many analogies to other fields as you can. Think of things to do. Find books on the subject. Pursue the topic as long as there is an interest and a need, or until a more important need comes up. If it turns into a long-term project, you may want to designate a certain day each week to devote to that topic.

The following is an example of a unit study we [the Flanagans] worked on for an entire year. It began with the question, "How much can we learn from a single verse of Scripture?" We chose the verse that says, "I have esteemed the words of his mouth more than my necessary food," Job 23:12. We wanted to find out if a unit study would be a better form of learning than using workbooks. We planned to take about two weeks to learn all we could related to this verse.

A look in the *Thompson Chain Reference Bible* revealed that the Bible has much to say about physical food. Each aspect of physical food could be studied, and analogies made to spiritual food. Some of those topics that we explored together were:

Its source   Sumptuous food
Prohibited foods   Meals
Varieties of food   Types of food
Admonitions concerning eating in the Old Testament

As we read the verses listed, we made several lists—

1. Foods good to eat
2. Foods bad to eat
3. Other commands concerning food and eating

We began to ask questions about our verse.

Are words ever more important than food? When?
What foods are necessary?
How long can we go without the necessary foods?
What effect do words have on the body, spirit, and soul?
Why is it important for ME to esteem His words?
What value do His words have?
What is the relationship between food and words? How are they alike?
When is food more important than words?
What would happen if you did not value God's words?
Can words sustain life?
Draw a picture that shows how you feel when someone esteems your words more than food.
How must God feel when you esteem His Words?

How can you show esteem?
Why should you pay attention to what God says?
Why should you pay attention to what others say?
Write a story about someone who loved food more than God's words.
Draw a picture to illustrate your story.
Try a group story—Once upon a time there was a boy who loved food more than he loved God's Word. . . .
What are the different parts and functions of the mouth?
How are words formed?
How can we live by the words of God?
Study attentiveness.
Is there value in the words of others?
How can you find value in the words of others?
Who in history loved food more than God's Word? Consequences?
Can food sustain life without His words?

Then further questions came up as we looked up the topic in resource books.

Food preparation	Food groups
Menu planning	Food storage
Healthy food	Vitamins
Food purchase	Junk food
Calories	Food handling
Diets	Cooking methods
Fasting	Energy
Food requirements	Following directions
Kitchen safety	Real foods
Orderliness	Cleanliness
Measurement	Nutritive value of foods
Reading recipes	Diseases related to diet
Meal etiquette	Cultural eating patterns
Digestive disorders	The digestive system
The excretory system	

Then we tried to make as many analogies between physical and spiritual food as possible.

What is spiritual food?
Why is it more important than all of the above?
Relate each of the physical aspects of food listed above to some aspect of our need for spiritual nutrition.

We studied grammar through word study projects with the key words in this verse. We used related verses for Scripture memory and handwriting practice. We developed skills in the areas of math, science, medicine, history, literature, home economics, stewardship, consumerism, physical education, language, etc.

In two weeks we only began our study. We covered every academic topic on our list and had fun doing it. The kids voted to get rid of workbooks after that. This study became the basis for a year-long Nutrition Education Project.

Our children are now very knowledgeable about food and nutrition. They plan, purchase necessary items, and prepare all of the family's meals without help. Even our eight-year old daughter grinds the wheat and makes bread weekly, unassisted. More importantly, they understand the value and necessity of spiritual food.

We challenge families to explore this topic as we did. Fathers, especially, are encouraged to lead their families in the initial Bible studies related to the project in order to allow the convicting power of the Holy Spirit to bring about permanent changes in the physical and spiritual eating habits of their families. They will soon discover, as we did, that we can't have the quality of life intended for us apart from regular reading, study, memorization, and meditation on God's Word. We also learned that God does care about what we eat.

—Julie Flanagan

BIBLE-BASED UNIT STUDIES CURRICULUM?

You've probably noticed by now that unit studies curriculum seems to be a Christian stronghold. You are right! Not only are the people inventing their own unit studies often Christian, but every packaged unit studies curriculum I have seen is Christian. This includes the Advanced Training Institute of America (Bill Gothard's group), Alta Vista, KONOS, Hewitt Child

Development Center, and the Weaver (all reviewed in detail in the next chapter).

Now, you don't have to be a Christian to use unit studies. A lot of what I read in *Growing Without Schooling,* a magazine primarily featuring liberal/progressive types, describes very effective family unit studies. The same could be said about *Home Education Magazine,* another home-schooling magazine not focused exclusively on Christians.

So why are all the packaged unit studies programs Christian?

Perhaps it has something to do with the desire to be "Bible-based." Studying topics starting from the Bible sounds like it would be easier to accomplish with a unit study approach. Thus every integrated Christian curriculum I have seen prides itself on being "Bible-based." In practice, topics are sometimes stretched a mite to fit them under a particular Bible verse. For example, it takes some ingenuity to see how we get from Genesis 11:14 to Architecture to Poetry and Library Skills to First Aid in the Weaver curriculum, or from the character trait of Attentiveness to a study of orchestra instruments in KONOS. This arises from the difficulty of squashing the public schools' predetermined secular curriculum into a Christian framework.

When a Christian curriculum developer makes the bold experiment of developing a list of objectives based on the Bible alone, such subjects as Transportation dwindle in importance, while Storytelling and Marriage Preparation mightily increase. (Actually, this description is beginning to look like the ATIA curriculum. ATIA *has* made the effort to rethink curriculum content as well as curriculum methodology.) As the list of NEA-demanded school subjects grows to include items like nuclear pacifism and condom use, now the time is certainly ripe for Christians (especially!) to rethink the area of *what* we want in our curriculum, not just *how* it should be taught.

UNIT STUDY HELPS

Christian Life Workshops
Bible Truth for School Subjects. Dr. Ruth Haycock. Four volumes, $42 plus 10% UPS shipping.

Would you like to turn your encyclopedia into a dynamite Christian unit studies curriculum? Here's how to do it. Either look up all Scripture references for every subject in a concordance, study them, and create a framework for approaching each subject. Or buy *Bible Truth for School Subjects*. It's a four-volume set of books that organizes all the passages of Scripture related to over thirty subjects of school study. For each subject you get a concept summary and Scriptural overview. By looking through the concept summary you can identify the places in your encyclopedia or regular text where passages of Scripture will be illuminating.

Ranging from Art to Zoology, Dr. Haycock gives the complete verse or passage (or a synopsis of a lengthy passage) along with historical information concerning the Bible's accuracy in areas under study. You'll be amazed at the amount of revelation the Bible offers on subjects like biology, mathematics, and athletics, subjects that most people think it doesn't address at all!

Volume I, *Social Studies*, covers history, geography, economics, government, leadership and administration, social relationships, the family, the church, and social problems. Volume II, *Language Arts/English*, gets into reading, writing, literature, speech, listening, and foreign languages. Volume III, *Science/Mathematics*, looks at astronomy, earth science, physics and chemistry, zoology, botany, human biology, and mathematics. The final volume, *Fine Arts and Health*, has creativity, arts and crafts, music, health, sex education, physical education, athletics, and death education—all from a point of view you'll never hear in public school.

Each volume of *Bible Truth for School Subjects* also includes a vast list of resources for further study, including books for students and teachers, tapes, curriculum guides, textbooks, resource units, supplementary materials, audiovisual materials, and periodicals. Each volume has its own index.

It's hard to see how anyone could go wrong with books like these; it's easy to see how someone might go wrong without them. This is the classic on integrating the Bible into school studies, whether at home or in the classroom.

NEW**
Konos Helps
$18/9 monthly issues. Back issues, $2.50 each.

Here is a *very* fancy and professionally-produced new newsletter for unit study families in general and KONOS families in particular. *KONOS Helps* is published by a lady who has written several insightful articles for my own newsletter—Kathy von Duyke—and her partner Nina Watts. If you like KONOS, you're gonna love this. Published nine months of the school year (with the blessing of the folks at KONOS), each issue of *KONOS Helps* features articles, games, crafts, costume patterns for sewers and non-sewers, recipes, music, and art suggestions, all based on one of the KONOS unit studies. 1989-90 issues cover Indians; Rocks, Plant, and Animal Classification; Kings and Queens; Christmas; Great Feats; The Eyes and Senses; Frontier and Pioneers; Plant and Animal Reproduction; and Olympics. You also get organization tips, language arts and math suggestions, toddler tips, a Dad's corner, and almost anything else useful you can think of. Plus a different free reproducible planning sheet in each issue. The suggestion in the first issue on how to keep from losing your library cards to rampaging toddlers was alone worth the price of a year's subscription! Obviously, the value of this newsletter is max if you're using KONOS, but even if you'd rather develop your own projects, it will help.

NEW**
TREND Enterprises, Inc.
Most bulletin board sets, $5.99. Require 4 x 6' bulletin board.

Here's a unit study tip I bet you haven't heard before! Why not plan your unit study around a bulletin board? Before you suggest that I have parted from my moorings, let me point out the advantages.

(1) Visuals and information all in one place. No running around gathering materials.

(2) Nothing to take out and put away.

(3) Large, bright format engenders interest.

(4) Accompanying teacher's guide has additional facts, activities, questions already prepared.

If you want to go beyond the information presented on the bulletin board, the launching points for your further investigations are already right there up on the wall. For example, TREND's "Weather Elements" bulletin board (currently up on my wall) easily leads into further study of clouds, air pressure, fronts, the water cycle, and weather folklore, among other things. These are among the topics introduced and illustrated by the visuals. It also comes with a manipulative: a circular model of the earth mounted on a brad that you can tilt toward or away from the sun to discover why we have different seasons in different places. I just tack the resource guide right up on the bulletin board and take it off when we want to pursue any of the topics further.

Why TREND bulletin board sets? Because they are inexpensive, colorful, easy to mount (pre-perfed!), available at teacher's stores everywhere, and come with resource guides. Also, TREND has a higher proportion of "teaching" bulletin boards than other suppliers I have seen, who mostly stick to motivational themes with very little teaching information. These bulletin board sets plus an encyclopedia equal a *lot* of instant unit studies!

CHAPTER TWENTY-TWO

PICKING A HOME STUDY PROGRAM FOR YOUR CHILDREN

When I produced the first edition of this chapter years ago, I included every home-school curriculum I could get my hands on. Neither I nor anyone else had enough years' experience with these programs to authoritatively separate the winners from the merely OK.

Well, the years have gone by and I've been watching and listening. At this point it is clear that some winners *are* emerging from the pack. It's also clear that a number of the small programs I wondered about including in the first edition just aren't worth mentioning in this one. For one thing, small "satellite" programs are now a dime a dozen, especially in California, where state laws encourage their proliferation. For another thing, with the home-schooling marketplace growing at such a phenomenal rate, any program that *remains* tiny in its enrollment just isn't that great.

So in order to make your curriculum-shopping less confusing, in this edition we are concentrating on tried-n-true major curriculum from major suppliers. These have all been around for a number of years and served many satisfied customers. They also represent as wide a spectrum of educational philosophies and choices as most of us could ever want. You can find suppliers who follow the traditional public school plan as well as those who emphasize projects and creative thinking. Some programs are back-to-basics. Some are classical. Some are in-between. Some are straight pub-

lic-school-at-home. And some programs are just completely different from anything else. There are big programs and small programs, old programs and new programs, time-tested programs and innovative programs, programs for elementary-age kids only and programs for high school students. Everything you could possibly desire in a home-school program is out there . . . and reviewed right here!

Now, let's help you narrow down your choices a bit.

If you are the disorganized type, you might benefit from the accountability of a "full-service" program. Full-service programs offer complete services: record-keeping, transcripts, counseling by letter, grading of papers, diplomas, and other options. Since you are required to send completed materials in periodically, you will have an outside incentive to keep on top of your foray into home schooling.

If your children aren't yet of compulsory attendance age, you don't need the full-service option. In fact, you may not need a real curriculum at all! Browse through the Preschool section in Volume 2 to find some low-key ways of starting your preschooler on learning at home. If you do want to get into the swing of regular home schooling, though, this is a great time to do it. Pressures and expectations are low (nobody expects your four-year-old to read), and you have more time while you have less children. Personally, I still think Calvert's kindergarten program (a readiness program) is the best way for novice home schoolers to get started.

If you are intending to teach a school-age child at home, and this is your first venture into home schooling, I recommend that you pick a good, solid curriculum and stick with it for at least one year. After several months you will probably start having ideas of how to improve it. Great! Save those ideas for *next* year, when you will have more teaching experience. Nothing is more deadly to fledgling home schoolers than the butterfly syndrome—flitting from resource to resource without settling on any one. By sticking with your first choice, you will (1) save money, (2) save mental anguish, and (3) learn perseverance and organization.

Those of us with more years' experience are often going to want to mix and match curriculum to provide completely individualized education for each child. For this approach, you need to turn to the curriculum suppliers who let you buy their curriculum without enrolling. Some of these companies (A Beka, Alpha Omega, Bob Jones, Rod and Staff, etc.) sell more materials this way than through full-service programs. The main difference from a full-service program is that you do not have to send in tests, etc., and no telephone counseling or advisory tutoring service is available. All you do is buy the curriculum and use it at your own pace and in your own way.

Regardless of which approach you end up using, it is really worthwhile to read this whole chapter. Get an overview of the basic curriculum options. This will greatly increase your confidence in your final choice, as well as giving you ideas for the future.

Please keep in mind that programs are not totally uniform; they vary from grade to grade, and often the supplier will upgrade his product (which may be a change for the better or the worse). However, you can expect that the basic educational philosophy will usually remain constant. Keeping all this in mind, I have looked at a cross-section of grades for each program, with particular attention to the "entry" grades (kindergarten and first grade), the "middle" grades (fourth through eighth), and the final grades. Unless stated otherwise, the reviews are based on actual inspection of those courses.

You would be wise to send for a current brochure and application form for the curricula you find interesting and make your final choice on that basis. Some suppliers also have sample packets, and you might want to spend a few dollars on one of those before investing in the entire program. Although prices listed were checked out as being valid at the time of writing, this guide is not intended as an order form. Its main purpose is to alert you to what's out there and also help you narrow down your choices.

To further assist your search, here are some lists by program type of the programs covered in detail in this chapter. Note that some of the programs fall into more than one category. The Advanced Training Institute of America program, for example, is both a full-service program *and* a unit studies program.

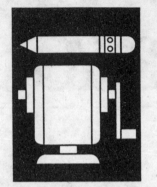

TYPE OF SERVICES OFFERED

FULL-SERVICE PROGRAMS

These range from full correspondence programs where you send in every lesson for grading to those that merely require periodic reporting of grades and accomplishments. They offer telephone and mail consultations, record-keeping, transcripts, and (sometimes) diplomas.

A Beka Correspondence School
A Beka Video Home School
Advanced Training Institute of America
American School
Calvert School (full-service optional)
Christian Liberty Academy (full service optional)
Clonlara School
Covenant Home Curriculum
Hewitt Child Development Center (optional after one year full-service enrollment)
Home Centered Learning (no curriculum, just services)
Home Study International
International Institute (full service optional)
Living Heritage Academy (uses Basic Education materials)
McGuffey Academy
North Dakota State Department of Public Instruction/Division of Independent Study
Oak Meadow School

Our Lady of the Rosary School
Our Lady of Victory
Seton Home Study School
Summit Christian Academy (uses Alpha Omega
   materials)
The Sycamore Tree
University of Nebraska-Lincoln/Independent
   Study High School

CURRICULUM PUBLISHERS

The advantages of just getting a curriculum without
enrolling in a program are *cost* and *flexibility*. In a program, you pay for all those telephone sessions and
graded tests supplied with enrollment. You also in
most cases have to do *all* the work the school sends,
even if it bores your young 'un to tears. On your own,
you can pick and choose which activities or exercises
you think are worth the effort, and you save some
money.

On the other hand, you might find a certain laziness seeping in, as many people find it harder to work
without supervision. That nagging feeling that the
school is waiting for this quarter's projects and tests can
be a helpful kick in the pants for the procrastinator.

Afterschoolers are definitely better off without formal enrollment, since a child can only stand to do so
much schoolwork and you have no need to prove anything to anybody. The exception is when Summer
School looms ahead and you'd much rather have your
eighth-grader take the Calvert math course—for credit.
Talk over such decisions with your school personnel,
as they can get huffy about assigning credits for courses they haven't approved.

A Beka Books (full service available)
Alpha Omega Publications
Basic Education
Bob Jones University Press
Calvert School (full service available)
Carden Educational Foundation
Christian Liberty Academy (full service available)
Christian Light Education (full service available)
Christian Schools International
International Institute (full service available)
KONOS Character Curriculum
Our Lady of the Rosary (full service available)
Pathway Publishers
Rod and Staff Publishers
School Supply Room/Gordonville Print Shop
The Sycamore Tree (full service available)

The Weaver Curriculum
Wilcox & Follett (bargain textbooks only)

BARGAIN CURRICULUM

For the penny-pinchers among us, here are sources for
discount used curriculum. If you like what you see in
this chapter, but can't afford it, see if one of the following companies has it on hand at discount!

Christian Teaching Materials Company (see Cata-
   logs chapter)
Rainbow Re-Source Center (see Catalogs chapter)
Wilcox & Follett

GRADES OFFERED

PRESCHOOL/READINESS

These are what we remember as old-fashioned kindergarten or nursery school—lots of play 'n clay. Readiness programs gently lead young children to explore
various art media, do simple dramatics, become familiar with colors and shapes, listen to stories and nursery
rhymes, and become acquainted with seasonal activities. Towards the end of the school year, counting and
letters are usually introduced in a very low-key way.

Some program providers have a "readiness"
kindergarten, while others label theirs "nursery school"
or "preschool." Don't be confused by the labels; use
the following list to discern which providers really offer preschool programs, whatever they are called.

A Beka Correspondence School (nursery school
   for 2- and 3-year-olds)
Advanced Training Institute (preschoolers have activities in Parent's Guide, but no separate program available for preschoolers)
Bob Jones University Press ("Beginnings" program
   for preschoolers)
Calvert School (kindergarten course is a readiness
   program)

Carden Educational Foundation (preschool)
Hewitt Child Development Center (readiness program for children under age 8)
Home Study International (preschool program)
International Institute (kindergarten course is a readiness program)
Our Lady of the Rosary (kindergarten course is a readiness program)
Smiling Heart Press (combined with kindergarten in one-volume curriculum)

ACADEMIC KINDERGARTEN

"Academic kindergarten" programs set themselves the task of teaching children to cipher and read. They may start off with readiness activities, but quickly progress to formal instruction in these two subjects. Generally such programs also include very simple history lessons and a variety of art and music activities.

A Beka Correspondence School (K4 and K5)
A Beka Video Home School (video kindergarten program)
Advanced Training Institute of America (need separate math and phonics)
Alpha Omega Publications (LITTLE PATRIOTS kindergarten program)
Associated Christian Schools/Landmark's Freedom Baptist Curriculum
Basic Education (choice of two academic learning-to-read programs)
Bob Jones University Press
Christian Liberty Academy (junior and senior kindergarten)
Christian Light Education
KONOS Character Curriculum (need separate math and phonics)
Home Study International
International Institute (full service optional)
Living Heritage Academy (uses Basic Education materials)
McGuffey Academy
Our Lady of Victory (kindergarten is called "grade 1A")
Seton Home Study School
Smiling Heart Press (combined in one manual with preschool)
Summit Christian Academy
The Sycamore Tree
The Weaver (Interlock program)

GRADES 1-6

A Beka Books (curriculum only)
A Beka Correspondence School
A Beka Video Home School
Advanced Training Institute of America
Alpha Omega Publications
Associated Christian Schools/Landmark's Freedom Baptist Curriculum
Basic Education
Bob Jones University Press
Carden Educational Foundation
Calvert School
Christian Liberty Academy
Christian Light Education
Christian Schools International
Clonlara School
Covenant Home Curriculum
Hewitt Child Development Center
Home Centered Learning
Home Study International
International Institute
KONOS Character Curriculum
Living Heritage Academy
McGuffey Academy
Oak Meadow School
Our Lady of the Rosary School
Our Lady of Victory
Pathway Publishers
Rod and Staff Publishers
School Supply Room/Gordonville Print Shop
Seton Home Study School
Smiling Heart Press (grades 1 and 2)
Summit Christian Academy
The Sycamore Tree
The Weaver Curriculum

MIDDLE SCHOOL

A Beka Books (curriculum only)
A Beka Correspondence School
A Beka Video Home School
Advanced Training Institute of America
Alpha Omega Publications
Associated Christian Schools/Landmark's Freedom
  Baptist Curriculum
Basic Education
Bob Jones University Press
Carden Educational Foundation
Calvert School
Christian Liberty Academy
Christian Light Education
Clonlara School
Covenant Home Curriculum
Hewitt Child Development Center
Home Centered Learning
Home Study International
International Institute
KONOS Character Curriculum (need separate
  grammar/language arts)
Living Heritage Academy
McGuffey Academy
Oak Meadow School
Our Lady of the Rosary School
Our Lady of Victory
Pathway Publishers
Rod and Staff Publishers
School Supply Room/Gordonville Print Shop
Seton Home Study School
Summit Christian Academy
The Sycamore Tree

HIGH SCHOOL

A Beka Books (curriculum only)
A Beka Correspondence School (full service)
A Beka Video Home School (full service)
Alpha Omega Publications (curriculum only)
Advanced Training Institute of America (full ser-
  vice; apprenticeship program)
American School (full service: state-accredited
  diploma)
Associated Christian Schools/Landmark's Freedom
  Baptist Curriculum
Basic Education (curriculum only)
Bob Jones University Press (curriculum only)
Carden Educational Foundation (curriculum only)
Christian Liberty Academy (full service available)

Christian Light Education (full service available)
Clonlara School (full service)
Covenant Home Curriculum (full service)
Hewitt Child Development Center (full service))
Home Centered Learning (no curriculum, just ser-
  vices)
Home Study International (full service)
International Institute (full service optional)
Living Heritage Academy (full service; uses Basic
  Education materials)
McGuffey Academy (full service)
North Dakota State Department of Public Instruc-
  tion/Division of Independent Study (full service;
  state-accredited diploma)
Oak Meadow School (full service)
Our Lady of the Rosary School (full service)
Our Lady of Victory (full service)
Seton Home Study School (full service)
Summit Christian Academy (full service; uses Al-
  pha Omega materials)
The Sycamore Tree (full service available)
University of Nebraska-Lincoln/Independent
  Study High School (full service; state-accredited
  diploma)

RELIGIOUS ORIENTATION

CATHOLIC PROGRAMS

Our Lady of the Rosary School
Our Lady of Victory School
Seton Home Study School

CHRISTIAN/EVANGELICAL PROGRAMS

A Beka Correspondence School
A Beka Video Home School
Advanced Training Institute of America
Alpha Omega Publications
Associated Christian Schools/Landmark's Freedom
  Baptist Curriculum

Basic Education
Bob Jones University Press
Christian Liberty Academy (full service optional)
Christian Schools International
Covenant Home Curriculum
Hewitt Child Development Center
International Institute (kindergarten only; rest of
  grades have separate Bible course)
KONOS Character Curriculum
Living Heritage Academy
McGuffey Academy
Smiling Heart Press
Summit Christian Academy
The Sycamore Tree (program run along evangelical
  lines, although owners are Seventh-day Adventists)
The Weaver Curriculum

CHRISTIAN/MENNONITE

Christian Light Education
Pathway Publishers
Rod and Staff Publishers
School Supply Room/Gordonville Print Shop

CIVIC RELIGION/OLD-FASHIONED, NON-DENOMI-NATIONAL

Calvert School
Carden Educational Foundation

"FREE LEARNING" PROGRAMS

Clonlara School
Home Centered Learning
Santa Fe Community School

SECULAR/PUBLIC SCHOOL

International Institute (grades 1-8)
North Dakota State Department of Public Instruc-
  tion/Division of Independent Study
University of Nebraska-Lincoln/Independent
  Study High School

SEVENTH-DAY ADVENTIST

Home Study International

WALDORF PROGRAMS (New Age flavor)

Oak Meadow School

ACADEMIC ORIENTATION

BACK-TO-BASICS

Associated Christian Schools/Landmark's Freedom
  Baptist Curriculum
Basic Education
Living Heritage Academy
Our Lady of Victory School

CLASSIC/TRADITIONAL

Calvert School (uses mix of classic and up-to-date
  materials)
Carden Educational Foundation
Christian Liberty Academy
Covenant Home Curriculum
McGuffey Academy
Our Lady of the Rosary School
Seton Home Study School
Smiling Heart Press

COMPUTER-ASSISTED INSTRUCTION

Basic Education
University of North Dakota/Division of Independent Studies (some courses)

"FREE" OR "INVITED" LEARNING

Clonlara School
Home Centered Learning
Santa Fe Community School

PRINCIPLE APPROACH

American Christian Academy

PUBLIC SCHOOL APPROACH

Home Study International
International Institute
North Dakota State Department of Public Instruction/Division of Independent Study
University of Nebraska-Lincoln/Independent Study High School

TEXTBOOK/WORKBOOK/WORKTEXT

Alpha Omega Publications
Associated Christian Schools/Landmark's Freedom Baptist Curriculum
Basic Education
Bob Jones University Press
Christian Light Education
Christian Schools International
Living Heritage Academy
Pathway Publishers
Rod and Staff Publishers
School Supply Room/Gordonville Print Shop
Summit Christian Academy (uses Alpha Omega materials)

UNIT STUDY PROGRAMS

Advanced Training Institute of America (K-6)
Alta Vista Homeschool Curriculum (K-7)

Hewitt Child Development Center (birth-grade 12)
KONOS Character Curriculum (K-8)
The Weaver Curriculum (Pre-K through 6)

VIDEO INSTRUCTION

A Beka Video Home School (all courses)
Basic Education
North Dakota State Department of Public Instruction/Division of Independent Study (some courses)
University of Nebraska-Lincoln/Independent Study High School (some courses)

WALDORF APPROACH (stresses fantasy and ecology)

Oak Meadow

CHAPTER TWENTY-THREE

MAJOR K-12 HOME STUDY PROGRAMS

A Beka Correspondence School

$300 Nursery (two- and three-year-olds), $300 K4 (four-year-olds), $400 K5, $450 1-6, $445 grade 7, $460 grade 8, $545 grades 9-10 (full program), $405-580 grades 11-12 (depending on electives). Nursery-grade 4 includes $75 deposit which will be refunded upon return of the curriculum. Book deposit for some upper-grade texts. Reuse discount, $50 less than the normal tuition.

Established: 1973.

Enrollment in 1988-89: A Beka texts are used by over 600,000 children in more than 17,000 Christian schools. Home school enrollment, around 2-3,000; families purchasing A Beka texts during 1989-1990, tens of thousands.

Curriculum: Purchase entire program or individual courses (grades 9-12). Books available without signing up for program.

Services: Record-keeping and teacher evaluations of student's work (students enrolled for credit only).

Special Requirements: Work must be sent in on regular basis, or pay reinstatement fee.

Unique features: Only home-schooling programs especially for 2-4 year-olds.

Tone: Correspondence school, strict. Mail-order sales department quite user-friendly.

Religion: Evangelical Christian. Creationist.

Emphasis: Patriotic, pro-free enterprise. Solutions to social problems presented.

Learning Style: Primarily auditory/visual.

Grades: Nursery (for 2- and 3-year-olds) through grade 12.

An offshoot of one of America's largest Christian day schools, A Beka's correspondence program is a ministry of Pensacola College, using the popular A Beka Book series of Christian texts that the college publishes. The Day School itself is recognized by both the State of Florida and the Florida Association of Christian Schools. (See also the entry under A Beka Video Home School, for A Beka's home video program.)

A Beka's rules are strict: no discounts, no payment plans, no refunds, no course alterations allowed. A Beka says, "Continued enrollment is contingent upon compliance with program guidelines."

A Beka provides a Teacher's Manual identical to that used in Christian classrooms with their A Beka materials. *This manual is only leased and must be returned at the end of the course.* A Beka also supplies all needed textbooks and materials; periodic grade reports; permanent school records; and advice and counseling as requested.

A Beka's approach is traditional and textbook-oriented. Curriculum is based on a classroom model. If followed exactly, it would be a whole school day's work for both parents and students. Count on spending some time adapting the lessons to your home situation.

Handwriting starts with manuscript. Cursive writing begins in grade 2. Writing and reading are taught together in kindergarten, which is a serious academic program also including fun stuff like art, music, and poetry.

A Beka's products are colorful and generally professional-looking. Some illustrations in some books are amateurish—this only bothered me in the early Science series, where realistic art is a plus.

The Teacher's Manuals are cumbersome in the home situation (although the course of study is well laid out). I hope that in time A Beka will produce its own Home Study manuals like many other suppliers have done.

Subjects we liked the least were lower-grades Language Arts and upper-grades Literature. Subjects we liked the best: Math, History, and Geography.

Expect to find a lot of questions with one right answer and not too many open-ended questions. A Beka uses a programmed approach, with the child drilled in correct responses, rather than a discovery approach. A Beka books thus frequently use "I" sentences. Example: "I must ask God to help my hands do what is right."

Lessons follow one another logically, so students should not become frustrated through lack of understanding. Though there is a lot of repetitive drill, the exercises are fairly interesting.

No record-keeping is required for nursery and K4. Beyond these grades the amount of record-keeping is average (returning work to school, grading daily work, keeping attendance records).

This entire program is available on video for grades K-12. See the A Beka Video Home School review in this section.

Home-schooling parents may now purchase individual subject area curricula, textbooks, tests, and teacher aids in all subjects for grades 1-12 without enrolling in A Beka Correspondence School. Send for the free A Beka Books catalog.

If you enroll in the Correspondence Program, prepare to move along at a brisk pace. A Beka expects you to administer weekly tests and keep right on top of things. Some people like being held to a schedule like this. But if you're the mellow type who dislikes tight schedules, or like to pick and choose workbook exercises instead of assigning them all, or need to move at the pace you set rather than having it set for you, you'd be better off bypassing A Beka's enrollment services and just buying the A Beka books you need direct from the catalog.

A Beka Video Home School
$650 plus $50 retainer. Everything included. No discounts. Tapes must be returned UPS prepaid and insured every two or nine weeks depending on grade. Full program available for grades K-12. Payment Plan: $380 down and $60 per month for 6 months.
Option for grades 7-12 subjects: individual courses may be ordered for noncredit. Tapes returned every nine weeks, as per above. Courses $250 each plus $30 retainer; $125 additional per course for each additional student within the immediate family using the course, excluding student books.

Established: 1986.
Enrollment in 1988-89: Around 4,000.
Curriculum: Lease entire program or (for grades 7-12) individual courses.
Services: Record-keeping and teacher evaluations of student's work (students enrolled for credit only).
Special Requirements: Tapes are only leased; must be repacked and returned on regular basis.
Unique features: Only home-schooling video program.
Tone: Strict.
Religion: Evangelical Christian. Creationist.
Emphasis: Patriotic, pro-free enterprise.
Learning Style: Visual/auditory. Not recommended for kinesthetic learners.
Grades: K-12.

You knew it was inevitable. We have video cooking classes, video rock, and now . . . video home school! Launched in 1986, A Beka's video program generated instant controversy. More on that later.

You get instructional videocassettes and A Beka's very popular texts and teaching guides. Kindergartners receive two and a half hours daily instruction from the videotape teacher, and children in grades 1-6 spend slightly more than three hours watching their tapes. Students also have homework assignments. You return completed work and tests at designated intervals of six to nine weeks, depending on grade level.

I can't give this program an academic rating without seeing it. However, you can expect that the video teaching is of superior private school quality. A Beka's textbooks are widely used and generally well-regarded. See the A Beka listing for further details.

You will need a VCR for each student enrolled, unless one tunes in mornings and the other does his work in the afternoons. This is not the program for large families.

Now for the controversy I promised you! Some people have raised questions about whether a video approach is right for home schooling. (1) They worry about the eyestrain involved. (2) They also feel that, in the one-on-one home-school situation, a child does not need to spend that much time being "taught" by anyone. (3) Lastly, they fear that children will miss out on home school's greatest advantage: personal attention from their parents.

As the mother of a TV-free family I sympathize with these concerns. However, I also recognize that most children watch a lot of TV, and they might as well be watching something edifying. As for A Beka, the first two problems can be minimized by simply not requiring the student to watch tapes or portions of tapes covering subjects he can handle on his own. Concerning objection 3, my feeling is that A Beka is carving out a new market—home school for families who otherwise wouldn't consider it. Such parents might put the tapes to their best use by watching with their children and learning how to teach from the A Beka teachers—thus eventually moving on beyond video into "normal" home schooling.

Accelerated Christian Education
See Basic Education

Advanced Training Institute of America
$400-$900/family (depending on number of children) includes training seminar and materials. Food and lodging while attending seminar not included.

Established: 1984.
Enrollment in 1989-1990: About 3,000 families.
Curriculum: Unique to ATIA. Includes required resource library you purchase directly from individual publishers. Curriculum only available to enrollees.

Special Requirements: Parents must attend two IBYC seminars to apply for program; must attend special one-week training seminar once accepted.
Unique features: *Wisdom Booklets* that cover academic topics from a Biblical frame of reference; father-led Bible studies; emphasis on training in 49 Christian character qualities; apprenticeship program; whole-family approach to learning; separate roles for boys and girls; leadership preparation.
Tone: Demanding but fairly flexible.
Religion: Evangelical Christian. Much emphasis on practical holiness. Creationist.
Emphasis: Patriotic, pro-free enterprise, heavy respect for "God-given authorities." Solutions to social problems discovered through inductive study.
Learning Style: All styles.
Grades: K-12. Post-high-school training is apprenticeship format.

A project of Bill Gothard's Institute in Basic Youth Conflicts, the ATIA program reflects Gothard's message. ATIA materials use the Bible as the core of all learning and from that core are intended to lead students to master all areas of study. The program stresses the father's leadership role and the mother's homemaking role. Enrollment is limited to qualifying families: a preliminary qualification is that both parents have attended the Basic Youth Conflicts Seminar and the Essential Life Goals Seminar (otherwise known as the Advanced, or Life Purpose, Seminar).

Parents attend an intensive one-week training seminar, which fills them in on the program's philosophy and instructs them in how to operate it.

The program itself is heavily Scriptural. Much stress is placed on character development and application of Biblical principles in daily living. Parents evaluate their children regularly using ATIA's computerized scanner forms.

The ATIA curriculum includes both *Wisdom Booklets* and *Wisdom Applications*. These unit studies start with a Scripture verse—e.g., "And seeing the multitudes . . . he went up into a mountain." The theme for this unit would be Seeing and Sight, and it would be studied from several perspectives: Linguistics (language, grammar, vocabulary, communication), History (archaeology, geography, prophecy, music, art, literature), Science (including math), Law (government, economics, logic), and Medicine (health, nutrition, behavior, counseling). Under the topic of Medicine, for example, ATIA's study asks the question, "How do the things we see affect our physical strength?" Then follows a description of the way adrenalin affects the bodily organs, along with exciting stories of the amazing things people have done when moved by adrenalin, pictures of the organs involved, etc. Topics picked for the *Wisdom Booklets* are meant to demonstrate the applications of the Scripture passage. Alternatively, verses chosen are meant to illuminate the subject area.

A *Parent Guide* accompanies each *Wisdom Booklet.* This guide includes introductory ideas, bibliography, cross-references in the required resource library (for further study), an answer key for projects and quizzes, extra unit study ideas, and creative ideas for teaching concepts to younger children.

Scripture itself is studied intensively through "Wisdom Searches." These are Dad's responsibility, and consist of the whole family together searching out what the Bible says about important topics. Each *Parent Guide* includes suggestions for doing this effectively and correlating it with its *Wisdom Booklet.*

The curriculum includes many other unique materials, such as the *Parts of Speech* guide which provides activities for teaching the parts of speech, and (for older children) the 18-lesson *Sentence Analysis* course; ATIA's 24 x 36" illustrated *Time Line Chart*; ATIA's *Hymn History Sing-Along Tapes;* and the projected *Basic Living Skills Notebook,* designed for parents to use in training children in the how-tos of child care, equipment, home maintenance and decorating, hospitality, nutrition, clothing, and personal care.

I should mention somewhere in here that all the materials are absolutely beautiful and intellectually intriguing. You won't find any fill-in-the-blanks here! Along with the strong Scriptural emphasis, the high quality and organization of the materials are probably why everyone I have talked to who has tried this program raves about it.

Hospitality and ministry are important parts of the program. ATIA wants children to be involved in their parents' ministry, not to be an excuse for not having any ministry. Also, ATIA believes in Biblical roles for boys and girls. The educational program for each sex is "designed to meet their specific and varied needs."

An important feature of the curriculum is the Life Purpose Program which helps young people (ages 15 and up) discover and commit themselves to a life calling with a ministry orientation. In the Life Purpose Program, students fill out journals based on 2 Peter 1:1-10. This passage stresses how faith, virtue (character), and knowledge enable you to be fruitful in the world. Once the student, based on his studies, obtains a sense of his particular life purpose, he enters into actual apprenticeship training.

The Life Purpose Program emphasizes that any vocation will be more significant if it is related to the goal of strengthening families, since the family is the foundation of both church and nation. To be effective in such a vocation, ATIA believes that students need specialized training in four areas: counseling, medicine, law, and business. Rather than going to college, where students must major in a designated field, ATIA Life Purpose students train under specialists in each of these fields. This Life Purpose training is a graduation requirement of the ATIA program.

ATIA's application booklet provides excellent information about the seminars and the ATIA curriculum, along with sample sheets from the curriculum.

Alpha Omega Publications
LITTLE PATRIOTS Complete Kindergarten Program, $129.95. $200/year for Alpha Omega grade 1-12 materials for each child (includes Teacher Guides, answer keys, and all other necessary material).

Established: 1978.
Families served in 1988-89: Over 22,000 home-schooling families. Alpha Omega curriculum is also used by over 60,000 students in Christian schools.
Curriculum: Published by Alpha Omega, except for LITTLE PATRIOTS program from Mile Hi Publications, of which Alpha Omega is the exclusive distributor. Curriculum available separately.
Support Services: None.
Special Requirements: None.
Unique features: Grades 1-12 materials use a worktext format that goes beyond fill-in-the-blanks. Very easy to use, helpful when teaching many children at once. Many high-school electives.
Tone: Friendly.
Religion: Evangelical Christian. Creationist.
Emphasis: Patriotic, pro-free enterprise. Social studies curriculum less Biblically-oriented than some others—problems more emphasized in some places than solutions.
Learning Style: Visual/auditory. Some kinesthetic projects/activities.
Grades: K-12.

Alpha Omega Publications is not exactly the new kid on the block. Way back in the days of President James Earl Carter, a team of over 250 Christian academic writers, most of whom held Masters or Doctorates, got together and produced an entire curriculum for grades 1-12. Why did they do this? Because, like so many others, they saw modern education slipping over the cliff and they wanted to provide a Christian alternative. At the moment Alpha Omega curriculum is being used by over 60,000 students in all fifty states and in twenty foreign countries. Most of these students are enrolled in small Christian schools. Alpha Omega has also more than doubled the number of home-school families it serves in the past two years.

Alpha Omega doesn't publish textbooks. Instead, they have gone the workbook route, with consumable booklets containing both texts and assignments. These they call LIFEPACS. Each subject for each grade has ten LIFEPACS, plus Teacher Handbooks and answer keys. You might scoff at answer keys, knowing you can always check out Junior's work without them, but when it's time to grade those hundreds and thousands of three-digit math problems, you will be grateful to Alpha Omega for providing them! Each grade has five subjects, plus the usual and not-so-usual high school electives of art, consumer math, home ec, Greek, and Spanish. It all is very professionally done in black and white.

Alpha Omega's English program, particularly in the upper grades, is excellent. Students not only read great literature, but learn the arts of good writing, speaking, and listening. The science curriculum is likewise excellent: lucid, logical, and thorough. Alpha Omega provides *real* lab experiments. If your children like to fool around with ice cubes and table salt, that's fine. But if your son is serious about Bunsen burners and ripple tanks and the like, Alpha Omega's got the stuff for him. You can buy most of the equipment and supplies for the experiments from Alpha Omega.

Social studies is a bit more spotty, following the public school formula of "widening circles" from the student to his family, his community, his nation, and the world. History and geography are also included, but the variety of authors works against a totally unified view of history and politics. The social studies curriculum was recently revised to be more in line with fundamentalist Christian beliefs.

The Bible courses contain theology, book studies, and practical applications from a generally consistent evangelical viewpoint.

First grade materials are full of "I like me" and original (nonclassical) fantasy stories. You decide whether you like this or not.

For kindergarten, Alpha Omega is a distributor of Mile-Hi Publishers' THE LITTLE PATRIOTS, a comprehensive, phonics-based program. Its analytical approach to the English language is based on Biblical principles. The program includes phonics, reading, writing, spelling, penmanship, numbers, and Bible. Teacher's Guides organize the daily work, while many worksheets and student workbooks provide in-depth practice. Researched and developed over more than 15 years, Alpha Omega considers it a proven and effective kindergarten program. For more info see the Preschool chapter.

Alpha Omega LIFEPACS are *not* self-instructional. Projects, compositions, essay questions, and other "thinking" assignments fill the curriculum. This makes for a superior education, but more work for parents and students.

Overall, I give Alpha Omega an A. For English and science, you could stretch this to an A+. Although the curriculum has weak areas, generally speaking the more I see of what's available to schools (both public and private), the better I like Alpha Omega.

If you want a correspondence program using Alpha Omega materials for grades 1-12, check out the Summit Christian Academy listing. Christian Light Education also has a revised Alpha Omega program for the Mennonite community.

UPDATED✱✱
Alta Vista Homeschool Curriculum
One-time family registration fee, $25. Each complete unit, $75 (each unit contains 15 lessons to be covered in approximately 1/2 year). Extra student workbooks, $25/unit. Earth and Space sample packet, $5. Shipping, 8% parcel post or 12% UPS.

Established: 1987.
Enrollment in 1988-89: Not available.
Curriculum: Published by Alta Vista College. Curriculum available separately.

Support Services: Training and accreditation for Washington State parents.
Special Requirements: None.
Unique features: Two-year units. All curriculum divided into five major study areas. Covers Social Studies, Science, and Bible only. Discovery approach, parent as facilitator more than as teacher.
Tone: Authoritative.
Religion: Mellow Evangelical Christian. Creationist.
Emphasis: Heavy emphasis on the validity of discovering God through His Creation. More "right-brain" activities than other Christian programs—logic and reason not as emphasized.
Learning Style: Kinesthetic/auditory/visual.
Grades: K-7.

Highly structured, ambitious integrated Christian curriculum with a lot of innovative features. Operating out of Alta Vista College, an evangelical graduate institution in Medina, Washington, the Alta Vista Homeschool Curriculum embraces four learning styles (intuitive, analytical, practical, and imaginative) in an attempt to balance right brain/left brain activities.

Alta Vista's curriculum is divided up into five major areas of study: Plants, Animals, Earth and Space, People as Individuals, and People as a Group. Each of these forms one unit area. This is quite different from the usual math/science/social studies/language arts setup—at first blush, anyway. As it turns out, Alta Vista expects you to purchase separate language arts and math curriculum (they carry some). So you are really dealing with social studies, ethics, Bible, and science. Now, rather than having a single grade level for each unit area, as is usually the case, the curriculum is divided into two-year tracks. In other words, you can order a K-1 Plants unit, or a grades 2-3 Plants unit, or one for grades 4-5, or grades 6-7.

Now here comes the "highly structured" part mentioned above. Each lesson has the *exact same structure*. In part one, the parent is asked to create or recall a personal experience for the child and help the child talk it over afterwards. Projects are suggested to help students make connections between what they already know and have experienced and the new material they will be studying. Part two is where the child is presented with what Alta Vista calls the "givens": facts and knowledge that normally make up the material of school studies. Part three is practicing the givens—using this new information, and experimenting to test the givens. Part four finds the student working out an application of his new learning, evaluating how useful it is, and teaching what he just learned to another person. These four steps are repeated for each of the fifteen lessons in each unit. To keep the unit a unit instead of fifteen entirely separate lessons, some background activities (like reading a particular book) continue through the unit.

We'll talk about this approach in a minute. But first, let's see what you get for your money. Your registration fee includes the large, thick instructor's manual. This introduces the Alta Vista perspective on Christian knowledge and educational philosophy (including a learning styles survey for your child), presents how-tos and alternative projects, shares some (semi-secularized) child development info, and gives you a lovely, large Scope and Sequence, similar in content to some other publishers' teaching guides. As for the units themselves: each unit includes parent instructions and student worksheets, along with a progress chart. Aside from the student worksheets, the rest of the material is reusable. Keeping in mind that each level (five units) represents two years of work, the curriculum's cost winds up between that of a full-service program and a one-book curriculum such as KONOS or Weaver.

As for appearance and ease of use, Alta Vista has done a *very* professional job. Because of the consistent user interface, you will find lessons very easy to prepare. Everything you need to present, including pre- and post-tests for each lesson and a choice of activities, is right there in the lesson. Activities rely on readily available household items.

The older format had separate parent instruction cards and parent and student manuals. The new format, described above, integrates all this into one set of instructions for each unit. As of this writing, the Plants, Earth and Space, and People as a Group units were published in the older format. The newly-formatted material will be available in 1990.

Now, about Alta Vista's approach. This curriculum stresses our experience of the creation, and God's self-revelation in the creation, in a manner unfamiliar to most Western Christians. Sometimes I do get the feeling that they are laboring to discover through the "back door" of creation what is easier to see through the written Word. The curriculum introduction, for example, invites you to look at a glass of water. "What do you see?" it asks, and then supplies a list of possible answers: • baptism • a cup of cold water • fishing rights • a thing of beauty • a water bill • the common cup • a babbling brook • the Red Sea • analytic chemistry • an emotional high • a thirst quencher • H_2O • water power • a block of ice • or one glass. This is then related to "the different ways humans experience God's world": • theological • ethical • juridical • aesthetic • economic • social • lingual • historical • analytical • emotional • biological • physical • kinematic • spatial • and numerical. The curriculum then goes on to examine each subject heading (plants, animals, etc.) under these classifications. It is good that on this list theology comes first, but it could be made clearer that theology also informs the other classifications rather than relying so heavily on the innate "law-order designed into Creation" (here I am paraphrasing Alta Vista's brochure).

In a similar vein, the Alta Vista curriculum depends rather more heavily on modern secular educational psychology than other programs. The role of parent as teacher is downplayed in favor of experience-based learning. According to Alta Vista's own calculations, "Over 50% of the learning is based on a personal experience with the subject matter and personal choice of options." You, of course, can tilt the curriculum more to the objective side by parental fiat, skipping over or neglecting some of the subjective material.

Alta Vista has made it easy for you to look into the unique features and philosophy of this curriculum. For three dollars you can send for the sample Earth and Space unit (specify grade level) and check Alta Vista out for yourself.

NEW
American Christian Academy
Track 1, $175. Track 2, price $100.

Established: 1989.
Home School Enrollment in 1988-89: 95.
Curriculum: ACA promotes using a Principle Approach curriculum and offers help in how to use it.
Special Requirements: Commitment to Biblical home education.
Unique features: Assistance in training parents how to teach their children.
Tone: Authoritative.
Religion: Traditional American Christian. Creationist.
Emphasis: Heavy emphasis on reason and logic, and on applying Biblical principles to personal and social issues.
Learning Style: Primarily auditory/visual. Heavy intellectual

emphasis on Biblical researching, reasoning, relating, and recording.
Grades: K-12.

The once and future American Christian Academy . . . Once upon a time there was a full-service program for home schoolers by this name that used the A.C.E. curriculum. I have been informed that it filed for bankruptcy in February of 1988, and turned its records and students over to McGuffey Academy. That is the ACA that was.

Here is the American Christian Academy that is. An entirely different company, located in an entirely different state, and using an entirely different curriculum, it has nothing to do with the original, now-defunct ACA. This ACA is a non-profit California corporation which has retained the American Christian History Institute (producer of Principle Approach materials and seminars) to direct an entire educational program for grades K-12 and home-schooling families.

The school facility occupies seven acres, with 10 classrooms and a full gym. It serves at present around 70 local families and offers a home-school program completely based on the Principle Approach. Day school tuition is $130/month for 10 months plus registration.

American School
$379 one year, $479 two years, $579 three years, $679 four years, for high-school program. Everything included. Payment plan.

Established: 1897.
Enrollment in 1988-89: 30,000.
Curriculum: Published by American School. Only available to enrollees.
Support Services: Lesson grading by correspondence, record-keeping, phone consultation.
Special Requirements: Students of compulsory attendance age must attach a note from their parents or guardians "explaining why this enrollment is necessary" and/or obtain an exemption from local school authorities.
Unique features: Immense array of courses. State-accredited high-school diploma program. 10-day free inspection of materials. Generous refund policy for uncompleted courses. American School will either refund your money or provide you with free additional training if you are required to take a qualifying exam within six months of completing their course and fail to pass it. 10 scholarships/year totaling $6,000 awarded to top graduates.
Tone: Friendly.
Religion: Mainstream secular.
Emphasis: Skills and knowledge useful in the job market.
Learning Style: Primarily visual (studying textbooks).
Grades: 9-12 and vocational training.

American School, widely known as "The School of the Second Chance," is a private school offering a high school diploma by mail. American School is accredited by the North Central Association of Colleges and Schools and by the Accrediting Commission of the National Home Study Council. It is recognized as a private secondary school by the State of Illinois.

The school's ads are aimed mostly at adults. However, students of compulsory attendance age may enroll by attaching a note from their parents or guardians "explaining why this enrollment is necessary" and/or obtaining an exemption from local school authorities.

Usually the first course the American School will send you is Psychology Today (unless you have already taken it somewhere else). This may be waived by students who would rather take another course or by those who, for religious reasons, may not feel comfortable with psychology.

American School lets you buy with confidence, allowing a ten-day free inspection of your courses and a generous refund policy for uncompleted courses. Also, take note of this! *American School will either refund your money or provide you with free additional training if you are required to take a qualifying exam within six months of completing their course and fail to pass it.*

American School offers an immense array of job-related and enrichment courses.

Each year, American School's Scholarship Committee awards 10 scholarships totalling $6,000 to its top graduates.

I have not seen most of their courses, but with over 2,500,000 customers since 1897 and a reported 98 percent satisfaction rate, American School must be competent.

Associated Christian Schools

Now sold under Landmark's Freedom Baptist Curriculum label. See that review.

UPDATED**
Basic Education

Established: 1974.
Enrollment in 1988-89: Approximately 30,000 home-schooled children. Basic Education is also used in over 6,000 schools in 78 countries.
Curriculum: Worktexts and computer.
Services: Available by enrolling in Living Heritage Academy.
Special Requirements: None.
Unique features: New computer and computer-video curriculum. Worktext program moves slower in the first two grades than other programs, moves ahead by ninth grade.
Tone: Friendly.
Religion: Fundamentalist. Creationist.
Emphasis: Morality, patriotism, free enterprise.
Learning Style: Visual. Back-to-basics. Rote and drill.
Grades: K-12.

Basic Education (also known as Accelerated Christian Education, or A.C.E.) is now marketing a brand-new computerized and computer-video interactive curriculum under the name "School of Tomorrow." I'll tell you about it in a minute. But first, let's take a look at the basics of Basic Education.

The Basic Education curriculum contains four core subjects—English, Math, Social Studies, and Science—taught through self-contained and self-instructional worktexts called PACES, SELF-PACS, and Self-Texts. PACES are four-color worktexts written in bite-sized pieces, especially suitable for slower learners. SELF-PACS are black and white worktexts designed for faster learners. Self-Texts are vocabulary-controlled worktexts (one book per subject per grade level) with separate Chapter Test and Answer Key booklets. Emphasis is heavily traditional and back-to-basics, rather than open-ended, unlike other programs that stress hands-on projects and thinking skills. The "biblical" and "theistic" courses (Basic Education's own labels) feature lots of drill and fill-in-the-blanks.

For the teacher, Basic Education is a very easy program to administer. Curriculum is mostly self-instructional, with the exception of the Basic Reading program, for which a complete Teacher's Manual is provided. No other teacher's guides are needed or provided.

Basic Education's program is equally easy for the early-grades student to follow. Layout is straightforward and logical, if unexciting, with a lot of repetition. Texts are printed in nice, clear type. High school students can choose from a variety of electives. Some high-school worktexts would benefit from being broken up into smaller units.

The Basic Reading program teaches 35 phonetic sounds through "visuals, coordination exercises, music, phonetic drills, writing of the letters, and stories" using an animal motif. Originally written for classroom teaching, Basic Reading is both a reading and readiness program, and requires a substantial amount of parent involvement.

In a school situation, Basic Education consists of children of all ages sitting at study carrels, studying individually at their own pace, with a few adults hovering nearby to help answer questions and grade tests. It is an extremely inexpensive way to start a new school and quite a departure from the recent age-segregated classroom model. The folks at Basic Education like to compare it to the traditional one-room schoolhouse; this, however, is not quite accurate, since the one-room schoolhouse featured more regular teacher interaction and kids sitting at desks (and reciting in "classes" of children studying the same book) instead of isolated in booths.

Another Basic Education difference: Basic Education moves more slowly through material in the first two grades than other programs. There is a reason for this; the curriculum writers felt that the reason so many children were failing in school was inadequate time spent on "the basics" before jumping into more advanced studies. Research seems to bear them out, since students taught using Basic Education test *lower* in the first two grades than children using other programs, but *higher* by grade 9 than children following the regular public-school schedule.

Some love Basic Education curriculum; some hate it. Critics complain that Basic Education does not teach real thinking skills, only rote facts, and that children can figure out the answers to the self-tests without ever reading the material. It is true that this program does not put the same stress on creativity as, say, Alpha Omega or Calvert. However, Basic Education still surpasses the public schools' results, since too often they teach *neither* thinking *nor* facts. Basic Education students have in fact been shown to significantly

outperform public school children on standardized tests.

It seemed to me that if parents make the effort to make sure students really study the material, the curriculum will do the job of teaching basic skills and facts in a Christian context, which is what it set out to do.

Now, let's take a look at the new "School of Tomorrow" curriculum from Basic Education. This is a very ambitious project designed eventually to bring the entire Basic Education curriculum into the computer and video age.

The first phase of the School of Tomorrow is AcceleTUTOR® I. The hardware is a Commodore computer with disk drive and special "audio datamaster" (e.g., cassette player). This phase provides computerized tests for all 12 grades of the PACE program, plus some introductory work in typing, word processing, database management, spread sheets, and BASIC and PASCAL programming. By virtue of the audio cassette interface, it also provides spelling practice. OK, but not terribly exciting.

Phase Two, the AcceleTUTOR® II, is a different animal. Here Basic Education leaps ahead of anything anyone else is doing in this area. They have designed a unique method that can take any existing video, add special codes to it, and make it computer-interactive with any IBM-compatible computer using their special plug-in video card. The software-driven board will work with any standard video player. (This approach is being made available to businesses that want to add computer testing/instruction to their training videos—if you are interested, call!) Their own AcceleTUTOR® II setup includes a Kaypro IBM-compatible and a Magnavox monitor that can switch back and forth from RGB (computer) mode to NTSC (video) mode. What you end up with are full-color videos that you can manipulate from your computer keyboard (go to beginning of lesson, go back to last part of video you were watching, skip to next lesson, etc.) and that self-interrupt with regular computer testing on what you just saw on the video. Questions include true/false, yes/no, fill-in-the-blanks, and multiple choice. The computer testing includes screen-sensitive help, the option of calling up a summary of the video's narration (in case the questions are a bit hard to answer), and ways to quit or move around in the video. You never have to fiddle with Fast Forward or Rewind. Each video will be correlated directly to an existing PACE; lesson numbers of the PACE appear in the lower portion of the screen. It all comes with an Applications Projects Manual (also available on floppy disk) that provides projects in the basic areas of word processing, spreadsheets, and database management. Basic Education claims that if your student completes all the suggested Applications Projects (which are integrated with the basic scope & sequence), he will graduate high school with the equivalent of two years' computer experience.

The School of Tomorrow equipment and programs are only available through Basic Education. Basic Education also sells a fine selection of commercial educational software for Commodore and IBM at good prices, and provides a scope and sequence showing how to integrate it to their curriculum.

Families wishing to enroll in a Basic Education full-service home-school program should contact Living Heritage Academy. Satellite schools may qualify for a school account with Basic Education itself; contact them directly for details.

Bob Jones University Press

Established: 1974.
Home-school families served in 1988-89: Tens of thousands (exact figures are not available).
Curriculum: Published by Bob Jones University Press. A few support materials from other publishers.
Support Services: Toll-free phone consultation. *Home School Helper* newsletter. Annual Home School Conference. Not an enrollment program—all these services are free to all comers.
Special Requirements: None.
Unique features: Academic Skills Evaluation Program available, using national standardized tests. Highest-quality textbooks and teacher support materials. Full line of science-lab equipment and supplies.
Tone: Extremely friendly.

Religion: Evangelical Christian.
Emphasis: Training students to think, as well as to master facts. Less overtly Biblical than some other programs.
Learning Style: Primarily auditory/visual. Good amount of kinesthetic input, especially in early grades.
Grades: Pre-K through 12.

Now here's a big-time company that's *really* friendly to home schoolers! Bob Jones has a toll-free number for questions about their curriculum and a gorgeous catalog loaded with everything you need from preschool through high school. Not only that, BJU's line of (often hardback) texts is widely conceded to be the overall best in Christian publishing.

BJU Press offers textbooks and teacher's editions in all subjects and grade levels. In addition, they offer texts in a number of special areas—computer science, speech, family living— where materials are not generally available.

BJU Press has worked very hard to make their materials consistent with a Christian approach for each subject discipline. (A concise statement on each discipline and on Christian education is available from the publisher.) This does not mean every page is loaded with Bible verses. The BJU Press educational approach balances learning facts, understanding concepts, developing reasoning skills, and nurturing Christian character, all for use in a real-world context.

This curriculum offers Bible from grades K4-12; reading, K-6; handwriting, K-6; spelling, 2-6; grammar and composition, 2-12; literature, 7-12; vocabulary, 7-12; history, 1-7 and 9-12; math, K-12 (includes geometry and two years of algebra); science, 1-12, including chemistry and physics.

You may buy teacher's manuals for any subject. Most of the teacher's editions include a complete student text in a looseleaf notebook. This could eliminate the need for a student book in some subjects. In other subjects, BJU's policy of printing most upper-grade texts as hardbacks (students do assignments in separate notebooks) means you buy the book only once and can use it again and again with all your children. In addition, Bob Jones University Press is currently working on teacher editions especially designed for home educators. Some of these will be available by fall of 1990.

Did I say Bob Jones University Press was friendly to home schoolers? How about this: *home schoolers may order at the wholesale price,* plus shipping and handling only. Catalogs and curriculum overviews are free on request (just call BJU's toll-free number, 1-800-845-5731).

UPDATED**
Calvert School
$215 K, $370 1-4, $395 5-8. Advisory Teaching Service, $182 1-4, $193 5-6, $203 7-8. New French course, $110 first student, additional students $35 each, Advisory Teaching Service $65. Video Lessons for the first grade, $150. Everything included. No discounts. No refunds once course begins.

Established: 1897.
Enrollment in 1988-89: 7,300.
Curriculum: About half-and-half Calvert School materials and materials from other publishers. Unique Calvert Manuals for each grade show exactly what to do and how to do it.
Support Services (optional): Lesson grading by correspondence, record-keeping, phone consultation.
Special Requirements: Students entering grades 4-8 who have not finished the previous grade using Calvert's Advisory Teaching Program must take a placement test. Each course may only be used with one student. Teacher's Manual must be returned or destroyed on completion of course.
Unique features: New video enrichment program for first grade. New French course for grades 4 and up. Classic emphasis. Super-excellent teacher manuals. All needed school supplies included.
Tone: Friendly.
Religion: Public school civic religion as it used to be (occasional references to God). Calvert is a private, non-sectarian, non-profit school.
Emphasis: Training students to think, as well as to master facts. Strong focus on Western cultural heritage, classic art, and creative writing.
Learning Style: All styles in early grades, progressing to mostly visual in later grades.
Grades: K (a readiness program)-8.

Calvert School is the granddaddy of home education programs. Over 350,000 pupils have enrolled in Calvert over the years, many of whom have gone on to demonstrate considerable excellence in their chosen fields. Justice Sandra Day O'Connor, for example, is a graduate of Calvert's kindergarten program.

Calvert operates its own highly successful day school, and all home-study materials are tested in Calvert's own classrooms. The school is fully accredited by the Maryland State Department of Education.

Before we get into the program itself, you should know that Calvert definitely has "it," that special ambience that emanates only from the old, the rich, and the excellent. We hear that the Calvert Day Class of 1927 contained twelve descendants of the signers of the Declaration of Independence, and we aren't surprised. As Pooh Bear might say, "It's *that* sort of school."

The Calvert program is a structured, textbook-oriented, traditional course of study. Academically it is very strong, with a commendable emphasis on developing creative thought and communication as well as basic skills. Calvert has a "Christian culture" flavor. Christianity is not taught, or presented as *the* truth, but it is not blatantly ignored or suppressed either. The historic accomplishments of Christians are recognized, and morality is generally pro-Christian. Evolution is not stressed, but appears now and again in some science courses.

Calvert's emphasis on creativity includes serious attention to art in the early grades and a unique series on painting, sculpture, and architecture appreciation in the upper grades. Other special emphases: Social studies means history and geography, not "Sam's Visit to Niagara Falls." History studies include mythology. Handwriting begins in the first grade with Calvert's own simplified cursive script. Parents are given a wealth of classic stories to read to their young offspring. Another nice touch, much appreciated by Calvert's many missionary families: *All* needed school supplies are included with each order—pencils, paper, crayons, art supplies, ruler, etc.

Textbooks in science and math are up-to-date. For language arts, Calvert often uses classics, some of which Calvert reprints itself. Lots of enrichment books and literature are included. *The Teacher's Manual is only leased from Calvert and must be destroyed or returned when the course is completed.*

New features for the 1990 school year:
• The first and second grade reading programs have been revised to restore a more classic phonics emphasis.
• A brand-new video enrichment program is also now available for first grade. These engaging tapes have a "Mr. Rogers" flavor, with snippets featuring dif-

ferent Calvert teachers giving show-and-tell style lessons in language arts, science, music, physical education, math, and fine art. They appear made for TV, with a lead-in and sign-off for each episode (not necessary on a home video!) along with very professionally-done shooting and staging. You might get a mellow piano player dressed in a rakish top hat introducing his "friends," the stringed instruments, or meet some animal babies, or practice hopping, skipping, and galloping. These lessons were designed to demonstrate concepts and activities that are hard to convey to young children in words alone. The set of three tapes costs $150 and is only available to families enrolled in Calvert's first-grade program.

• Calvert also now offers a beginning French course, consisting of five audio cassette tapes, a student workbook, a parent instruction manual, and all necessary supplies. Students in grades 4 and up may enroll in Beginning French. You do not need to enroll in Calvert to take the French course. The Advisory Teaching option is available for this course.

Calvert's optional Advisory Teaching Service includes test grading, record-keeping, and correspondence by mail or phone with a certified teacher who will give suggestions and advice to the home study student and to the home teacher.

Calvert requires more work from the home teacher in the early grades than most programs. To help you through this period, each lesson includes *everything* you need to teach it. Potential trouble spots are identified and solutions given. If you follow Calvert's excellent advice *exactly*, you can hardly go wrong.

For the student, Calvert is an excellent program. The format is straightforward, crisp, and logical and the lessons are interesting. Tests are bound into the Manual after every 20 lessons, so the student can see where he is heading and what progress he is making.

Each grade becomes progressively more self-instructional, as the student learns to take control of his own education. Thus the parents work less in the end than at the beginning. Also, required record-keeping is minimal.

Calvert's lesson manuals are an education in themselves—for the parents! Any home-school parent who uses Calvert for a young child will pick up some excellent teaching tips and techniques as a bonus. After using Calvert kindergarten, I felt competent to teach my children on my own.

Calvert is equally useful for the very bright student and the slower student, thanks to the excellent step-by-step approach. Many poor performers in

school have gone on to do outstanding work after enrolling in Calvert.

Calvert deserves an A+ academic rating. A child can graduate from Calvert's eighth grade course, take a few achievement tests, and go straight to the college of his choice. Think about it!

NEW**
Carden Educational Foundation
Basic Carden Course, 15 hours of on-site instruction to groups of 10 or more, $120/person attending. Teacher instruction cassettes, around $13 apiece. All books, cassettes, manuals, and teacher's editions are quite inexpensive.

Established: 1934.
Enrollment in 1988-89: About 10,000 pupils in 75 schools.
Curriculum: Classic. Uses "living books" approach stressing cultural heritage, plus many readers and books written by Miss Carden.
Special Requirements: Purchasers requested to take Carden Basic Course if at all possible. This requirement may be waived; however, you would be very wise to read Miss Carden's books and listen to the teacher instruction cassettes before beginning this program.
Unique features: Programs for 3- and 4-year-olds. Strong phonics/reading comprehension approach. Classic literature, cursive writing, music (including sightsinging), classic music and art appreciation, and French begin in grade 1. Dramatics and playlets. Individualized approach based on heavy teacher involvement.
Tone: Firm but friendly.
Religion: Civic religion. Bible workbooks and plays available separately.
Emphasis: Cultural heritage, respect for individual, character-building (with emphasis on the student's Stamina Quotient, e.g., persevering with cheerfulness).
Learning Style: All styles.
Grades: Nursery school-11.

I introduced you to Miss Mae Carden in Chapter 11. She was one formidable lady, a great educator with a sense of humor and respect for children coupled with high academic and moral standards. The 75 schools she helped establish all over the United States have got to be the best-kept secret of modern education, mainly because the trustees of the Foundation set up after her death don't believe in materialistic self-promotion. (Now when's the last time you heard anything like THAT??!!)

Standing firmly in the classic educational tradition born out of 1900 years' experience in Christendom, the Carden materials stress the importance of understanding over memorizing, beauty over expediency, learning for its own sake rather than artificial rewards, and structured learning over letting children drift as their whims take them. The curriculum is designed "incrementally"; that is, children are given a chance to digest new material before being pressured to use it, and are given sufficient opportunity to practice with it until it becomes second nature. Teachers are encouraged to show children the meaning of their lessons in terms of "the needs of life," which to Miss Carden did not mean "how to get a better job" so much as "how to find out who you are and what you can contribute to the world."

Thus, starting with the earliest grades, children are introduced to classic art and music (and learn art and music techniques), put on playlets for each other, read or listen to classic literature, learn French (cassettes are provided to ensure correct pronunciation), and enjoy poetry, along with traditional courses in science and math. Upper-grades students study the history of Greece and Rome as well as the history of the USA. Handwriting starts with cursive in the first grade, and reading instruction includes a very strong phonics course (zero failures to read in Carden schools!) combined with an emphasis from the first on *thinking* about what you read. The Carden readers are value-laden and extremely comforting, written as they were in a world when nobody worried about AIDS, divorce, or nuclear war. These sorts of problems are not dumped on children in the Carden curriculum.

The brochure you will receive from the Carden Educational Foundation states that materials may only be purchased by those who have received Carden training. The people at Carden do recognize, however, that some of us live in remote areas or have trouble getting together 10 like-minded people for 15 hours of training; so you can write for a waiver of this condition. Indicate you are a home schooler and the circumstances that prevent you from attending a Carden Basic Course.

Carden materials were all designed for classroom use, meaning that the teacher's manuals are not the simplest books to zip through. If you can't attend Carden Basic Training, you will be well-advised to obtain the teacher instruction cassettes for subjects and grades you want to teach, as these will greatly enhance your ability to get the most out of Carden materials.

Christian Liberty Academy

$150 Jr, Sr K; $230 grades 1-8; $270 grades 9-12. CLASS now requires a modest "book fee" surcharge for high school electives. Otherwise, everything included. Book credit when younger student reuses materials. No discounts. No refunds once books shipped. Family Administration Plan enrollment option, $130 K, $200 grades 1-8, $240 grades 9-12. School Starter Kit (for Christian schools), $70.

Established: 1968.
Enrollment in 1988-89: 22,000.
Curriculum: Eclectic. Uses books and materials from 25 different (mostly evangelical Christian) publishers. CLASS is also now publishing an increasing amount of its own textbooks and readers. These last are available separately—write for brochure.
Support Services (optional): Schoolwork review by correspondence, grading, record-keeping, quarterly report cards, administration of a Basic Skills Test, phone counseling, legal advice and assistance, and diplomas on completion of grades 8 and 12. Family Plan enrollment option includes testing and curriculum only.
Special Requirements: Students using full enrollment option in grades 1-12 must complete all pages in every workbook, with the exception of math and grammar texts.
Unique features: Latin and foreign languages available starting in grade 7. Individualized program for each student. Heavy academic emphasis in kindergarten programs. Quarterly newspaper. Other special materials sent out free to CLASS families from time to time.
Tone: Firm but friendly.
Religion: Sturdy evangelical Christian. Creationist.
Emphasis: Patriotic, pro-free enterprise. Strong focus on American Christian heritage, character development, and basics.
Learning Style: Primarily visual/auditory. Not recommended for kinesthetic learners.
Grades: Junior and Senior Kindergarten-12.

Could it be an omen? Christian Liberty Academy has bought a public school campus! With an active enrollment of 20,000 home study students, Christian Liberty Academy Satellite Schools (CLASS) is seeing its program grow faster than any other in the USA. Christian Liberty operates its own day school where courses are originated and evaluated by its staff of well-educated professionals.

Here we have a strongly traditional, basics-oriented program with a heavy non-denominational Bible emphasis. CLASS curriculum covers more subject areas than many others: traditional math, phonics, reading, writing, Biblical studies, geography, history, the Constitution, science, and even languages (optional). Kindergarten programs include art, music, and character development.

CLASS places great stress on self-discipline and mastery of material. *All* of the workbooks provided for the many subject areas must be completed in their entirety, with the exception of math and grammar. Parents may write requesting program alterations, but you should not count on making any substantial program changes if you purchase full enrollment services.

Students receive individualized programs based on their test results (for grades 2-12) and on the information parents provide about their children's current level of skills (kindergarten and grade 1). Parents grade daily work; major tests and completed daily work are returned to CLASS. CLASS keeps records, issues quarterly report cards, and grants eighth grade and high school diplomas. CLASS also provides a large handbook for parents, with information on how to administer the program, and teacher's editions for some subjects. Parents are expected to produce their own lesson plans. You do this by taking the total number of pages in each book, dividing them by the number of days in the school year, and completing that number of pages

per day. Simple! Study guides are now provided for all courses, eliminating the hassle CLASS parents used to face of making up lesson plans for courses without study guides.

Textbooks are up-to-date—even the Latin texts!

Expect to spend ten to twenty hours getting acquainted with the books and the Handbook. You will also be designing lesson plans to meet your family's particular needs. CLASS provides a sample of a proper lesson plan, and you take it from there. This takes much more time at the beginning, but gives the family more educational freedom.

CLASS is a *lot* of work for the student. You get a wealth of texts and workbooks to complete. Even four- and five-year-olds have a serious academic program, where they learn to read, write (in manuscript), add, and subtract, as well as doing normal kindergarten art, music, and so on. Each CLASS grade covers work other schools don't assign this early. Thus CLASS grade 2 is more like public school grade 3 and their senior kindergarten is actually a serious first grade program.

Latin and foreign languages are available starting at grade 7, for students who have already successfully completed a year of CLASS.

CLASS sends out special materials for homeschooling parents from time to time. Examples: a *Home Education Journal* devoted to legal issues, a book on Biblical principles, a monthly newspaper.

I like the freedom of making my own lesson plans, and in my view when it comes to questions of government, family, and the like, CLASS is among the most Biblical programs on the market. CLASS operates as a ministry; therefore tuition is low and their concern for families is high.

A friend reports immense satisfaction with the first grade program. The kindergarten and grade 2 programs (which we have used) are also excellent—many books for your money, all of them carefully chosen. Quality seems to continue through all grades. Quibbles: Some of the workbooks are voluminous and repetitive. You have to provide your own science equipment. The language arts approach in the upper grades could be more creative and fun (try supplementing with some Alpha Omega LIFEPACS).

Academically, I give CLASS an A. If you want a really solid, economical Christian curriculum with lots of "meat" both spiritually and academically; if you want the flexibility of designing your own schedule; if you have the confidence to teach without elaborate study guides; if you and your children enjoy hard work, CLASS is a program for you.

Christian Light Education

Three enrollment options (see below). Curriculum materials are extra for all options. Curriculum cost is approximately $120/year/pupil.

Established: 1979.
Enrollment in 1988-89: 1,260 in Option 3 (see description below), plus hundreds more in the other Options, for which a count is not maintained.
Curriculum: Revised Alpha Omega LIFEPACS, plus some textbooks published by CLE.
Support Services: Option 1: Basic Information Teacher Training Kit—$20, and, if you have a first-grader, *Basics for Beginners,* the training program for teaching the Learning to Read program—$7.50 and the Teacher Handbook for that program—$4.95. Option 2: *Basics for Beginners* (if needed), one-week parent-training program, available by mail or at CLE's regular late spring and summer training sessions—$75. Option 3: *Basics for Beginners* (if needed), parent training program, record-keeping, telephone counseling (you call and describe problem and they get back to you), California Achievement Test, and diploma upon completion of high school—$100. Free one-day regional fall workshops for all home schoolers.
Special Requirements: None.
Unique features: Lab supplies available for all science courses. Strong role distinctions for boys and girls. Materials feature people in Mennonite dress. Canadian social studies. Large variety of high school electives.
Tone: Friendly.
Religion: Conservative Mennonite.
Emphasis: Pacifist, down-to-earth, nonpolitical, family- and farm-oriented.
Learning Style: Primarily auditory/visual. Borderline for kinesthetic learners.
Grades: Junior and Senior Kindergarten-12.

Christian Light Education is a part of the ministry of Christian Light Publications, a provider of school materials to the conservative wing of the Mennonite community. Mennonites are followers of Menno Simons, a sixteenth-century religious leader who practiced believers' baptism, pacifism, and unworldliness.

The Pennsylvania "Dutch," or Amish, are one well-known Mennonite group.

Christian Light offers a worktext approach, based on their own revision of the very popular Alpha Omega worktexts, plus some of Christian Light's own hardcover textbooks and resource books. The revised Alpha Omega texts are more attractive than the original, with heavy kivar-like paper covers and colored ink used within. As revised, their curriculum is more down-to-earth; family-centered stories replace Alpha Omega's fantasy stories in the lower grades, for example. Pictures reflect Mennonite community values: women have uncut, covered hair, dress is very modest, we see nice large families.

You can purchase a variety of high school electives, including consumer math, home economics, art, Greek, and Spanish, and four Canadian social studies units, in the usual worktext format. Christian Light also carries courses in typing, carpentry, auto mechanics, small engines, survival car care, woodworking, and bookkeeping. These courses are based on textbooks from other publishers, and Christian Light provides brief guides explaining how to fit them into its program.

Religious orientation is gently Mennonite (they don't beat you over the head with it). Traditional family values and sexual roles are stressed. The curriculum is creationist, pacifist, and determinedly nonpolitical.

The curriculum emphasizes the basic skills as well as offering a strong program in science and social studies. First grade starts with the intensive phonics *Learning to Read* program, which is easy to teach and inexpensive (less than $20 without Answer Key). As a whole, this largely self-contained curriculum stresses thinking skills. Christian Light believes in individuality (learn at your own pace) and personalized studies (matching content and teaching methods to the student's needs and abilities).

Teacher handbooks and answer keys are available for almost every subject. Some of these are Alpha Omega's original versions, which were designed with classroom use in mind. Still, they are easy to follow. The worktexts are also very easy to follow. Students can do most work without too much adult teaching.

Christian Light's record-keeping requirements for option 3 families are straightforward. (Families using other options do not send records to CLE.) You send in brief monthly reports of work done, including reports of test scores, work in other planned educational activities, and time in each. From this CLE maintains a student file including the student's academic and attendance records. Additional attendance books and record-keeping forms are available to make life easier.

The original Alpha Omega materials are very good in English and Science, and Christian Light hasn't hurt these areas any. The Social Studies emphasis is different, reflecting Mennonite concerns. I consider Christian Light's changes to the early-grades material to be an improvement.

Christian Light sells all needed materials for its science courses (with the exception of commonly-available items like soda straws, toothpicks, etc.). This places their science program head and shoulders above most others. The *free* CLE sample packet includes a catalog and info on science equipment and school supplies. A larger $10 sample kit is also available.

Children can progress rapidly with Christian Light's material, and they will truly learn how to learn. Academically, I give Christian Light an A.

For those favoring Mennonite religious and political beliefs, Christian Light is a "best buy."

Christian Schools International

Established: 1920.
Home-schooling families served in 1988-89: Figure not available.
Curriculum: Published by Christian Schools International.
Support Services: None.
Special Requirements: None.
Unique features: No-nonsense approach, very reasonable prices.
Tone: Firm.
Religion: Reformed Christian with a *Christianity Today* flavor.
Emphasis: Mainstream approach to social problems. Peer-segregated classroom focus.
Learning Style: Auditory/visual.
Grades: K-12.

Another full-service schoolbook supplier, this time from a Reformed Christian perspective. In keeping with this background, CSI's products appear to be more functional and intellectual than most others.

CSI doesn't offer math or reading textbooks, but covers most other subjects and grades.

One excellent CSI offering is their *Writing Rainbow* series, reviewed in the Writing and Composition section. This opens up the art of composition both logically and creatively. Their hardbound science series for upper elementary grades is on a par with Bob Jones' science series—very well organized and easy to use, with a lot of training in thinking and observation. The series takes a pop approach to "overpopulation" and other ecological issues some may prefer to skip. New in 1989 is a preschool-8 Bible series entitled "The Story of God and His People." It takes a chronolgical, story-based approach, with sequenced picture cards for K-2 and a Bible dictionary for grades 3-5.

All the CSI textbooks are very reasonably priced and easy to order.

Clonlara School Home Based Education Program

$350 per family for all services. Books and supplies extra. Standardized achievement testing extra. Refunds: $35 fee for cancellation within six days after registration form received by Clonlara.

Established: 1979.
Enrollment in 1988-89: 1,200 families.
Curriculum: Eclectic.
Support Services: Clonlara's *The Learning Edge* newsletter, contact with other Clonlara families, a pen pal network for your children to plug into if desired, continual consultation with Clonlara staff on academic and other questions, record-keeping, transcripts, and diploma upon graduation. The Clonlara staff handles all interactions with local school and other authorities for each enrolled family.
Special Requirements: Secondary school students are expected to perform 300 hours of volunteer service in the community.
Unique features: Much more parental/student control than other full-service programs.
Tone: Friendly.
Religion: Serves all religious groups.
Emphasis: Progressive/liberal.
Learning Style: All styles.
Grades: K-12.

The Home Based Education Program operating out of Clonlara's independent alternative day school is a program for the progressive, do-it-yourself type.

You get a curriculum to use as a starting point for a program you tailor yourself, a *Math Skills Guidebook*, and a *Communication Skills Guidebook*, plus Clonlara's menu of support services (see above).

You create your own individualized program with the help of Clonlara's curriculum listing and as much guidance from the Clonlara staff as you desire. The listing tells you what subjects to study and what the objectives are in each area. Some families take it just as it stands, some don't bother with it at all, and some change it around to suit themselves. This latter is the option Clonlara recommends most: to use it as a working paper.

Clonlara's *Skills Guidebooks* are diagnostic tools that cover the basics. You can find out where your children stand by checking off their accomplishments on the chart in the *Math Skills Guidebook* and seeing if they are on track for their ages in the *Communications Skills Guidebook*.

The choice of textbooks and other materials is left entirely to the family. Clonlara suggests you go beyond texts by making wide use of the public library and building up your home library.

Clonlara stresses manipulative learning tools and real-life experiences in place of endless workbookery. You choose the texts you do use based on the student's achieved grade level in each subject, not his age. You can order texts from any school publisher through Clonlara.

Each month you send in a Monthly Home Study Record to Clonlara, or if you prefer, a daily or monthly log, along with narrative reports. Clonlara teachers review these, and respond when necessary. A cumulative file folder (student record) is kept for each student. Clonlara provides report cards, transcripts, and a private school diploma on graduation. Graduation occurs when a student has completed his credits and exit examinations, regardless of his age. A Clonlara diploma is widely accepted.

Parents and students are not pressured into completing x amount of work and mailing it to Clonlara. Neither do you have to wait for Clonlara's judgment upon your work. Passage to another grade or subject does not hinge on Clonlara's approval. You decide what you are ready for and when you are ready for it.

The Clonlara staff bristles with official credentials, up to and including the Ph.D. Dr. Pat Montgomery, Clonlara's director, is very active in the alternative school movement, and has served as a president of the National Coalition of Alternative Community Schools. Pat currently serves on the executive committee of the National Homeschool Association.

Families who follow John Holt's lead rank high on the list of those who find Clonlara compatible. This includes those who can "do it themselves" but want a friendly school's guidance and backup and those who want to try the structure of a traditional program without the pressure of deadlines and punishments (such as withholding grades). Progressive types looking for a relaxed program will probably be most comfortable with Clonlara.

UPDATED✶✶
Covenant Home Curriculum

K $195, grades 1-8 $250. Tutorial fee and grade auditing service: K $55, grades 1-8 $85. Grades 9-12: regular enrollment with grade auditing included, $361 postpaid; enrollment without auditing services, $286 postpaid; each 2-year course, $76 additional. Grades 1-12 Diagnostic C.H.A.T. tests ("Little Windows on Progress") $14-18/student. Add $9.50/student for shipping. Extracurricular materials also available.

Established: 1972.
Home schoolers enrolled in 1988-89: 279.
Curriculum: Innovative blend of hands-on materials, classic literature.
Support Services: Grading, record-keeping, report cards, assigned telephone tutor you may call during specified school hours.
Special Requirements: None.
Unique features: Wide range of study helps and non-textbook material accompanying strong traditional core. Individualized curriculum (each subject may be at a different grade level). Westminster Shorter Catechism with study guide available for grades 5-7. More heavy-duty Bible study courses than other programs. Inexpensive diagnostic tests developed by Covenant. English includes diagramming. Many classics read. You only need to send in materials on quarterly basis.
Tone: Academically rigorous. College prep emphasis. Alternative high-school program allows extra time, less material to cover.
Religion: Traditional Reformed Christian. Creationist.
Emphasis: Classical. Strong emphasis on mastering the tools of learning. Pro-free enterprise and Christian culture.
Learning Style: All styles in early grades, progressing to mostly visual in upper grades.
Grades: K-12.

Covenant Home Curriculum has been tested and developed over a fifteen-year period in their K-12 Christian day school in suburban Milwaukee. Consciously designed to promote a classic Christian worldview, this eclectic curriculum strongly emphasizes classic literature (third- to sixth-graders get abridged versions of works like *A Tale of Two Cities* and *Pride and Prejudice*, upper-graders get full-length classics), writing and speaking skills, a reverently scientific outlook on life, and in-depth Biblical knowledge. The curriculum includes many extras: a *Preceptor's Manual* for parents that explains how to administer the program; study guides especially prepared for home schoolers; simple diagnostic tests; study helps, such as Covenant's own *Guide to Writing Book Reports*, and (Covenant's most unusual feature) a wide selection of extracurricular material, such as science, art, and history coloring books and historical biographies. New among these latter are a series of historical paper dolls used in the kindergarten and first grade history programs, and a truly innovative Christian art program called *Art Masters* (more info on this in Volume 4).

Before we get too much farther into this review, let me mention Covenant's new alternative high school program, designed for those who like to learn at a slower rate of speed. This is Covenant's attempt to "keep the quality while reducing the quantity." Essentially, the student is given the option of taking his high-school math and science courses for two years rather than one, meaning he has twice the time to master the material. With this innovation, Covenant has shown its commitment to maintaining quality standards of learning while recognizing that not all of us learn at the same speed.

Covenant's approach reminds me of Charlotte Mason's (see the Introduction to Home Schooling chapter): lots of emphasis on mastering the tools of learning, much time spent with classic literature and engaging the child's scientific interest, combined with drill and discipline. I also noticed with some interest that their classic literature selections are very similar to those used in the Carden schools. Great minds think alike!

Kindergarten is a reading and discovery curriculum. History books are read to children in grades K and 1, working up to grade 3, where history finally becomes a full-credit course.

Science includes not only a basic science text, but appealing science readers that tell the story of, for example, weather, or, say, follow the life cycle of an elephant or oak tree. Upper-grades science work covers natural science, biology, physics, and chemistry (one subject per grade), along with hands-on investigations and a solid grounding in creation science. Students electing the alternative high-school program can take either Science of the Physical Creation or Biology for two years.

Upper-grades history concentrates on presenting a Biblical (pro-free enterprise and freedom) worldview, and covers government and economics as well as history.

The math courses continue CHC's strong college prep emphasis. Algebra starts in grade 8 (your choice of Saxon Algebra or a Brand X text) and proceeds to more algebra (grades 9 and 10), trig and geometry (10 and 11), calculus (11th grade) and prepping for the College Boards (grade 12). In addition, your student can choose from a number of alternative math books and courses, some designed especially to help those who struggle with math. Students electing the alternative high-school program can either take Business Math and Math for Your Career, or spread Algebra I or Plane Geometry over two years. (College-bound students should take both Algebra and Geometry.)

The language arts curriculum is CHC's pride and joy. Earlier grades focus on developing basic punctuation and grammar skills and developing a love of reading, with many short classics included in the standard curriculum as well as A Beka readers and McGuffeys. Upper-grade students study grammar (including diagramming), spelling, poetry, vocabulary, composition, etymology (grades 5-9), and serious classics (books are included with the program). To accompany these, Covenant now offers a series of *Classic Critiques*. Designed for parents, these brief write-ups point out the reasons the book is considered a classic and provide discussion questions and Biblical analysis of the book. Covenant also offers a wide range of high-school literature and composition electives, plus two years of elective Latin. A two-year high-school course on the Westminster Shorter Catechism is also available.

Covenant Home Curriculum provides individualized curriculum (each subject may be at a different grade level), phone counseling, short turn-around grading time, and report cards. Additional help, in the form of reading comprehension books and test preparation materials, is available. You have an assigned telephone tutor whom you may call during specified school hours for a quick response.

All texts and workbooks include answer keys and teaching guides. You get a *lot* of books for your money, including titles from A Beka, Thoburn Press, Raintree

Press (American publisher with a user interface like that of EDC's Usborne books), Modern Curriculum Press, Educators Publishing Service, Christian Schools International, Saxon Algebra, Bob Jones University Press, and other reputable, quality publishers. All Covenant Home Curriculum materials are very professional and good-looking

Covenant only asks you to return *quarterly* tests for grading, unlike some other programs that require weekly or monthly reporting.

I am increasingly impressed with Covenant Home Curriculum, especially now that they are flexing to accommodate slower students. (Or shall we say, to accommodate non-supersonic learners!) Their high-school program looks particularly good. This time around, Covenant gets an A.

Hewitt Child Development Center

Regular Program, $275. Alternate Program, $145. High Achievers Regular Program, $375. High Achievers Alternate Program, $215. Special Needs Program, $475. Readiness Program, $95. Early Childhood Training Program, $95. Books extra for all options except the Early Childhood and Readiness programs. Book costs generally range from $125 to $250 per student.

Established: 1983.
Enrollment in 1988-89: 4,000.
Curriculum: Innovative blend of hands-on materials and Hewitt activity guides. Some textbooks and workbooks used as resource material.
Support Services: Depends on option chosen. Regular Program includes two program evaluations, telephone and mail counseling, semi-annual testing with the PASS test for grades 3-8 (see Testing chapter), and some record-keeping. Alternate program does not provide follow-up counseling or evaluations, but may be upgraded to Regular Program at any time.
Special Requirements: None.
Unique features: Special programs for "special" and "gifted" children. Low-key programs for young children. Choice of traditional textbook program (designed so as to involve little writing) or more hands-on program for 6- and 7-year-

olds. Stress on community service and home business for older students.
Tone: Friendly.
Religion: Evangelical Christian. Creationist.
Emphasis: Hands-on, project-oriented, creative thinking.
Learning Style: All styles. Particularly suited to kinesthetic learners.
Grades: Birth through grade 12.

The Hewitt Research Foundation's Child Development Center program is based on the concept of "better late than early." Swimming against the cultural stream that threatens to tear infants from the very breast to plug them into formal learning situations, Hewitt maintains that readiness can't be rushed and that it's better to put off formal studies until an age when the student is sure to succeed.

Hewitt's philosophy revolves around preparing you to educate your child rather than preparing your child to be educated. Hewitt says, "Place the child at his optimum learning level and then allow him to proceed at his own rate." This is done as much as possible with real-world learning and hands-on projects. Although texts and some workbooks are used, they are meant as resource material, not as the primary source of instruction. Many Hewitt materials, such as the activity guides that accompany texts, are exclusively theirs.

How do you offer a curriculum that starts at birth? With an Early Childhood Training Program for parents of babies and toddlers! Hewitt teaches you how to teach yours. For children aged five to seven, Hewitt has an informal Readiness Program that emphasizes nature study, practical work, field trips, and art. In keeping with the better-late-than-early philosophy, the Readiness Program does not teach formal reading and writing skills.

If your child is above the readiness level, and has not previously been enrolled in a Hewitt course, he must enroll in the Regular Program. This is the full-service option. Hewitt's Alternate Program, which does not include counseling and evaluations, is available only to families of elementary students who have been enrolled with Hewitt for one year and are thus familiar with their philosophy, books, and methods. A Hewitt teacher will design an individualized curriculum for your child with this option. Alternate Program enrollees may upgrade to the Regular Program at any time. All secondary students must enroll in the Regular Program.

Unlike other programs, Hewitt has special services for families with exceptional children on both the high-need and high-achievement ends of the spectrum. The teachers involved in these programs "have met special education requirements and are thoroughly equipped to give you well-thought-out and skillfully-prepared support for your special child." This includes children labeled as developmentally delayed, dyslexic, or as having "attention-deficit disorder" (a fancy term for little boys who hate sitting still), as well as those with physical conditions such as Downs Syndrome. Honors classes are available to high achievers in the secondary program. Hewitt offers specialized testing in both the Special Needs and High Achievers programs.

Students, especially those enrolled in the secondary program, are encouraged to establish a cottage industry, become involved in civic or volunteer work, or be involved in a vocational program. Hewitt strongly promotes this kind of practical work education as an excellent way of both building character and preparing the student for the realities of making a living. Their *Home Education Guide* provides a list of potential cottage industries. Secondary students are expected to manifest self-motivation and are required to mail four reports to Hewitt for each subject throughout the year.

Hewitt's new newsletter, *Treasure Trove*, is really sharp and eye-catching. Geared towards children, each issue presents upbeat articles on such subjects as pets, exhibits to visit around the country, healthful living, craft projects, penpal and get-acquainted columns, and poems, stories, and other submissions for home-schooling children. Each issue also includes a page or two of information for parents.

For the student, Hewitt's approach definitely is less stressful. Hewitt wants to avoid meaningless rote work (e.g., filling out dozens of workbook pages on a subject the student has already mastered). Heavily visual/intellectual learners may prosper more with a more rigorous traditional approach, but active little boys and tomboys, special-needs children, and kinesthetic learners of all ages will find a friend at Hewitt. For students in these categories, I give this curriculum an A.

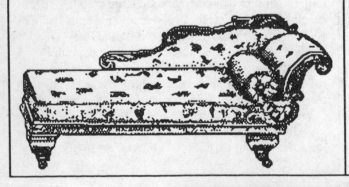

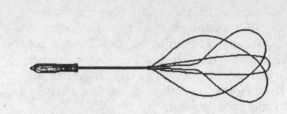

Home Centered Learning
Family membership: $90 per year. Additional services extra.

Established: 1980.
Enrollment in 1988-89: 500.
Curriculum: Eclectic.
Services: Kits, guides, record-keeping, Year Book, ID card, newsletters, and materials required by California law.
Special Requirements: None.
Unique features: "Shell" program designed to help parents increase their teaching skills and meet California requirements. You design your own curriculum.
Tone: Friendly.
Religion: Secular.
Emphasis: Director John Boston is a firm believer in the educational philosophy of John Holt, Ivan Illich, and Dr. William Glasser.
Learning Style: All styles.
Grades: K-12.

Here's one program *without* a preset curriculum for you California types! A state-attested private school Administrative Unit (this all means something in California!) that believes in "invited teaching." For the yearly enrollment fee, a family gets • California private school affidavit filed • transfer of records• Curriculum Guide • Attendance Sheet • maintenance of teacher's records • Earthquake safety program (all these so far are required by California law) • student ID card • a page in the Year Book • a Getting Started Kit • six issues of *Growing Without Schooling* • membership in the National Homeschool Service and California Coalition of People for Alternative Learning Situations (CC-PALS) • six issues of HCL newsletter • and a choice of one year's subscription to *Home Education Magazine*, the *NALSAS* newsletter, *The Teaching Home*, or becoming an Associate of the National Coalition of Alternative Community Schools. Other services offered at cost plus 10 percent.

A credentialed teacher with a Master's in Education directs the private school Administrative Unit program, which is now accredited with NALSAS through NCACS. Families are free to choose the methods used in implementing curriculum under the private school law of California.

UPDATED**
Home Study International

$66.70 Preschool, $175.45 supplies and 113.40 tuition K, $500-$600 grades 1- 6. Shipping extra, K-6. Grades 7-8, $148/subject plus supplies and shipping. Grades 9-12, $113.40 per subject per semester unit plus supplies and shipping. $40 processing fee, grades K-12. Excellent catalog lists all materials used in each grade. Parents only purchase items they lack.

Established: 1909.
Accreditation: Accrediting Commission of the National Home Study Council and approved by the Maryland State Department of Education.
Enrollment in 1988-89: 2,500.
Curriculum: Eclectic mix of Seventh-day Adventist texts and public school texts.
Services: Test grading and record-keeping, advice, report cards, and certificates of promotion or diplomas.
Special Requirements: None.
Unique features: Excellent teaching guides for every subject in every grade. Strong health curriculum teaches first-aid and survival skills.
Tone: Firm.
Religion: Seventh-day Adventist. Creationist.
Emphasis: Morality.
Learning Style: Visual in grades 1-12. All styles in preschool and kindergarten.
Grades: Preschool-12.

Established as a service to Seventh-day Adventists, Home Study International has grown into a major supplier of home-school programs. The staff consists entirely of certified teachers, many of whom have a Master's or Ph.D.

This is a standard, structured, school-at-home program. Young students are taught by their parents; older students are expected to work directly with the HSI staff under their parents' guidance.

Materials used include a number of Seventh-day Adventist (S.D.A.) texts as well as some standard public school texts. Most books are up-to-date. In early grades, HSI has its own adapted version of the Ginn 720-Rainbow readers. All the S.D.A. texts I saw were professionally done and colorful.

HSI's own materials are conservative and pro-family. Some of the public school texts HSI uses are less so.

Religiously, HSI is creationist and evangelistic. Some Christian books are used and the Bible is taught. Seventh-day Adventists believe that their founder, Ellen White, was a prophet of God, and her writings are quoted in some Bible and Health sections of the curriculum, as well as occasionally in the Parents' Guides.

The HSI preschool readiness program is really neat. It includes a very rich music program (with five cassettes thrown in), lots of arts and crafts activities, nature awareness, physical education, math readiness, and more! The heart of the preschool program is a super Parents' Guide, with *week-by-week* activities laid out—a very sensible approach! Like all HSI's programs, this includes optional Christian and Adventist teaching.

HSI's new kindergarten program includes a character development emphasis: faith, virtue, knowledge, temperance, patience, godliness, brotherly kindness, and love. Elementary students are graded beginning in kindergarten. Subjects include art and music, Bible (optional), health/science, language, math, physical education (grades 3-6), reading, social studies, spelling, and handwriting. You can see there is a lot of work here!

HSI's upper grades cover fewer subjects and use fewer books, but still require a lot of work. Students of high school chemistry, for example, are expected to spend seven to ten hours a week on that one subject.

HSI's Parents' Guides are *great*. Most lessons include stated objectives and list materials needed to do the assignment. Upper-grades lessons consist of a "commentary" section intended to substitute for the normal classroom lecture followed by assigned exercises. Guides directed to the student himself are written in a breezy style, while those addressed to parents are more serious in tone.

HSI has some terrific ideas that others would do well to emulate. Example: Professionally-drawn Bible Activity Sheets printed on card stock enable young learners to make projects like an Ark (with animals!) that look great and will really hold together. Example: The health curriculum teaches survival and first aid skills. Example: Like U of Nebraska, HSI provides a lab kit so upper-grades science students can do *real* experiments.

HSI has an entirely new math program in grades 1-3 for the 1989-1990 school year. Strong emphasis on back-to-basics problem-solving, using Harcourt, Brace, Jovanovich's *Mathematics Today*. Grades 3-6 math is the "new math" and reading is only partly phonetic.

HSI will appeal most to families who prefer modern educational methods and who appreciate HSI's professional materials and consistent Adventist flavor.

International Institute

$75 K, $125 grades 1-8. Books $100 K, $275 grades 1-8. Advisory Council $60 (n/a for K). 50% off tuition for 3rd student, 4th and rest FREE! (All applications must be received at same time to qualify for tuition discounts.) Also, 20% off tuition and Advisory Council for full-time Christian workers. Course reuse option, $35 plus approximately $35 for new student workbooks.

Established: 1960
Enrollment in 1988-89: 950.
Curriculum: Almost entirely public school texts.
Services (optional): Grading, counseling, record-keeping, certificates of promotion.
Special Requirements: None.
Unique features: Christian program with public school texts. Very low cost for large families, especially the families of Christian workers. Inexpensive "reuse" option.
Tone: Friendly.
Religion: Evangelical Christian. Textbooks are secular.
Emphasis: Same as in public school.
Learning Style: All styles in kindergarten, primarily visual/auditory in other grades.
Grades: K-8.

Founded as a program for missionaries' children, over the years tens of thousands of students have used International Institute's courses. The staff consists of qualified Christian educators who look upon this as a ministry.

International Institute is unusual among Christian-founded programs in that at present it uses secular materials almost exclusively. With the exception of the Bible program, texts are chosen from among those approved by the public schools.

As far as International Institute knows, no student who has completed a course under the direction of its Advisory Service has ever been turned down or put back by any school anywhere.

Because International Institute uses up-to-date public school texts in grades 1-8, those courses amount to public school at home, without the extraneous public school classes on values clarification and sex ed and so on, and with an optional Bible course added. International Institute's philosophy is that the Christian teacher is competent to integrate Christian teaching in each subject herself.

The publishers International Institute chooses are among the more conservative philosophically (although there is still a lot of stress on "feelings" and self-disclosure, and subjects such as drug education are introduced). Format is textbook-workbook, with all teachers' editions supplied.

International Institute has an inexpensive Advisory Service. A professional elementary instructor grades tests, evaluates Achievement tests, makes suggestions, and assists you with problems. International Institute will also keep a file on each student, issue transcripts, and grant a certificate of promotion on completion of a grade to those using the Advisory Service.

Kindergarten is a readiness program *and* a basic reading program. Kindergarten includes some Christian materials: a coloring book and several Bible story books. Public school math, readiness, basic reading, "listening and talking," and phonics materials are used, and all supplies are included (writing supplies, scissors—even gold stars!).

Handwriting starts with pre-cursive and graduates to cursive in grade 2.

International Institute provides an attractive Teacher's Manual for each grade, with weekly, daily, and hourly lesson plans. Their lesson plans are simple and straightforward. Because teaching hints are not incorporated in the lesson plans, but listed separately, it becomes much easier to tailor individual lessons to the student's working speed.

If you follow the instructions in the teachers' editions exactly, you will work yourself to death. You, of course, will not do this, because unlike the poor victims who teach in public schools you can stop "teaching" as soon as your student has learned the material. Armed with the teachers' editions you can do as much or as little teaching as needed.

Students can expect to work hard in an International Institute course. Textbooks are drill-oriented and there is a lot of review.

International Institute offers a novel "reuse" option. On receiving International Institute's approval and payment of a reuse fee, International Institute will send you just the workbooks at their cost plus handling. International Institute also allows you to return any undesired book sent with the course for a full refund. Also note the extremely low cost for large families, especially the families of Christian workers.

International Institute promises fast shipping—"within a few days of receiving your order (except in the rush months of July and August when it takes a few days longer)." Books lost or damaged in transit are replaced free.

Missionary mothers who want to start a kindergarten (or any grade level) program for national or missionary children can purchase additional student books for this ministry at cost. The same privilege is available for stateside mothers who wish to teach two or more students at the same grade level.

Students who are at or above normal grade level to begin with can progress well in public school-required skills in this curriculum.

Until International Institute switches over to Christian texts, families with strong feelings against public schools may find the present health, science, and reading materials not what they wish. This also applies to those who are looking for a course that overtly integrates Christianity into every subject area. If you do not fall into these categories, consider if you:

(1) have a large family and are looking for an economical curriculum,

(2) appreciate being supplied all teachers' editions,

(3) want a course that should be credible in the eyes of public educators.

**IMPROVED
KONOS Character Curriculum
Volume 1, Volume 2, and Volume 3, with lesson guides, $75 each. Lesson guides may be purchased separately for old (pre-revision) volumes, $15 per volume. Corresponding laminated time line figures for each volume, $59.95 each. The dated lines on which to place time line figures are included in Volume 1 Time Line or can be purchased separately for $9.95. Any volume plus its corresponding time line, $124.95. Bible Time Line figures, about 190 characters, $59.95. Artists and Composers time line figures, about 90 figures, $25. *KONOS Compass*, $20. Seminar, *How to Use Konos Curriculum*, 6 one-hour cassettes, $25. Writing Tapes, 2 one-hour cassettes teaching composition, $8.50. Starter kit includes Volume 1 plus its time line, *KONOS Compass*, seminar tapes, and writing tapes, all for $165. Add 10% shipping, minimum $2. Foreign orders, add 20% shipping.

Established: 1986.
Families using KONOS in 1988-89: Estimated at 8,000 families.
Curriculum: Large spiral-bound volumes of correlated unit studies for K-6, plus time line figures for each volume.
Services: How-to tapes, live seminar.
Special Requirements: None.
Unique features: KONOS' own time lines and unit studies.
Tone: Firm.
Religion: Evangelical Christian. Creationist.
Emphasis: Learning by doing and discovery.
Learning Style: Kinesthetic. Visual and auditory styles used as well.
Grades: K-8.

I respect people who keep improving their products. The KONOS staff has done this again, not only revising the early volumes I reviewed in the last edition of this book, but also providing lesson guides designed to help "even unorganized moms teach using the discovery and doing methods."

All KONOS volumes are a cross between a lesson plan book, super textbooks covering dozens of subjects, and an encyclopedia. The volumes no longer merely list activities, but give detailed explanations and nuggets of information to keep teacher study to a minimum. The greatly improved Table of Contents and the neater packaging of subunits make the revised KONOS volumes much easier to use.

These new lesson guides break the multitude of activities down into weeks and sometimes even days. These guides really help, because the KONOS curriculum is Unit Studies to the nth, and you can go crazy trying to figure out which activities to do when!

The curriculum's launching pad is character trait themes. Each month's activities follow the theme for that month. The themes for Volume 1 include Attentiveness, Obedience, Orderliness, Honor, Trust, Stewardship, and Patience. Under the theme of Attentiveness, for example, children study how eyes and ears work (science), tell and retell the Bible story of Samuel (Bible, reading comprehension, creative expression), make a straw oboe and paper kazoo (music, art), read Davy Crockett's biography (history, reading), practice tracking (nature study), learn Indian sign language (language), and study Indian customs (social studies)—among many other things!

Every activity has the corresponding subjects listed next to it in the margin. Examples: "Hammer a nail into wood. The next time rub the nail with soap and see if there is a difference." This activity has "Science" listed in the margin. "How old was Noah when he started building the ark?" = Math. "Make your own sandpaper" (instructions follow) = Art and Science. "Learn Indian sign language and picture writing" (directs you to a book on the subject) = Language.

Since KONOS is not an umbrella school but a curriculum, you don't really have to do anything you don't feel up to (including role-playing ol' Dan'l).

New: KONOS has just come out with the *KONOS Compass,* an in-depth scope and sequence which • provides an overview of all three volumes • compares KONOS to state requirements, so you can be sure you are covering everything required by law • gives planning and scheduling suggestions • contains a math and language arts checklist by grade level • plus lots of other useful info for KONOS users and prospective KONOS users, including a detailed introduction to the KONOS philosophy. The *KONOS Compass* even has instructions on how to teach creative writing, so now you don't need a separate language arts curriculum. The overviews make it a *lot* easier to take in the curriculum. I recommend that you purchase the *Compass* if you are considering using KONOS.

KONOS relies on library books, which are free, for its supplementary literature and resource material. This makes it much cheaper than a standard curriculum. Count on spending several hours a week in the library looking up books in the card catalog and hunting them down on the shelves. A wealth of resource books are listed after every section. All these activities and resources make the KONOS manuals *huge.* Volume 1 has 440 pages, Volume 2 has 447, and Volume 3 is almost 600 pages. A lot for your money!

For parents who opt to own rather than borrow (i.e., moms with low energy, no transportation to the library, or who work on the mission field) KONOS has a satellite business in the works which will sell the best available books as resources for each unit. KONOS already supports another satellite business, *KONOS Helps,* a newsletter published by two KONOS users nine months out of the year. (See "Unit Study Helps" in the Unit Studies chapter.)

KONOS covers all elementary and middle school topics in the combined three volumes, excluding phonics and math. (Remember, the new *KONOS Compass* includes language arts instruction.) Each of the three volumes contains two to three years' worth of activities for all the K-8 members of your family.

Obviously Attentiveness and Obedience are wonderful things to learn, but can any sort of planned school experience really teach them? KONOS' answer is that by emphasizing a character trait for an entire month, parents will at least convey to their offspring that they are serious about that trait.

Since unit studies alone are not always sufficient to build up the necessary learning framework, KONOS has lots of historical Time Line packets to pull together the history and literature. (See them reviewed in the History chapter of Volume 2.)

Volume 1 of KONOS, as I said, is more-or-less a launching pad based on character traits. You study a lot of interesting things, but not in any readily discernible order. In Volume 2, material is presented in a more chronological order. You'll study famous scientists and inventors by reading biographies and thinking through their experiments. What experiment would *you* concoct to determine whether the earth was flat or round? Hmmm . . . You'll also study colonial history through the eyes of the ethnic groups who settled here. Build a fire using tinder, flint, and steel. Try dressing like a Dutch housewife. Play Puritan games (I kid you not!). All this, plus practical living skills, astronomy, paper designs, a study of ants, model sailboat building, knot tying . . . is there *anything* interesting, useful, or fun that this curriculum doesn't cover? Everything is in a Christian context, with Bible verses to memorize and serious questions to discuss (like, why was it wrong for the Aztecs to sacrifice children to their gods?). All is logically laid out, easy to follow, and most of the materials and books you will use are free, thanks to the KONOS practice of library-rummaging.

Even though all three volumes are multi-level K-8, Volume 3 is definitely heavy on activities for older children. Under the character trait of Resourcefulness, for example (a trait every teenager should have!), your child studies inventors and their inventions, covering the Industrial Revolution as well as ninth-grade physical science. Under Cooperation (another vital teen virtue!) you study the normal fourth-grade states-and-regions, as well as the "body systems" portion of tenth-grade biology. For this reason, the authors recommend using the books chronologically even though they do not build on each other.

The KONOS writers believe in exposing Christian children to non-Christian ideas and values; thus the curriculum includes some activities (e.g., role-playing misbehavior) that I personally would skip.

Academically, KONOS deserves an A. (Remember, *it does not teach basic math and phonics. You need to buy those materials separately.*)

If you buy this curriculum, don't overdo it! The writers have included more suggested activities and field trips than you probably will be able to manage. Pick and choose, and have fun!

NEW**
Landmark's Freedom Baptist Curriculum
$450 Plan A, $300 Plan B, $150 Plan C. Books included. Shipping extra. $50 off students 2, 3, etc. in plans A and B. No refunds. The ACS Scope and Sequence tells you what is taught at various levels in the curriculum: $5. ACS Samplepac includes books from various grades and levels as well as a Scope and Sequence; this costs $29. Cassette tape entitled "Christian School Curricula: Good, Better and Best" compares ACS with other Christian school materials: $5. If you want any of these, don't forget to include 15% shipping and handling.

Established: 1979.
Enrollment in 1988-89: 500 families plus 200 schools.
Curriculum: Worktexts.
Services: Three options. Under Plan A, ACS provides all books, answers, and tests; evaluates tests and assignments; keeps student records; sends report cards each semester; and awards diplomas when work is completed. This plan includes free testing. Plan B includes everything in Plan A except for placement testing and evaluation of the student's work. In Plan C ACS provides books, answers, and tests, and it's up to you to do the rest.
Special Requirements: None.
Unique features: Lots of drill, diagramming, and Scripture memory. Composition skills emphasized.
Tone: Friendly.
Religion: Baptist/fundamentalist. Creationist.
Emphasis: Morality, patriotism, free enterprise.
Learning Style: Visual.
Grades: K-12.

Associated Christian Schools curriculum under a new label. The program is now administered by Landmark Baptist Church, a church with a day school, college, and radio station. Enrollment in the day school is 350. The college (at time of writing) had thirty students on-campus and ninety taking its video courses. With the addition of Landmark's video college courses, this is now a K-college program.

Associated Christian Schools was founded by well-known Baptist author Dr. Donald Boys to provide an "educationally sound and biblically true" curriculum for Christian schools. With the help of 54 writers (almost all of whom hold Masters or Doctorates), he produced a complete K-12 program. Now Dr. Boys has selected Landmark Baptist Church and College in Haines City, Florida to carry on the curriculum. Dr. Earle E. Lee, president of Landmark Baptist College and author of several of the ACS courses, will be overseeing the continued development of this popular curriculum, which is available under the Landmark's Freedom Baptist Curriculum (LFBC) label for both home schoolers and day schools.

The LFBC program is mainly a worktext series. Areas covered are Bible, English, Math, Science, History, Geography (no "social studies"!), Literature, and Penmanship. Their *Right Start* program for kindergartners uses a strong phonics approach.

As a "back to basics" program, LFBC employs a lot of drill, diagramming, and Scripture memory work. Every area is approached from an explicitly Christian perspective. Literature studied is classical and Christian. Composition skills are emphasized.

LFBC curriculum is designed to be as easy as possible for the teacher to use. All the lessons for one week appear in one chapter of the subject's large work-text. This eliminates the need for setting goals or drawing up lesson plans. Also, LFBC is "the only publisher of school material that provides weekly quizzes."

The LFBC material is user-friendly. Texts are addressed directly to the student and marked with good humor and wit. Lessons are straightforward and follow each other logically.

LFBC claims that their material "is more of a challenge than ACE [Accelerated Christian Education, listed in this guide under Basic Education] or AOP [Alpha Omega Publications]." As far as ACE is concerned, I believe this is correct, but I would question whether LFBC is more challenging than AOP. Some areas, such as math and English, may be considered roughly comparable. AOP's reproduction and layout are superior to LFBC.

Dr. Don Boys says "If you are not a Fundamentalist and a political conservative, you probably will not be satisfied with the LFBC Curriculum." If you *are* the above and are looking for a fully-integrated, easy-to-use Christian curriculum that emphasizes straight-arrow morality and Baptist doctrine, check out LFBC.

Living Heritage Academy

$135 Learning-to-Read Kit, $27.50 second student. $250 ABC's of A.C.E., $75 second student. $325 tuition levels 1-8, $375 levels 9-12. $20 enrollment fee. $30 Diagnostic Test fee. Resource books, electives extra. 5% off on second student and rest. 5% prepayment discount.

Established: 1983.
Enrollment in 1988-89: 5,541.
Curriculum: Basic Education's worktexts.
Services: *Home Study Handbook* for parents, diagnostic testing, record-keeping.
Special Requirements: To enroll you must send a copy of the student's birth certificate and a recent picture with the appropriate fees and a completed application form for each child.
Unique features: Choice of high school courses (Basic College Prep, Academic, or Vocational). Discounts for additional students in same family.
Tone: Friendly.
Religion: Non-denominational Christian. Creationist.
Emphasis: Patriotic, pro-free enterprise.
Learning Style: Visual.
Grades: K-12.

Living Heritage Academy is Basic Education's own home-school correspondence program. See the Basic Education writeup.

McGuffey Academy

Registration fee, $20/student. Test fee, $30/student. Tuition, grades 1-8, $350; grades 9-12, $375. $15 discount for each additional child. 10% prepay discount. Workbooks included; textbooks purchased separately.

Established: 1987
Enrollment in 1988-89: 350.
Curriculum: "Classic" curriculum used in 19th-century public schools (grades 1-4); Basic Education, Alpha Omega, and other curricula also available.
Services: Individualized program developed for each student. Mail and phone consultation, reporting forms, diploma upon graduation. Seniors receive College Testing Registration forms.
Special Requirements: None.
Unique features: Tuition payment options: by year, semester, or quarter.
Tone: Firm.
Religion: Evangelical Christian. Creationist. Traditional.
Emphasis: Patriotic, pro-free enterprise.
Learning Style: Visual/auditory. Emphasis on logic and reason.
Grades: K-12.

McGuffey's Readers. Ray's Arithmetic Series. Harvey's Grammars. Spencerian Penmanship. For a longish while now, Mott Media has been quietly republishing these classic schooltexts used a century ago in American classrooms. Now there is a home-school program based on these classics.

Young children start off with Mott's phonics materials, including the *Phonics Made Plain* flashcards and Mrs. Silver's workbooks. Fourth-graders get to sink their teeth into *Harvey's Grammar,* and grammar work continues until eighth grade. Everyone uses *Ray's Arithmetics* (the series spans Pre-K through college) and *Spencerian Penmanship.* Social studies includes Mott's *Sower Series* of biographies of famous people. Etc.

Scattered throughout the *Big Book of Home Learning* volumes you will find reviews of the books mentioned above. In general, they share a disciplined, structured approach to learning. *Ray's Arithmetics* heavily stresses word problems (real-life problems) and are accompanied by an excellent teaching guide. The *McGuffey Readers* are not ideally suited to early phonics instruction, but do contain much character-building material, along with excerpts from many great classics. All these books were written with dedicated, hard-working teachers in mind and are definitely not self-instructional. With the exception of the *Spencerian Penmanship* workbooks, they are all reusable.

It will take some time for you to get used to the slightly antique vocabulary, but most of those purchasing these books are really after the considerably more Christian worldview these books represent. We're not talking about exercises like, "If you add one Bible to two Bibles, how many Bibles do you get?" but about a pervasive regard for honesty, integrity, compassion, decency, and so on—what *used* to be known as the American spirit in the days before progressive education and values clarification. That old-time spirit does come through loud and clear, and any child whose parents take the effort to nurture him or her with these books will undoubtedly soak it up. As to how much help the Academy will provide in guiding you through the work—you get a series of teacher/student workbooks correlated with the subjects taught at each level, plus a Scope and Sequence with tips on how to present the curriculum. These aids should help, because the books are not the easiest to tackle on your own, although historically they have been proven on millions of children to provide excellent results.

Those nostalgic for the little red schoolhouse will undoubtedly want to send for more information about McGuffey Academy.

UPDATED✶✶
North Dakota State Department of Public Instruction
Division of Independent Study
$27/semester course, North Dakota residents. $47/semester course, nonresidents. Books and supplies extra (about $13-$40 for most courses). $5 handling fee on all course registrations. Wide range of video supplements priced at about $10 total per video tape, for a total price ranging from $20 for Intro to Computers (8 lessons on 2 tapes) to $180 for Russian I (36 lessons on 18 tapes). Current video selection includes Local History, North Dakota History, Russian I and II, Spanish I-IV, French I and II, and Psychology. All tapes 60-minute VHS. You may preview a one-part video for each course free if returned within 30 days.

Established: 1935.
Enrollment in 1988-89: 4,347.
Curriculum: Traditional public school format with textbooks and assignments, plus new video supplements.
Support Services: Total correspondence program including grading of each lesson, record-keeping, and report cards.
Special Requirements: Students presently enrolled in high school or who are of compulsory school age must have their local school administrator sign the application and approve a supervisor for them, who must be a certified teacher. This does not apply to non-credit students. Applicants for the diploma must have a transcript of their previous work sent to the Independent Study Program.
Unique features: Six different languages: Latin, German, Spanish, French, Norwegian, and Russian. All except Norwegian and German now have video supplements. Wide variety of practical courses in basic vocational fields. Very low prices. State-accredited diploma. Biology I and II and Chemistry I and II now come with lab kits. New computer-assisted Spanish course.
Tone: Straightforward, no-frills.
Religion: Secular.
Emphasis: Practical.
Learning Style: Visual for textbook courses, visual/auditory for video supplements.
Grades: 9-12 and some vocational courses.

Four thousand students are currently enrolled in this Independent Study program, making it one of the biggest in the country. So why has nobody ever heard of the North Dakota Independent Study program? It could be maidenly modesty, but I think it's likely that the educational house is divided against itself. Home education is just starting to get really big, and the people in state education have not yet begun to wake up to what a wonderful way this is of making a name for their program.

Getting down to brass tacks, what does North Dakota's Division of Independent Study have to offer? It's one of the few *state-accredited high school programs*, for one thing. That means that if your local school superintendent agrees to the plan, you can get a *real live diploma* through DIS. They have lots and lots of *nifty electives*, for another thing: stuff like creative writing, and journalism. North Dakota offers six languages: Latin, German, Spanish, French, Norwegian, and Russian (these courses include cassettes). They also have quite a variety of useful-looking art, business education, agriculture, home economics, and practical/mechanical courses. Not only that, but DIS's prices are extremely low. Book and supply charges are also slight (the program uses standard public school texts), and many textbooks can be returned afterwards for a one-half refund of the purchase price.

DIS courses are rather easy, as far as the assignments go. If you can understand the texts and syllabi you can breeze right along. Science might be an exception to this rule, though the experiments are also easy to do.

DIS includes lesson wrappers in which you return the assignments (you pay the postage). You don't have to keep attendance records or grade anything.

Now, you're asking, what are the drawbacks? There are some, I am sorry to say. Some of the courses are not designed for success. You need a large vocabulary, for example, to understand the directions for the vocabulary improvement exercises. The algebra course seemed to have new terms and concepts on every page. The science text I saw was dull, dull, dull and the experiments were rinky-dink. In general, the problem is lack of organization: too many (sometimes unrelated) facts to learn, not enough underlying structure. More emphasis on long-term memory (concepts and memory pegs) would help a lot. I'm not saying you can't learn from these courses, but they do not soar to sublime heights. Students with learning problems would be better off with University of Nebraska-Lincoln. Also, you need special permission to get your lessons returned to you.

On the brighter side, the Student Guides are livened up with copious appropriate cartoons. Science courses now come with lab supplies. Some of the study topics are quite interesting, such as a section on regional dialects in the Language and Composition course. The old-fashioned flavor of some of the courses is (to me, anyway) quite endearing. Also, I recently discovered that you don't have to have the approval of a school administrator—or a certified teacher overseeing your studies—if you choose to enroll for non-credit. This is good news for those of us who would like to supplement our home programs with DIS electives without signing our souls away.

The most recent selection of DIS courses I saw, although the directions were still couched in somewhat-difficult school vocabulary, looked more promising. *Developmental English*, for example, a basic grammar course, was well laid-out and easy to follow. *Personal Management for Independent Living* also covered much essential territory for a student facing life on his or her own: insurance, taxes, employment policies, choosing quality clothing, nutrition, how to make out a check, dealing with banks and credit agencies, even some necessary social graces! Once you got past the somewhat languid introduction with its unnecessary stress on personal autonomy and free-floating values, this course covers a lot of ground. And DIS is now developing video supplements for selected courses, with a goal of eventually providing videos for all of its 131 courses. Again, these are more of a lecture format: the Russian teacher says the words, but does not act out the sentences. Thus, you get part of the educational benefit of a video (hearing a foreign language), but not all (no connection of words to images).

DIS is now experimenting with a new computer-assisted Spanish course. Again, this could be made far more interactive. Most screens are just text from the course curriculum, although in some you can click on, say, days of the week and hear them pronounced in Spanish. You move back and forth between the Spanish teaching video and the computer.

Academically, at present DIS gets a good solid B.

If you want a secular high school diploma at a low, low cost and you can get permission from your local school superintendent, or if you are interested in some of DIS's unusual courses, check out this program.

Oak Meadow School

Tuition, $225/family. Curriculum alone, $60-145 each K-4, $100-150 grades 5-12. Class Teacher Fee, $60/quarter K-4, $90/quarter 5-8, $75/semester/subject 9-12.

Established: 1975.
Enrollment in 1988-89: 1,000.
Curriculum: Hands-on, artistic, fantasy-oriented..
Services: Enrollment, transfer of records, parent training and a newsletter, phone counseling, and communication with school officials when necessary. Class Teacher provides feedback and evaluations.
Special Requirements: K-4 full enrollment option, parents correspond with Class Teacher once a month. Upper-grades students correspond directly with Class Teacher twice monthly.
Unique features: Everything.
Tone: Strict.
Religion: Pantheistic.
Emphasis: Self-awareness, learning by doing.
Learning Style: Kinesthetic and affective.
Grades: K-12.

Oak Meadow curriculum is based in the early grades on the educational teachings of Rudolf Steiner and continues in the later grades with an extremely strong emphasis on self-awareness and closeness to the earth. Following Mr. Steiner's theories, Oak Meadow places more importance on art and "right brain" learning, including the use of fantasy, than any other program.

Oak Meadow curriculum has a semi-Christianized "New Age" flavor. This is particularly apparent in the areas of the upper-grade curriculum that deal with ecology and our relationship with animals. In the early grades, the stress is on developing qualities of imagination and perception in the child. Thus math becomes the story of four little gnomes named Add, Sub-tract, Multiply, and Divide; the alphabet is taught through fairy tales that associate each letter with a real or fantasy object; science is first approached through nature experiences; and so on. Art, music, and crafts all play an important part in the elementary curriculum.

As much as possible, "learning by doing" is built into the curriculum. Thus sixth-grade children study other countries by cooking their food, making their clothes, doing their crafts, learning conversational French, and so on. Science follows a hands-on discovery approach. Much attention is given to self-awareness, including many personal writing assignments with the student disclosing his feelings about a variety of situations.

Materials used are unique to Oak Meadow's program. Young children learn to play the recorder and sing a variety of uplifting songs, including a number of Christian hymns. Many books about nature and animals are included at the various levels. Some of these books are pantheistic to the point of being strange. One upper-grades book, for example, tries to make a case for animals, including flies, being able to communicate meaningfully with people (!). Curriculum for all grades is self-contained.

Oak Meadow does use textbooks, generally not from major publishers. Exceptions are some excellent University of Nebraska-Lincoln courses and math materials.

Students in grades K-4 "play" more than "work." Most assignments are informal and can be done anytime, and there is no pressure to meet deadlines. Once students reach grade 5, the parents are considered support and resource people and the Class Teacher takes over most teaching work.

Upper-grade students do have to work, although the amount of paperwork is less than many traditional programs require. In grades 5-8 Oak Meadow curriculum strongly emphasizes "human values and ideals." Subjects are approached from the angle of how they affect people (subjectively) rather than as collections of objective facts. Grades 9-12 finally concentrate more on facts and the intellectual approach.

Oak Meadow provides materials, legal enrollment, transfer of records, Home Teacher training and a newsletter, and communication with school officials. In addition, every child has a Class Teacher. For grades K-4 the parents correspond with the Class Teacher; in grades 5 and up the student works directly with the Class Teacher, and the parents move into the background.

In keeping with a "noble savage" emphasis, Oak Meadow children learn how to forecast their local weather, how to track animals, how to paint meaningful pictures, and a number of other things that do not find their way into standard school texts. On the other hand, students get less practice and drill in the basics than those enrolled in more traditional programs.

Oak Meadow's kindergarten and grade 1 materials are usable by just about anyone fond of a fairy-tale approach to education, but Christians and others will have to censor them lightly to omit the pantheism. The upper grades appear designed mainly for New Agers.

NEW★★
Our Lady of the Rosary
Registration: new students, $20 first child, $10 second child, all others free; present student, $10. Full enrollment: Pre-K $75, K $175, 1-2 $350, 3-8 $390, 9-12 $450. Some old books must be returned. "Kindergarten for Catholics" religion program, $29.95. Religion only: 1-8 $60 plus shipping, 9-12 $95 plus shipping. High school electives, some materials extra. 10% discount on second and other children. Extensive selection of materials, all can be purchased individually.

Established: 1983.
Enrollment in 1988-89: 995.
Curriculum: 100% Catholic materials.
Services: Grading, evaluations, report cards, awards, diploma, phone counseling.
Special Requirements: Some irreplaceable old books must be returned. OLR also strongly suggests that you confine TV viewing to educational programs only.
Unique features: 100% Catholic curriculum. All books accompanied by teacher's manuals/lesson plans written by certified teachers. Scholarships available as donations make them possible. Monthly payments allowed.
Tone: Friendly.
Religion: Traditional Catholic.
Emphasis: Morality and loyalty to Catholic faith.
Learning Style: All styles, more kinesthetic approach than most.
Grades: K-12.

Did you know your local Catholic school might not even be using Catholic texts? Yep, it's true. As the Our Lady of the Rosary catalog truthfully notes,

> For many years Catholic authors have not written Catholic textbooks. Catholic books are no longer required in Catholic schools and are no longer permitted where state or federal funds are provided.

The truth is that a lot of what passes for Catholic education today is really warmed-over New Age Hug-a-Planet goo. "So," Catholic parents ask themselves, "how are we going to raise our children Catholic when the folks down at the parish school seem never to have heard of the Baltimore Catechism?"

That question seems to be occurring to a lot of people today. So now you have a choice of *three* (count 'em!) Catholic home-school programs. And boy, is Our Lady of the Rosary *Catholic!* The whole catalog will recall memories of Sister Monica in her long, black habit. Starting with materials for parents on how to teach Catholicism to their children, you have here a complete pre-kindergarten through high school old-timey Catholic curriculum. Stories of saints for all grade levels. Communion and confirmation preparation. Latin. Home Economics courses with Catholic patterns (even altar cloths and vestments!). All this plus traditional math and grammar, Catholic science texts, penmanship, Catholic history, geography, and (in high school) a course intriguingly titled "Christian Culture and World Civilization." You also get high school electives—e.g., typing and computer intro; "Philosophy of History" in grade 12; and a catalog of Catholic gift items. Some of these materials were produced by OLR; others are out-of-print texts they unearthed; some are still in print. The out-of-print material has to be returned when you are finished with it.

I don't have space here to review all of OLR's unique materials, so let's just look at a few:

• OLR offers religion-only programs for all grades, for those who want to supplement regular school or another program with Catholic education. Their "Kindergarten for Catholics" program has lessons, Bible stories, art and creative activities, resource books, and a 22 x 23" "My Jesus and I" full-color wall chart with forty large pictures and text outlining basic Catholic devotional beliefs.
• OLR's "Kindergarten Music" course is exceptionally well-designed for home schools. It starts with a nice overview of the whole course that

lists songs, instruments (you will be making several simple instruments during the year), listening selections (classics available at most libraries), and a glossary of terms. The program, like other OLR courses, is divided by months and weeks, and the songs are (naturally) Catholic.

• OLR's "Math Kit for Home Schoolers" starts at counting (with manipulatives provided) and goes right up to the eighth grade level. In one book you get the equivalent of curriculum and teacher guides for K-8. The kit comes with a set of linking cubes (for counting and arithmetic operations) and a fractions board. A very nice, simple approach that anyone can use.

As you can see, OLR is more activity-oriented than similar programs.

OLR now also has a magazine ($12/year for a subscription) and graduation ceremonies. OLR also has a reduced-cost "Satellite Program" option that includes everything except teacher services.

Our Lady of Victory School
$200 1A-6, $250 7-12. 10% off second student and rest. Books and supplies extra ($65-$125, depending on the grade). Optional Iowa Test extra. $25 registration fee. Repurchase option: up to 50% of cost of reusable books. School year enrollment only.

Established: 1978.
Enrollment in 1988-89: 1,100.
Curriculum: Catholic. Some non-Catholic texts.
Services: Grading, record-keeping, transcripts, phone and mail counseling.
Special Requirements: Parents are "required to duplicate our typical classroom as closely as possible." Special permission is needed for deviations from the OLV schedule,

which must be followed during the regular nine-month school year. In other words, you may only enroll in September and must follow a classroom schedule thereafter. The lesson plan is also an attendance record that must be checked off as "done" and mailed in every two weeks. Students are encouraged to follow dress code requirements, and parents are asked to send a photo of their uniformed child to the school. OLV reserves the right to dismiss students for unsatisfactory conduct.
Unique features: Emphasis on discipline in all areas of the program.
Tone: Firm, but flexible.
Religion: Traditional Catholic.
Emphasis: Catholic morality and worldview.
Learning Style: Thinking and reasoning. Visual.
Grades: K-12.

Our Lady of Victory is an extremely traditional Catholic day school. The Home Study program has a staff of twenty (plus, of course, all the parents who do the actual teaching!).

OLV's program is

> the typically Catholic school format that was used successfully across the nation up until about 1960. We do not experiment with your child's mind. We give traditional grades, including F's if they are deserved. But, we don't abandon the "F" student or place them in an "educationally handicapped" group; we place them at the grade level they can handle and then we encourage them to advance from there.

Lots of memorization and drill work is included in OLV's program, and lots and lots of Catholic theology (so much so that when one priest saw an OLV second-grader's religion books he quipped, "Is he studying for a degree in theology?").

A fair number of out-of-print Catholic texts are used, which must be returned to the school at the end of the year. Some non-Catholic texts are also used. As much as possible, OLV attempts to avoid purely secular materials, relying exclusively on Catholic literature in the upper grades.

OLV believes students should work hard and develop self-discipline. Parents are also required to stick to a rigorous schedule. The amount of work in and of itself is not crushing, and many families have written to say they enjoy the program.

Record-keeping is straightforward, and can mostly be done on the lesson plan itself.

OLV's kindergarten is a real learning experience, not time for play. Therefore cursive handwriting begins in kindergarten (which they call "grade 1A" to show they are taking the kindergarten student seriously). 1A students also learn reading, simple math, and other serious academic fare.

OLV has a strong "basics" program, although they seem weaker in science than some others. Theology and Catholic devotion are the heart of the curriculum; in these areas students will be exceptionally well trained. Academically, give them a B+ to A-.

If you are not a Catholic you are unlikely to enjoy OLV, as so much of the curriculum *is* Catholicism. If your number one concern is that your children grow up Catholic, and you are leery of any exposure at all to secular thinking, OLV and you are a happy match.

NEW
Pathway Publishers

Established: 1970.
Number of children using these texts in 1988-89: About 4,000.
Curriculum: Textbooks for the traditional Amish community.
Services: Monthly magazines for parents and teachers.
Special Requirements: None.
Unique features: Extreme wholesomeness of texts.
Tone: Firm and caring.
Religion: Amish. Creationist.
Emphasis: Farm lifestyles, political non-involvement, family togetherness, strict morality.
Learning Style: Thinking and reasoning. Visual.
Grades: K-12.

Pathway Publishers is both a source for hundreds of titles for the Amish community published by other companies, and their own marvelously character-building series of grade 1-8 readers, with accompanying workbooks, teacher's manuals, and answer keys. Pathway also publishes a variety of other religious and educational books, including story books, Amish history, devotions, and so on. Their full catalog includes children's books, nature books, song books, cookbooks (yum!), and farm-and-garden books. Much of this would not appear in a standard school curriculum—Pathway does not consider itself primarily a "school" publisher—but then again, you *Big Book* readers aren't standard people!

Rod and Staff Publishers

Established: 1958.
Enrollment in 1988-89: Rod and Staff says, "We really do not know how many are purchasing books. We know we have 41,500 on our mailing list of people who purchased or asked for a catalog of textbooks. This list increased approximately 10,000 in the last year."
Curriculum: Textbooks and workbooks.
Services: Newsletter.
Special Requirements: None.
Unique features: Extreme wholesomeness of texts.
Tone: Firm and caring.
Religion: Mennonite. Creationist.
Emphasis: Farm lifestyles, political non-involvement, family togetherness, strict morality.
Learning Style: Thinking and reasoning. Visual.
Grades: K-12.

Do you *care* what your child learns? Rod and Staff, a large, serious publisher of Mennonite schoolbooks, says, "We do!" This company has been printing Christ-centered textbooks for approximately twenty-five years. As one might expect, their books are very traditional and are filled with pictures of people in Mennonite dress. Home schoolers of all faiths enjoy them—Rod and Staff is one of the most popular home-school sources.

These textbooks are academically sound and character-building. No iffy stuff whatever. Subjects include:
• reading • English • math • penmanship • science
• spelling • health • social studies • history • Bible
• and supplementary materials for most of the elementary grades.

Their straight-arrow seriousness does not deprive the Rod and Staffers of wit. My son and I had a happy five minutes giggling over this exercise from one of their books:

(In a section of the *Bible Nurture and Reader* series on Giving Thanks:)

Q: You have to work after school and do not have much time to play.
(pick one)
a. Be thankful you can work and help at home.
b. Be thankful you do not like to work.
c. Be thankful you know how to grumble a lot and show your mother how much you hate to work. (!!!!)

Rod and Staff is a publisher, not a correspondence school. However, their teacher's manuals are designed to assist the inexperienced. Hundreds of home schoolers across the country are using these books successfully.

In keeping with an unworldly Christian outlook, all Rod and Staff materials are very reasonably priced.

Santa Fe Community School
$120 per child per year covers the cost of SFCS correspondence services and record-keeping. Books and supplies extra.

Established: 1974
Enrollment in 1988-89: 200.
Curriculum: You develop it with their help.
Services: Record-keeping, transcripts, diploma, legal assistance, phone and mail consultations.
Special Requirements: Parents keep journals of the children's projects and progress and send them in from time to time.
Unique features: Great freedom in curriculum selection.
Tone: Friendly.
Religion: Liberal.
Emphasis: "Free" learning.
Learning Style: All styles.
Grades: K-12.

This small alternative school, familiar to readers of *Growing Without Schooling*, was one of the first to legally shelter home schoolers. In the early days, Ed Nagel, the director of Santa Fe Community School, was quite busy galloping about on a white horse rescuing families from overzealous state officials. One father he rescued had actually been served with a warrant for his

arrest! (The happy ending: upon Santa Fe enrollment, all charges were dropped.)

Accredited by the Rio Grande Educational Association, Santa Fe Community School is a state-recognized alternative nonpublic school operating a regular educational program since 1968, now year-round. Ed Nagel, the director, believes strongly in noncompulsory learning.

Santa Fe Community School is not a correspondence school. It assists parents in developing their own educational programs. The parents become "volunteer teachers" of the school, and the "home school" is considered an extended part of Santa Fe's regular program.

Santa Fe describes its program as "Boarding/Day/Home-School/Community . . . Multi-Cultural . . . Womb to Tomb."

Like most programs of this sort, Santa Fe requires that the parents keep journals of the children's projects and progress and report on their program from time to time. Work required varies with the family's interests and energy level.

To apply, send name, address, birthdates of children, phone number, and the name and address of the school(s) last attended, plus inclusive dates and grade levels.

School Supply Room/Gordonville Print Shop

Established: Years ago.
Enrollment in 1988-89: Not available.
Curriculum: Textbooks and workbooks.
Services: None.
Special Requirements: None.
Unique features: Extreme wholesomeness of texts.
Tone: Firm and caring.
Religion: Mennonite. Creationist.
Emphasis: Farm lifestyles, political non-involvement, family togetherness, strict morality.
Learning Style: Thinking and reasoning. Visual.
Grades: 1-8.

A supplier of Mennonite texts, grades 1-8, that is even cheaper and simpler than Rod and Staff. Send large SASE for price list/order blank.

What do they have? Dick and Jane in the first grades. German-English materials. Lots of Christian materials. School supplies. Some secular textbooks. All you get is a mimeo sheet with the prices on it in green ink. Surprisingly, it is not hard to figure out what you want from the extremely laconic descriptions. Example: "Color Book-Workbook;50 States;Maps;State Flowers;State Birds;Cap.; Popu.;1.50." And where else can you get the *McGuffey Primer* in German?

Mary Kay Clark with priest friend and Julie Luchey, Administrative Assistant

Seton Home Study School

$125 K, $340 grades 1-12. Books and supplies: $50 for K, $90 grades 1 and 2, $100 grades 3-7, $110 grades 8-12. Single high school courses: $90 plus materials. Registration fee: $30 first student, $20 second, $15 third, rest FREE! Discount on tuition: 10% off second student, 15% off third, 20% off fourth, 50% off rest. 10% prepayment discount.

Established: 1981.
Accreditation: Seton is accredited by the National Home Study Council. It is the only Catholic home-study program accredited by the Council.
Enrollment in 1988-89: 2,200.
Curriculum: Workbook/textbook with Seton lesson guides. Some materials produced by Seton; some out-of-print Catholic texts that must be returned; some evangelical Christian texts.
Services: Grading, record-keeping, transcripts, diploma, extensive phone and mail consultation services.
Special Requirements: None.
Unique features: An L.D. specialist on staff who sends supplemental materials to families with slow learners. Freedom to skip already-learned sections of course work.
Tone: Very friendly and caring.
Religion: Traditional Catholic. Creationist.
Emphasis: Morality, loyalty to Catholic faith, and academic preparation for college.
Learning Style: All styles and abilities.
Grades: K-12.

Seton, a traditional Catholic school stressing academics, was established as an outgrowth of Seton Junior/Senior High School, located in Manassas, Virginia. The size of Seton's home-school enrollment has more than doubled in the past two years under the guidance of Seton's extremely well-qualified teaching staff. The director of Seton, Mary Kay Clark, is not only the possessor of a Ph.D. but a home schooler as well, and the curriculum reflects her understanding of the special advantages of home schooling.

Seton's program is textbook-oriented, generally classical, flexibly structured, and very Catholic. "On all levels," Seton says, "it is important to remember that the primary purpose of home school is to teach proper Catholic attitudes about life, Catholic values, and the ability to see the integration of Catholic truth in all areas of knowledge and of daily living." Thus Seton emphasizes traditional Catholic distinctives: the Mass, the Rosary, prayers to Mary and the saints, and so on. The curriculum is also creationist and patriotic.

Seton also offers single courses in upper-grade subjects, and a religion course for grades 1-12.

Except for workbooks, *the books and lesson plans must be returned at the end of the course.* You may keep the kindergarten materials.

Kindergarten is a readiness *and* phonics program which includes handwriting. Each kindergarten lesson tells you what materials are needed and the objectives for the lesson (this is a good feature).

Seton's program is very thorough in all areas. Books come from a variety of publishers—some Catholic, some evangelical, some secular. From an academic standpoint, their choices are good.

Placement is by the Stanford Test at no extra charge. Seton gives its students the Stanford Achievement Test at the end of their school year.

Educationally, Seton has a more relaxed attitude than other programs. The Seton staff believes in mastering a concept and then moving on, rather than continuing to fill out unnecessary workbook pages. They also believe strongly in individualized instruction and make special provisions for accelerated and slow students.

Seton's staff bends over backwards to help parents. Their teaching aids are excellent, in my opinion. Curriculum is constantly revised and improved. Also, Seton maintains a small bank of educational software available to parents at a nominal fee.

Seton is very involved with its families. The director arranges a phone consultation with every family before sending out their books, in order to better understand the family's individual needs. Seton staff includes a learning disabilities specialist.

Although Seton tries to integrate Catholicism into its program as much as possible, to the point of publishing some textbooks themselves and using out-of-print Catholic texts in some subjects, the program is very strongly college-geared. Therefore they introduce classical and modern secular literature as well.

Students are given placement and achievement tests, quarterly exams, periodic progress reports, permanent records on file, transcripts if necessary, and advice and counsel from the Seton staff. Graduates from this program are awarded a diploma. Parents are provided with course materials, lesson plans, teaching aids, and tests (which Seton grades).

Parents receive a suggested lesson plan and a blank lesson plan notebook. They then devise a schedule that meets their own needs. Each subject has its own teaching aids and enrichment suggestions. Parents fill out attendance forms and grade daily assignments. Quarterly tests and completed daily work are sent to Seton. Parents can expect to work hard, but to find their work interesting.

Students are given a great deal of material to cover, but unnecessary repetition of mastered exercises is not required, thus eliminating much school drudgery.

Seton has a full-time lawyer on staff and is in close touch with legislative realities. If problems arise, Seton deals directly with school officials, providing not only lesson plans but their objectives and curriculum guidelines.

New: Seton's home-school computer bulletin board. Call (703) 635-7528 twenty-four hours, seven days. Set your program to 300, 1200, or 2400 baud; no parity; 8 data bits; and 1 stop bit.

Academically, overall Seton rates an A.

Families looking for a classical Catholic program which emphasizes individuality and flexibility will find Seton very attractive.

NEW**
Smiling Heart Press
Pre-K and K, one book, $50. Grade 1, $50. Grade 2, $50. Add 10% shipping.

Established: 1987.
Families using this curriculum in 1988-89: About 5,000.
Curriculum: One-book curriculum with lesson plans, suggested resources, teaching material, etc. Uses no textbooks; correlated to library books and encyclopedia. All suggested resources for this program are available through Home School Books and Supplies company. Volumes are correlated to make it easier to teach children in different grades at once.
Services: None.
Special Requirements: None.
Unique features: Extensive listing of suggested children's books to read in each volume, with info about each. Practi-

cal writing every week. Correlated with *World Book Encyclopedia*. Strong history lessons. Functional art projects culminate in thrice-yearly puppet shows. Geography songs. Thankfulness list. Daily calendar activities. Math practice through pretend store shopping.
Tone: Warm.
Religion: Evangelical Christian. Creationist.
Emphasis: Patriotic, pro-free enterprise.
Learning Style: All styles.
Grades: Pre-K through 2.

Written by home-schooling mom Ann Ward, Smiling Heart Press's *Learning at Home* curriculum covers all subjects in just one oversized spiral-bound manual for each grade level. Preschool and kindergarten are bound together in one volume; grades 1 and 2 each have their own manual.

For preschool you get a really rich program of learning activities, including: Bible concepts (four times a week), reading readiness (four times), arithmetic readiness (four times), God's world (social studies—twice), character building (once), health, safety, manners (once), art (twice), music (twice), physical education skills (four times), Bible memory verses (four times), and stories (four times). This schedule should take you an hour and a half four days a week. Friday is set aside just for field trips.

As is typical with rich curricula, *Learning at Home* requires considerably more work than just opening a manual and turning to the proper page. You have to collect materials for the activities, find books at the library, schedule field trips if desired, and so on. Author Ann Ward has made this somewhat easier by providing card catalog numbers for the books she recommends. This means you can find another book on the same topic easily if the one you're looking for isn't there, and you won't have to spend hours flipping through cards or microfiche. Also, for people with less time and more money, she has arranged with Home School Books and Supplies to have them carry *all* the resource materials recommended in this program. Not all these materials appear in their catalog, due to space considerations; however, you can request them just the same.

The kindergarten program in the back of the manual includes a kindergarten arithmetic section and a reading section based on Romalda Spaulding's approach in *The Writing Road to Reading*. To this you can add the preschool activities, but that means you will be flipping back and forth between three sections of the manual. However, this may be worth the effort to you, especially if you are teaching both a preschooler and kindergartner together.

First grade and second grade continue to build on this approach. Each volume starts with an overview, by subject, of the entire year's program. Each day's work is broken down into calendar time (including praying and adding to the Thankfulness List), a short Bible unit study (example: looking at plants/poem about plants for the Third Day of Creation), language arts (reading phonograms, writing, grammar, spelling), music, art, arithmetic, health-manners-responsibility, physical education, history-geography-science (first grade covers American history from 1600-1700; second grade covers American history from 1700-1800), and Bible memory. Some of these subjects are covered on all days; others are not. Friday is left open, as in the preschool-kindergarten program, for field trips and service projects.

Children have a three-ring notebook in which they keep their "Thankfulness List," a journal, a calendar (many activities are based on this calendar), a lists of books read, and notes from each subject. Daily calendar activities may include saying the Pledge to the Bible, saying the days of the week and months of the year, counting from 1-31 while pointing at the calendar square, counting the ordinals from first to thirty-first, saying today's day and date, recording today's temperature and weather, and various number-line counting activities.

For practical application in learning to write, instead of completing book lessons, every week first- and second-graders write a short letter to grandparents or an older person or shut-in, write a journal entry, and copy a short passage into the notebook. First-grade art takes a similarly functional approach, with art projects focused on preparing puppets and backdrops for the three puppet shows presented through the year (Pilgrims, Christmas story, Easter story). Second-graders do a variety of art projects. Second-graders also work on exercises to prepare them for (possibly) obtaining the President's Council on Physical Fitness Award.

Both the first- and second-grade programs coordinate with the preschool-kindergarten program in terms of what is studied when, making it easier to teach several children at once.

Every volume is very professionally-done, easy to use, and covers the territory with enough activities and questions to draw out real thinking but not so much that you or your children will be overwhelmed. Christian families that like structure and that can manage to locate or purchase the needed resources will like this program.

Mel Hassell

Summit Christian Academy
$125 K, $385 1-12. Materials included. $30 registration fee. $30 testing fee, grades 3 and up. LIFEPACS only, order just the ones you wish. Complete curriculum for a year, including Teacher Guides and answer keys, $150. Individual subjects, $16.95; if you throw in answer keys and teacher handbooks, it comes to around $30/subject. Requests and letters answered within two days. $5 for walking program: specify K-3 or 4 and up. Foreign language programs for younger children, 3 levels, about $20 a level. Supplementary material available without enrollment.

Established: 1981.
Enrollment in 1988-89: Over 1,000.
Curriculum: Kindergarten program uses Smiling Heart Press, *Writing Road to Reading*, and *Letterland Math*. Alpha Omega worktexts in grades 1-12.
Services: Diagnostic testing, Parent Teacher Handbooks, grading of major tests, record sheets for parents, quarterly progress reports, record-keeping, consultation and advice, and a high school diploma for those fulfilling their requirements. Also, Teacher's Manuals and answer keys come with each AOP subject. Special Requirements: Parents return grades to Summit every nine weeks.
Unique features: Foreign languages in younger grades (Spanish, French, and German). For physical education, special "walking" programs for K-3 and 4 and up. Two-step testing program.
Tone: Friendly.
Religion: Evangelical Christian. Creationist.
Emphasis: Patriotic, pro-free enterprise.
Learning Style: Visual/auditory. All styles in kindergarten.
Grades: K-12.

This Christian program was founded by Mel Hassell, an ex-Marine who wants to make Summit the "biggest and best" home-school program in the country. I'm no prophet, so can't tell you whether he'll succeed, but I am impressed with what he and his staff have accomplished so far.

Summit is a complete home-school program using Alpha Omega materials for grades 1-12. These are the very popular Christian worktext materials being used worldwide by more than 60,000 students. For kindergarten, Summit has a program built around Romalda Spalding's excellent *Writing Road to Reading*, reviewed in this book's Reading section, Smiling Heart Press's excellent *Learning at Home* one-book curriculum, and *KinderMath* from Letterland Phonics. Plus, you can buy Summit's curriculum without enrolling, if you so desire, and it costs no more than if you ordered it directly from the publisher. See the listing under "Alpha Omega Publications" for a full description of the materials that Summit uses in grades 1-12.

Foreign languages (French, German, and Spanish) are now available in the younger grades. Summit also has a unique physical education program based on walking, with two skill levels: K-3 and grade 4 and up.

Students enrolled in Summit score in the top 10 percent on the Iowa Test of Basic Skills, and their graduates are scoring in the top 15 percent on A.C.T. college entrance exams. Summit says, "We know of no other school that has produced these results."

Families are urged to join the Home School Legal Defense Fund.

You get a twofold testing program in grades 3 and above. Upon enrollment Summit sends you the WRAT. This achievement test tells what your child has learned to date. Next, individualized placement is achieved using AOP Diagnostic Tests. Also, during the spring and fall optional Iowa Tests of Basic Skills are given if families request them.

Parents can expect to do a lot of teaching in the earliest grades, but considerably less later on. Alpha Omega material, while not self-instructional, allows the student to take more responsibility for his own education as he matures.

Students will find the AOP materials challenging. Although AOP uses a worktext format, its material is comparable in quality to that of the better textbooks. There are a significant number of thought questions requiring essay answers or leading to projects.

Record-keeping required is fairly extensive: however, Summit makes your job easier by providing all the necessary forms. Parents return grades to Summit every nine weeks.

Academically, give Summit an A.

Bill and Sandy Gogel

The Sycamore Tree

$35/month/family (10-month basis). Books and supplies extra (expect $150-200 per child). $50/child registration fee. 10% discount on all catalog items for enrolled families.

Established: 1982
Enrollment in 1988-89: Not available.
Curriculum: Wide-open. Sycamore Tree carries literally thousands of resources. You may purchase any resource without enrolling.
Services: Assistance in developing an individualized program, assistance in selecting Bible-centered curricular materials, record-keeping, testing, advice and counseling, support groups in each area where Sycamore Tree families are located, a student body card indicating your child is enrolled in a private school, group legal insurance, high school diploma, and a 10 percent discount on all items from their catalog. Sycamore Tree also publishes a monthly newsletter from September to June full of enrichment material—fifty to seventy pages per issue.
Special Requirements: Parents enrolled in program keep attendance records, provide quarterly progress reports and student work samples, write lesson plans (with guidance from Sycamore Tree), and oversee the student's program.
Unique features: Totally individualized curriculum. Student learns at his own pace.
Tone: Very friendly.
Religion: Evangelical Christian. Creationist.
Emphasis: Health, character-building.
Learning Style: All styles.
Grades: K-12.

Sycamore Tree is an alternative, individualized Christian program established by Bill and Sandy Gogel, who between them hold about every teaching credential imaginable. Sycamore Tree also sells a wide variety of nifty Christian (and other) educational materials. Send for their catalog!

Sycamore Tree charges tuition on a per-*family* basis, payable monthly (on a ten-month basis, usually September-June). Thus they don't have or need a refund plan for tuition. Families get what they pay for and if they decide they don't like it, all they have to do is stop paying. (The Gogels, of course, hope you won't do this!) There is also a $50/child registration fee.

Books and supplies are extra, but families are not required to get their materials from Sycamore Tree (although in most cases they would be wise to do so). All materials may be returned for a refund within fifteen days.

The student's workload will reflect his and his parents' desires, since each program is totally individualized.

Sycamore Tree's catalog will make any true-blue home schooler drool with desire. The range of materials they have chosen to offer reflects sound taste and judgment. *You may order from the catalog without enrolling.*

Sycamore Tree materials are educationally sound and interesting. Here's just a sample of what they offer. The Alpha Omega curriculum. The Rod and Staff curriculum. Some "Home-Grown Kids" products, like Math-It and Winston Grammar, that are used in Hewitt's program. A wide variety of neat science and art equipment, including the best drawing text I have ever seen for young children. Foreign language materials. A whole host of Christian teaching aids that are hard to find elsewhere. I have not even begun to list the topics their catalog covers. You will just have to request one and see for yourself.

With all this variety of excellent materials to choose from, a family that *knows what it wants* should have no trouble setting up an "A+" individualized program.

University of Nebraska-Lincoln
Independent Study High School
Division of Continuing Studies

$58.50/semester course, Nebraska residents. $68/semester course, nonresidents. Books and supplies about $30-$40/course. Science supplies run $40-$100/course. Shipping extra.
Established: 1929,
Enrollment in 1988-89: 11,000.
Curriculum: Syllabus, textbook, workbooks, and supplies.
Services: Grading and evaluations (all students), testing and state-accredited diploma (credit students).
Special Requirements: Students under 18 who want to take courses for credit and transfer the credit to their local school must secure the written permission of their local school administrator to enroll and obtain a "approved person" to supervise their program.
Unique features: All supplies provided for every course, including science courses. A limited number of scholarships are available.
Tone: Friendly.
Religion: Secular. Evolutionary.
Emphasis: Respects cultural heritage.
Learning Style: Visual.
Grades: 9-12.

Those who believe public schools need megabucks to produce quality education ought to take a look at University of Nebraska-Lincoln's independent study program for high school students. Here, for an absolutely minimal financial investment, students can obtain the best *public* school education (in my opinion) in America today. No computers, no band practice or football team, no Olympic-size swimming pool, no "gifted and talented" kids playing Dungeons and Dragons—not only do UNL students survive without these things, somehow they surpass their schoolbound fellows!

UNL provides a state- and regionally-accredited high school diploma. Students under eighteen must secure the written permission of their local school administrator to enroll and obtain a "approved person" to supervise their program. This applies only to those seeking credit from their local public school; courses are available to anyone who wants them.

All students get course syllabi, the texts and supplies they ordered, and the privilege of instruction and comments on their written work from an Independent Study High School teacher. Those enrolled for credit must also take tests under supervision. The texts used come from standard public school suppliers. UNL writes its own excellent syllabi.

Each course is so well laid out that students should experience no frustration. Although the workload corresponds to that in a public school classroom, there is no busywork. Courses are self-instructional, and parents need not get involved. Since UNL is a state- and regionally-accredited program, if your school superintendent approves your enrollment, attendance and other record-keeping should not be needed. Also, UNL grades all tests.

This is a fully legal, accredited program.

You can get *all* the supplies for every course from UNL, *including equipment and materials for all the science courses*. For this reason alone I would give UNL's science courses preference over those from any other program except Alpha Omega. Any science materials not provided should be locally available, and are clearly listed under the catalog entry for that course. Thus the student gets a real science course with real experiments, not just a book.

UNL uses the best public school texts, and their syllabi are excellent. The syllabus writers make a real attempt to be objective, and while the result in some areas (I am thinking particularly of English and the social sciences) of necessity reflect secular thinking, it is still a whole lot better than you're likely to find in your local school.

As learning tools, the syllabi I saw were extremely well organized. Each step is clearly presented, each possible learning obstacle is illuminated and explained, goals and objectives are stated explicitly, and there are even self-check tests to help you decide whether you need to review any areas before you take a test.

Academically, the UNL program rates an A.

Those looking for a high-quality, traditional, secular high school course will be pleased with the UNL program.

UPDATED✲✲
The Weaver Curriculum
Pre-K (includes manipulatives, visuals, manuscript pages, and music tape), $95. Volume 1 K-6, $115. Volume II K-6, $115. Volume III, $115. *Teaching Tips* manual, $30. *Skills Evaluation for the Home School*, $15. Sample 10-day lesson, $4 (Pre-K), $5 (Vol. I). Add 8% postage ($1.25 minimum). Supportive resource materials for each volume available at discounts.

Established: 1984.
Number of families using the curriculum in 1988-89: Not available.
Curriculum: One-book unit study manual with many supplemental resources available.
Services: *Teaching Tips* manual, *Skills Evaluation* manual available separately.
Special Requirements: None.
Unique features: K-6 format (with supplements for 7-12) mean all the children in the family can (in theory!) study the same subjects at the same time.
Tone: Friendly.
Religion: Fundamentalist/evangelical Christian. Creationist.
Emphasis: Unit studies follow Bible in chronological order.
Learning Style: All styles.
Grades: Pre-K through 6, with supplements for 7-12.

Here comes another all-in-one integrated curriculum. Like some others, the Weaver Series, produced by Becky Avery, takes Scripture as the starting point for a wealth of activities and research projects in the science/social studies/enrichment areas. Also like some others, it is multi-level: that is, children of grade levels K-6 (and with the new supplements, available May 1990, students in grades 7-12) can study the same subject at the same time. Also like the others, the volumes for early grades need phonics and math supplementation. (Pre-K is complete.)

Now . . . what makes Weaver different? Besides the pages color-coded for each grade level, that is. For one thing, you don't need a separate grammar course. The new *Wisdom Words* grammar and composition course is an "application approach to learning" that stresses daily creative writing exercises, use of reference skills, and use of multisensory methods and manipulatives where possible. It's all in one book for K-6, color-coded to coordinate with the Weaver, and comes free with each volume (it's also available separately for $30).

For another thing, the Scriptures used as the starting point for each unit are in sequential order. The preschool-kindergarten manual starts at Genesis 1 and continues through Genesis 10. Volume 1 covers Genesis 11-50, Volume 2 does the same for Exodus and the Books of Law, and Volume III covers Joshua, Judges, and Ruth. All these are cross-referenced to other Bible verses, so you cover more of the Bible than you initially expect.

Another feature is the teacher materials. These include *Teaching Tips and Techniques* and *Skills Evaluation for the Home School*. The latter is written up in the Curriculum Guides chapter; the former is a 248-page book full of how-tos for all subjects, motivation techniques, developmental stages, and general teaching how-tos. Also, in June 1990 a complete lesson plan guidebook will be available. This will give daily lesson plans for each chapter of The Weaver Curriculum, list supplies needed for the activities, incorporate Wisdom Word directives, and provide additional literature suggestions, resource-set references, and time-saver suggestions. You can be sure that such a lesson-plan book will make using this program *much* easier!

This curriculum was originally developed through comparing and collating three widely-used curriculum guides. It is now developed "through the guidance of the Holy Spirit, the use of a framework, the advice of four professional educators (all with Ph.D.'s), and one Christian psychologist." Each new Weaver resource is tested by thirty pilot families and gone over by two editors before it is published. What you get at the end of this process is a program that includes Bible, social studies, general language arts, grammar, composition, vocabulary, health, field trips, art, memory verses, penmanship, music (Pre-K only), reading suggestions, and spelling.

Volume I includes these topics: City, Architecture, Language, History, Transportation, Famine—Water, Plants, Animals, Stewardship of Money, Solar System and Stars, Covenant/Character Sketch, Family (life cycle and reproduction), Character Sketch of Isaac and Rebekah, Character Sketch of Jacob (focusing on deceit and its consequences), Character Sketch of Joseph (including a study of slavery). By Volume III you are getting into topics like Exploration, Espionage and Communications, How History Is Recorded, Fortifications, Music, Thinking Skills, Time, Conquest of the Land (correlated with U.S. history 1790-1861), Idolatry, and Judicial Systems. Each volume also covers some aspect of world history.

You can get a complete resource set for each volume. These books are drawn from a wide range of publishers, are multi-level, and are completely evolution-free. A Resource Catalog describing these comes with the free Weaver catalog.

The Weaver also has a very attractive Bible-based unit study program for the preschool and kindergarten set. The price includes a copy of Kathy Diehl's *Johnny STILL Can't Read . . . But You Can Teach Him at Home,* a music tape, and a manuscript writing program. You can also get an optional Resource Set that includes a lot of colorful beginning nature books, a Sesame Street paper dolls book with seasonal outfits, and a Bible flannelgraph set.

Much "integrated" material stumbles over its choice of integration point. The Interlock program, based on Genesis 1-10 and with heavy emphasis on the days of creation, is blessed with a natural sequence of items to study: first God as Father, Son, Holy Spirit, and Trinity, then light, air, sun, moon, stars, animals, vegetables, man, and so on. Your preschool or kindergarten child is literally (and systematically) introduced to everything in creation through the course of this program. I was impressed!

The Interlock program also has lots of poems, exercises, songs (to familiar tunes), and fun movement activities built in, which is nice. I hate having to jump up every minute to find another story or poem book, as is common with most preschool programs. Other features of note: lessons are provided for only three days a week, thus allowing you to proceed at a more relaxed pace. Lots of hands-on and art activities. Introductory section of manual helps you check out your child's readiness skills, with activities prescribed to shore up each area of weakness.

The list of subjects covered is impressive: social studies, science, language arts, arithmetic, observation projects, art, physical ed, health, Bible memory work, music, phonics, and penmanship. Separate activities are provided in some subjects for preschool and kindergarten children. These activities are not "mushed" together, but individually labeled by subject and presented in a standard order each time, which makes for much less confusion.

New: The Interlock Program has been reworked so that you don't need to do any lesson planning. Previously you had to produce your own lesson plans for the last 12 weeks of the program. This is a real improvement!

Bottom line: The Weaver Curriculum is for dedicated Christian families who want a chronological Bible-study approach, have the time to spend on lots of family activities, and aren't fond of textbooks.

Wilcox & Follett
Free 150-page catalog. Most used textbooks priced at around $2-$4.

You won't beat these prices! Used and rebound textbooks from most publishers, grades K-12, current and older editions. Wilcox & Follett also carries new workbooks to accompany your bargain textbooks. Toll-free number for credit card orders only. Single copy or class-size orders both welcome. Quick shipping. All from "The Nation's Largest Wholesaler of Elementary and High School Textbooks."

HOME SCHOOL ORGANIZATIONS WORLDWIDE

CHAPTER TWENTY-FOUR

HOME SCHOOL ORGANIZATIONS IN THE U.S.A.

Every time I revise this book, I am amazed how fast home schooling is growing. What fun to read the information questionnaires I sent out all over the world and see not only so many new home school groups, but the fantastic growth of the old groups! Groups that a few years ago only had a few dozen member families now have hundreds. Groups that had hundreds now have thousands. Even in states like Michigan with its unreasonable (and probably un-Constitutional) restrictions on home schooling, the typical home school state convention draws over a thousand people.

Your local and state home school groups do more than take your $10 or $20 and mail you a newsletter. They lobby legislators, sit in on court trials if necessary, set up conventions and educational fairs, organize field trips, present media events, and act as your resource network. Home schoolers who fail to tap into this rich source are not only denying themselves many wonderful opportunities, but are failing to support the sacrificial efforts of those who are succeding in making home schooling thoroughly legal and respectable.

Obviously, the more members a state group can claim, the more impact it can have on legislators and the media. Now is the time to join the movement. Stand up and be counted!

HOME SCHOOLING IN THE U.S.A.

As home schoolers gain political savvy, a uniform type of state group is springing up: equipped with newsletter, phone tree, support groups, media chairmen, field trips, state convention, and so on. This is the kind of group that works, and it's a joy to belong to. If your state doesn't have this kind of group, see if you can make contact with a state that does have one, and copy their format.

Following are listings for all fifty states. These are as up-to-date as possible.

In this edition I have included a new information section for every home-school group. This information includes the year it was founded, the number of members, whether or not it has a newsletter, newsletter circulation (this is the actual number of families on the newsletter mailing list), information about the yearly convention if applicable, whether or not the group lobbies for better home-schooling laws, information about support groups (these are local groups distinct from the state group), how the group rates its state's political climate from 1-10 (1 is lousy, 10 is couldn't be better), and information on the legal requirements for home schooling in that state.

A note on the number of home schoolers out there: Keep in mind that the total number of home schoolers in every state far exceeds the number of official home-schooling group members. This becomes obvious when, for example, attendance at the state convention is triple the membership number, as often happens. So you can't arrive at an accurate figure for home schoolers in the U.S.A. by simply adding up the membership numbers of the state groups. After all, *Teaching Home* magazine has a card deck that goes to 100,000 home-schooling families, which is more than the total number of members for all the state groups in the country!

My own best guess is that 150,000 to 250,000 families are now consciously home schooling a total of from 500,000 to 750,000 children. This number is doubling roughly every eighteen months, according to my files.

As ever, groups grow and change—and sometimes, so do their addresses. If you have trouble contacting the group that interests you, try another in the same or a neighboring state. They can probably tell you where to find help. If you write for info, please enclose a dollar or two to pay for the time spent answering your letter, and an SASE. And if you call, remember that you are likely to be answered by a private individual working out of his or her private home; so time your calls accordingly. These little courtesies are what keep the overworked home-school leaders from grinding to a halt.

ALABAMA

Alabama Home Educators, Inc.
P.O. Box 160091
Mobile, AL 36616
Founded: 1984
Number of members: Non-membership service organization
Newsletter: *The Voice*, Rt. 3 Box 37-B, Tallassee, AL 36078
  Circulation: 250
Yearly convention time: varies. Last time's attendance: 350

Lobby? Yes
Local support groups function independently from the state organization and have their own special events.
Political climate: Rating (1-10): 5
Standardized testing? N Teacher oversight? N Register? Y
Records: Attendance records.

Alabama Home Educators (AHE) is a non-profit service organization founded in 1984 to provide information to the estimated 4,000 parents desiring to educate their children at home in Alabama. To protect the privacy of home schoolers AHE has no individual membership. The organization consists of twelve district representatives serving on the board of directors and seven officers.

Currently most home schools must operate as satellites of a church school since the only other legal option is for the parent to be state-certified. Each support group or church school in a district functions independently from AHE and plans its own meetings, field trips, seminars, and other activities. Communication between the state and local leadership is maintained through letters from the president to the director of each district. The director is then responsible for relaying information to participating support groups and church schools. If your group would like to stay informed of state home schooling issues, send a long SASE to the above address and subscribe to *The Voice*.

Newsletter: *The Voice*, published quarterly, $8/year. It contains legal reports, book reviews, resource information, editorials, legislative reports, letters, cartoons, kids' pages, news of support group activities, and discounted products for sale.

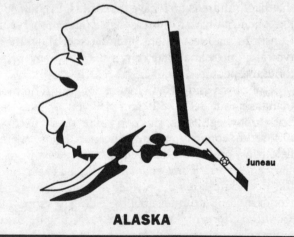

ALASKA

Alaska is unusual in that the state allows home schooling under state auspices (they supply texts, etc.). If this kind of situation meets your needs, contact the State Department of Education.

Alaska Private & Home Educators Association
P.O. Box 70
Talkeetna, AK 99676
(907) 733-2482
Founded: 1987
Number of members: 178 families
Newsletter: *APHEA Update*
  Circulation: 250 - published with *The Teaching Home*
Yearly convention time: October. Last time's attendance: 175
Lobby? Yes
Number of support groups: 12
Annual convention and occasional regional seminars - everything else encouraged at the local support group level.
Political climate: Rating (1-10): 7
Standardized testing? Y Teacher oversight? N Register? Y
Records: 180 day attendance, immunization records (religious exemption allowed), testing at 4, 6, 8 grade levels.

APHEA is a coalition of parents and others who have agreed to a positional statement and have banded together to promote educational excellence by providing alternatives to the government-operated schools.

Membership: $25/year includes a subscription to their magazine. Open to anyone who is willing to sign a declaration of agreement to their positional statement.

ARIZONA

Arizona Families for Home Education
P.O. Box 4661
Scottsdale, AZ 85261
(602) 948-7310
Founded: 1982
Number of members: N/A
Newsletter: *Arizona Families for Home Education*, 10 monthly issues/year, $12 suggested donation. Homey, mimeoed lists of home-schooling events and resources.
  Circulation: 1200
Yearly convention time: June. Last time's attendance: 550
Lobby? Yes
Number of support groups: 25
Political climate: Rating (1-10): 4
Standardized testing? Y Teacher oversight? N Register? Y
Records: Minimal

A non-profit educational corporation. Functions: Legislative watchdog/lobbying, yearly convention.

Christian Home Educators of Arizona
3015 S. Evergreen Rd.
Tempe, AZ 85282
(602) 897-7688
Founded: 1990
Number of members: N/A. Dr. Harold Wengert estimates there are 5,000+ home schoolers in Arizona.
Newsletter: Co-published with *Teaching Home*. $15/6 issues.
Yearly convention: Co-sponsored with Arizona Families for Home Education
Lobby? No
Number of support groups: 37
Supports groups are locally autonomous. These provide such amenities as science fairs and field trips.
Political climate: Rating (1-10): 8
Standardized testing? Y Teacher oversight? N Register? Y
Records: None

Christian Home Educators of Arizona is a fee-for-service group. They provide information and education on biblical principles of home schooling and family growth; sponsor seminars and workshops; co-sponsor the state curriculum fair; work with local churches on setting up support groups; and offer starter kits and other information for novice home schoolers and those who move to Arizona. A board of five families oversees CHEA; Dr. Harold Wengert, one of the founders of Alpha Omega Publishers, is its president.

ARKANSAS

Arkansas Christian Home Education Association
P.O. Box 501
Little Rock, AR 72203
(501) 834-7729
Founded: 1981
Number of members: 350

Newsletter: *The Update* is available separately for $10/six monthly issues.

  Circulation: 400
Yearly convention: May. Last time's attendance: 300-400
Lobby? Yes
Book Fair. Regional science fairs and high school coopera-tives.
Number of support groups: 35
Political climate: Rating (1-10): 5
Standardized testing? Y Teacher oversight? N Register? Y
Records: No record-keeping required. Families must regis-ter by August 15th (for the school year) or December 15th (for the second semester). Standardized testing is in April. If your child does poorly, you can request a retest. If he still does poorly, but there are extenuating circumstances (e.g., child has learning problems or was sick a lot) you can request a waiver of the testing results.

Functions: lobbying, support groups, legislative watchdog, community events, media appearances. Membership dues: $20/year, which includes the newsletter. ACHEA could use at-home volunteer help—give them a call. Nice friendly folks.

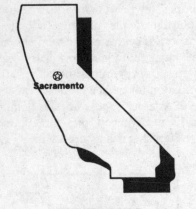

CALIFORNIA

Christian Home Educators Association of California
P.O. Box 28644
Santa Ana, CA 92799-8644
(714) 537-5121
Founded: Fall 1982
Number of members: 1,800
Newsletter: *The California Teaching Home*, bimonthly, $15/year.
  Circulation: 2800 - published with *The Teaching Home*
Yearly convention time: July. Last time's attendance: 2600
Lobby? No
Bi-monthly support network newsletter, annual leadership conference, legislative consultant monitors laws and pub-lishes a newsletter, local radio program planned beginning winter 1990.
Political climate: Rating (1-10): 8
Standardized testing? N Teacher oversight? N Register? N

Records: No home-school statute. Most home educators operate as private schools or join independent study pro-grams.

CHEA is a well-organized nonprofit organization providing info, support, and training to the California home education community. Functions: support, net-work, media appearances, speakers bureau, annual statewide/regional convention, legislative monitoring, leadership training, special workshops and area con-ventions, helpful materials for California home educa-tors. Call their informational telephone number for a ten-minute informational message (updated monthly) which describes currently available services and litera-ture as well as statewide current events.

Membership: $25/year. Includes *Teaching Home* subscription, 10% discount on materials and conven-tion, discount coupon book, and members only newsletter.

Send for CHEA of California's free brochure.

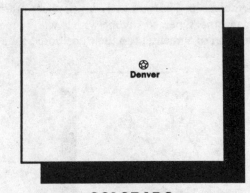

COLORADO

Colorado Home Schooling Network
7490 W. Apache
Sedalia, CO 80135
(303) 688-4136
Founded: April 1981
Contact: Judy Gelner
Newsletter: *Colorado Homeschooling Network Newsletter*. $5/year, 12 monthly issues. Address for subscriptions: CHSN, c/o Nancy McGuire, 365 Hooker, Denver, CO 80129.
Most functions are now done in conjunction with CHEA (Colorado Home Educators Association), an association of groups.
Political climate: Rating (1-10): 8
Standardized testing? Y Teacher oversight? N Register? Y
Records: Attendance records, test and evaluation results, immunization records. Records must be produced given fourteen days notice. Can have a private school hold your records instead of a public school.

Colorado Home Schooling Network is a service organization with no membership dues. They offer a legal packet, *Homeschooling in Colorado*, for $6.25. Order from Judy Gelner. Send SASE for free brochure.

Homes Offering Meaningful Education (HOME)
1015 S. Gaylord, #226
Denver, CO 80209
(303) 777-1082
Founded: 1985
Number of members: 20-25 families
Newsletter: *Christian H.O.M.E.* - published with *The Teaching Home*
Yearly convention time: June. Last time's attendance: 700
Lobby? Yes
Political climate: Rating (1-10): 8
Standardized testing? Y Teacher oversight? N Register? Y
Records: Register with local school district only. Attendance, immunizations, and test data.

A Christian home-school support group (meets monthly). Functions: legislative watchdog, conventions/curriculum fair, monthly field trips, monthly activity days, resource library. Co-publishes its newsletter with *The Teaching Home* ($15/year for both).

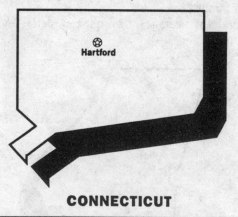

CONNECTICUT

Connecticut Home Schoolers Association
c/o Nancy Williams
Box 464
Chester, CT 06412
(203) 526-5005

Founded 1983. Over 100 on mailing list. Functions: lobbying, support groups, legislative watchdog, media appearances, group field trips, guest speakers. Membership dues: $12/year if you can afford it, less if you can't. At-home volunteer help is gratefully accepted.

Newsletter: *Hearth Notes*, bimonthly, free with membership.

Education Association of Christian Homeschoolers
Box 446
Broad Brook, CT 06106

Address supplied from *Teaching Home* state groups list.

Emanuel Homestead Home Education Resource Center
P.O. Box 355
S. Woodstock, CT 06267
(203) 974-2416 Thursday 2-6 P.M. and Friday noon-4 P.M.

Services for all New England and New York. Helps support groups get started. Free quarterly periodical (supported by donations), *The Godly Home—Constitution of the Christian Family*. You can drop in in person (call first!) to see their variety of textbooks, resources, supplemental materials and supplies, as well as guidance in setting up an individualized program and recommended reading material. Workshops, regional (New England) home schooling conferences.

T.E.A.C.H. The Education Association of Christian Homeschoolers
P.O. Box 446
Broad Brook, CT 06016

Address supplied through Emmanuel Homestead. Offers support-group contacts and information regarding ongoing education legislation alerts.

DELAWARE

Tri-State Home School Network
Box 7193
Newark, DE 19714
(303) 368-4217
Fax: (302) 886-1553—ask for Rich Ogburn
Founded: 1987
Number of members: 50 families

Yearly convention: No. Delaware home schoolers attend the Maryland and Pennsylvania conventions.
Lobby? Informally
Number of support groups: 12
Political climate: Rating (1-10): 8 or 9
Standardized testing? N Teacher oversight? N Register? N
Most home schools in Delaware are registered as private schools or satellite programs. Requirements for solo home schooling vary from school district to school district.

A Christian home-school support group: motto, "Jesus is Lord over church and home." Area covered: northern Delaware with some members from southeastern Pennsylvania and eastern Maryland. Monthly meetings on the fourth Tuesday; monthly field trips. Helps home schoolers obtain standardized tests. No membership fee structure at present, but very open to lots of new members!

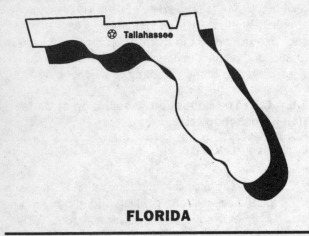

FLORIDA

Florida at Home
7615 Clubhouse Estates Dr.
Orlando, FL 32819
(407) 422-5357
Founded: 1986
Yearly convention time: May. Last time's attendance: 350
Lobby? Yes
Curriculum Fair in May, also Gregg Harris's Christian Life Workshop in September with 700 attending in 1989.
Political climate: Rating (1-10): 7
Standardized testing? N Teacher oversight? N Register? N
Records: Standardized testing is optional. Registering with the state is also optional. Record-keeping requirement "depends on organization."

Florida Parent-Educators Association
9245 Woodrun Road
Pensacola, FL 32514
(904) 477-9642
Founded: 1984

Number of members: 1,500 families
Newsletter: *The FPEA Almanac*
  Circulation: 2,000
Yearly convention time: April. Last time's attendance: 500
Lobby? Yes
Number of support groups: 54
Political climate: Rating (1-10): 5
Standardized testing? N Teacher oversight? N Register? Y
Records: Portfolio must be maintained and made available for inspection on request (in writing, fifteen days notice).

FPEA is organized statewide in nine districts, with elected officers and board of directors. Annual business meeting in September. State curriculum fair in April.

Functions include: lobbying, legislative watchdog, maintain relations with state Department of Education, intervention as needed with local public school officials, media appearances, conferences, and curriculum fairs. Provides local contacts for new home schoolers and encourages local support groups, church sponsorship, and private-school cooperation.

Membership dues: $15/year, includes subscription to newsletter, *The FPEA Almanac*, six or more issues yearly. Newsletter only, $10/year. Group memberships $5 per family.

Send 45¢ postage for sample newsletter and brochure.

GEORGIA

Georgians for Freedom in Education
5986 Randy Lane
Ellenwood, GA 30049
(404) 832-1910
Founded: 1983
Number of members: 350. 1,200 families are on the mailing list.
Newsletter: *Georgians for Freedom in Education*
  Circulation: 350

Yearly convention time: March. Last time's attendance: 300
Lobby? Yes
Political climate: Rating (1-10): 7
Standardized testing? Y Teacher oversight? N Register? Y
Records: Declaration of intent, testing every three years, yearly assessment, monthly attendance.

Functions: lobbying, support groups, legislative watchdog, community events, media appearances, monthly lecture series during school year, weekly field trips, consultation services.

Membership dues in this classy, professional group are $10/year and include the bimonthly newsletter, snappily entitled *Georgians for Freedom in Education* (well, you can't win them all!). The group has over twenty professional advisers, but can use volunteer help.

Send an SASE for the most impressive free home school brochure in the USA. The group's seal features an eagle instructing its eaglet; both have a "don't-tread-on-me" look. Frankly, I'm glad I'm on the right side and don't have to tangle with this group!

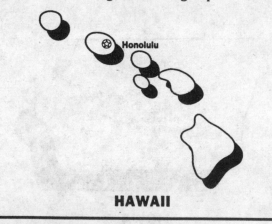

HAWAII

Christian Homeschoolers of Hawaii
91-824 Oama St.
Ewa Beach, HI 96706
(808) 689-6398
Founded: 1986
Number of members: 200
Contact: Arleen T. Alejado
Newsletter: *Na Makua Ho'olako*
  Circulation: 250
Yearly convention time: April/May. Last time's attendance: 325
Lobby? Yes
Number of support groups: 10
Convention is a curriculum fair. Art fair, spelling bee, mom's lunch, presentation night.
Political climate: Rating (1-10): 8
Standardized testing? Y Teacher oversight? N Register? Y

Records: Standardized testing optional. Records need not be submitted, but must be on file.

Hilo Home School Association
P.O. Box 469
Mt. View, HI 96771
(808) 968-8434
Founded: 1989
Number of members: 25 families
Contact: Judith Wilson
Newsletter: *Hilo Homeschool Association Newsletter*
  Circulation: 25
Lobby? No
Number of support groups: 1
Bi-monthly meetings, field trips.
Political climate: Rating (1-10): 7
Standardized testing? Y Teacher oversight? N Register? Y
Records: Testing required for grades 3, 6, 8, 10. Bibliography of books used. Beginning and ending date of program. Number of instruction hours per week (should average three or more per day). Subject areas to be covered. Method used to determine mastery.

Home-school support group meeting twice a month on the Big Island.

IDAHO

Idaho Home Educators
Box 4022
Boise, ID 83711-4022
Founded: 1982
Number of members: 300+
Newsletter: *The Bulletin* - published with *The Teaching Home*
Lobby? Yes
Support groups, orientation meetings, curriculum swaps, conventions, media appearances, field trips, lobbying, in-service training, phone chain.
Political climate: Rating (1-10): 9
Standardized testing? N Teacher oversight? N Register? N
Records: No record-keeping required
Free statement of purpose for SASE.

ILLINOIS

Illinois Christian Home Educators
P.O. Box 261
Zion, IL 60099
Founded: January 1984
Newsletter: Co- published with *The Teaching Home*, $15/year for both.
Support groups, legislative watchdog, media appearances, seminars.
Free contact support group listing with SASE.

No membership dues. ICHE is anxious to find home educators who can swing a pen to write for their newsletter, co-published with *Teaching Home*.

ICHE support groups meet monthly and also provide resource centers and current news, as well as monthly field trips for the children.

"Legal Information for the State of Illinois," "Questions and Answers Concerning Home Education," $1.50 each. Other resources available.

INDIANA

Indiana Association of Home Educators
P.O. Box 17135
Indianapolis, IN 46217
(317) 782-3397
Founded: 1983

Number of members: 3,500 on mailing list
Newsletter: *Indiana Teaching Home*—copublished with *The Teaching Home*. Cost: $15/year.
Yearly convention time: February. Last time's attendance: 1200
Lobby? No
Number of support groups: 65
Conventions, state-wide seminars, graduation ceremonies.
Political climate: Rating (1-10): 8
Standardized testing? N Teacher oversight? N Register? N
Records: None required by state law. Indiana is an "equivalency" state with no official regulations at this time.

Functions: support groups (sixty-five listed in a recent newsletter!), legislative watchdog, community events, media appearances, conventions. Send an SASE to request that your name be added to IAHE's mailing list, and they will inform you of special seminars, legislative updates, and other pertinent info concerning home education in Indiana. (Personally, I'd slip in a couple of bucks to help pay for this service.)

Send SASE for complete list of support groups in your area.

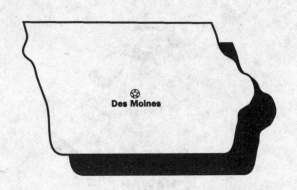

IOWA

Iowa Home Educators' Association
P.O. Box 213
Des Moines, IA 50301

Founded: 1983
Number of members: 325
Newsletter: *Iowa Home Educators Newsletter*
  Circulation: 400
Yearly convention time: March. Last time's attendance: 600
Lobby? Yes
Number of support groups: 10
Curriculum Fair in March, Thanksgiving/Harvest Outing in November
Support groups, field trips, legislative watchdog, celebrations! Annual picnic, Science Fair, seminars, field trips.

Political climate: Rating (1-10): 1
Standardized testing? N Teacher oversight? Y Register? Y
Records: Register with local school district. Record-keeping varies with the school district. Every child in the state of Iowa must be taught by certified teachers.

Iowa Insights
301 N.W. Sharmin
Ankeney, IA 50021
(515) 965-1270

State home schooling newsletter, copublished with *Teaching Home*. Nice looking. Includes children's writing, community events calendar, legislative updates. Make $15 check payable to Clarence Townsend and mail to the above address to get both *Iowa Insights* and *Teaching Home*.

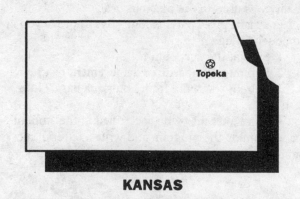

KANSAS

Kansans for Alternative Education
19985 Renner Rd.
Spring Hill, KS 66083
(913) 686-2310
Founded: 1984
Number of members: 800 families
Newsletter: *Kansans for Alternative Education*, sent to members eight times a year (monthly January-April, bimonthly otherwise).
Yearly convention.
Lobby? Yes
Political climate: Rating (1-10): 5
Standardized testing? N Teacher oversight? N Register? Y
Records: Register as non-accredited private school.

KAE's functions: lobbying, linkage between support groups, legislative watchdog, media appearances, and a state conference.

Membership dues are $10/year and include the newsletter and access to the groups's educational, legal, and legislative resources.

Kansas Home Educators
3201 Berry Road
Kansas City, KS 66106
(913) 722-2386
Political climate: Rating (1-10): 5
Standardized testing? N Teacher oversight? N Register? N
Records: Registering with the state is optional. Recommended for the family's own protection.
Information contact only. Send SASE when writing.

Kansas Home Educators is a contact organization only. KHE provides information on resources, nearest groups, referrals to other area groups or leaders, state information, etc.

Teaching Parents Association
100 E. 109th St. N.
Valley Center, KS 67147
(316) 755-2159
Founded: 1980
Number of members: 300
Newsletter: *TPA Newsletter*
 Circulation: 300
Yearly convention time: May. Last time's attendance: 400
Lobby? Yes
Home School Fair and Talent Show, All City Home-School Choir
Political climate: Rating (1-10): 5
Standardized testing? N Teacher oversight? N Register? N
Records: Registration not required, but recommended. Record-keeping not required, but recommended.

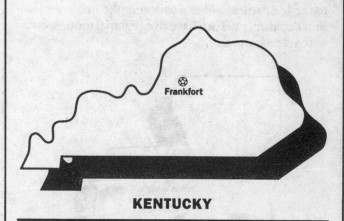

KENTUCKY

Kentucky Christian Home Schooling Association
1301 Bridget Dr.
Fairdale, KY 40118
(502) 363-5104
Founded: 1985
Number of members: 82
Newsletter: *Homeschool Messenger*
 Circulation: 50

Yearly convention time: May or July.
Lobby? No
Number of support groups: 9
Science Fair, Graduation/Promotion, field trips, support group meetings, Field Day, yearbook.
Political climate: Rating (1-10): 10
Standardized testing? N Teacher oversight? N Register? Y
Records: Attendance records.

Kentucky Home Education Association
580 Ruckerville Rd.
Winchester, KY 40391
(606) 744-6404
Founded: 1989
Number of members: 300 families
Newsletter: *KHEA Newsletter,* published quarterly for $12/year membership fee.
  Circulation: 600
Yearly convention time: September. Last time's attendance: 200
Lobby? Yes
Refer people to area support groups. Curriculum fair, etc. in the works.
Political climate: Rating (1-10): 8
Standardized testing? N Teacher oversight? N Register? Y
Records: Register with your local school superintendent informing him of your intention to home school and that you will be teaching for a 175-day year, six hours/day, and that you will teach certain core subjects.

This brand-new group was founded as a legislative watchdog while the new education laws are being written, to give testimony on behalf of home schoolers to the legislature, and as a liaison to the public education department. They have five regional groups, each with its own director.

Baton Rouge

LOUISIANA

Louisiana law allows for home schooling in one of two ways. A parent may either establish a private school or register with the state in the Home Study program. De-

pending on the choice, differing legal requirements must be met.

To establish a private school, parents must write a letter to the Superintendent of Education at the State Department of Education notifying the department that the school exists and how many students will be attending. This must be done every year. It is recommended, though not legally required, that the school incorporate, be officially named, and keep good records.

To register in the home study program, parents should first write to the State Department of Education to request a home study application. The application is easy to complete. They then return the application to the Department of Education with a birth certificate for each child taught. Parents will receive notification of approval. Parents have to reapply each year and include with the application proof that a curriculum of quality was used in the previous year.

Louisiana gives parents four ways to prove you are home schooling:

1. Submit the curriculum;
2. Submit a standardized achievement test score;
3. Submit test score from Louisiana Basic Skills Test;
4. Have a teacher who is certified in the student's grade examine the program and write a letter of recommendation.

Christian Home Educator's Fellowship (C.H.E.F)
P.O. Box 14421
Baton Rouge, LA 70898-4421
(504) 642-2059
Founded: 1985
Number of members: 150 families
Newsletter: *Chef Report,* included in $10 membership.
  Circulation: 150—co-published with *The Teaching Home*
Yearly convention time: April. Last time's attendance: 220
Lobby? No
Number of support groups: 2
Mission outreaches, skating parties, science fairs, graduation, workshops, campouts, picnics, speech club, field trips, activity co-ops, resource library, group standardized testing.

Political climate: Rating (1-10): 8
Standardized testing? Y Teacher oversight? N Register? Y
Records: None. Standardized testing and teacher over-sight are either/or choices. Louisiana home schoolers have five choices of how they choose to be monitored. Functions: support groups, legislative watchdog, community events.

Louisiana Citizens for Home Education
3404 Van Buren
Baker, LA 70714
(504) 775-5472

Founded January 1982. Not presently active on a statewide level, due to favorable legal climate. Contact for legal information or referral to local support groups.

MAINE

Which state was the first in the nation to have a gover-nor-signed proclamation of National Home Education Week? You guessed it . . . Maine. And they've started a movement. Last year Missouri became the second! Both states held Home School Education days at their state capitols with information packets and buttons to wear supplied to legislators. Get on the bandwagon, folks! Don't let your state be the last in line!

Maine Homeschool Association
P.O. Box 3283
Auburn, ME 04240
(207) 777-1700
Founded: 1988
Number of members: 1,400
Newsletter: *Re-Maine-ing at Home*
  Circulation: 1,400
Yearly convention time: June. Last time's attendance: 1,025
Lobby? Yes
Number of support groups: 36
Political climate: Rating (1-10): 6

Standardized testing? N Teacher oversight? N Register? Y
Records: Minimum, not overly burdensome.

Used to be Maine Home Study Association.

Guardians of Education for Maine (GEM)
H.C. Route 68
Box 124
Cushing, ME 04563
(207) 354-6336
Founded: 1978
Newsletter: *GEM/News*
  Circulation: 300
Yearly convention time: October. Last time's attendance: 50
Lobby? Yes
Political climate: Rating (1-10): 2
Standardized testing? N Teacher oversight? N Register? N
Records: Changing because the education department has power to write regulations with the force of law.

GEM describes itself as "an information gathering and disseminating center concerning many phases of education, but home schooling holds a special place."

Christian Homeschool Association of Maine
P.O. Box 5496
Augusta, ME 04332
(207) 872-2015
Founded: 1985
Newsletter: *Home Happenings* (quarterly)
Yearly convention time: September.
Lobby? Yes
Political climate: Rating (1-10): 2
Standardized testing? N Teacher oversight? N Register? N
Records: Changing because the education department has power to write regulations with the force of law.

MARYLAND

Maryland Association of Christian Home Education Organizations
P.O. Box 1041
Emmitsburg, MD 21727
(301) 662-0022

Founded: 1984
Lobby? Yes
Number of support groups: 15-20
Political climate: Rating (1-10): 7
Standardized testing? N Teacher oversight? Y Register? Y
Records: Portfolio of work.

MACHEO is planning to begin publishing a newsletter, and to hold their first convention in 1990.

Maryland Home Education Association

9085 Flamepool Way
Columbia, MD 21045
(301) 730-0073
Founded: 1980
Number of members: 1,000
Yearly convention time: April. Last time's attendance: 450
Lobby? Yes
Number of support groups: 22+
Functions: Locally organized events.
Political climate: Rating (1-10): 9
Standardized testing? N Teacher oversight? N Register? Y
Records: Options: (a) Keep portfolio and meet with schools 1-3 times/year; (b) Calvert or Homestudy International with teaching services, no school meetings; or (c) set up as a religious satellite school that complies with MD bylaws, no school meetings.

Membership dues of $10 includes newsletter. Newsletter will be sent to anyone who requests it. Functions: conferences, networking, resource clearinghouse.

MASSACHUSETTS

Massachusetts Home Learning Association

P.O. Box 1976
Lenox, MA 01240
(413) 637-2169
Founded: 1987
Number of members: 100
Newsletter: *Massachusetts Home Learning Association Newsletter*
   Circulation: 200
Lobby? No

Periodic picnics. Other get-togethers.
Political climate: Rating (1-10): 8
Standardized testing? N Teacher oversight? Y Register? Y
Records: Register with school district. Record-keeping varies with school district.

Massachusetts Home Schooling Association of Parent Educators

15 Ohio St.
Wilmington, MA 01887
(508) 658-8970

Address provided by *Teaching Home*. Yearly convention in April.

MICHIGAN

Christians United to Reclaim Education/C.U.R.E.

P.O. Box 71050
Madison Heights, MI 48071-0050
Founded: 1985
Newsletter: *C.U.R.E. News,* five times/year, $10. News of activities, legislative report, reprints of articles discussing a wide range of social and political issues from a distinctly Christian perspective.

Information Network for Christian Homes

4150 Ambrose N.E.
Grand Rapids, MI 49505
(616) 364-4438
Founded: 1984
Number of members: N/A
Newsletter: *Information Network News*
Yearly convention time: April. Last time's attendance: 1,100
Lobby? Yes
Number of support groups: 25
Functions: state convention, support groups, legislative action.
Political climate: Rating (1-10): 2
Standardized testing? N Teacher oversight? Y Register? N
Records: None.

MINNESOTA

Minnesota Association of Christian Home Educators
Box 188
Anoka, MN 55303
(612) 753-2370
Founded: 1984
Number of members: 800
Newsletter: *Paper MACHE* (cute) comes out quarterly. Subscription rate is $12 for nonmembers. Although it's small, it's typeset on fancy paper, betokening good things to come from this group. Circulation: 1,200
Yearly convention time: April. Last time's attendance: 1,000
Lobby? Yes
Number of support groups: 61
Special function: Annual picnic
Political climate: Rating (1-10): 8
Standardized testing? Y Teacher oversight? N Register? Y
Records: Quarterly report cards for parents without a four-year college degree.

Functions: support groups, educational field trips, annual picnic, media appearances, seminars, conventions. Dues are $12/year and include the newsletter, discounts on seminars, a membership certificate, and an information packet. Unlike most home-school organizations, MACHE has a professional staff of six. However, they will be happy to accept volunteer help with their mailings, especially computer-assisted addressing.

Send SASE for MACHE's free brochure.

T.E.A.C.H Institute and Accrediting Association
4350 Lakeland Ave. North
Robbinsdale, MN 55422
(612) 535-5514
Founded: 1983

Number of members: 160 families, 277 children—588 total members
Contact: Robert Newhouse
Newsletter: *T.E.A.C.H. Outreach*
  Circulation: 204
Yearly convention time: August or June.
Lobby? Yes
Number of support groups: 10
Christmas festival, Spring Awards Night, Track and Field Day, Photo Day, Curriculum Exchange (June), Orientation (three days—August), fall and winter retreats to the Environmental Learning Center for outdoor education in the forest.
Political climate: Rating (1-10): 9
Standardized testing? Y Teacher oversight? N Register? Y
Records: Non-accredited—quarterly report card, 170 days in session, daily schedule. If accredited by T.E.A.C.H.—accountable only to T.E.A.C.H. Institute (self-governing).

T.E.A.C.H. is a home-school accrediting agency. They have twelve teacher consultants who visit each family's home once a month to help them with planning, evaluating, and troubleshooting problems. When a family is accepted into TEACH, they no longer have to report to their superintendent of schools.

T.E.A.C.H. also provides support groups, annual events, graduation, field trips, and parent training sessions.

Registration: New families—$50 first child, $25 each additional, $100 maximum. Alumni—$20/child, $60 maximum. Associates—$25/family (associates participate in activities, but are not accredited).

Annual tuition: Plan A—$450 first child, $225 second child, $100 each additional child. Plan B—$350 first child, $175 second child, $100 each additional child. Associates—$150 first child, $50 each additional child.

Newsletter: *T.E.A.C.H. Outreach,* monthly, $15/year for non-enrolled families.

MISSISSIPPI

Mississippi Home Schoolers
Box 2067
Starkville, MS 39759
(601) 324-2668
Founded: 1983
Number of members: 800 on mailing list
Newsletter: *Mississippi Home Schoolers*
  Circulation: 200—co-published with *The Teaching Home*
Yearly convention time: April. Last time's attendance: 400
Lobby? Yes
Number of support groups: 30
Political climate: Rating (1-10): 7
Standardized testing? N Teacher oversight? N Register? Y
Records: none

Support groups and information, and legislative watchdog. Sponsor an annual conference and curriculum fair.

Handbook for Mississippi Home Schoolers gives legal tips, resources, philosophy, how-tos, and lots more for $6. A leaflet, "There's No Place Like Home," an intro to home schooling for outsiders, is just 10¢ plus postage. Newsletter ($15/year) also covers Alabama, Georgia, and Louisiana, and is co-published with *Teaching Home*.

MISSOURI

It's all in how you pronounce it. Am I living in the state of Missouri or the state of Misery? We ask ourselves these questions in the hot, humid, miserable summers and the cold, cruel, miserable winters. Situated in the Missisippi River valley, my hometown of St. Louis gets its share of both northern winters and southern summers. (And don't forget the tornadoes!) As one lady wrote in to our local paper, "The only way a tourist will ever see Missouri is while his family is heading through it on their way to Florida or Colorado."

One big reason for sweating it out in the home of the heat wave (well, St. Louis is not Texas, but we make up for the few degrees difference by building our entire town out of sun-soaking red brick) is the good people in Families for Home Education. Any group of people who can spend six hours jammed together in a schoolbus on a field trip to Amish Country, and still smile at each other, is worth knowing. I may be just lucky, but so far I have never met a Missouri home schooler I haven't liked. (Come to think of it, I've never met *any* home schoolers I haven't liked!)

Families for Home Education
21709 E. Old Atherton Rd.
Independence, MO 64058
(816) 796-0978
Number of members: 1,000 families
Newsletter: *Heart of America Report* is really more of a magazine than a newsletter.
Yearly convention in June.
Lobby? Yes
Political climate: Rating (1-10): 9
Standardized testing? N Teacher oversight? N Register? N
Teach 1,000 hours/year, 600 in core subjects. Keep a home-school log.

This is it, folks: the one and only Missouri state home-school group. At last count, we had over 1,000 member families, but I can personally attest that there are many times that many home schoolers in this state, since four out of five of my home-schooling friends haven't yet joined FHE, the rascals! Dues are $30 a year, which entitle the happy member to support groups, legislative watchdogging, a yearly conference and regional conferences, media representation, monthly magazine including local news from your regional director, voting privileges, and earnest lobbying on your behalf.

FHE offers many useful items, such as:

• "Home Schooling?" pamphlet that answers the most frequently asked questions, like "What about socialization?" Five for 25¢.

• FHE's *Academic Freedom Handbook* makes the case for home schooling as unregulated private schooling. Thanks partly to this pamphlet, Missouri now has the best home schooling law in the country. We are required to provide 1,000 hours of instruction (600 of core subjects) and to keep a log showing these hours, but allowed complete freedom in what areas we cover and what hours of the day we work, and protected from the intrusions of the Division of Family Services. Handbook is $2.

• *Heart of America Report* brings brand-new home schoolers up-to-date on all aspects of home schooling in Missouri. Includes legal info, sample daily log page, how to get started, advice on home schooling in the office or with several children, apprenticeships, philosophy, and a whole lot more! Free with paid membership.

Mail $30 membership check (payable to "FHE Educational Fund") to the FHE address above. Mail orders for individual items (check payable to "FHE Educational Fund") to FHE Mail Service, 400 E. High Point Lane, Columbus, MO 65203. On individual items, add 15 percent shipping.

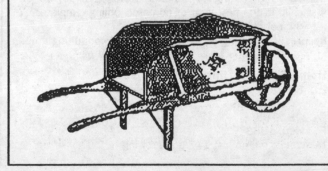

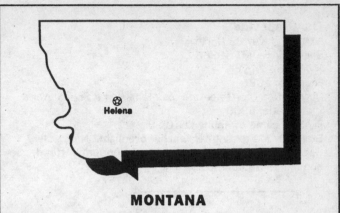

MONTANA

Home Schoolers of Montana
Box 40
Billings, MT 59101
(406) 248-6762
Founded: 1982
Number of members: 100 families
Newsletter: Co-published with *Teaching Home*
Yearly convention time: varies.
Lobby? Yes
Local support group? Yes
Spelling bees, science fair, legislative show 'n tell (home-schooled kids bring their projects to the capitol), field trips.
Political climate: Rating (1-10): 7
Standardized testing? N Teacher oversight? N Register? Y
Records: Don't have to register as such, just notify county superintendent. Keep attendance and immunization records.

Membership group. Functions: support groups, conventions. Dues, $5/year. Copy of Montana Home School Law, 50¢. Newsletter, *Homeschoolers of Montana Journal*, $15, copublished with *Teaching Home*.

Montana Coalition of Home Educators
P.O. Box 654
Helena, MT 59624
(406) 357-2893
Founded: 1988
Number of members: No individual membership
Newsletter: none (gets info through *The Grapevine* and *Teaching Home* insert)
Yearly convention time: March usually. Last time's attendance: 450
Lobby? Yes
Number of support groups: 30+
Legislative day rally in odd years, convention in even years.
Political climate: Rating (1-10): 8
Standardized testing? N Teacher oversight? N Register? Y
Records: Don't have to register as such, just notify county superintendent. Keep attendance and immunization records.

The Grapevine
1702 Highway 83 North
Seeley Lake, MT 59868
(406) 754-2481
Founded: 1986
Newsletter: *The Grapevine, Montana Home School News*
  Circulation: 300
Political climate: Rating (1-10): 8
Standardized testing? N Teacher oversight? N Register? Y
Records: Notify the county superintendent. Attendance and immunization records.

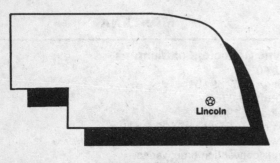

NEBRASKA

Nebraska Home Educators Association
5000 Grand View Ln.
Lincoln, NE 68521
(402) 476-9925
Founded: 1986
Number of members: 250
Newsletter: *NHEA Newsletter*
  Circulation: 250
Yearly convention time: April. Last time's attendance: 400
Lobby? Yes
Number of support groups: 9
Curriculum fair, state convention. Local support groups sponsor field trips, science and used book fairs, workshops and special classes, art fairs, and many special activities for junior and senior high such as banquets and classes.
Political climate: Rating (1-10): 7
Standardized testing? N Teacher oversight? N Register? Y
Records: Must report curriculum, school calendar, parents' names and educational background, names and ages of children.

NEVADA

Nevada has a rather strange home-schooling law. You have four options: (1) Hire a full-time teacher. (2) Parents who are certified teachers or who would be qualified to be certified teachers (whether or not they have a current certificate) can home school without any further requirements. (3) Use an approved correspondence course. (4) Use anything you want, but for the first year of home schooling pay for twenty-five hours of consulting with a certified teacher. If your child shows progress, you can go solo from then on.

Nevada home schooling is divided up along geographic lines, as follows.

Nevada Home Schools - Northern Division
Box 21323
Reno, NV 89515
(702) 323-0566
Founded: 1985
Number of members: 100 families
Newsletter: *Northern Nevada Home Schools Gazetter*
  Circulation: 70-100
Yearly convention time: Spring. Last time's attendance: 200+
Lobby? No
Number of support groups: 10
Science Fair, exhibition, curriculum fair, annual picnic. Field trips. Occasional co-op classes.
Political climate: Rating (1-10): 6
Standardized testing? Y Teacher oversight? Yes, for the first child in the first year of home schooling Register? Y, with the county school district
Records: Consulting teacher keeps log of consulting time.

Home Schools United - Vegas Valley
P.O. Box 26811
Las Vegas, NV 89126
(702) 870-9566
Founded: 1983
Number of members: 177 and growing

Newsletter: *Home Schools United Newsletter*, monthly, $12/year.
Circulation: 177
Lobby? No
Number of support groups: 6
Back to Home School Picnic, Demonstration/Exhibit Fair, promotion and graduation ceremony.
Political climate: Rating (1-10): 5
Standardized testing? Y Teacher oversight? Y Register? Y
Records: Teacher oversight first year only.

Information packet, $6. This group has a resource center with used textbooks which members can borrow.

Silver State Education Advocates
2516 Janelle Dr.
Sparks, NV 89431
(702) 356-7058
Founded: 1989
Number of members: 180
Newsletter: *SSEA News*, co-published with the *Northern Nevada Home Schools Gazette*
Lobby? Yes

SSEA is the legislative advocacy group for Nevada. They monitor the legislature and the state school board and are available to offer advice to families if any legal problems arise. They also hope to influence the legislature favorably in the area of home-schooling law. Membership dues are $20/year.

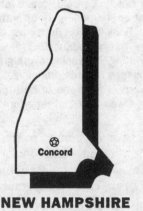

NEW HAMPSHIRE

New Hampshire Home Educators Association
9 Mizoras Drive
Nashua, NH 03062
Founded: 1983
Number of members: Association only
Newsletter: *N.H. Homeschools Newsletter*
Lobby? No
Have had resource fairs in the past.

Political climate: Rating (1-10): 8
Standardized testing? N Teacher oversight? N Register? Y
Records: Legislation introduced 1/90.

This group consists of a few families that try to organize meetings, promote communication between home schoolers, and provide information. It also maintains contact with the State Department of Education. Send SASE for the info sheet.

The *New Hampshire Home Schools Newsletter* is available for $3 (six issues, bimonthly) from Abbey Lawrence, P.O. Box 97, Center Tuftonboro, NH 03816.

Christian Home Educators of New Hampshire
Box 1653
Hillsboro, NH 03244

State group that co-publishes its newsletter with *The Teaching Home*

NEW JERSEY

New Jersey Unschoolers Network
2 Smith Street
Farmingdale, NJ 07727
(201) 938-2473

Founded in 1977. Nancy Plent, the director, points out that "strictly speaking, a network doesn't have 'members.'" The mailing list has over 2,000 addresses.

Functions: support groups, community events, media appearances, workshops, statewide gatherings, resource clearinghouse, and general help and goodwill. No membership dues. The Unschoolers Network could use volunteers at times to answer letters from students. Volunteers produce the monthly bulletin. UN is seeking articles from NJ residents about favorite places for family outings.

Newsletter: *Unschoolers Network*, costs $7/year for three issues. It's a pretty hefty tome as these things go, and contains advertising and articles with a *Growing Without Schooling* flavor. Everyone shares, nobody puts anyone down.

Booklet: *Famous Home Schoolers* gives short thumbnail biographies of famous men and women who were home schooled.

Education Network of Christian Home-Schoolers of New Jersey (E.N.O.C.H.)
65 Middlesex Rd.
Matawan, NJ 07747
(201) 583-7128
Founded: 1989
Newsletter: *E.N.O.C.H.*
  Circulation: 1,199 - co-published with *The Teaching Home*
Yearly convention.
Lobby? No
Number of support groups: 14
Political climate: Rating (1-10): 9
Standardized testing? N Teacher oversight? N Register? N
Records: None; however, keeping a journal is recommended.

Brand-new organization. They are planning their first leadership conference early February 1990. Memberships, conventions, and other activities are to be discussed and established at that meeting.

Subscribe to the New Jersey version of *The Teaching Home* for information about E.N.O.C.H.

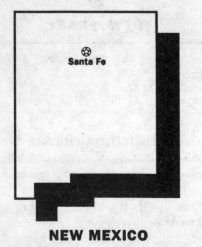

Santa Fe

NEW MEXICO

New Mexico Christian Home Educators
5749 Paradise N.W.
Albuquerque, NM 87114
(505) 897-1772
Founded: 1984
Number of members: 200. Over 1,300 on their statewide mailing list.

Newsletter: two newsletters: *N.M. Teaching Home*
  Circulation: 200 - published with *The Teaching Home*
Second newsletter: *Family Voice*, circulation 400, monthly, provided to support groups.
Yearly convention time: April or May. Last time's attendance: 400
Lobby? No
Number of support groups: 25
Lobby individually. Set up and network with support groups, media promotion, liaison with state and local school authorities, legislative watchdog, legal information. Annual state convention/curiculum fair, statewide speaker's bureau.
Political climate: Rating (1-10): 4
Standardized testing? Y Teacher oversight? N Register? Y
Records: Calendar showing when 180 days of home education will occur, immunization forms, and attendance forms submitted. No logs or other records required.

Dues of $20/year include newsletter co-published with *Teaching Home*. Free brochure with SASE.

New Mexico Family Educators
P.O. Box 13383
Albuquerque, NM 87192
(505) 892-5783 or (505) 265-3019
Founded: 1982
Number of members: 120 families
Newsletter: *NMFE Gazette*
  Circulation: 150
Lobby? No
Number of support groups: 8
Social studies fair, craft sale, talent show, science fair, participate National Spelling Bee, National Geographic Bee, Pizza Hut "Book-It," Fun Run, classes, etc.
Political climate: Rating (1-10): 5
Standardized testing? Y Teacher oversight? N Register? Y
Records: Attendance records, immunization records. Bachelor's degree required for one or both parents. Can apply to the state for a waiver of that requirement.

Functions: support groups, media appearances, and general clearinghouse and contact point for people interested in the joys of home schooling. Annual events: Science Fair, History/Geography Fair, Talent Show, etc. NMFE could use volunteer help with the newsletter and mailings, plus office help filing things and dynamic go-getters to organize some fun activities.

Newsletter is given out free at monthly meetings, or mailed to paid members.

Membership: $10. Gets you the monthly newsletter and reduced prices at all activities and classes. Introductory packet of N.M. Home School information is available for long SASE and $2.

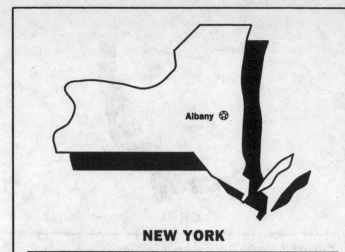

NEW YORK

Home Schoolers Exchange
R.D. 1, Box 172E
East Chatham, NY 12060
(518) 392-4277
Founded: 1984
Number of members: 50 families
Newsletter: *Home Schoolers' Exchange*
  Circulation: 50
Lobby? Yes
This organization is a local support group. Workshops for children.
Political climate: Rating (1-10): 5
Standardized testing? Y Teacher oversight? N Register? N
Records: Register with local school district. Quarterly reports, attendance records.

Founded in the freezing month of February 1984, HSE is nonetheless a warm and growing group. Functions: support groups, field trips and workshops for children, lending library, community events, an information exchange, and current legislative info. Dues are $12/year and includes the bimonthly newsletter and workshop announcements. Meetings are open to the public.

Loving Education at Home (LEAH)
P.O. Box 332
Syracuse, NY 13205
(518) 377-6019
Founded: 1983
Newsletter: *New York State LEAH Newsletter*
  Circulation: 1,100 - co-published with *The Teaching Home*
Yearly convention in Syracuse each April. Last time's attendance: 1,000
Lobby? No
Number of support groups: 55+
Newsletter published in *Teaching Home* every other month and as a state newsletter the months in between. Field trips, parties, science, art, and history fairs, sports—within support groups, graduation, monthly meetings.
Political climate: Rating (1-10): 6
Standardized testing? Y Teacher oversight? N Register? N
Records: By August 1 send letter of intent to school district. Quarterly reports. End of year assessment.

LEAH is the statewide group for New York.

LEAH membership dues of $10 per family entitles your family to: bimonthly state newsletter; free mailings concerning upcoming seminars and other important news; legal updates; free handouts and info at the LEAH meetings. This small fee helps cover all the services LEAH offers for families around the state: maintaining the Hotline, cost of printing and mailing materials, correspondence, etc. So do it—join, already!

LEAH will send you a support group starter packet for $1 to cover shipping, or a list of statewide support groups, also for $1. Their legal manual covers what you need to know to home school in NY State and is only $5.00. Also available: tapes of previous seminars, resource materials, and even LEAH T-shirts for your whole family!

Membership dues vary from local chapter to local chapter.

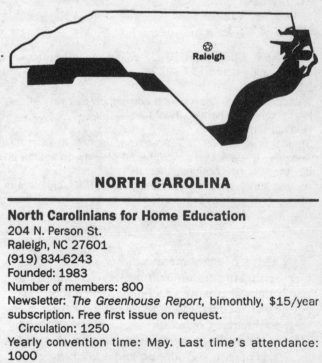

NORTH CAROLINA

North Carolinians for Home Education
204 N. Person St.
Raleigh, NC 27601
(919) 834-6243
Founded: 1983
Number of members: 800
Newsletter: *The Greenhouse Report*, bimonthly, $15/year subscription. Free first issue on request.
  Circulation: 1250
Yearly convention time: May. Last time's attendance: 1000
Lobby? Yes
Number of support groups: 61
Regional workshops, graduation/senior trip. Local art, sci-

ence, and history fairs. Local field days. Local group classes, LD coordinator, capitol tours.
Political climate: Rating (1-10): 9
Standardized testing? Y Teacher oversight? N Register? Y
Records: 9-month attendance, immunizations, test records.

NCHE is organizing local support groups across the state. They also serve as a legislative watchdog and do media work and conventions.

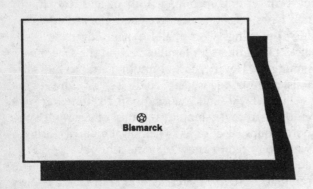

NORTH DAKOTA

North Dakota Home School Association
P.O. Box 539
Turtle Lake, ND 58575
(701) 448-9193
Founded: 1984
Newsletter: *NDHSA Newsletter* (monthly) - published with *The Teaching Home*
Lobby? Yes
Curriculum fair (will become a convention this year—Gregg Harris seminar), home school fair.
Political climate:
Standardized testing? Y Teacher oversight? N Register? Y
Records: Three options available. If parents do not fall under the first two options, then their program must be under the supervision of a certified teacher. Records: courses taught, achievement test results, immunization records.

NDHSA operates more as a network than as a membership organization. Functions: lobbying, support groups, legislative watchdog, conventions, plus advice and encouragement to those who need it. No membership dues are required, but gifts are gratefully accepted. Benefits of membership include the newsletter, legal counsel, and support and encouragement. NDHSA has some professional staff members, but could also use volunteer help.

OHIO

Christian Home Educators of Ohio
P.O. Box 9083
Canton, OH 44711
(216) 673-7272
Founded: 1983
Newsletter: *Ohio Home School Companion*
  Circulation: 1,000
Yearly convention time: June. Last time's attendance: 1,750
Lobby? No, they cannot directly lobby, but they direct their families toward legislative action and also can legally educate their legislators about home schooling.
Number of support groups: many.
The support groups around the state are autonomous and hold many local activities.
Political climate: Rating (1-10): 8
Standardized testing? N Teacher oversight? N Register? Y
Records: Notification to the superintendent of your intent to home school; inform him of curriculum used and proposed outline of study; some form of academic assessment required at the end of the year, not necessarily standardized testing.

Large, well-organized group with state conventions, support groups, and the like. Legislative watchdog, media appearances. Over 1750 people attended the last state convention, at $35 a throw, to give you some idea of the membership's size and dedication. Legal info packet describes Ohio's new reasonable regulations, $2.50. Newsletter comes with $25/year membership fee. Sample free.

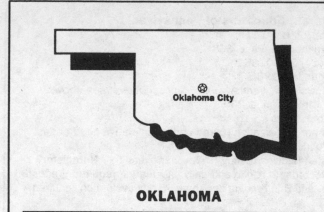

OKLAHOMA

Coalition of Christian Home Educators of Oklahoma

P.O. Box 471032
Tulsa, OK 74147-1032
(918) 455-6284
Founded: 1984. Reorganized: 1989
Newsletter: *CCHO News* - published with *The Teaching Home*
Lobby? Yes
Number of support groups: Around 100
Capitol Day (meet at state capitol to display students' accomplishments, curriculum, etc. and speak with legislators)
Political climate: Rating (1-10): 8
Standardized testing? N Teacher oversight? N Register? N
Records: none

Functions: support groups, legislative watchdog, community events, media work, statewide workshops and seminars. Dues of $15/year include a subscription to *Teaching Home*, in which CCHO's state newsletter is inserted. Send SASE for free brochure.

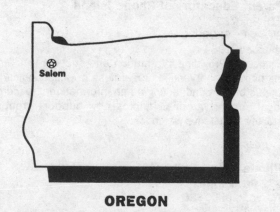

OREGON

Oregon Christian (Home) Educators' Association Network (OCEAN)

2515 N.E. 37th
Portland, OR 97212
(503) 288-1285
Founded: 1986
Number of members: Over 1,000
Newsletter: *The Oregon Network News*, co-published with *Teaching Home*, $15/year for both.
  Circulation: 850
Lobby? Yes
Number of support groups: 58
N.W. Curriculum Exhibition (annual—May or June), The Home School Winter Workshops (annual—February or March), and The Home School Student Convention (annual—April or May)
Political climate: Rating (1-10): 8
Standardized testing? Y Teacher oversight? N Register? N
Records: Annual test results and attendance records.

You're automatically a member of OCEAN if you're active in a local Oregon home-schooling support group. No membership dues. Functions: support groups, legislative watchdog, media appearances, conventions. Some nifty annual events in Oregon: a curriculum exhibition in Portland that draws 1,200 paying attendees and a Home School Student Convention and Winter Workshop.

OCEAN provides communication between Christian support groups in Oregon, as well as training and assistance for support group leadership.

Parents' Education Association

P.O. Box 1482
Beaverton, OR 97075
Founded: 1983
Number of members: 1,000+
Newsletter: *Line Upon Line*
  Circulation: 1400
Lobby? Yes
Political climate: Rating (1-10): 7
Standardized testing? Y Teacher oversight? N Register? N
Records: Yearly standardized test submitted to local education service district.

PEA is a political action committee that provides home school information and does periodic mailings. Support groups, legislative watchdog, media work. Their newsletter has some of the best reporting on the real political and spiritual issues in education today that I have seen. They are doing an excellent job of presenting and organizing their views politically as well.

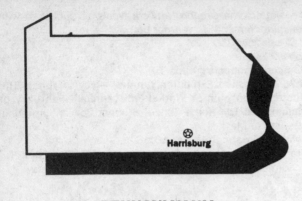

PENNSYLVANIA

Pennsylvania Homeschoolers

c/o Howard and Susan Richman
R.D. 2 Box 11
Kittanning, PA 16201
(412) 783-6512
Founded: 1981
Number of members: No formal "membership"
Newsletter: *Pennsylvania Homeschoolers*
  Circulation: 1200
Lobby? Yes
Number of support groups: 50+
Local and regional science fairs, history fairs, arts festivals, essay contests, legislative breakfasts, major curriculum fairs, etc.
Political climate: Rating (1-10): 7+ and improving.
Standardized testing? Y Teacher oversight? Y Register? Y
Records: Standardized testing grades 3, 5, and 8. Log and portfolio of student work and written evaluation must be turned in at end of year to local superintendent. Hearings available if the district thinks the education is not adequate.

Twelve hundred Pennsylvania families subscribe to the newsletter as well as many folks from outside the state. Functions: lobbying, networking with the support groups, legislative watchdog, media work, publishing, speaking at local support groups and conferences, small group and individual testing service, year-end evaluation of home education programs, and yearly "Homeschooling Weekend" conference/family time at Richmans' Farm. No membership dues.

Newsletter: *Pennsylvania Homeschoolers*, $10/year (four issues), $2.75/sample issue. This quarterly newsletter is thirty-two or more pages long and includes resources, calendars of events, support group listings, legislative updates, practical articles by homeschooling parents, and a children's writing section! (Neat idea—it's *their* education, after all!)

Booklet: *Guide to PA Homeschooling Law*, $4 + 24¢ sales tax, thirty-two pages.

Parent Educators of Pennsylvania

R.D. 2 Box 141
Wrightsville, PA 17368
(717) 252-0286
Founded: 1985
Newsletter: *Pennsylvania Homeschoolers*, see above.
  Circulation: 1,200
Lobby? Yes
State organization retired until a legislative need arises.
Political climate: Rating (1-10): 8
Standardized testing? Y Teacher oversight? N Register? Y
Records: Portfolio and daily log. Testing required grades 3, 5, and 8 in reading and math. Yearly evaluation required.

Seventy state coordinators. Legislative watchdog. The statewide organization is officially retired until a legislative need arises. Newsletter: subscribe to *Pennsylvania Homeschoolers*, above.

RHODE ISLAND

Parent Educators of Rhode Island

P.O. Box 782
Glendale, RI 02826
Founded: 1984
Functions: Providing information and support to all incoming home school families regardless of philosophical or religious background; acting as an informational resource for local support groups; helping new support groups get started; legislative watchdog.

Rhode Island Guild of Home Teachers

272 Pequot Ave.
Warwick, RI 02886
(401) 737-2265

Address provided by *Teaching Home*.

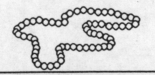

SOUTH CAROLINA

South Carolina Home Educators Association
P.O. Box 33
Goose Creek, SC 29445
(803) 761-3076
Founded: 1989
Number of members: Non-membership, service organization for the 800+ home schoolers of SC.
Newsletter: *Palmetto P.E.N.* (Parent Educators Newsletter)
  Circulation: 200
Yearly convention time: June. Last time's attendance: 528
Lobby? Yes
Number of support groups: 18
Workshop—Gregg Harris or other national speaker
Political climate: Rating (1-10): 1
Standardized testing? Y Teacher oversight? N Register? Y
Records: Plan book, diary or other written record of subjects taught, a portfolio of student's work and record of evaluations, a semi-annual progress report including attendance records, individualized assessments of student's progress in each basic instructional area must be submitted to the school district.

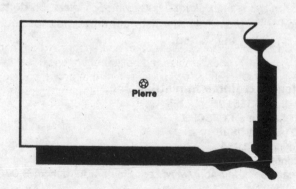

SOUTH DAKOTA

South Dakota Home School Association
1606 South 4th Ave.
Sioux Falls, SD 57105
(605) 334-2213
Founded: 1983
Number of members: 75

Newsletter: *South Dakota Home School Association Newsletter.* Monthly.
  Circulation: 150
Lobby? Yes
Political climate: Rating (1-10): 8
Standardized testing? Y Teacher oversight? N Register? Y
Records: A yearly visit in which you are asked to show curriculum, schedules, etc.

Functions: support groups, legislative watchdog, media work. Dues are $10/year and include the newsletter and voting privileges.

Western Dakota Christian Home Schools
Box 528
Black Hawk, SD 57718-0528
(605) 787-5928
Founded: 1983
Number of members: 100
Newsletter: *Western Dakota Christian Home Schools*
  Circulation: 100
Yearly convention time: April. Last time's attendance: 150
Lobby? Yes
Art Fair, Music Festival, Speech and Drama Fair, Science Fair, Spelling Bee, Field Day, Book-It, roller skating.
Political climate: Rating (1-10): 7
Standardized testing? Y Teacher oversight? N Register? Y
Records: File exemption from public school certificate yearly. Home visit by designee from the state required every one to two years.

Reorganized group offers support groups, legislative watchdogging, and statewide network, plus greater accountability for individual families. Membership dues $15/year.

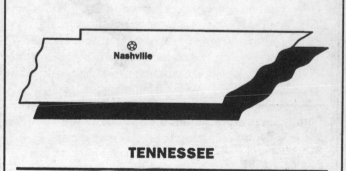

TENNESSEE

Tennessee Home Education Association
3677 Richbriar Court
Nashville, TN 37211
(615) 834-3529
Founded: 1984
Number of members: About 900

Newsletter: Published with *The Teaching Home*, $15/year (six issues).
Yearly convention time: March. Last time's attendance: 500
Lobby? Yes
Number of support groups: 75-100
Political climate: Rating (1-10): 4
Standardized testing? Y Teacher oversight? N Register? N
Records: Basic attendance records. Registering with the state is one option. You may also be affiliated with a church school. The state requires a B.A. degree to teach high school. The law provides for a waiver, but the superintendent of schools has yet to grant one. HSLDA has launched a class action suit to remove this "unconstitutional requirement."

Functions: lobbying, support groups, legislative watchdog, community events, media work, curriculum fairs, statewide and area conferences.

Tennesse home schooling is divided into seven regions. In each of these seven regions, the following are offered: Science fair, art and talent shows, graduation ceremonies, beginning and veteran home schooling work shops.

Dues are $10 and do not include the newsletter. You must subscribe for this separately.

Five local newsletters announce field trips and support group activities. Ask about these.

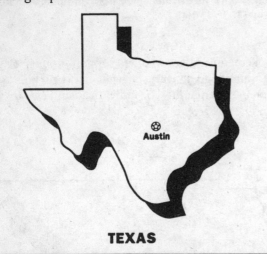
Austin

TEXAS

Family Educators Alliance of South Texas
1400 N. Flores
San Antonio, TX 78212
Founded: 1989
Number of members: 580 on mailing list
Lobby? Yes
Convention held in 1988. Attendance 800.
Number of support groups: 21
Track meet, book fair in June 1990 (to become an annual event), office with curriculum displays, lending library,

computer set up to disseminate information on coming events.
Political climate: Rating (1-10): 9
Standardized testing? N Teacher oversight? N Register? N
Records: Have written curriculum in reading, grammar, spelling, math, and good citizenship; use the curriculum in regular bona fide manner.

Another brand-new organization. They had not even installed their phone when they supplied their information. They hope to have a newsletter soon.

Home Oriented Private Education (H.O.P.E.) for Texas
P.O. Box 43887
Austin, TX 78745
(512) 280-4673
Founded: 1986
Leadership: 5-member board
Newsletter: *Texas Home Educators Newsletter*
  Circulation: 2,200 - published with *The Teaching Home*
Lobby? No
Number of support groups: 300
No activities. Cooperate with the other state organizations to do the Texas Home Education Week—the first full week of May.
Political climate: Rating (1-10): 10
Standardized testing? N Teacher oversight? N Register? N
Records: None

HOPE for Texas (formerly CHEA of Texas) co-publishes the *Texas Home Educators Newsletter* with *The Teaching Home*, $15/year, six issues. It also publishes the *Handbook for Texas Home Schoolers*, $5 donation. Also provides other helpful information for families just getting started.

Hearth & Home Ministries, Inc.
P.O. Box 835105
Richardson, TX 75083
(214) 231-9838
Founded: 1984
Contact: Kirk and Beverly McCord
Yearly book fair April/May. Last time's attendance: 3,038
Lobby? No
Book fair is a buying event. Have workshops, but no plenary sessions.

Hearth & Home Ministries (formerly the Texas Association for Home Education) has been in existence since 1984. It is a nonprofit, tax-exempt, Christian ministry established for the purpose of informing

Texas families about home education. No membership dues; funded through seminars and individual donations. Kirk and Beverly McCord, well-known in homeschooling circles, direct the ministry. Function: Running the annual Home School Book Fair (over 3000 people attended the 1989 one), now in its sixth year. Also publishes the downright essential *Home Education: Is it Working?*, an attractive little footnoted booklet that documents statistical studies on home education and otherwise proves that home education is working. *Home Education: Is it Working?* is general in nature and can be used in all fifty states. Five-copy minimum when ordering by mail, $1 each, or $75/100.

Southeast Texas Home School Association (SETHSA)
5620 FM 1960 W. Box 354
Houston, TX 77069-4202
(713) 586-8897
Founded: 1984
Number of members: 1,500 families
Newsletter: *Teaching Pioneer* available through support groups.
Number of support groups: 30+

Functions: Put on seminars, and help families in their area get started in home schooling.

UTAH

Utah Christian Home Schooling
3190 South 4140 West
West Valley City, UT 84120

Small group founded in 1985. Functions: support groups, legislative watchdog, community events, media work, conventions. Membership dues, $5 a year. Newsletter co-published with *Teaching Home* ($15/year, six issues).

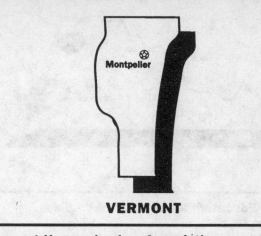

VERMONT

Vermont Homeschoolers Association
c/o Rich and Cindy Larson
R.F.D.
Wells, VT 05774
Founded: 1985
Number of members: 80
Newsletter: *VHSA*
   Circulation: 80. Occasionally sent to 500.
Lobby? Yes
Informal support groups.
Political climate: Rating (1-10): 8
Standardized testing? N Teacher oversight? N Register? Y
Records: Submit curriculum. End-of-year evaluation by one of several choices, written screening for disabilities before entering home-school program.

Vermont Home Schoolers Association
Spruce Knob Road
Middletown Springs, VT 05757
(802) 235-2620
Founded: 1985
Newsletter: *VHSA News*
Lobby? Yes
Number of support groups: 8
Political climate: Rating (1-10): 8
Standardized testing? N Teacher oversight? N Register? Y
Records: None

Try Emanuel Homestead Center (see Connecticut listing) for more help in locating other home schoolers.

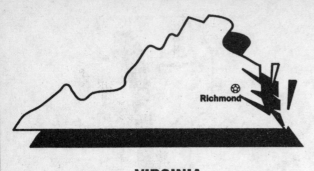

VIRGINIA

Home Educators Association of Virginia
P.O. Box 1810
Front Royal, VA 22630-1810
(703) 635-9322
Founded: 1984
Number of members: 1,800+ on mailing list
Newsletter: *Home Educators Association of Virginia Newsletter*
  Circulation: 600+
Yearly convention time: June. Last time's attendance: 1000
Lobby? Yes
Number of support groups: 45
Events: High school graduation, annual Home Education Convention
Political climate:
Standardized testing? Y Teacher oversight? N Register? Y

HEAV's functions are lobbying, support groups, legislative watchdog, and media work.

Dues are $15/year and include the newsletter, support-group information, and legislative updates.

Interesting sidelight: Mary Kay Clark, the director of the Seton Home Study Program for Catholics (reviewed in the Curriculum Buyers' Guide), was one of HEAV's founders.

Newsletter: *HEAV Newsletter* goes only to members. It comes out bimonthly. Free brochure for SASE with 65¢ stamp.

Virginia Home School Manual, 100+ pages, $10 for members, $13 for non-members.

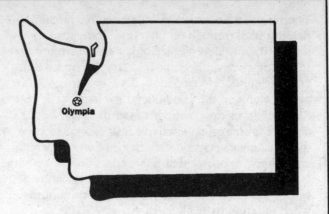

WASHINGTON

Homeschoolers's Support Association
23335 269th Ave. S.E.
Maple Valley, WA 98038

Open-minded support group. Newsletter: *Homeschoolers' Voice.*

Family Learning Organization of Washington
P.O. Box 7256
Spokane, WA 99207-0256
(509) 467-2552
Founded: 1983
Newsletter: *Family Learning Exchange (FLEx)*
  Circulation: 300
Biennial convention time: June. Last time's attendance: 1,800
Lobby? Yes
Political climate: Rating (1-10): 9.5
Standardized testing? Y Teacher oversight? N Register? Y
Records: Test scores must be kept, but not reported.

Originally founded in 1983 as the Family Learning Association, and later known as the Washington Association of Home Educators, FLO is a service organization for home educators in Washington. Functions: family learning advocacy, lobbying and serving as legislative watchdog, community events, support group network, liaison with school districts, news and information, media appearances, testing services, research, workshops, and courses on home schooling.

Newsletter: *Family Learning Exchange (FLEx)*, $15/year.

For more information or a list of publications (such as the immensely appealing 132-page *Home Educator's Resource Guide for Washington State*), please send an SASE.

Washington Homeschool Organization (WHO)

P.O. Box 938
Maple Valley, WA 98038
(206) 432-3935
Founded: January 1986
Number of members: 800
Newsletter: *W.H.O.'s News*
  Circulation: 1,000
Yearly convention time: June. Last time's attendance: 2,000
Lobby? Yes
Convention, high school graduation.
Political climate: Rating (1-10): 8
Standardized testing? N Teacher oversight? N Register? Y
Records: Standardized testing optional. Parent keeps results. Can take a non-test assessment. Immunization records.

Statewide support and information network offering support and information to all home schoolers. WHO began in January 1986 as the Washington State Homeschool Committee, an informal group providing a chance to get home-school leaders together after their succesful legislative effort. WHO now reaches over 3,000 home-school families. WHO organizes an annual convention, supports home-school research, produces a weekly radio program, and is the primary contact for state legislative and educational boards.

W.A.T.C.H. (Washington Association of Teaching Christian Homes)

P.O. Box 554
Colville, WA 99114
(509) 684-3270
Founded: 1989
Newsletter: *The W.A.T.C.H. Word* - published with *The Teaching Home*
Yearly convention time: In planning.
Lobby? No
Activities: Still being worked out.
Political climate: Rating (1-10): 7
Standardized testing? Y Teacher oversight? N Register? Y
Records: None. Register with local school board.

Another brand-new home-school organization. We'll have to W.A.T.C.H. this one (Bill's pun, not mine)!

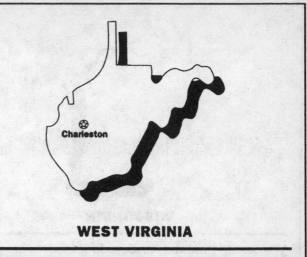

WEST VIRGINIA

West Virginians for Religious Freedom

P.O. Box 7504
Charleston, WV 25356
(304) 776-1948
Founded: 1982
Number of members: 500 churches
Newsletter: *Watchword*
  Circulation: 500
Lobby? Yes
Seminars on freedom issues. Training for lobbying.
Political climate: Rating (1-10): 7
Standardized testing? Y Teacher oversight? N Register? N
Records: none

West Virginia Home Education Association

P.O. Box 266
Glenville, WV 26351
(304) 462-8296
Founded: 1986
Number of members: No membership
Newsletter: *WVHEA Report*
  Circulation: 125
Yearly convention time: varies. Last time's attendance: 200
Lobby? Yes
Number of support groups: N/A
Annual test, Administration Seminar, student sessions available at annual conference.
Political climate: Rating (1-10): 9
Standardized testing? Y Teacher oversight? N Register? N
Records: none

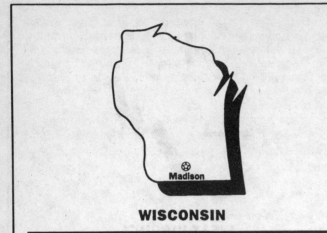

WISCONSIN

Wisconsin Parents' Association, Inc.

P.O. Box 2502
Madison, WI 53701
Founded: 1983
Number of members: 675 families
Newsletter: *W.P.A. Newsletter* (quarterly). Bulletins are sent out as needed.
  Circulation: 800
Yearly convention time: April. Last time's attendance: 950
Lobby? Yes
Number of support groups: 15
Functions: lobbying, support groups, legislative watchdog, media work, yearly conference, regional coordination.
Political climate: Rating (1-10): 9
Standardized testing? N Teacher oversight? N Register? Y
Records: Minimal

Dues are $15/year and include the newsletter, access to the regional coordinators, slot on the phone tree, and discount on printed materials such as the very informative *W.P.A. Handbook on Home Education in Wisconsin.*

WYOMING

Homeschoolers of Wyoming

P.O. Box 2197
Mills, WY 82644
(307) 235-4928

Founded: 1988
Number of members: 475 on mailing list.
Newsletter: *Home St. Journal* (Casper area newsletter—contains state news)
  Circulation: 50 - published with *The Teaching Home*
Yearly convention time: July. Last time's attendance: 150
Lobby? No
Number of support groups: 15
Yearly convention, fine arts fair, science fairs.
Political climate: Rating (1-10): 7
Standardized testing? N Teacher oversight? N Register? Y
Records: none

U.S.A. NATIONAL ORGANIZATIONS

National Coalition of Alternative Community Schools (NCACS)

58 Schoolhouse Road
Summertown, TN 38483
(615) 964-3670
Founded: 1976
Number of members: 1,000+ individuals and schools
Newsletter: *Skole*
Yearly convention.
Membership: Patron $200, Sustaining Member $100, Friend $60 (all three receive the newsletter and NCACS directory free). Voting Member $30, Associate Member $20. Subscription to *Skole*, the NCACS journal, $15; single issue $6.
NCACS directory: $12.50 for non-members, $7.50 associate members, free to voting members.

NCACS has just produced a new directory of alternative schools, the first in two years. It includes an introduction to the NCACS, a list of 600 educational alternatives in forty-seven states and sixteen countries (all "democratic" and "non-discriminatory"), alternative boarding schools and colleges, a section of innovative projects and ideas, plus a special section on resources for home schools suggested by good old Pat Farenga at Holt Associates.

National Association for the Legal Support of Alternative Schools (NALSAS)

P.O. Box 28223
Santa Fe, NM 87501
(505) 471-6928
Yearly membership dues, $20. Directory, $12.50.
Resources for alternative schoolers. Insurance fund.

Ed Nagel is a man of many hats. Besides serving as the director of Santa Fe Community School he is also the director of the National Association for the Legal Support of Alternative Schools, otherwise known as NALSAS.

NALSAS serves as a resource for those in the alternative school movement who find themselves embroiled in confrontations with state authorities. Its commodity is information, in the form of people to contact, legal briefs, legislative proposals, and a file of articles that support their position. NALSAS also operates a legal insurance fund. Premiums are quite low. Inquire for details.

Families interested in the alternative school philosophy and home schooling are advised to look into becoming a satellite of a nearby alternative/free/community school that already is legally in operation in their state. You can buy a current *Directory of the National Coalition of Alternative Community Schools* from NALSAS.

National Center for Home Education

P.O. Box 125
Hwy 9 at Rte. 781
Paeonian Springs, VA 22129
(703) 882-4770
Fax: (703) 882-3628
Founded: 1990
Newsletter: TBA. NCHE hopes to provide extensive networking and information services, primarily for state groups
Yearly convention: Beginning in 1991, NCHE will host an annual home education leaders' symposium.
Functions: Polling state groups and reporting their positions in Washington, D.C.; coalition-building with non-home-schooling organizations on behalf of home schooling; monitoring legislation in all fifty states; networking between state organizations; national resource referral center; media relations; leadership fellowship and training; database of home-school speakers; awards to promote home school recognition; national leaders' newsletter.

This new organization seeks to provide national services for local state groups. It is not a membership organization, but a service group funded by Home School Legal Defense Association. HSLDA will provide two full-time staffers and its executives will also donate a portion of their time. Like HSLDA, NCHE is a organization based on Christian principles. Also like HSLDA, it serves both the Christian and non-Christian home-schooling communities.

Journalists seeking accurate input on home schooling should put this group on their list of contacts.

National Homeschool Association (NHA)

P.O. Box 58746
Seattle, WA 98138-1746
(206) 432-1544
Founded: 1988
Number of members: 650. Constituency 1,000+
Newsletter: *National Homeschool Association Newsletter*
  Circulation: 1,500
Yearly convention time: August or September. Last time's attendance: 100
Lobby? No
Membership: $15/year, includes quarterly newsletter, access to all programs and networking services, voting privileges, business discounts. Sample newsletter, $2. 1989 *Travel Directory*, $3.75.
Services: Resource file, apprenticeship/mentor program, single parent network, student exchange program, travel directory, business discount program.

NHA assures us that, in spite of their name, they are laying no claims to being *the* voice representing home schoolers in America. Their purpose is merely to support and encourage all home schoolers, and to be a clearinghouse of information.

CHAPTER TWENTY-FIVE

HOME SCHOOL ORGANIZATIONS OF CANADA

Canadian Alliance of Home Schoolers
195 Markville Road
Unionville, Ontario L3R 4V8
(416) 470-7930
Founded: 1979
Number of members: 500
Newsletter: *Child's Play*
Lobby? Yes
Media work, community events, conventions.

This is a national networking and membership organization. Half a thousand members at present. Functions: lobbying, support groups, media work, community events, conventions. Membership, $17/year. Newsletter, *Child's Play*, included in membership fee.

Christian Educational Consultants
P.O. Box 283, St. Vital Postal Station
Winnipeg, Manitoba R2M-5C8
(204) 326-6836
Founded: 1980
Newsletter: *The Christian Family Advocate*
  Circulation: 5,000

Education Advisory
2267 Kings Avenue
W. Vancouver, BC V7V 2C1
(604) 926-9081

Political climate (British Columbia): Rating (1-10): 9
Standardized testing? N Teacher oversight? N Register? Y
Records: None. A new law "engrains in legislation parents' rights to home educate. Upon registering with a school (private or public) they qualify for certain services and resources."

Covering the Western provinces, Education Advisory provides information packets, advice. Free brochure with SASE. Donations fund the work.

Manitoba Association for Schooling at Home
89 Edkar Crescent
Winnipeg, Manitoba R2G 3H8
(204) 334-4763
Founded: 1982
Number of members: 100 families
Newsletter: *M.A.S.H. Newsletter/Communique A.M.E.D.*
  Circulation: 125
Lobby? Yes
Children's activities and excursions, art workshop and showing, bimonthly meetings, legislative monitor, etc.
Political climate (Manitoba): Rating (1-10): 9
Standardized testing? Y Teacher oversight? N Register? Y
Records: Standardized testing for three years. Report bimonthly.

Functions: support groups, legislative watchdog, media work. Newsletter included in $10 annual membership dues.

Round Up
R.R. #6
Calgary, Alberta T2M-4L5
(403) 285-9855
Founded: 1987
Newsletter: *Round Up*
  Circulation: 135
Help and encouragement to those starting to home school in Canada.
Political climate: Rating (1-10): 8
Standardized testing? N Teacher oversight? N Register? Y
Records: Varies with each school district.

Nancy McElroy saw a need for a newsletter in Canada that would provide practical and encouraging information for home-educating moms. She was en-couraged to fill the need herself by starting *Round Up*. Her vision for *Round Up* is for it to become a Canadian *Teaching Home*.

CHAPTER TWENTY-SIX

HOME SCHOOL ORGANIZATIONS OF OTHER LANDS

I am delighted to be able to include listings from so many countries in this edition of the *Big Book*. Home schooling is evidently growing by leaps and bounds worldwide!

One interesting source of new overseas home schoolers is American military personnel serving abroad. Another, more traditional group of home schoolers is foreign missionaries. These home schoolers are usually pretty much on their own, due to the nature of their work. That's why I have no "Navy Home Schoolers" or "Costa Rican Missionary Support Group" in the listings below.

If your country or group is not included, please do write me c/o the publisher and tell me about yourself, so I can put you in the next edition!

AUSTRALIA

Alternative Education Resource Group
39 William Street, Hawthorne
Melbourne, Victoria 3122
Australia
(03) 818-3674
Founded: 1976
Number of members: 300
Contact: Sue Simpson
Newsletter: *Other Ways*
  Circulation: 400

Yearly convention time: Varies. Last time's attendance: 100
Lobby? No
Number of support groups: many
Events are organized locally by the support groups.
Political climate: Rating (1-10): 8
Standardized testing? N Teacher oversight? N Register? Y
Records: Varies

Functions: Support groups, community events, conventions, and media work. Membership, $15/year Australian. Newsletter included in membership fee. Newsletter alone, $15 Australian.

Christian Home Schools of Australia
P.O. Box 161
Balwyn, Victoria 3103
Australia
From U.S.: 011-61-71-481179 From Aus: 071-481179
Fax: 011-61-71-482129
Founded: 1984
Number of members: 300
Newsletter: *CHSA*
  Circulation: 100 - published with *The Teaching Home*
Lobby? Yes
Number of support groups: 6
Autonomous support groups organize science fairs, field trips, etc.
Political climate: Rating (1-10): 1
Standardized testing? Y Teacher oversight? Y Register? Y

Records: In many states parents must be government-registered, certified, college-degreed teachers. Some states are more tolerant. Due to these oppressive and inherently unjust laws, most Australian home schoolers do not register with the government.

Homeschoolers Australia
P.O. Box 346
Seven Hills, NSW 2147
Australia
From U.S.: 011-61-26-293727 From Aus: (02) 629-3727
Founded: 1986
Number of members: 200 families
Yearly convention time: December.
Lobby? Yes
Number of support groups: 20
Monthly meetings. Information service, library. Science day in July. Other activities variable.
Political climate: Rating (1-10): 5
Standardized testing? N Teacher oversight? N Register? Y
Records: Children's work for two years, daily diary, detailed programs, yearly inspector's visit.

No membership dues. Functions: support groups, legislative watchdog, community events, media appearance.

NEW ZEALAND

New Zealand Home Schooling Advice Network
120 Eskdale Rd.
Auckland 10
Australia
4805570
Founded: 1981
Newsletter: *Prunes*
Political climate: Rating (1-10): 7
Standardized testing? N Teacher oversight? N Register? Y
Records: minimal

Why is this group's newsletter named *Prunes?* Call or write and find out! The group was founded in 1981 and provides support groups, keeps an eye on the legislators, does community events and conventions, and talks to the media when necessary. Newsletter subscription, $10 N.Z.

Christian Home Schoolers of New Zealand
4 Tawa St.
Palmerston North
New Zealand
(063) 74-399
Founded: 1986
Lobby? Yes
Support groups have their own activities.
Political climate: Rating (1-10): 7
Standardized testing? N Teacher oversight? N Register? Y
Records: No official mandatory requirements. Must teach "as efficiently and well" as the state schools. "Efficiently" and "well" are not legally defined.

Christian Home Schoolers of New Zealand is a non-membership, service organization. They try to promote the home schooling concept through lobbying, press releases, and occasional conferences.

The following three organizations work with Christian Home Schoolers of New Zealand to lobby and keep in close touch.

Keystone
P.O. Box 61
Pukekohe
New Zeland

Newsletter for home schoolers. Glenys Jackson, editor.

Christian Home Education Support Ministries
25 Harrisville Rd.
Tuakau, New Zealand

Contact: Peter Butler
Curriculum advice and materials.

A.C.E. Parent Home Education Programme
P.O. Box 291
Dannevirke
New Zealand

Contact: David Worboys

New Zealand Home School Association, Inc.
2094 B. Great North Rd.
Avondale, Aukland, 7
New Zealand

Contact: John O'Brien, president
Paid membership, elected officers, newsletter.

We heard about this organization from Craig Smith of Christian Home Schoolers of New Zealand (above).

UNITED KINGDOM

Education Otherwise
25 Common Lane
Hemingford Abbots, Cambridgeshire PE18 9AN
England
0480-63130
Founded: 1977
Number of members: 2,000 families
Newsletter: *Education Otherwise*
  Circulation: 2,000
Yearly convention time: January, May, and September. Last time's attendance: 20 families.

Special events: Camping and local outings.
Lobby? Yes
Support groups? Yes.
Political climate: Rating (1-10): 5
Standardized testing? N Teacher oversight? N Register? N
Records: None.

The name of this self-help group, Education Otherwise, is taken from the Education Act, which states that *parents* are responsible for their children's education, "either by regular attendance at school or otherwise." Functions: support groups, legislative watchdog, community events, media work, conventions. Dues: £10 U.K., £15 overseas.

Membership includes • *School Is Not Compulsory*, a booklet containing sections on the law and advice about approaching the Local Education Authority (LEA) • bimonthly newsletter • *Early Years*, a booklet containing accounts of members' experiences and suggested learning activities for children under thirteen • a Contact List with names and addresses of members who have chosen to be listed, along with children's names and birthdates and, where applicable, the skills and resouces they offer other members • Advice and Information Exchange.

INDEXES

HOW TO USE THE INDEX OF SUPPLIERS

These indexes were designed to give you both the necessary information to order products and catalogs, and to give you an idea of each company's services and policies. Besides addresses, the indexes of suppliers contain telephone numbers, types of payment accepted, price of catalog or brochure (if any), refund policy, and a general description of the company's product line. This information will (we hope!) help you become a more informed shopper.

HOW TO BE A PERFECT CUSTOMER

First, please do not call a toll-free number except to order, unless the index entry specifically says that the supplier is willing to use his toll-free line for inquiries.

Each call on a 800 number costs the supplier a substantial amount, and it is frustrating to have callers rack up your phone bill for questions that could have been answered just as well by letter.

A number of suppliers have asked me to mention that it is necessary to add state sales tax when you order from a supplier in your home state. Not sure what the tax is? The supplier's order form will tell you.

It is always wise to get the supplier's catalog or brochure before ordering. Prices change, and so do refund policies. You are less likely to be disappointed if you carefully check these out before ordering.

When requesting information by letter, an SASE (self-addressed stamped envelope) is always appreciated. This does not apply to requests for free catalogs, since these seldom fit in a standard envelope.

Companies that offer free catalogs do so in the hope that we will become interested in and buy their products. By all means, send for any catalogs you think might be useful. Just remember that catalogs are expensive to print and mail, so give the supplier a fair chance to sell you something in return!

If you experience a problem with a supplier, please contact them about it more than once before assuming they have deliberately mishandled your order. Errors do happen. The Post Office may not have delivered the letter containing your original order, or may have lost the letter you wrote complaining about your order. Phone messages can be mislaid. Verify all information: enclose copies of your cancelled checks, product invoices, and packing slips.

Remember the rule of charity, even when dealing with businesses: "Do unto others as you would have them do unto you." Then you will be a Perfect Customer!

EXPLANATION OF CODES USED IN THIS INDEX

Credit card information: we list credit cards accepted by each supplier. "VISA" means (of course) they take the VISA card. "MC" means they take MasterCard. "AmEx" means they take American Express. "CB" stands for "Carte Blanche." Some companies also take Discover, OPTIMA, and other lesser-known cards.

Please note that many suppliers *only* allow the use of their toll-free lines for credit card orders. In-state calls must also be made on the local telephone number rather than the toll-free number. You may also need to have a certain minimum size of order to qualify for ordering over the toll-free line.

Local telephone number: when you see a toll-free number followed by two letters, a colon, and another number, that means that callers from that state must use that local number. Example: "OR: (503) 343-0123" means Oregon callers must use the (503) number.

Other methods of payment: "Check or M.O." means the company *only* takes checks or money orders; they do not take credit cards. All companies that take credit cards also take checks and money orders. "School P.O." means they accept purchase orders from *legitimate, institutional* schools. Do not try to get around this by sending a P.O. on your home school's letterhead! (Home schoolers who do this give us all a bad name.) Similarly, "Business P.O." means they accept purchase orders from *legitimate* businesses.

Although it is not explicitly stated in many instances, most suppliers offer wholesale terms to retailers and catalogers. Call or write the supplier for information if you are interested in retailing their products.

Some suppliers list office hours during which they answer their phone. In such cases, "EST" stands for

Eastern Standard Time; "PST" stands for "Pacific [West Coast] Standard Time"; and "CST" stands for "Central Standard Time."

SASE stands for "self-addressed stamped envelope." "Long SASE" means a self-addressed business-size (#10) envelope.

Catalog/brochure prices: many catalogs and brochures are free. Some companies charge for their catalogs, though. A number of those who charge for their catalogs refund the catalog price on the first order you place with them. Thus, "Catalog, $1, refundable on first order," means that although you have to send $1 in advance to get the catalog, you get to deduct $1 from your first order from that catalog.

Returns policy: generally, companies either offer unconditional guarantees (return product within the time limit for any reason), or have a guarantee that applies only to products returned in "resalable condition." This means the product must not be tattered, written on, or look used, since the supplier expects to sell it again.

Sometimes you are also required to return the product in its original packaging or with a copy of your invoice. This is to ensure that it does not arrive back damaged and to help the supplier quickly locate and refund your account on his computer system.

Some suppliers' guarantees require you to get permission first to return the item. This means you must call or write first and receive a return authorization from the company *before* sending the item back.

We sincerely hope you find this index information helpful. Please keep in mind that businesses do move and change their telephone numbers and order policies; that's one reason why the *Big Book* is periodically revised! Generally, if a successful business moves, it arranges to have its mail forwarded. If there is no forwarding address, or it has expired, the company very likely has ceased to exist. (All companies in this index were verified shortly before the book was printed.)

WHERE TO FIND MORE HELP

Please also be kind to your humble reviewer. I no longer have the resources to answer requests for new business addresses, or to give personalized curriculum consultations. (Did I mention we're expecting our eighth child?)

Your local home school support group, on the other hand, exists to offer this very kind of help. Go ahead and give them a try!

INDEX OF AMERICAN SUPPLIERS

A Beka Correspondence School
Box 18000
Pensacola, FL 32523-9160
1-800-874-BEKA (2352) M-F 8-4:30 CST VISA, MC
(904) 478-8480 ext. 2062
Fax: (904) 478-8558
Free brochure. No refunds.
Home school program.

A Beka Video Home School
Box 18000
Pensacola, FL 32523-9160
1-800-874-BEKA (2352) M-F 8-4:30 CST VISA, MC
(904) 478-8480 ext. 2062
Fax: (904) 478-8558
Free brochure.
Home school video program.

A&D Bookstore & Educational Supply
621 West Sixth Ave.
Amarillo, TX 79101
Free catalogs.
Sunday school and school supplies.

ABC School Supply
P.O. Box 4750
Norcross, GA 30091
(404) 447-5000 weekdays. VISA, MC
Fax: (404) 447-0062
Free catalog. Returns: Within 30 days. 15% service charge if company not at fault.
School supplies pre-K-6.

Achievement Basics
800 South Fenton Street
Denver, CO 80226
(303) 935-6343 Check or M.O.
Free brochures.
Junior Business and speaking.

Advanced Training Institute of America
Box 1
Oak Brook, IL 60522-3001
(708) 323-9800
Fax: (708) 323-6394
Check or M.O. Free catalog.
Home education program.

Afore-the-Wind
Box 84
South Gillies, Ontario P0T 2V0
Canada
(807) 345-4455 Check or money order
Free brochure. Returns allowed within 60 days in
resalable condition or if flawed. Mail order only.
Limited number of copies remain.

Aletheia Publishers
P. O. Box 1437
Tempe, AZ 85281
Check or M.O.
Free brochure.
Child training book.

Alpha Omega Publications
P.O. Box 3153
Tempe, AZ 85281
1-800-821-4443 Ask for Dept. OMP
AZ: (602) 438-1092
Fax: (602) 438-2702
Free catalog.
Christian curriculum.
Home school program.

Alta Vista College
Curriculum Office
P.O. Box 55535
Seattle, WA 98155
(206) 368-9914 6-3 PST M-Fri. Check or M.O.
Free leaflet.
Home school curriculum.

American Christian Academy
P.O. Box 805
Anderson, CA 96007
(916) 365-2950
Check or M.O.
Home school program.

American Christian History Institute
P.O. Box 648
Palo Cedro, CA 96073
(805) 987-1887 Check or M.O.
Principle Approach book by James Rose.

American Citizen
950 North Shore Dr.
Lake Bluff, IL 60044
1-800-448-8311 Visa, MC, AmEx
IL: (708) 295-8088
Free catalog.
Book catalog.

American Reformation Movement (ARM)
P.O. Box 85125 MB 138
San Diego, CA 92138
Check or M.O. Donations accepted.
Witty and insightful newsletters on topics relating
to home schooling and family issues.

American School
850 East Fifty-Eighth St.
Chicago, IL 60637
(312) 947-3300
Payment plan. Free brochure.
High school correspondence program.

Arthur Bornstein School of Memory Training
11693 San Vicente Blvd.
Los Angeles, CA 90049
1-800-468-2058 VISA, MC, AmEx
(213) 478-2056
Fax: (213) 207-2433
Free brochures.
Memory training books and tapes.

Audio Forum
96 Broad St.
Guilford, CT 06437
1-800-243-1234 VISA, MC, AmEx, DC, CB
(203) 453-9794 CT, AK, HI
Fax: (203) 453-9774
Free catalogs. Returns within 3 weeks, full refund.
Spoken word cassettes.

Baker Book House
P.O. Box 6287
Grand Rapids, MI 49516-6287
(616) 957-3110 VISA, MC
Fax: (616) 676-9573
Free catalog.
Christian book publisher.

Barbara M. Morris Report
P.O. Box 2166
Carlsbad, CA 92008
Check or M.O.
Books.

Barnes & Noble Bookstores, Inc.
126 Fifth Ave.
New York, NY 10011
1-800-242-6657 24 hours. VISA, MC, AmEx, DC, CB
(212) 633-3300
Free catalog. Minimum charge order $15. Returns within 30 days, full refund.
Discount mail-order books.

Basic Education/Accelerated Christian Education
P.O. Box 1438
Lewisville, TX 75067-1438
1-800-873-3435
(214) 462-1776
Fax: (214) 462-8681
Free brochure.
Full-service Christian worktext supplier.
Home school program.

Black Fox Productions
Box 246
Booneville, CA 95415
(707) 895-3241
Check or M.O. No returns.
Homeschooling for Excellence book.

Blue Bird Publishing
1713 E. Broadway #306
Tempe, AZ 85282
(602) 968-4088 VISA, MC.
Free brochure.
Publisher of home school and home business books.

Bluestocking Press
P.O. Box 1014
Dept F3
Placerville, CA 95667-1014
(916) 621-1123 VISA, MC. US funds only.
Free info with large SASE.
Series of books on what to read and where to find it. Special report on how to sell educational products to alternative educational markets.

Blumenfeld Education Letter
P.O. Box 41561
Boise, ID 83711
(208) 322-4440 7 days, 24 hours. VISA, MC.
Newsletter.

Bob Jones University Press
Customer Services
Greenville, SC 29614
1-800-845-5731 weekdays. VISA, MC, C.O.D.
Free catalog. Orders and info on toll free line.
Returns: Resalable condition, with permission, within 30 days.
Christian texts and school supplies.
Christian Student Dictionary.
Reading list K-12.

Book-of-the-Month Club, Inc.
P.O. Box 8803
Camp Hill, PA 17011-8803
They bill you.
Biggest, oldest book club.

Books for All Times, Inc.
P.O. Box 2
Alexandria, VA 22313
(703) 548-0457 Check or M.O.
Publisher of Joe David's books, *Glad You Asked!* and *The Fire Within*.

Brook Farm Books
P.O. Box 277
Lyndon, VT 05849
Check or M.O.
Publisher of *The First Home-School Catalogue*.

Builder Books
P.O. Box 5291
Lynnwood, WA 98046
(206) 745-2545 Check or M.O.
Catalog $1.
Fine assortment of home-school materials, many discounted.

Bureau of Educational Measurements
Emporia State University
Emporia, KS 66801-5807
(316) 343-1200 ext. 5297 8-5 CT. Check or M.O.
Free catalog. Returns with permission.
Supplier of testing material.

Cahill & Company
950 North Shore Dr.
Lake Bluff IL 60044
1-800-448-8311 9-5 M-F CST. Credit card orders
only. VISA, MC, AmEx.
IL: (708) 295-8088
Book catalog.

Calvert School
Tuscany Road
Baltimore, MD 21210
(301) 243-6030
Fax: (301) 366-0674
Free brochure with detailed outline of subjects
and topics.
Home school program

Carden Educational Foundation
P.O. Box 659
Brookfield, CT 06804
(203) 740-9200 Check or M.O.
Free catalog. Returns, 30 days, resalable condi-
tion, call first.
Complete private school curriculum.

Catalogue Revue
144 South First St.
P.O. Box 4507
Burbank, CA 91503
Check or M.O.
Source for obtaining mail order catalogs

Center for Applied Research in Education, Inc.
P.O. Box 430
West Nyack, NY 10995
Check or M.O.
Guided research units.

Charlotte Mason Research & Supply Co.
P.O. Box 172
Stanton, NJ 08885
Check or M.O.
No returns.
Books and resources promoting Charlotte Ma-
son's educational philosophy.

Chasselle, Inc.
9645 Gerwig Lane
Columbia, MD 21046
Free catalog.
School supplies.

Chesterbrook Educational Publishers, Inc.
16 Industrial Blvd.
Paoli, PA 19301
1-800-327-8400 VISA, MC, AmEx, Discover.
(215) 640-9885
Where There's a Will There's an A video seminar.

Christian Book Distributors
Box 3687
Peabody, MA 01961-3687
(617) 532-5300 VISA, MC.
Free sample catalog.
Returns: Shipping mistakes, defective products.
Membership $3/year.
You don't have to be a member to order.
Discount Christian books/Bibles.

Christian Liberty Academy
502 W. Euclid Ave.
Arlington Heights, IL 60004
(708) 259-8736 Check or M.O.
Returns: Within 30 days, 10% restocking charge.
Home-school program.

Christian Life Workshops, Inc.
P.O. Box 2250
Gresham, OR 97030
(503) 667-3942 Check or M.O.
Brochure with SASE. Returns: 100% refund,
except shipping and handling.
Home school workshops on tape. Books.
Organizer. Seminars. *Bed & Breakfast Directory*.

Christian Light Publications
1066 Chicago Ave.
P.O. Box 1126
Harrisonburg, VA 22801-1126
(703) 434-0750 VISA, MC. Free catalog.
Fax: (703) 434-0769
Science equipment, curriculum, and school sup-
plies, Mennonite-approved books.

Christian Schools International
3350 E. Paris Ave., S.E.
Grand Rapids, MI 49512
Canada: 1-800-637-8288 US: 1-800-635-8288
VISA, MC. Free catalog.
Fax: (616) 957-5022
60-day examination privilege for prepaid and credit
card orders.
Christian textbooks.

Christian Teaching Materials Co.
P.O. Box 647
Santa Ynez, CA 93460
Inventory list, $2.
New & used home-school materials.

Clonlara School Home Based Education Program
1289 Jewett
Ann Arbor, MI 48104
Home-school program.

Community Learning Center
2144 Vermont St.
Ramona, CA 92065
Check or M.O.
Free brochure.
Publisher of *Explore* curriculum guide.

Conservative Book Club
15 Oakland Ave.
Harrison, NY 10528
Check or M.O or they bill you.
Monthly reviews to members.
Discount book club.

Constructive Playthings
1227 E. 119th St.
Grandview, MO 64030
1-800-255-6124 VISA, MC.
MO: (816) 761-5900
Fax: (816) 761-9295
Free home catalog.
Play furniture, toys, school supplies pre-K-3. Free toy guide for parents. Free catalog of Jewish educational materials.

Conversa-phone Institute, Inc.
One Comac Loop
Ronkonkoma, NY 11779
(516) 467-0600 Check or M.O.
Fax: (516) 467-0602
Sells through distributors.
Recorded courses, self-help.

Covenant Home Curriculum
3675 N. Calhoun Rd.
Brookfield, WI 53005
(414) 781-2171
Check or M.O.
Free brochures.
K-12 curriculum. Quarterly tests.

Crossway Books
9825 W. Roosevelt Rd.
Westchester, IL 60154
(708) 345-7474
Check or M.O. Free brochure.
Publisher.

Dale Seymour Publications
P.O. Box 10888
Palo Alto, CA 94303
1-800-872-1100/1-800-222-0766 (CA) (orders)
(415) 324-2800 Check or M.O.
Fax: (415) 324-3424
Publisher of educational and teacher's books.

Delphi Schools, Inc.
20950 SW Rock Creek Rd.
Sheridan, OR 97378
1-800-626-6610 MC, Visa, AmEx
Sells *The Leipzig Connection.*

Didasko
65 Middlesex Rd.
Matawan, NJ 07747-3030
(201) 583-7128 Check or M.O.
Imported math and science manipulatives, and readers.

Dove Christian Books
1425 Aurora Road
Melbourne, FL 32935
1-800-456-7076 (orders)
(407) 242-8290
Fax: (407) 259-6035
Returns: Resalable condition, call first. Distribute throughout Nigeria, S. Africa, Ghana, S. America, Singapore, Australia, New Zealand, and others.

Dr. Steve Deckard
11144 Riaza Apt. #5
St. Louis, MO 63138
(314) 355-1675 Check or M.O.
Publisher of *Home School Laws All 50 States.*

E-Z Grader Co.
P.O. Box 24040
Cleveland, OH 44124
(216) 831-1661 collect. Check or M.O.
Fax: (216) 831-1667
Samples. Free brochure. Returns: Resalable condition, within 30 days.

Eagle Forum Education Fund
Alton, IL 62002
(618) 462-5415 Check or M.O.
Free brochure lists items, prices only.
Phonics kits.

EDC Publications
Division of educational development corporation
P.O. Box 470663
Tulsa, OK 74147
1-800-331-4418 VISA, MC.
OK: (918) 622-4522
Free color catalog. Returns: after 60 days, less
than 12 months, resalable condition, 15 percent
restocking charge, written authorization.
Home party plan.
Usborne books.

Education Services
6410 Raleigh St.
Arvada, CO 80003
Check or M.O.
Biblical Psychology of Learning (a great book), al-
so guides to reading, math, etc.

Educational Freedom Foundation
20 Parkland Avenue
Glendale, MO 63122
Check or M.O.
Contributions tax-deductible.
Magazine.

Educational Oasis
Good Apple
Box 299
Carthage, IL 62321-0299
(217) 357-3981
Check or M.O.
Magazine for middle grades/junior high.

Educators Publishing Service
75 Moulton St.
Cambridge, MA 02138-1104
1-800-225-5750 VISA, MC.
MA: (617) 547-6706
Free brochures.
Indicate grade level you need.
Language arts and parent helps.

The Elijah Company
P.O. Box 12483
Knoxville, TN 37912-0483
(615) 691-1310 Check or M.O.
Returns: In resalable condition, within 30 days.
Home school distributor of *How to Tutor, Alpha-
phonics, Keyboard Capers, Type It, Spelling Dictio-
nary,* Star Shirt.

Encyclopaedia Britannica, Inc.
Britannica Centre
310 S. Michigan Ave.
Chicago, IL 60604
Write to the above address, or look in telephone
book under "Encyclopedias" for your nearest Britannica representative. No mail-order sales.

Executive Gallery
380 Dublin Ave.
Columbus OH 43215
1-800-848-2618 VISA, MC, AmEx, DC, Discover,
company purchase order
Organizers.

Fleming H. Revell Co.
Old Tappan, NJ 07675
Check or M.O.
Publishes *Peanut Butter Family Homeschool.*

Footstool Publications
P.O. Box 161021
Memphis, TN 38186
(901) 382-1918 Check or M.O.
Blackboard Blackmail book.

**Foundation for American Christian Education
(FACE)**
Box 27035
San Francisco, CA 94127
(415) 661-1775 Check or M.O. or they'll bill you.
Principle Approach to America's Christian history.
Reading list, lots of other materials.

Frank Schaffer Publications, Inc.
23740 Hawthorne Blvd
Torrance, CA 90505
1-800-421-5565 VISA, MC, or school P.O.
Fax: (213) 375-5090
Sold in teachers' supply stores and catalogs.
Colorful and entertaining workbooks, puzzles, etc.
for preschool and elementary grades.

Gazelle Publications
5580 Stanley Drive
Auburn, CA 95603
(916) 878-1223
Check or M.O.
Fax: (916) 888-8627
Free brochure (Long SASE appreciated). Returns: 100 percent satisfaction guaranteed.
Home school books.

Good Apple
Box 299
Carthage, IL 62321-0299
1-800-435-7234 VISA, MC, or school P.O.
(217) 357-3981
Free catalog.
Magazine, school materials publisher.

Great Christian Books
1319 Newport Gap Pike
P.O. Box 3499
Wilmington, DE 19804-2895
(302) 999-8317 VISA, MC.
Fax: (302) 999-9786
Discount Christian books.
Membership $5/year U.S., $8 Canada, $12 overseas.

Growing Without Schooling
2269 Massachusetts Ave.
Cambridge, MA 02140
(617) 864-3100
Check or M.O.
Sample issue $3.50. Subscription $20.
Home school magazine.

Hearth & Home Ministries, Inc.
P.O. Box 835105
Richardson, TX 75083
(214) 231-9838 Check or M.O.
Minimum order of 5 copies of *Home Education: Is It Working?* Donation of $1/booklet required.
Quantity price 75¢/booklet (100 or more).

HearthSong
P.O. Box B
Sebastopol, CA 95473 1-800-779-2211
1-800-325-2502 VISA, MC, AmEx, Discover.
Fax: (707) 829-9232 *as of Jan 2002*
Free 40-page full color catalog.
"A catalog for families."

Hewitt Child Development Center
P.O. Box 9
Washougal, WA 98671-0009
(206) 835-8708
Check or M.O.
Home-school curriculum supplier.

Hewitt Research Foundation
P.O. Box 9
Washougal, WA 98671
Check or M.O.
Free catalog.
Innovative home-school materials.

Holt Associates
2269 Massachusetts Ave.
Cambridge, MA 02140
(617) 864-3100 VISA, MC.
Catalog for SASE and 45¢ postage.
Books of interest to home schoolers.
Music and art supplies.

Home Centered Learning
P.O. Box 92
Escondido, CA 92025-0020
(619) 749-1522
John A. Boston, Educational Administrator
Home-centered learning program.
Send large SASE for information.

Home Education Press
P.O. Box 1083
Tonasket, WA 98855
(509) 486-1351 Check or M.O.
Free 16-page catalog of publications, books, and resources for SASE.
Publisher of *Home Education Magazine*.
Free home-school bookshelf catalog.

Home Life
P.O. Box 1250
Fenton, MO 63026-1250
Check or M.O.
Fax: (314) 225-0743
Free catalog. Returns: Resalable condition, 60 days.
Home education and family books. Organizers. TV-free video players.

Home Run Enterprises
12531 Aristocrat Ave.
Garden Grove, CA 92641
No phone orders. Brochure with SASE.
Make check out to Home Run Enterprises.
"Math Mouse" games, curriculum manual.

Home School Books and Supplies
24324 Miller Rd.
Stanwood, WA 98292
(206) 629-2978 Check or M.O.
Free catalog.
Home school supplier.

Home School Legal Defense Association
P.O. Box 159
Paeonian Springs, VA 22129
(703) 882-3838 Check or M.O.
Free brochure.
Home school legal defense.

Home School Researcher
Dr. Brian Ray
School of Education, Seattle Pacific University
Seattle, WA 98119
(503) 754-4031 or 754-2511
Home education researcher, publishes newsletter.

Home School Supply House
3524 Est Mitchell
Petoskey, MI 49770
(616) 348-2620 Check or M.O.
Free catalog.
Home school supplier.

Home Study International
P.O. Box 4437
Silver Springs, MD 20904-0437
(301) 680-6570 VISA, MC.
Monthly payment plans, grades K-12.
Good refund policy.
Home school program.

Homespun Tapes, Ltd.
Box 694
Woodstock, NY 12498
1-800-33-TAPES VISA, MC, COD (USA only)
(914) 679-7832
Fax: (914) 246-5282
Catalog $1, free with order.
Music instruction on audio and video cassettes.

Honeymoon Point
P.O. Box 124
Hope, Maine 04847
Check or M.O. Free brochure with SASE.
Home school T-shirts.

Hoover Brothers Educational Equipment and Supplies
P.O. Box 1009
Kansas City, MO 64141
(816) 472-4848 MC, C.O.D. Catalog $7.50.
School supplies.

ICER Press Bookstore
P.O. Box 877
Claremont, CA 91711
(714) 596-3928 Check or M.O.
School at Home book

Ideal School Supply Company
11000 S. Lavergne Ave.
Oak Lawn, IL 60453
1-800-323-5131
IL: (708) 425-0800
School supplies, all subject areas, K-8.
Order from school suppliers.

Instructor and Teacher
P.O. Box 6099
Duluth, MN 55806-9799
(218) 723-9200 Check or M.O.
Teacher's magazine. Activity resources catalog.

International Institute
P.O. Box 99
Park Ridge, IL 60068
or
N6128 Sawyer Lake Rd.
White Lake, WI 54491
(715) 484-5002
Check or M.O. Free brochure.
Full refund on undesired books.
Home school program.

International Montessori Society
912 Thayer Ave.
Silver Spring, MD 20910
(301) 589-1127 Check or M.O.
Free brochure.
Montessori books, course, newsletter, conferences.

Kappan
P.O. Box 789
Bloomington, IN 47402-0789
Check or M.O. or they bill you.
Magazine for intellectual teachers.

Kay Milow
14713 Echo Hills Dr.
Omaha NE 68138
(402) 895-3280 Check or M.O.
Quantity discounts.
Home Schoolers Complete Reference Guide.

Kaye McLeod
4623 Fortune Rd. S.E.
Calgary, Alberta T2A 2A7
Canada
(403) 272-3658
Check or M.O.
Daily/School Planner for Children.

Keys to Excellence
Perception Publications, Inc.
1814 W. Seldon Lane
Phoenix, AZ 85021
(602) 946-6454
Check or M.O. or order from school supplier.
Readiness workbook series.
Cassette training for parents to help their children
achieve academically.

KONOS
P.O. Box 1534
Richardson, TX 75083
(214) 669-8337
Check or M.O. U. S. funds only. No phone orders.
Free brochure and order form.
Curriculum, time lines, "how to" tapes, writing
tapes, seminars.

KONOS Helps
P.O. Box 9523
Newark, DE 19714-9523
Check or M.O.
Unit-studies resources and ideas, organization
tips, etc. for KONOS families.

Laissez-Faire Books
942 Howard St.
San Francisco, CA 94103
1-800-326-0996 VISA, MC 9-6 M-F 12-5 Sat. PST.
(415) 541-9780
Free catalog.
30-day unconditional guarantee.
Libertarian bookseller.

Lakeshore Curriculum Material Center
P.O. Box 6261
Carson, CA 90749
1-800-421-5334 CA: 1-800-262-1777. VISA, MC,
AmEx.
Info: (213) 537-8600
Free catalog. Returns: Within 30 days, unused
goods.
School supplies pre-K through 3, special ed.

Landmark's Freedom Baptist Curriculum
2222 E. Hinson Ave.
Haines City, FL 33844-4902
(813) 421-2937. VISA, MC, Discover.
Free brochure.
Home school program.

Larson Publications
4936 Route 414
Burdett, NY 14818
(607) 546-9342
Check or M.O.
Publisher.

Learn, Inc.
113 Gaither Dr.
Mt. Laurel, NJ 08054-9987
1-800-729-7323 Ext. 120 VISA, MC, AmEx.
Inquiries: (609) 234-6100
Fax: (609) 273-7766
Free catalog. Returns: Within 30 days.
Self-study and classroom audio and video courses.
Free preview.

Learning At Home
P.O. Box 270
Honaunau, HI 96726
(808) 328-9669 VISA, MC.
Free catalog.
K-12 books and workbooks.
Math manipulatives, science and art supplies.
Curriculum and teaching guides.

LibertyTree Network
134 98th Ave.
Oakland, CA 94603
1-800-872-4866 VISA, MC, AmEx. 24 hrs 7 days.
Credit card orders only.
Inquiries: (415) 568-6047 M-F 8:30-5:30 PST
Fax: (415) 568-6040
Free catalog.
Store Hours: M-F 8:30-5:30, Sat. by appointment.
David Teroux's libertarian book 'n tape 'n game 'n
gift catalog.

Lifetime Books & Gifts
3900 Chalet Suzanne Dr.
Lake Wales, FL 33853
(813) 676-6311 7-9 PM EST
Check or M.O.
Fax: (813) 676-1814
Always Incomplete Catalog and *Usborne Catalog*
$2.

Light of Faith Christian Academy
c/o Jim and Ann Morris
716 Central
Joplin, MO 64801
Check or M.O.
Home-school record-keeping system using 3 x 5
cards.

Literary Guild
Garden City, NY 11530
Check or M.O. They bill you.
Best-seller book club.

Little, Brown and Company
34 Beacon St.
Boston, MA 02106
(617) 890-0250
Check or M.O.
Publisher.

Living Heritage Academy
P. O. Box 1438
Lewisville, TX 75067-1438
1-800-873-3435
(214) 462-1776
Fax: (214) 462-8681
Installment plan.
No refunds once program opened.
Home school program.

Lollipops
Good Apple
Box 299
Carthage, IL 62321-0299
Check or M.O.
Magazine for preschool/early childhood teachers.

Lord's Fine Jewelry
P.O. Box 486
Piedmont, OK 73078
(405) 373-2877 VISA, MC
Free brochure. Returns: Guaranteed craftsman-
ship; call first.

Lucas Learning, Inc.
2406 Park Central Blvd.
Decatur, GA 30035
1-800-526-5000 Operator 20. Credit card orders
only.
(404) 987-8804
Memory products.

Lulli Akin
305 Conway Rd.
St. Louis, MO 63141
(314) 434-7048 Sat. mornings.
Check or M.O.
ERB testing materials.

Master Books
P.O. Box 1606
El Cajon, CA 92022
1-800-999-3777 VISA, MC.
CA: (619) 448-1121
Free brochure.
Creation Science books, videos.

McGuffey Academy
1000 E. Huron
Milford, MI 48042
(817) 481-7008 Check or M.O.
Home school program.

Mel and Norma Gabler, Educational Analysts
P.O. Box 7518
Longview, TX 75607
(214) 753-5993
Check or M.O.
Donation for materials.
Analyses of curriculum, textbooks & programs.

Mountain Meadow Press
P.O. Box 447
Kooskia, ID 83539
(208) 926-4526 Check or M.O.
Publisher.

Multnomah Press
10209 SE Division St.
Portland, OR 97266
1-800-547-5890 OR: 1-800-452-6994 Check or M.O.
(503) 257-0526
Fax: (503) 255-1690
Books sold in Christian bookstores.

NACD (National Academy of Child Development)
P.O. Box 1001
Layton, UT 84041
(801) 451-0942 VISA, MC.
Free catalog, brochure.
Satisfaction guaranteed.
Physical therapy/behavior modification programs, tape sets.
On-site evaluations.

National Association for the Legal Support of Alternative Schools
P.O. Box 2823
Santa Fe, NM 87501
(505) 471-6928
Resources for alternative schoolers. Insurance fund.

North Dakota State Dept. of Public Instruction
Division of Independent Study
State University Station
Box 5036
Fargo, North Dakota 58105-5036
(701) 237-7182 Check or M.O.
No payment plan.
Refunds: First two weeks. Processing fee of $5 retained.
High school correspondence program.

Oak Meadow School
P.O. Box 712
Blacksburg, VA 24063
(703) 552-3263 9-4 M-F EST VISA, MC.
Returns: Within 15 days for curriculum. No refunds after 2 months.
Parent Sensitivity Training.
Full-service home school curriculum supplier, K-12.

Our Lady of the Rosary School
904 West Stephen Foster
Bardstown, KY 40004
(502) 348-1338 VISA, MC
Fax: (502) 348-0811
Free catalog. Returns: With letter of authorization.

Our Lady of Victory School
14412 San Jose St.
P.O. Box 5181
Mission Hills, CA 91345
(818) 899-1966
Check or M.O.
Repurchase option.
Quarterly payment plan.
No refunds on registration.
Home school program.

Parent-Child Press
P.O. Box 767
Altoona, PA 16603
(814) 946-5213 VISA, MC. Minimum credit card order $10.
U. S funds only.
Montessori philosophy, art materials.

Pathway Publishers
RR #4, Box 266
La Grange, IN 46761
Check or M.O.
Publisher of Amish textbooks.

Pecci Educational Publishers
440 Davis Court #405
San Francisco, CA 94111
(415) 391-8579 Check or M.O.
Free brochure.
Reading program and Super Seatwork.

Pennsylvania Homeschoolers
RD 2 Box 117
Kittanning, PA 16201
(412) 783-6512
Check or M.O.
Brochure with SASE.
Returns: Resalable condition, within 30 days.

Pinkerton Marketing Inc.
209 Change St.
New Bern, NC 28560
MC, VISA.
Publisher of *The Great Book of Catalogs*.

Prometheus Nemesis Book Company
P.O. Box 2748
Del Mar CA 92014
Fax: (619) 944-0845
Check or M.O.
Book publisher.

Publishers Central Bureau
One Champion Ave.
P.O. Box 1262
Newark, NJ 07101
VISA, MC, AmEx. $10 minimum.
Discount books.

Quality Paperback Book Club
Middletown, PA 17057
They bill you.
Book-of-the-Month subsidiary.

R & E Publishers
P.O. Box 2008
Saratoga, CA 95070
(408) 866-6303 VISA, MC.
Fax: (408) 866-0825
Free catalog.
Books about children and schooling.

Rainbow Re-source Center
610 East Elm Street
Taylorville, IL 62568
(217) 824-5647 (3:00-9:00 PM Central)
Check or M.O.
One catalog, $1. One year (8 issues), $6.
Used home-school materials.

Reliable Corporation
1001 W. Van Buren St.
Chicago, IL 60607
1-800-621-4344 (orders) VISA, MC, or open account.
1-800-621-5954 (cust. service)
Fax: 1-800-621-6002
Good service with guarantee. Free shipping with most orders.

Research Publications
P.O. Box 39850
Phoenix, AZ 85069
1-800-528-0559 Business hours only. VISA, MC.
AZ: 1-252-4777 collect.
Bulk order discounts.
Sam Blumenfeld's books.

Riverside Schoolhouse
HCR 34 Box 181-A
Bemidji, MN 56601
(218) 751-8227 Visa, MC
Free Catalog. Other publishers' catalogs available free of charge, but include something for postage if not ordering anything. Returns: Resalable condition, no questions asked within 10 days, call first after 10 days.

Rod and Staff Publishers
Crockett, KY 41413
(606) 522-4348
Check or M.O.
Free catalog listing texts. Returns: With permission, 10 percent restocking charge.
Christian schoolbooks. Mennonite.

Rutherford Institute
P.O. Box 510
Manassas, VA 22110
Check or M.O.
Free magazine. Donations welcome. Worthy group.
Nonprofit legal association, defends religious liberties.

Santa Fe Community School
P.O. Box 2241
Santa Fe, NM 87504-2241
(505) 471-6928
Home study program.

School Supply Room
Gordonville Print Shop
3121 Irishtown Rd.
Gordonville, PA 17529
Check or M.O.
List of texts, send large SASE.
Mennonite texts.

Scott, Foresman & Company
1900 E. Lake Ave.
Glenview, IL 60025
1-800-554-4411
(708) 729-3000
Public school textbooks.

Servant Publications
P. O. Box 8617
840 Airport Blvd.
Ann Arbor, MI 48107
(313) 761-8505
Fax: (313) 761-1577
Major credit card.
Free catalog.
Book publisher.

Seton Home Study School
612 Crosby Road
P. O. Box 396
Front Royal, VA 22630-3332
(703) 636-9990
Check or M.O.
Home school program.

Shekinah Curriculum Cellar
967 Junipero Drive
Costa Mesa, CA 92626
(714) 751-7767
Check or M.O.
Catalog $1.
Refunds: Resalable condition, within 15 days.
Co-op buying plan.
"Quality books and teaching aids for home educators."

Shining Star
Division of Good Apple
Box 299
Carthage, IL 62321
1-800-435-7234 VISA, MC.
Free catalog.
Returns: Permission required.
Christian educational materials, magazines.

Smiling Heart Press
P.O. Box 229
Corbett, OR 97019
Check or M.O. made out to Ann Ward.
Free brochure with SASE.
One-book preschool curriculum.

Summit Christian Academy
P.O. Box 802041
Dallas, TX 75380
1-800-362-9180. VISA, MC.
(214) 991-2096 for inquiries.
Payment plan.
Free brochure.
Home school program.

Sunburst Communications, Inc.
39 Washington Ave.
Pleasantville, NY 10570
1-800-431-1934 Canada: 1-800-247-6756 VISA, MC, C.O.D.
NY: (914) 769-5030 collect.
Call toll-free number for free catalog. Customer satisfaction guaranteed. Lifetime replacement of defective parts.
Free software updates.
Creative educational software.

Sycamore Tree
2179 Meyer Place
Costa Mesa, CA 92627
(714) 650-4466 (info) (714) 642-6750 (orders)
VISA, MC.
Fax: (714) 642-6750
Catalog $3. Includes $3 rebate good toward first purchase.
Full-service home school supplier.
Home school program.

Teaching Home
P.O. Box 20219
Portland, OR 97220-0219
Check or M.O.
Home schooling mag. Christian.
State editions co-published in over twenty states and Australia as of '89.

Timberdoodle
E. 1610 Spencer Lake Road
Shelton, WA 98584
(206) 426-0672 Check or M.O., or COD.
Free catalog.
Returns: 60 days, resalable condition.
Educational materials.
Fishertechnik kits.

TREND Enterprises, Inc.
P.O. Box 64073
St. Paul, MN 55164-0073
1-800-328-0818
MN: (612) 631-2850
Fax: (612) 631-2861
Stickers, wipe-off books, more.

Trinity Foundation
P.O. Box 169
Jefferson, MD 21755
(301) 371-7155 Check or M.O.
Free catalog, brochures.
Returns: only defective books.
Newsletter, tapes, books.
Publisher.

University of Nebraska-Lincoln
Independent Study Department
Division of Continuing Studies
Lincoln, NE 68583-0900
(402) 472-1926
Fax: (402) 472-1901
Full-service H.S. diploma course.
Science equipment, courses.

Warren Publishing House, Inc.
Totline Books and Newsletters
P.O. Box 2250
Everett, WA 98203
1-800-334-4769 VISA, MC.
Fax: (714) 543-7801 (Totline)
Free catalog. Refunds: 30 days.
Materials for preschool, kindergarten.

Weaver Curriculum Series
2752 Scarborough
Riverside, CA 92503
(714) 688-3126
Check or M.O.
Free catalog.
Integrated curriculum K-6.

Wilcox & Follett Book Company
1000 W. Washington Blvd.
Chicago, IL 60607
1-800-621-4272. Check or M.O., or school P.O.
IL: 1-800-621-1474 Chicago: 666-5856
Free catalog.
Elementary and high school used textbooks; current and older editions; workbooks. In business for over 100 years.

Wisdom Publications
P.O. Box 3154
LaVale, MD 21502
(301) 759-3218 Check or M.O.
Publishes *Home School Digest*

World Book, Inc.
Educational Services Department
Merchandise Mart Plaza
Chicago, IL 60654
(312) 245-3456 Check or M.O. Orders over $25 may be billed.
Encyclopedia. Workbooks. Learning aids. Posters.

INDEX OF FOREIGN SUPPLIERS

Realizing that you overseas and Canadian readers prefer to shop in your own countries, I asked every distributor listed in this book for a list of their non-USA distributors. The results, while scanty, might be of help to some of you. The American company is listed first, with its distributor's name (and, where available, address) second.

As you can see, any of you who are interested in starting an importing business featuring American home-education materials have a wide-open market. Most other countries do not have as well-developed home-schooling movements as the U.S.A., and consequently Americans are blessed with more than our fair share of innovative products designed for home use. Why not even things out a bit? And when you get your business going, let me know so I can list it in the next edition!

AUSTRALIA

Baker Book House
S. John Bacon
P.O. Box 223
9 Kingston Twon Close
Oakleigh, Victoria, 3166
Australia
(03) 563-1044

Conversa-phone Institute, Inc.
Lift Australia Pty. Ltd.
P.O. Box 401
Unit 8-1 Vuko Place
Warriewood, NSW 2102
Australia

Multnomah Press
Bookhouse Australia
P.O. Box 115
Fleminton Markets, N.S.W. 2124
Australia

Dove Christian Books
Buchanan/Omega, Ltd.

CANADA

Alpha Omega Publications
Academic Distribution Services
528 Carnarvon St.
New Westminster, B. C. V3L 1C4
Canada
(604) 524-9758

Baby Love Products
5015 - 46 St.
Carmrose, Alberta T4V 3G3
Canada
(402) 672-1763 8-5 M-Sat. MC, Visa, AmEx
Fax: (403) 672-6942 Credit card orders only
Tremendous assortment of wholesome baby
products, including great choices in cloth
diapering.
Sells *Catalogue of Canadian Catalogues.*

Baker Book House
G. R. Welch Co. Ltd.
960 Gateway
Burlington, Ontario L7L 5K7
Canada
(416) 681-2760

Conversa-phone Institute, Inc.
Distribution Fusion III
5455 Rue Pare Suite 101
Montreal, Quebec H4P 1P7
Canada

Dove Christian Books
Word, Inc., Canada

Educators Publishing Service
Educators Publishing Service
66 Scarsdale Rd.
Don Mills, Ontario M3B 2R7
Canada
(416) 755-0591

Kaye McLeod
4623 Fortune Rd. S.E.
Calgary, Alberta T2A 2A7
Canada
(403) 272-3658
Check or M.O.
Daily/School Planner for Children.

Learn, Inc.
Hume Publ.
4100 Yonge Street
Willowdale, Ontario M2P 2B9
Canada
(416) 221-4596
Fax: (416) 221-4968

Multnomah Press
Beacon
104 Consumers Dr.
Whitby, Ontario L1N 5T3
Canada

Pathway Publishers
Pathway Publishers
Route 4
Aylmer, Ontario N5H 2R3
Canada

Shining Star
Beacon Distributors, Ltd.
104 Consumers Drive
Whitby, Ontario L1N 5T3
Canada
(416) 668-8884

ENGLAND

Audio Forum
Audio Forum
31 Kensington Church Street
London W8-4L1
England
01-937-1647

Charlotte Mason Research & Supply Co.
Scripture Press

Conversa-phone Institute, Inc.
L.C.L. Benedict Ltd.
102-104 Judd Street
London NC1H-9NF
England

Dove Christian Books
Kingsway

EDC Publishing
See Usborne Publishing listing

Multnomah Press
Scripture Press Found.
Roans Rd., Amersham-On-The-Hill
Bucks HP6 6JO
England

Usborne Publishing Ltd.
20 Garrick St.
London WC2E 9BJ
England
British producer of popular books sold under EDC
Publishing label in the U.S.A.

NEW ZEALAND

Baker Book House
Omega Distributors, Inc.
Box 26-222
69 Great South Road
Remuera, Aukland
New Zealand
548-283

Dove Christian Books
Buchanan/Omega, Ltd.

Multnomah Press
Omega Distributors
P.O. Box 26-222
Epsom, Aukland
New Zealand

SOUTH AFRICA

Baker Book House
Christian Art Wholesale
20 Smuts Ave., Box 1599
Vereeniging
Republic of South Africa
(016) 21-4781/5

Multnomah Press
ACLA
Box 332
Roodeport 1725
Republic of South Africa